Using FoxPro

John W. Zumsteg

que®

CORPORATION

LEADING COMPUTER KNOWLEDGE

Using FoxPro™

Copyright © 1990 by Que® Corporation.

Library of Congress Catalog No.: 90-60380

ISBN 0-88022-514-9

92 91 90   8 7 6 5 4 3 2 1

Interpretation of the printing code: the rightmost double-digit number is the year of the book's printing; the rightmost single-digit number, the number of the book's printing. For example, a printing code of 90-1 shows that the first printing of the book occurred in 1990.

Using FoxPro is based on FoxPro Version 1.0

"Peace of mind isn't at all superficial to technical work. It's the whole thing."

—Robert M. Pirsig
Zen and the Art of Motorcycle Maintenance

Publishing Director

Lloyd J. Short

Acquisitions Editor

Karen A. Bluestein

Product Director

David Maguiness

Book Design and Production

Dan Armstrong
Bill Basham
Claudia Bell
Brad Chinn
Don Clemons
Sally Copenhaver
Tom Emrick
Dennis Hager
Tami Hughes
Bill Hurley
Jodi Jensen
Larry Lynch
Lori A. Lyons
Jennifer Matthews
Cindy Phipps
Joe Ramon
Dennis Sheehan
Louise Shinault
Bruce Steed
Mary Beth Wakefield
Nora Westlake

Production Editor

Jo Anna W. Arnott

Editors

Sandra Blackthorn
Jay McNaught

Technical Editor

Lawrence Peters

Indexer

Hilary Adams

Composed in Garamond and OCRB Bold by Que Corporation.

John Zumsteg

John Zumsteg has worked with microcomputers and database management programs since their introduction to the computing world. Experienced on a range of computers, he prefers desktop computers and systems like FoxPro because they bring computing power to everyone. Mr. Zumsteg has developed many PC database systems, primarily in the airline industry, and is currently the Director of Management Information Systems for Horizon Air, the regional airline of the Northwest United States. In this role, he is responsible for the design, development, and implementation of large and complex database programs, as well as conducting classes in all areas of PC applications.

CONTENTS AT A GLANCE

TABLE OF CONTENTS ▽

II   Intermediate FoxPro

III   Advanced FoxPro

ACKNOWLEDGMENTS ▼

Any book, and *Using FoxPro* is no exception, is a lot of work by many people. I wish to thank those who helped me put this book together.

First, thanks to my friends and family who encouraged me to write *Using FoxPro*, and then endured my near-terminal grumps as it was being written.

Many fine people at Que Corporation encouraged, prodded, assisted, and cajoled me into writing the best book I could. These include David Maguiness, Karen Bluestein, Renee Ackerman, Jo Anna Arnott (what patience!), and the many editors who often knew, better than me, how to write what I was thinking. Also, thanks to Larry Peters for editing the technical aspects of *Using FoxPro*.

Thanks to Dean Myers and Computerland of Portland, Oregon, for providing several state-of-the-art PCs to research and write this book. With the difficulty they have had getting these PCs back (one does get used to powerful computers), they may be regretting their decision, but thanks anyway.

Mostly, a special thanks to Terrie Lynn Solomon of Que Corporation, whose faith in me resulted in this book. Without Terrie's encouragement, I would never have written *Using FoxPro*. Thanks, Terrie.

TRADEMARK ACKNOWLEDGMENTS

Que Corporation has made every effort to supply trademark information about company names, products, and services mentioned in this book. Trademarks indicated below were derived from various sources. Que Corporation cannot attest to the accuracy of this information.

Apple, Mac, and Macintosh are registered trademarks of Apple Computer, Inc.

COMPAQ is a registered trademark of COMPAQ Computer Corporation.

dBASE III PLUS and dBASE IV are trademarks of Ashton-Tate Corporation.

FoxBase+, FoxBase+/386, FoxBase/Mac, and FoxPro are trademarks of Fox Software, Inc.

MS-DOS is a registered trademark of Microsoft Corporation.

OS/2 is a registered trademark of International Business Machines Corporation.

UNIX is a trademark of AT&T.

Introduction

FoxPro brings to the PC world of database programs a unique combination of power and ease of use. With FoxPro, you can develop database applications to perform simple and complex jobs, and you can do it without learning an esoteric "language." FoxPro's windowing environment, brought from the Macintosh, makes complex database applications far easier than with any other database manager.

Just what is a database or a database manager? If you have information that can be defined in some organized way, you have a database. If the volume of that information makes it impossible for you to make sense of it, you need a database manager. A database manager is a program that stores the data in your computer and enables you to look at that data in various ways—sorted, viewed in whole or part, and reported any way you need. FoxPro gives you the power to do all this.

A good database manager does more than store and report data; it gives you new ways to look at the data, better capabilities to see the meaning of that data, and quicker ways to access what you need. FoxPro has an extraordinary amount of power, allowing complex database systems to be developed. A good-sized company could be run on a FoxPro-based Management Information System.

Unlike many other programs, FoxPro is fun to learn. Every step brings more power to your computer, and improves your ability to mold and manipulate your data to meet your needs.

How To Use FoxPro and This Book

Learning a new computer program can be an exercise in frustration. You know that the new program is going to pay great dividends in productivity and skill, but initially you may encounter obstacle after obstacle. I call the first stage of learning a new program "fritter time"; you just seem to fritter time away trying to get to those gains in productivity. *Using Fox-Pro* is designed to reduce fritter time to a minimum.

The Audience

Users of FoxPro and FoxBase+ span a wide range of experience, but this book concentrates on those who can be categorized as beginning users to intermediate users.

Users who have never used a database manager—or even a personal computer—will be able to start with this book and build a comfortable level of skill with FoxPro or FoxBase+.

Users who have "played around" with FoxPro or FoxBase+ and now need to do some serious work will be able to use *Using FoxPro* as a guide to learning how to organize and implement a database, no matter how simple or sophisticated.

Users who are experienced with FoxBase+ and who need to make the transition to FoxPro will find this book helpful in learning the graphical user interface approach that FoxPro takes. Learning to use FoxPro's windows, dialog boxes, and pull-down and pop-up menus is certainly easier with *Using FoxPro* as your guide.

The Approach

Using FoxPro is divided into three parts, which correspond roughly to "beginning FoxPro," "beginning-to-intermediate FoxPro," and "intermediate FoxPro" sections. Each part begins with a *quick start*, which is a hands-on, step-by-step guide to achieving results with FoxPro. By going through the quick starts only, you can learn enough about FoxPro to use the program productively. After the quick start in each part are several chapters that delve more deeply into the topics introduced in the quick start. In these chapters, you will learn enough about the topic at hand to use the many options and powerful capabilities of FoxPro and FoxBase+.

If you're new to the database management world, you should start at the very beginning, working through Quick Start 1. This quick start will give you an overview of database management: how to design and define your database; enter, edit, and view data; and report on that data. Then work through the chapters in Part I to deepen that knowledge and become familiar with the ways to use FoxPro. When you're familiar with these basic capabilities, you can repeat this process in Part II to learn how to tap the real power of FoxPro.

Users with some familiarity of FoxBase+ or another database management program also should go through Quick Start 1 because it is the easiest way to learn how FoxPro is different from other programs. This quick start will help you become comfortable with FoxPro's user interface.

When you're comfortable with your basic knowledge of FoxPro's capabilities and user interface, proceed to Quick Start 2, where you will learn to tap FoxPro's real power: its capacity to work with many related files. The chapters in Part II cover data entry, editing, viewing, and reporting on more sophisticated and complex database structures. This area is where FoxPro and FoxBase+ really stand out, providing power capabilities with unmatched ease of use.

More advanced users can use Part III, which covers how to use FoxPro and FoxBase+ to create simple programs and applications. Many users will eventually feel the need to reach this level of expertise, and Quick Start 3 will start them toward that goal.

Like FoxPro, which can be used by people with any level of computer and database management expertise, *Using FoxPro* has something for you if you're new to the computer world or new to database management, or if you are experienced in other programs and want to learn FoxPro. In *Using FoxPro*, you learn how to design a database and how to use FoxPro to bring that database into being. You learn how to create reports, queries, and data-entry screens. If after harnessing these FoxPro capabilities you find a need for more sophisticated applications, *Using FoxPro* also provides an introduction to using FoxPro's sophisticated programming language.

Some Database History

Computers originally were used for number-crunching, but it was not long before databases made their appearance. Nearly every computer application in the commercial world requires data storage; accounting systems store information about customers, orders, accounts payable and receivable, inventory, and myriad other sources of data. Microcomputers applications are no different; the storage and retrieval of data quickly became a primary purpose of microcomputers.

But those first databases were not easy to use. Ashton-Tate's dBASE II required that every command be entered from the keyboard in a highly structured syntax. dBASE III and dBASE III Plus, the most well-known microcomputer database programs, improved on that cryptic command approach, but the concept was the same.

In 1986, Fox Software introduced FoxBase+, which was a dBASE III Plus look-alike. FoxBase+ was faster and had some additional features, primarily for people developing sophisticated turn-key applications. Foxbase+

evolved into FoxBase 2.10, and FoxBase 2.10 evolved into FoxPro, but with an unusual detour resulting in a revolutionary, easy-to-use interface for such a powerful product.

Fox Software decided, in 1987, to port FoxBase 2.10 to the Apple Macintosh. Originally, the company wanted to move FoxBase as is, keeping the same command-line interface of the PC version. However, Fox Software ended up rewriting the program to make use of the intuitive, mouse-based Macintosh interface. When the company wanted to upgrade FoxBase +, Fox Software ported the Foxbase/Mac system to the PC—windows, mice, and all.

Differences in computing power and database management capabilities between FoxPro and other database programs are minor, but the ease-of-use of FoxPro makes it a superior product.

Who Should Read This Book?

Anyone using FoxPro will benefit from *Using FoxPro*. Novices will be able to start from square one, learning the necessary concepts and techniques to get FoxPro up and running productively. The quick start chapters provide tutorials to give new users immediate successes with FoxPro. Following chapters build on that foundation, providing more detailed and in-depth knowledge to allow more sophisticated use.

For the user already familiar with other database management programs (including FoxBase 2.10), *Using FoxPro* provides the bridge to new ways to accomplish old tasks. At the same time, the more experienced reader will learn how to use the more powerful FoxPro features.

How To Use This Book

Because FoxPro uses a novel user interface, the first topic for any new user of FoxPro is navigating in that interface. For this, you should start at Quick Start 1. In fact, all users should go through this section, because it provides essential information about navigating in FoxPro, which is unlike any previous version of FoxBase or any other database PC system. If you have any experience with Macintosh software (particularly if you have used FoxBase/Mac), you will find this familiar ground.

The novice will be best served by working through each section of the book, using the program while you work. Nothing can match the learning experience of actually trying something and seeing it work.

More experienced users, after learning how to navigate in windows, can jump to sections of particular interest. Note, though, that FoxPro does a lot of things differently and better that FoxBase+ and its competitors; there is much to learn here for even an experienced user.

Most of all, have fun! FoxPro brings an incredible amount of database power to you and your PC, but it is an enjoyable program to learn and to use.

Part I

FoxPro Fundamentals

Includes

Quick Start 1: Getting Started with FoxPro

An Overview of FoxPro

Designing and Creating a Database

Entering, Editing, and Viewing Data

Summarizing and Sorting Data

Creating Basic Reports

Getting Started with FoxPro

FoxPro provides an amazing amount of database power, yet that power is easier to use than any other database program. This quick start shows you how to get started with that power in the quickest, easiest fashion. Much of what you will do in this quick start receives more attention in the rest of the book, but if you follow along with this tutorial, you will learn enough to get going with FoxPro.

Creating a Database

Let's start with a hypothetical situation. Your boss wanders into your office and comments that, because she bought you that fancy computer to help you be more productive, she would like to see you doing something besides flying an F-15 in pursuit of MIG-23s. In fact, she would really like to see some reports on your company's customers and, later on, maybe a way to track contacts with those customers. After assuring her that you can do that, you gulp and decide it's time to learn FoxPro. Turning to your trusty, if somewhat unfamiliar computer, you prepare to delve into database management, FoxPro style.

To create and use your first FoxPro database, follow these steps:

1. Assuming that you have FoxPro installed on your computer in a directory named FOXPRO, enter the following commands:

   ```
   CD \FOXPRO
   MD CUST
   CD CUST
   PATH = \FOXPRO
   FOXPRO
   ```

This series of commands moves you to the FOXPRO directory, creates a subdirectory named CUST, moves to that directory, sets a path so that MS-DOS can find FoxPro, and invokes the FoxPro program. You should see the FoxPro opening screen (see fig. QS1.1).

Fig. QS1.1.
The opening
FoxPro screen.

Across the top of the screen is a menu bar, with the options System, File, Edit, Database, and so on. You use these menu options to tell FoxPro what to do. FoxPro functions are grouped into these areas and become available through menus that pop up when you select the top level menu.

In the lower right corner of the screen is a bordered box, with the word Command across the top. This is a window. FoxPro, revealing its Macintosh heritage, is a strongly window-oriented program. Nearly all you do with FoxPro will be in various windows. FoxPro has a View window, to look at information about the databases you're using; a Browse window, to view a database's information; and other windows in which FoxPro will do the things you ask of it. Most windows can be moved and resized, to enable you to customize FoxPro to your liking.

2. Next, using the mouse, move the mouse pointer to the File option in the menu and press the left mouse button. FoxPro displays the File pop-up menu, shown in figure QS1.2.

   You also can open the File pop-up menu from the keyboard by pressing the F10 key, which activates the Main menu. Use the left- and right-arrow keys to move across the menu to the File option, and press Enter. You will see the File pop-up menu shown in figure QS1.2.

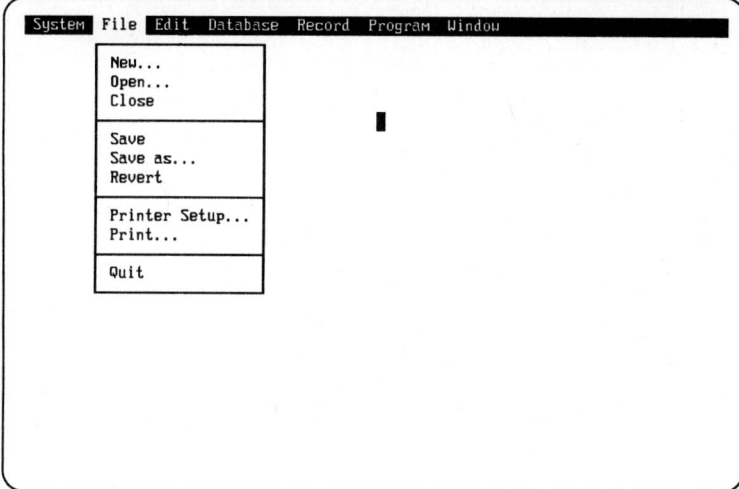

Fig. QS1.2.
The File pop-up
menu.

3. Next, you need to tell FoxPro that you want to create a new database. Choose New from the File menu by either highlighting that option and clicking it with the mouse, or by pressing N to select New.

4. FoxPro displays the New dialog (see fig. QS1.3). Select Database to tell FoxPro that you are creating a new database. Then choose OK. FoxPro displays the Structure dialog, shown in figure QS1.4.

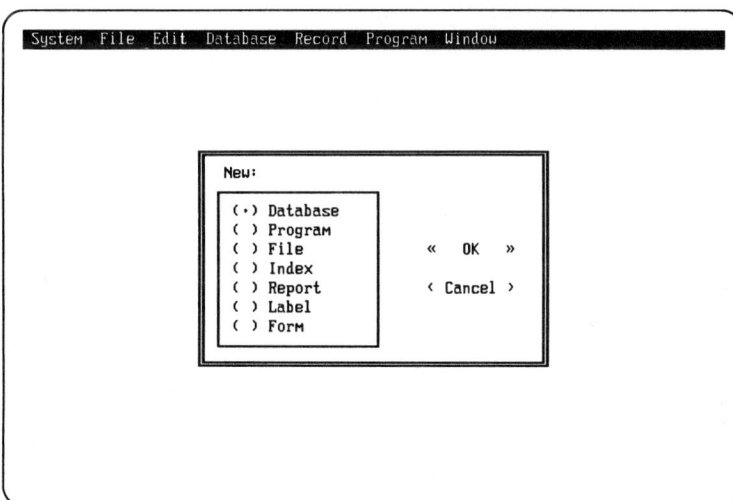

Fig. QS1.3.
The New dialog.

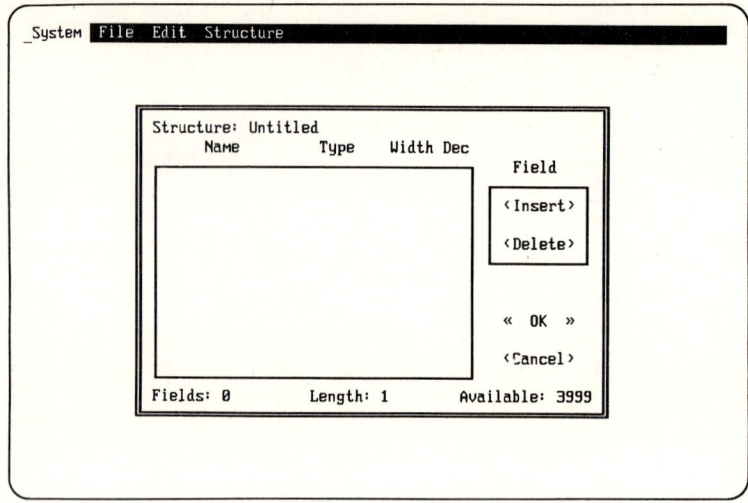

Fig. QS1.4.
The Structure
dialog.

Before you get to this point, you will have thought about your database and what it must contain. Database design can be as simple as writing down the fields of information you want to keep in the database. FoxPro is now waiting for you to enter that database design into the Structure dialog.

5. In the `Field Name` column, enter *cust_name*, telling FoxPro that you want to create a field in the database with that name. Press the tab key to move to the next column, the `Type` column. FoxPro has several different type fields, which you can see by pressing Enter or by pulling down the mouse pointer from the Type box. Leave this field as a Character field, the default.

6. Move to the Width field and enter *30*. This tells FoxPro to reserve 30 characters for the CUST_NAME field. Press Enter to move to the first field of the next line. Continue entering fields, field types, and field widths, using the following definitions:

Field Name	Type	Width	Decimal
CUST_NAME	Character	25	
ADDR_1	Character	25	
ADDR_2	Character	25	
CITY	Character	15	
STATE	Character	2	
ZIP	Character	9	
PHONE	Character	10	

CONTACT	Character	10	
CREDIT	Numeric	8	2
LAST_PUR	Date	8	
LAST_AMT	Numeric	8	2
PREFERRD	Logical	1	

When you enter the Type for the CREDIT and LAST_AMT fields, select Numeric from the Type menu by using the pop-up menu and highlighting Numeric, or by pressing the letter N; FoxPro fills in the rest.

Do the same for the Date fields, choosing Date from the menu, or by pressing D and letting FoxPro fill in the rest of the field type. The Structure window should look like the one in figure QS1.5.

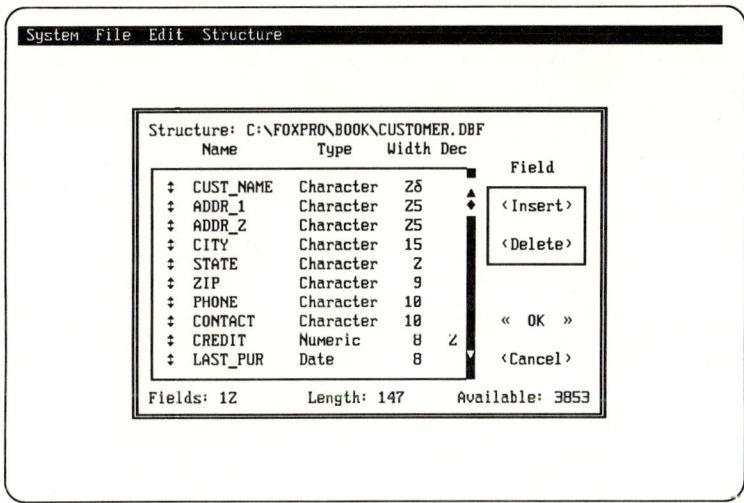

Fig. QS1.5.
The CUSTOMER database defined in the Structure dialog.

7. Next, choose OK. The Save As dialog appears so you can name your new database. Enter *customer* and select Save. Foxpro saves your database design and asks you if you want to enter records now. Choose Yes.

Congratulations! You have just created a real FoxPro database, ready to receive data and go to work for you.

Regular editing functions are available while entering or editing data in all FoxPro fields, either in the database or any of the dialogs requiring text entry. The backspace key is a "destructive" backspace. It moves the cursor one character to the left and erases that character. The right- and left-arrow keys move the cursor right and left, without erasing characters. The

Home key moves the cursor to the first character in the field; the End key moves it to the last character. The Ins key toggles Insert mode on and off. Press it once to insert characters into the text. Press it again to overwrite existing characters.

Now you can enter some data into the database by following these steps:

1. In the data-entry window (see fig. QS1.6), the cursor is in the field labeled Cust_name. Enter a customer name in this field. You can enter any characters or numbers, either upper- or lowercase.

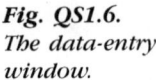

Fig. QS1.6.
The data-entry window.

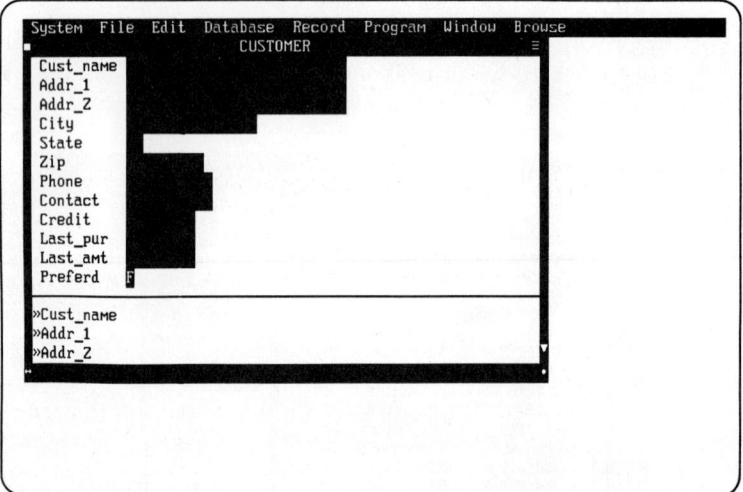

2. When you're finished entering a name in the CUST_NAME field, press Enter to move the cursor to the next field, ADDR_1. Enter an address and continue, entering a second address line if you want, and the city, state, and ZIP code.

3. When you have finished the first record, which occurs when you press Enter on the last field, FoxPro presents you with a data-entry field for the second record, just below the first. Enter the second record, and continue to enter more records, making up names and addresses until you have entered at least 15 records into the database.

4. Close the data-entry window by pressing Esc, or by moving the mouse pointer to the Close box in the upper left corner of the window and clicking. You're now ready to look through your database with the Browse command.

5. To view the information in your database, select Browse from the Database window. FoxPro displays the Browse window, shown in figure QS1.7.

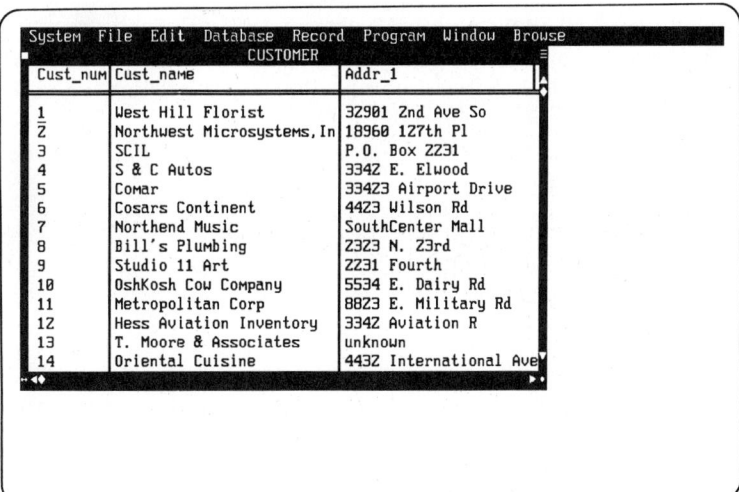

Fig. QS1.7.
The Browse
window.

Although the word "browsing" carries connotations of afternoons spent at the mall, it is an apt description of how you look at the information in a database. You can stroll through the database, looking at this record and that field, going back and forth to look at different things. FoxPro's Browse command enables you to do just that, and throws in the capability to add, edit, and delete data from the same window quickly.

Exploring the Window

Browse through the database by scrolling lines upward and downward. Move the mouse pointer to the right margin of the window, which is called the Vertical Scroll Bar. Move the pointer to the scroll-down symbol near the bottom of the scroll bar and click. You will see the database lines in the window move up one line. This is called scrolling down. The Browse window is a window on your database and, by clicking the scroll-down symbol, you move that window down one line in the database. You can move it back up by moving the mouse pointer to the scroll-up symbol at the top of the scroll bar and clicking.

If you are working from the keyboard, use the up- and down-arrow keys to scroll. As you press the up- or down-arrow keys, the highlight will move to the first or last record in the Browse window, respectively. Continue to press the up- or down-arrow keys to scroll the window up or down.

Move the mouse pointer to a place on the Vertical Scroll Bar that is between the scroll-down symbol and the thumb (the diamond shape in the scroll bar) and click. Your window will move a full screen down through the database. If the window shows 10 lines, scrolling down a page causes the window to move down 9 lines; the line that was last on the page now becomes the first line. Clicking in the scroll bar between the scroll-up symbol and the thumb scrolls the window up one screen.

From the keyboard, you should use the PgUp and PgDn keys to move the window up and down a full screen in the database. The first time you press PgUp or PgDn, the highlight moves to the first or last record visible in the Browse window. Pressing PgUp or PgDn again causes the window to scroll a full page up or down.

Using the thumb is most advantageous in large databases. If you drag the thumb halfway down the scroll bar, the Browse window will show the records halfway through the database. If you drag the thumb three-quarters of the way down the bar, the window will show the records three-quarters of the way through the database. The position of the thumb in the Vertical Scroll Bar corresponds to the position in the database of the records appearing in the Browse window.

Keyboard users looking for a way to use the thumb will be disappointed; this feature is one of the very few FoxPro features available to mouse users and not keyboard users.

To scroll the window to the right, move the mouse pointer to the bottom margin of the window, which is a Horizontal Scroll Bar. Place the pointer over the scroll-right symbol and click. The window now shows fields that were not visible before, and the first field, CUST_NAME, has disappeared (see fig. QS1.8). Clicking on the scroll-left symbol moves the window to the left.

From the keyboard, you can scroll right and left by using the Tab and Shift-Tab keys. Press the Tab key several times in succession; the highlight moves across the fields and, when it reaches the right-most field, causes the window to scroll to the right to bring more fields into view. Shift-Tab reverses the process.

You can drag the window anywhere off the screen. Move the mouse pointer to the top margin of the window, press the left button and move the mouse while holding the button down. The entire window moves with the mouse pointer. Figure QS1.9 shows the window moved partly off the screen.

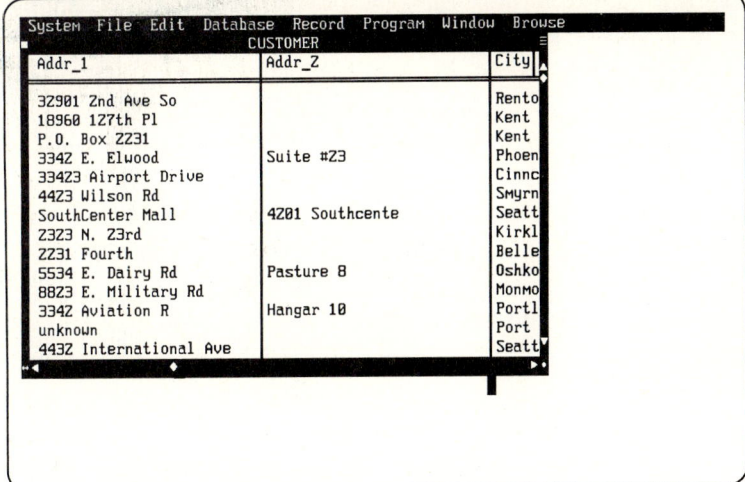

Fig. QS1.8.
The Browse window after scrolling to the right.

From the keyboard, you can move the screen by pressing Alt-W to activate the Window pop-up menu, and selecting Move. You also can go straight to the Move option by pressing Ctrl-F7. The window will start flashing and you can move it with the arrow keys. Press Enter to stop the Move process.

```
System File Edit Database Record Program Window Browse
                                              CUSTOMER
                               Cust_num Cust_name                      Addr_1
                               1        West Hill Florist              32901 2nd Ave
                               2        Northwest Microsystems,In       18960 127th Pl
                               3        SCIL                           P.O. Box 2231
                               4        S & C Autos                    3342 E. Elwood
                               5        Comar                          33423 Airport
                               6        Cosars Continent               4423 Wilson Rd
                               7        Northend Music                 SouthCenter Ma
                               8        Bill's Plumbing                2323 N. 23rd
                               9        Studio 11 Art                  2231 Fourth
                               10       OshKosh Cow Company            5534 E. Dairy
                               11       Metropolitan Corp              8823 E. Milita
                               12       Hess Aviation Inventory        3342 Aviation
```

Fig. QS1.9.
The Browse window, dragged partly off the screen.

To change the shape of the window, move the mouse pointer to the small dot in the lower right corner of the Browse window. This is the Sizing symbol. Use the mouse to drag the symbol. You will see the window change shape as you drag. When the window is the shape and size you want, release the button.

To change the shape of the window from the keyboard, select Size from the Window pop-up menu, or press Ctrl-F8. The border of the window flashes, and when you press the arrow keys, the bottom right corner moves, sizing the window. Again, press Enter to stop the process.

The last thing you can do to a window is zoom it, making it fill the whole screen. Move the mouse pointer to the Zoom symbol in the upper right corner of the Browse window and click it. The window "zooms" to fill the whole screen (see fig. QS1.10). Click the Zoom symbol again and the window returns to its old size.

To zoom from the keyboard, select Zoom from the Window pop-up menu or press Ctrl-F10. Repeat the process to return the window to its original size.

Fig. QS1.10.
Zooming a
window to fill
the screen.

```
 System  File  Edit  Database  Record  Program  Window  Browse
                              CUSTOMER
 Cust_name              Addr_1                   Addr_2
 West Hill Florist      3Z901 2nd Ave So
 Northwest Microsystems, In 18960 127th Pl
 SCIL                   P.O. Box ZZ31
 S & C Autos            3342 E. Elwood           Suite #Z3
 Comar                  33423 Airport Drive
 Cosars Continent       4423 Wilson Rd
 Northend Music         SouthCenter Mall         4201 Southcente
 Bill's Plumbing        Z3Z3 N. Z3rd
 Studio 11 Art          ZZ31 Fourth
 OshKosh Cow Company    5534 E. Dairy Rd         Pasture 8
 Metropolitan Corp      8823 E. Military Rd
 Hess Aviation Inventory 3342 Aviation R         Hangar 10
 T. Moore & Associates  unknown
 Oriental Cuisine       443Z International Ave
 Pickett's House of Music
```

If you have ever worked with a Macintosh computer, moving, sizing, and zooming windows is second nature to you. In the PC world, FoxPro is the first database management program to use windows extensively and efficiently.

Although windowing programs are built for mouse users, you can still use windows from the keyboard.

Using the Window

Besides giving you a way to look at your database, the Browse window enables you to edit and delete information in the database. To do some basic editing and deleting in your CUSTOMER database, follow these steps:

1. Move the mouse pointer to the CUST_NAME field in the first record and click. The entire record is highlighted and the field is selected. On a color monitor, the characters in the field change to yellow, showing the selected field. You can now edit the field. When you're finished, click somewhere in the window and the new information is accepted.

   From the keyboard, use the arrow and Tab keys to move to the CUST_NAME field in the first record. You can edit it normally.

2. To delete characters, move to the ADDR1 field in the first record and select the field. Place the cursor over the first character of the field and drag the mouse to the end of the field (holding the mouse button down while moving the mouse). On a color monitor, the entire field is now on a red background, indicating that all the characters have been selected. Press Del to remove all the information in the field (see fig. QS1.11).

   To delete characters from the keyboard, hold the Shift key down while using the right- and left-arrow keys to move the highlighted (red) portion of the field. When you have highlighted what you want to delete, press Del to remove it.

```
 System  File  Edit  Database  Record  Program  Window  Browse
                             CUSTOMER
  Cust_name                  Addr_1                 Addr_2

  West Hill Florist
  Northwest Microsystems, In 18960 127th Pl
  SCIL                       P.O. Box 2231
  S & C Autos                3342 E. Elwood         Suite #23
  Comar                      33423 Airport Drive
  Cosars Continent           4423 Wilson Rd
  Northend Music             SouthCenter Mall       4201 Southcente
  Bill's Plumbing            2323 N. 23rd
  Studio 11 Art              2231 Fourth
  OshKosh Cow Company        5534 E. Dairy Rd       Pasture 8
  Metropolitan Corp          8823 E. Military Rd
  Hess Aviation Inventory    3342 Aviation R        Hangar 10
  T. Moore & Associates      unknown
  Oriental Cuisine           4432 International Ave
  Pickett's House of Music
```

Fig. QS1.11. Deleting all the information in a field.

3. To restore the information you just removed, select Undo from the Edit menu. Undo enables you to reverse many actions you have just taken. Any time you make a mistake, check to see whether Undo is available. Some actions cannot be undone; if this is so, the Undo option will be dimmed in the menu, indicating that FoxPro cannot undo your last action.

4. You delete a record from the database by pointing to the space between the left-most field in the window and the left margin and clicking. A Deleted Record symbol appears (see fig. QS1.12).

   From the keyboard, you can delete the record by selecting it and choosing Delete from the Record menu. In the Delete dialog, choose `Delete`. The Deleted Record symbol appears in the Browse window.

Fig. QS1.12.
The Deleted
Record symbol
next to a record
marked for
deletion.

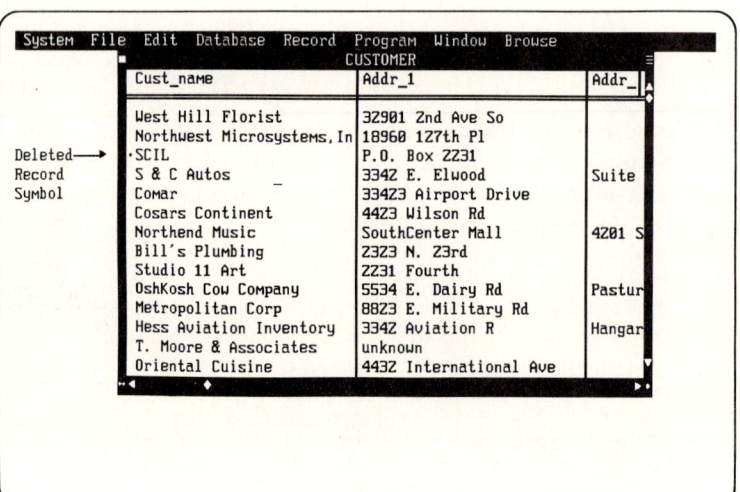

5. You can bring back the record marked for deletion by repeating the process for deleting it. Place the mouse pointer in the space left of the left-most field in the Browse window and click. The Deleted Record symbol disappears and the record is returned to the database. From the keyboard, select the record and choose Recall from the Record menu (Recall replaces Delete in this menu if the selected record is marked for deletion) or press Ctrl-U again. Deleting a record is a toggle action—do it once and the record is marked for deletion; do the same thing again and the marking is removed.

6. To remove all marked records permanently, choose Pack from the Database menu. FoxPro displays a dialog asking you to confirm that you really want to Pack the database. Choose Yes. Packing the database permanently removes the records marked for deletion.

7. Finally, choose Append from the Record window. FoxPro will open the data-entry window, enabling you to enter more records into the database. Add a record or two for practice, then close the data-entry window by pressing Esc or clicking the Close Window symbol in the upper left corner.

You have created a database and added, edited, and deleted records from it. An index on a database tells FoxPro in what order to show the data. You can tell FoxPro to set up an index on the CUST_NAME field. When you open the database and tell FoxPro to use that index, all records are listed in alphabetical order, even though they may have been entered randomly. If you create an index on the ZIP field, the records will appear in ZIP code order. An index is automatically updated whenever you add or delete a record, or change the entry in the field on which the database is indexed. To create an index for your database, perform the following steps:

1. Choose View from the Window menu. The View window opens (see fig. QS1.13).

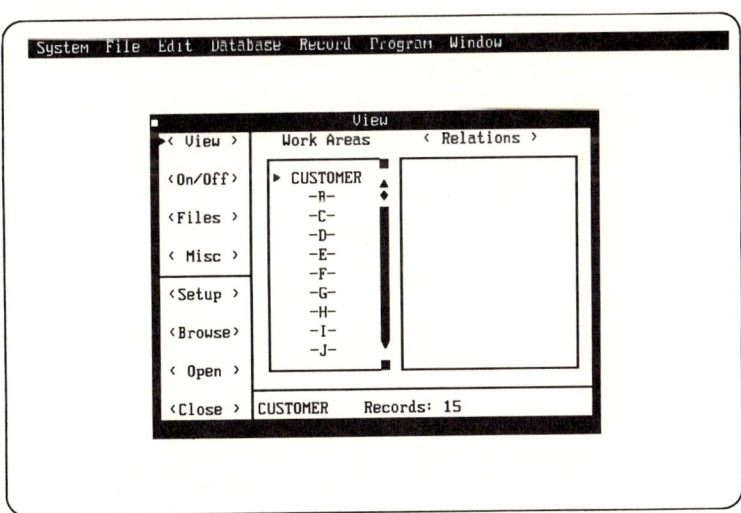

Fig. QS1.13.
The View
window.

2. Select Setup and the Setup dialog appears, as shown in figure QS1.14. In this dialog, you specify information that will be attached to the CUSTOMER database. Choose Add to tell FoxPro you want to add an index to the database.

Fig. QS1.14.
The Setup dialog.

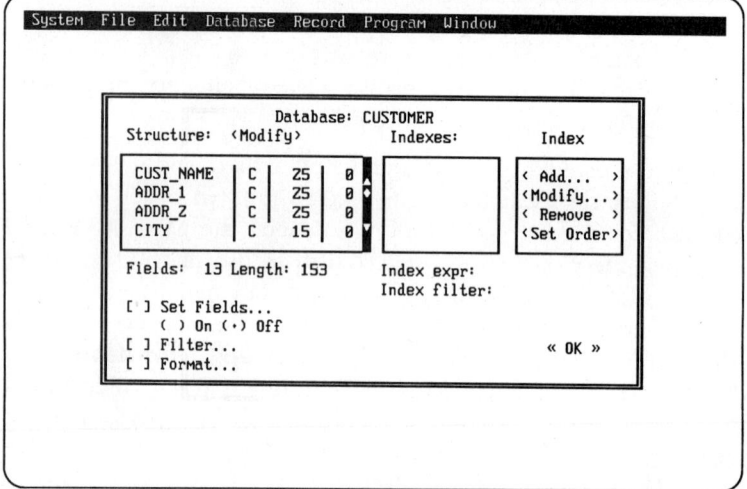

3. Next, you see the Open Index File dialog (see fig. QS1.15). FoxPro doesn't know whether you're going to create a new index or use one that already has been created (in an earlier FoxPro session). Because this will be a new index, choose New.

Fig. QS1.15.
The Open Index
File dialog.

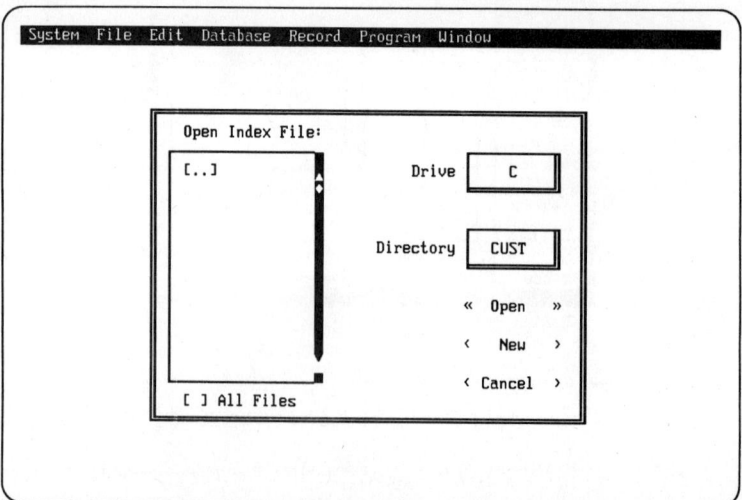

4. The Index On dialog appears (see fig. QS1.16). To create an index on the CUST_NAME field, select CUST_NAME in the scrollable list and press Enter or double-click CUST_NAME. CUST_NAME appears on the Expr line. Select OK and the window closes.

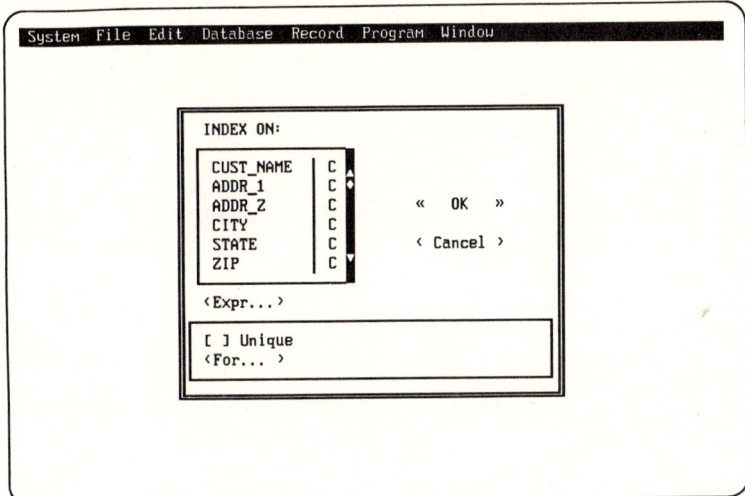

Fig. QS1.16.
The Index On
dialog.

5. You move to the Save As dialog, where you must enter a file name for this index file. Enter *custname* and choose Save to save the file. CUSTNAME becomes the DOS file name for the index file. Because it must adhere to the DOS rules for file names (eight characters long), you should leave out the underscore you used as a name in the database.

6. FoxPro now indexes the database. Choose Browse from the Record window and you will see that the database is presented in alphabetical order by the CUST_NAME field (see fig. QS1.17).

FoxPro also can sort a database, physically rearranging the records into the requested sort order. In a small database, sorting and indexing are similar, but in larger databases, sorting can take much longer. FoxPro indexing is so efficient that you will seldom, if ever, need to sort a database.

Generating Reports from the Database

FoxPro provides a sophisticated Report Writer, capable of reporting on multiple databases in an almost unlimited number of ways. Fortunately,

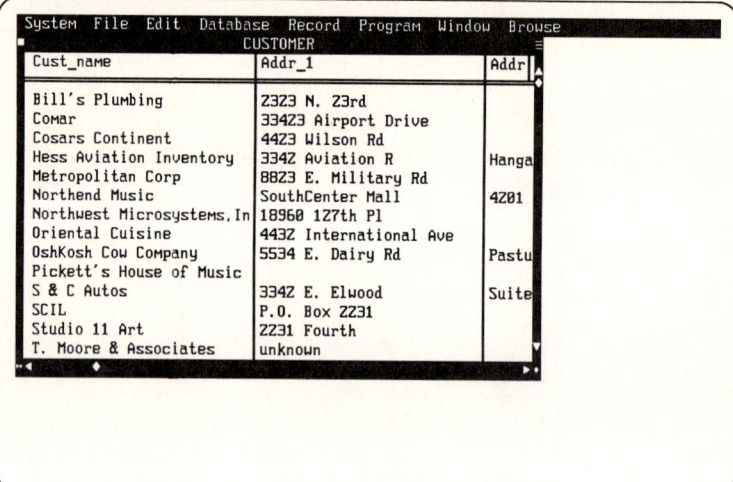

Fig. QS1.17.
The CUSTOMER
database,
presented
alphabetically by
the CUST_NAME
field.

the Report Writer also gives you a quick and easy way to create simple reports from one database. Now, to satisfy the boss, create and generate your first FoxPro report:

1. Choose New from the File menu. In the File New dialog, select Report and OK. FoxPro responds by presenting the Layout window, shown in figure QS1.18. The Layout Window is like a table top on which you arrange elements of your report: fields from the database, labels for the fields, titles, and lines.

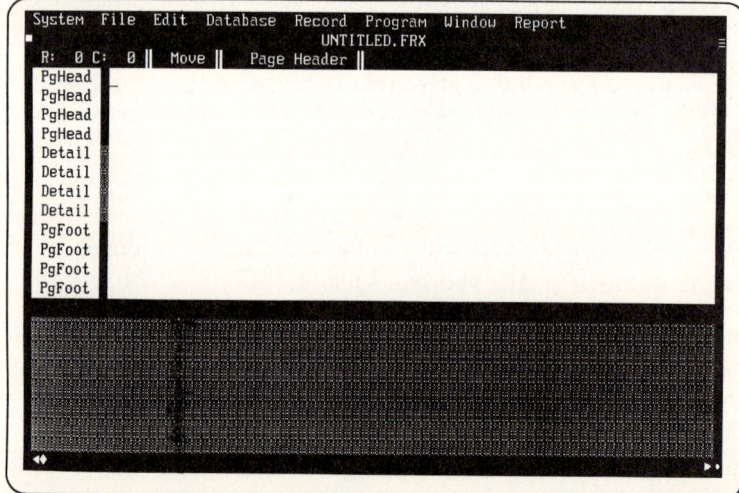

Fig. QS1.18.
The Layout
window.

2. Choose Quick Report from the Window menu. In the Quick
   Report dialog that appears, choose Form Layout (see fig. QS1.19).

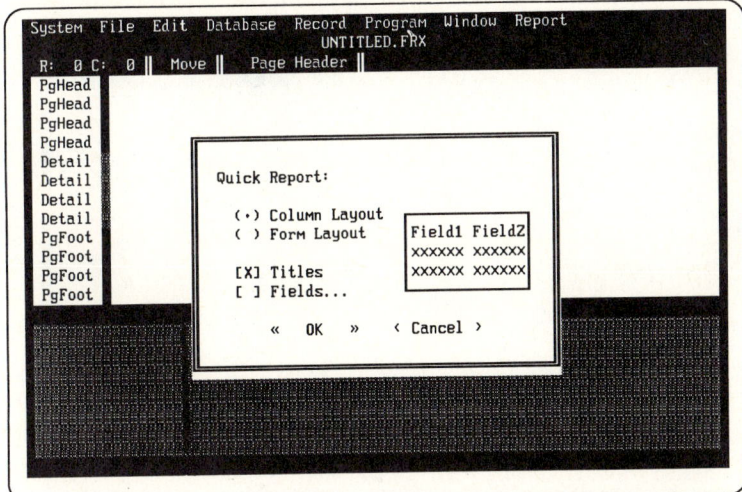

Fig. QS1.19.
The Quick Report
dialog.

3. FoxPro creates a default report by placing the database fields and
   labels on the Layout window, as shown in figure QS1.20.

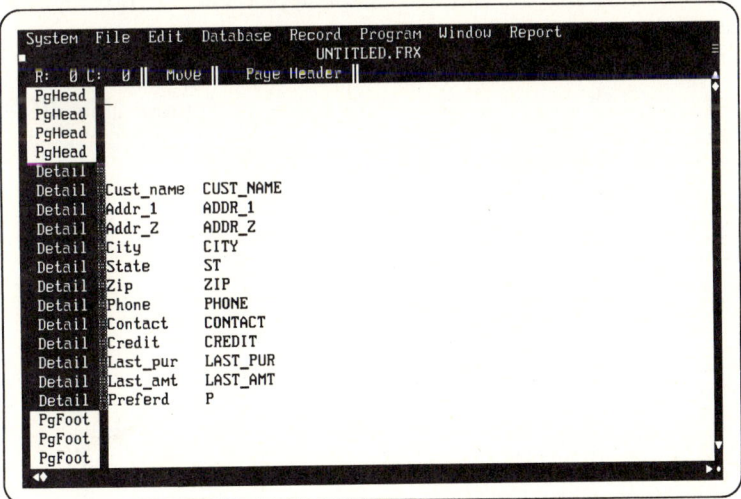

Fig. QS1.20.
The Layout, with
the default Quick
Report fields in
place.

To see how this report would look if you ran it right now, choose Page Preview from the Report menu. FoxPro runs the report and places the output in a Page Preview window (see fig. QS1.21).

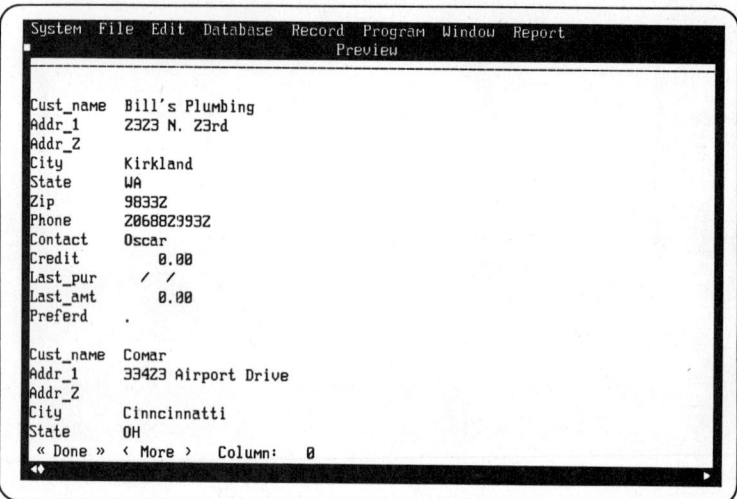

Fig. QS1.21.
Page Preview of the Quick Report.

As you can see, your report is a success. It is, however, a little on the plain side. Close the Page Preview window by choosing Done in the lower left corner to return to the Layout. To improve the appearance of your report, follow these steps:

1. First, replace the cryptic field labels with something you and other users will better understand. Make space for these labels by moving the database fields to the right. Move the CUST_NAME field by dragging until the field is about 15 columns to the right of its original position. If you're working from the keyboard, place the cursor on the CUST_NAME field and press Shift-space bar. You can use the arrow keys to relocate the field. Repeat this process with all the database fields, moving them to the right so that you have room for meaningful labels. When you're finished, the layout should look like the one in figure QS1.22.

2. Next, place the cursor on the label CUST_NAME and, while holding down the Ctrl key, click the mouse button or press the space bar. You now can change the text in the label with the standard FoxPro editing functions. Change this label to Customer Name. Press Enter to end the editing function. Move this field next to the CUST_NAME database field.

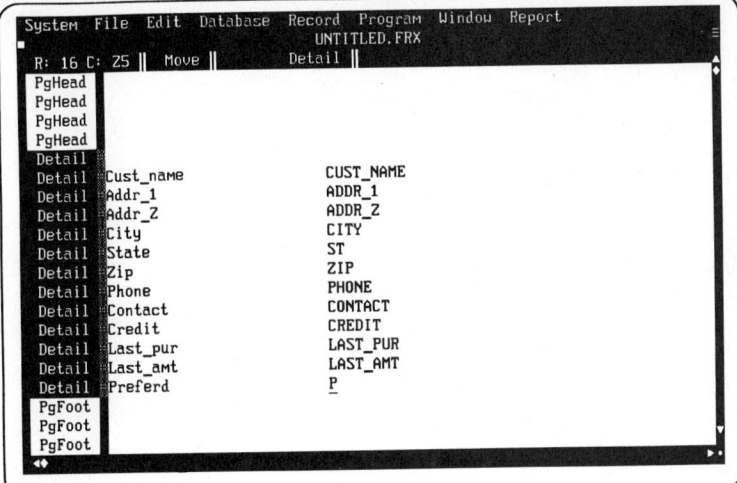

Fig. QS1.22.
Moving the
database fields
on the Layout.

Note that there is a minor bug if you enter the text-edit mode by pressing Ctrl-space bar; FoxPro will add a space at the cursor position. You must delete this space by pressing the Backspace key.

Continue editing and moving the labels until the layout looks like figure QS1.23.

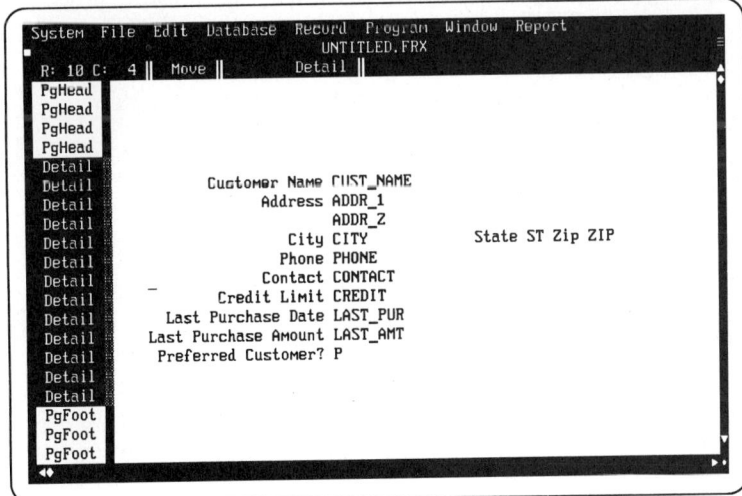

Fig. QS1.23.
Changing and
moving the field
labels on the
Layout.

Now, choose Page Preview from the Report window to see what your report looks like (see fig. QS1.24).

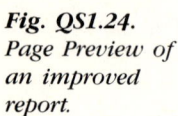
Fig. QS1.24.
Page Preview of
an improved
report.

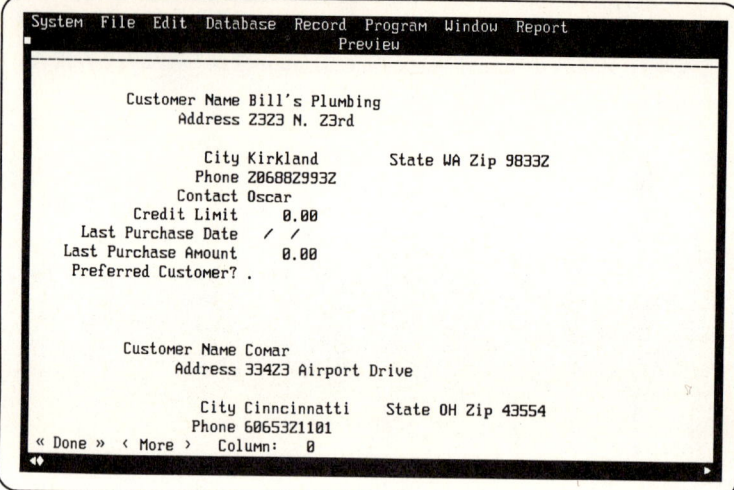

Much better, but the addition of a title and some lines will improve it even more:

1. Return to the Layout by choosing Done.

2. Move the cursor to the second line in the PgHead Band. Choose Add Text from the Report menu. An object named TEXT OBJECT appears on the Layout view at the position of the cursor. Press Shift-Enter or Shift-Click to edit this object and change the name to Customer Database Report. Move the new title to the center of the page.

3. Move the cursor to the left margin of the bottom line of the PgHead Band and choose Box from the Report menu. If you have a monochrome monitor, you will see the Box dialog, shown in figure QS1.25, asking what type of box to add.

4. Choose the default, Single Line. When you do so, you return to the Layout, which now contains a highlighted box object. Size the box by placing the cursor anywhere on the box frame and pressing Ctrl-space bar. The box will blink. The right and bottom sides of the box will move; use the arrow keys to move these sides until the box is the size you want. Press Enter to accept the box size.

   With a mouse, the process is different. Choose Box from the Report menu. Then place the cursor where you want to start the box or line and drag the mouse pointer to where the line or box should end. As you move the mouse around the Layout you can see how the box changes shape.

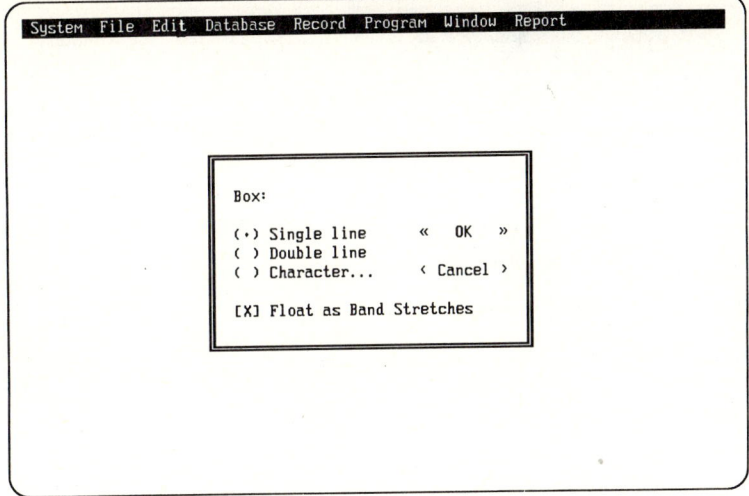

Fig. QS1.25.
The Box dialog,
showing the
different types of
box borders
available on
monochrome
monitors.

Horizontal and vertical lines are created by making a box and sizing it so that it has only one dimension. Figure QS1.26 shows the Layout for a more polished report of the CUSTOMER database.

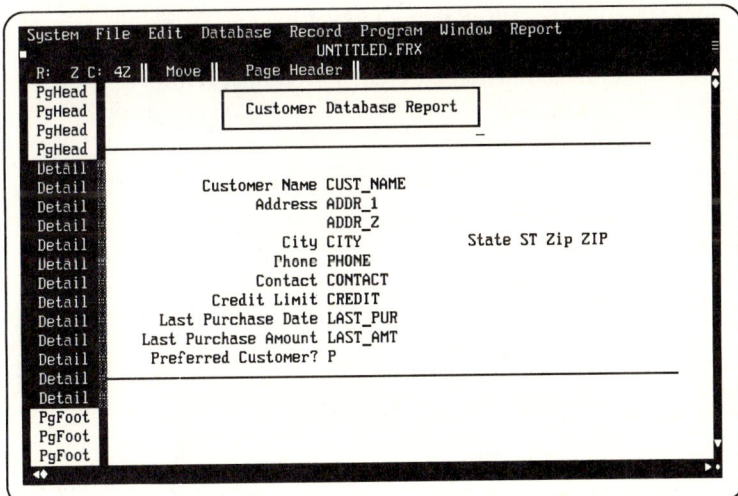

Fig. QS1.26.
Layout of a
polished report.

If you want to see how this report will appear in page preview, choose Page Preview from the Report menu (see fig. QS1.27).

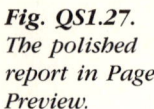

Fig. QS1.27.
The polished
report in Page
Preview.

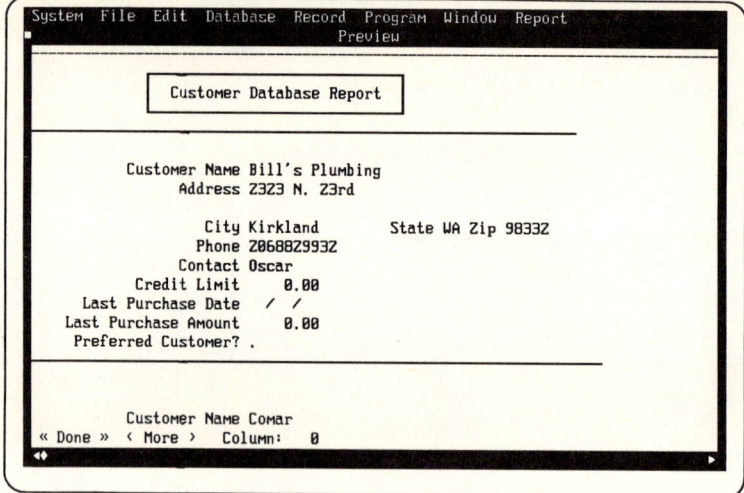

This new version is a much more readable report, certainly proof that your computer is good for more than playing F-15 pilot.

Finally, you will want to save and run your report:

1. Choose Save from the File menu. When the Save As dialog appears, enter the name *REPORT1* in the text box and choose Save (see fig. QS1.28). FoxPro saves your report with the name REPORT1.FRX (it automatically appends the FRX extension, which FoxPro uses to identify this as a report file).

Fig. QS1.28.
Saving the report
as REPORT1.

2. Close the Layout window by pressing Esc or clicking the Close Window symbol. You are returned to the FoxPro screen.

3. Choose Report from the Database menu to run your report. You will see the Report dialog, shown in figure QS1.29, in which you tell FoxPro which report to run.

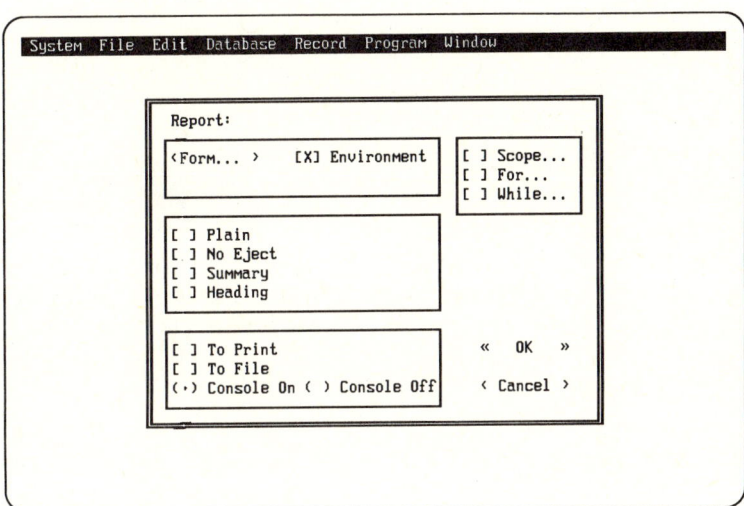

Fig. QS1.29.
The Report
dialog.

4. Click Form. FoxPro shows you the Report File dialog (see fig. QS1.30). Select REPORT1.FRX by clicking it or by using the Tab key to highlight it, then choosing OK. When you return to the Report dialog, the report name is entered below Form.

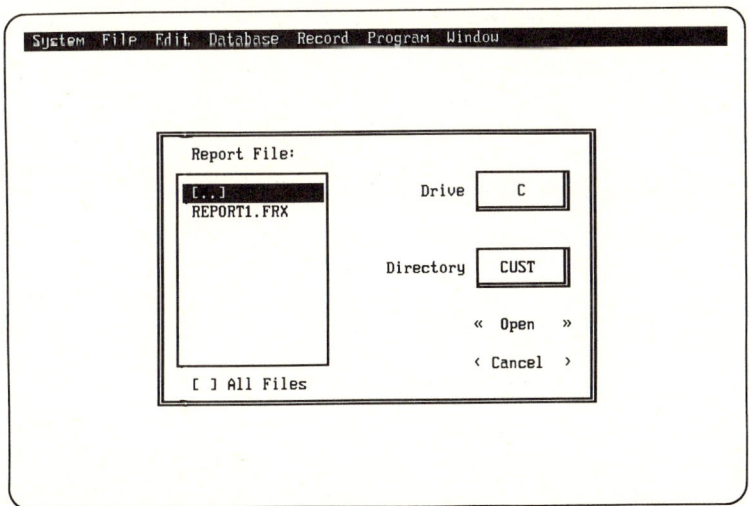

Fig. QS1.30.
The Report File
dialog, used to
choose which
report to run.

5. If you want to print this report on your printer, select To Print; otherwise the report will go only to the screen. Select OK, and FoxPro prints the report. Unless you choose Console Off, FoxPro will print the report to the screen as it prints it to the printer.

The purpose of all database programs is output—it doesn't do much good to store valuable and necessary information without a way to print it or view it on-screen. FoxPro provides a quick and easy way to create elegant reports.

Summary

FoxPro is a visually oriented program. Each action you choose from the menus causes FoxPro to respond, often with a window asking for more information. Unlike any other database system available on IBM PC compatible computers, FoxPro does not ask you to learn complicated command structures that must be entered from a command line. Developing and using databases in FoxPro requires that you know only what choice to make from the Main menu; from there, FoxPro presents the options and the choices you need to make.

In this quick start, you have learned how to design a database and define it in terms FoxPro understands. You can enter information into the database, edit, delete, and extract it in the form of reports. FoxPro's strength is that it gives you the power to do all this on increasingly sophisticated databases without much more effort. Throughout the range of database complexity, you will use the same basic tools and operations.

1

An Overview of FoxPro

FoxPro is the latest in a line of database management programs from Fox Software. FoxPro's *user interface*—the way the program interacts with the user—breaks completely from other past and current database programs. Other database management programs require you to learn and enter commands from a prompt, but FoxPro uses a visually oriented *graphical user interface*. Whether you're a new or experienced database user, you will find that FoxPro's windows, menus, and fill-in-the-blanks approach is easy to use and enables you to be more productive.

What Is a Database?

A *database* is simply a collection of data with some organization to it. A database can be a file cabinet, a stack of file cards, or a notebook. A computerized database is simply a collection of data organized and placed into computer files instead of notebooks or file cards. The advantage of computerizing a database is your ability to easily change the data, view it in different ways, and generate accurate reports. A computer lets you access the same data you had in your notebook, for example, but faster, more accurately, and in more ways than you could have when the data was in written form.

FoxPro enables you to use the two most important types of PC database files: flat files and relational database files.

Flat Files

If you store the number, name, address, and telephone number of every employee in your company, you have a *flat file* because the file has only two dimensions. Its width represents one record in the file, and its length represents the number of records in the file. Figure 1.1 illustrates a flat file. Programs that work only with flat files are called *file managers*.

Fig. 1.1.

A flat file.

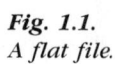

```
                  ◄──── Flat File's "width" ────►

              Employee│  Employee         Phone
              Number  │    Name          Number

              00001   │ JONES, W.L.      443-3342
              00002   │ WILSON, R.B.     334-2231
              00003   │ ZABY, M.M.       331-2203
              00004   │ ROCKETT, R.W.    335-4423
      Flat    00005   │ KENNEDY, B.W.    449-3312
     File's   00006   │ COLE, D.W.       442-3302
    "length"  00007   │ PICKETT, W.L.    334-9923
              00008   │ LENNON, M.W.     224-9903
              00009   │ FLEMING, R.H.    883-9923
              00010   │ STEWART, U.B.    334-9903
              00011   │ STEWART, L.L.    334-9903
              00012   │ SOLOMON, R.R.    443-5534
              00013   │ SIPPI, L.W.      449-0001
              00014   │ KEHOE, J.C.      550-3342
```

Relational Files

The power of FoxPro is in its capacity to work with files that are related; FoxPro is a relational database manager. How can files be related? How can those relationships make a database more powerful? Suppose that you already have created the employee number, name, and phone number file shown in figure 1.1, and now you want to store information about your company's organizational structure—namely, which employees work in which departments. You can create another flat file that includes the employee number, the department in which that employee works, and the employee's title. These two files are related, and the employee number field is the tie between them. In database design, you can illustrate this relationship as shown in figure 1.2.

In this example, you have one record for each employee. If you want a report of each department's employees, with phone numbers, you need to tell FoxPro that the two flat files are related. Then FoxPro can get the right information from each file. When FoxPro looks at a record in the

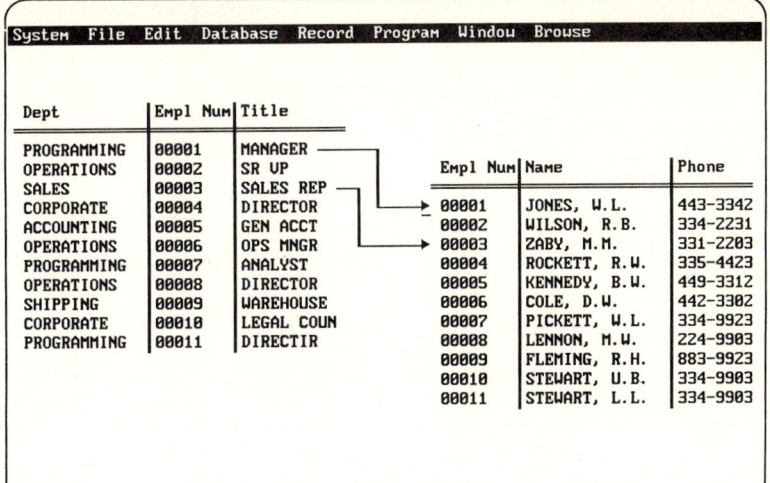

Fig. 1.2.
Two related files.

department file, the program looks at the employee number and automatically finds the record in the employee file with the same employee number. No matter how much you move through the department file, FoxPro keeps the employee file in sync, making available any information for that employee (see fig. 1.3).

```
System  File  Edit  Database  Record  Program  Window  Browse

                    DEPTMENT
   Dept                Empl_num  Titl

   PROGRAMMING         00001     MANAG
   OPERATIONS          00002     SR UP
   SALES               00003     SALES
   CORPORATE           00004                        EMPLOYEE
   ACCOUNTING          00005     GEN A     Empl_num  Empl_name      Phone_num
   OPERATIONS          00006     OPS M
   PROGRAMMING         00007     ANALY     00001    JONES, W.L.     443-3342
   OPERATIONS          00008     DIREC     00002    WILSON, R.B.    334-2231
   SHIPPING            00009     WAREH     00003    ZABY, M.M.      331-2203
   CORPORATE           00010     LEGAL     00004    ROCKETT, R.W.   335-4423
   PROGRAMMING         00011     DIREC     00005    KENNEDY, B.W.   449-3312
                                           00006    COLE, D.W.      442-3302
                                           00007    PICKETT, W.L.   334-9923
                                           00008    LENNON, M.W.    224-9903
                                           00009    FLEMING, R.H.   883-9923
                                           00010    STEWART, U.B.   334-9903
                                           00011    STEWART, L.L.   334-9903
```

Fig. 1.3.
Two related
FoxPro files.

The great advantage of a relational database manager over its predecessors (which require such connections between files to be defined when the database is created) is that you can set up the relationships as you need them. You can add another flat file and tell FoxPro about a relationship between that file and others. Or you can tell FoxPro that two files are related in one way for one purpose and then change that relationship when you need to. Relational database managers give you flexibility.

The Backgrounds of FoxBase +, FoxBase +/Mac, and FoxPro

In this section, you briefly examine the history of Fox Software's database products: FoxBase +, the company's first database program; FoxBase +/ Mac, the result of the company's move into the Macintosh world; and Fox-Pro, the company's current database program, which brings the Mac interface to the PC.

FoxBase +: A Look-Alike of dBASE III PLUS

In 1986, Fox Software introduced its first database product—FoxBase +. This product was one of several dBASE III PLUS look-alikes. FoxBase + had the same user interface and functionality as the industry leader, with one major improvement: FoxBase + was about five times faster than dBASE III PLUS when running programs written in the database language and doing important database functions such as sorting and indexing. Fox-Base + accomplished this supercharging by converting the program's source code into an intermediate type of code that ran much faster.

FoxBase + eventually evolved into Version 2.10, which was even faster and added a number of features not included by its competitors. Most of these features, though, were of benefit only to programmers who were developing full "turn-key" systems in FoxBase +. For the beginning to intermediate nonprogramming user, FoxBase + Version 2.10 was still a dBASE III PLUS clone, with the continued advantage of being faster in many areas.

FoxBase+/Mac: FoxBase+ in the Macintosh Interface

In 1988, FoxBase+ took an interesting detour into the world of the Apple Macintosh. Originally, Fox Software planned to convert FoxBase+ to the Macintosh environment with only minor changes; the result was to be FoxBase+ running on the Macintosh. In the process, though, FoxBase+ got the Macintosh "religion." In the end, FoxBase+ was almost completely rewritten for the Macintosh, to take full advantage of the Mac's graphical user interface. FoxBase+/Mac uses windows, dialog boxes, and all the other easy-to-use features for which the Macintosh is famous. When the time came for Fox Software to upgrade FoxBase+ in the PC world, the Macintosh version of FoxBase+ was the base.

FoxPro: Bringing the Macintosh Interface to the PC

Although Fox Software originally planned to convert FoxBase+ to the Macintosh, the company ended up going the other way—converting Fox-Base+/Mac back to the PC world. The program then took the name Fox-Pro. The user interface of FoxPro is a direct translation of the Macintosh interface. Windows, dialog boxes, radio buttons, and pull-down and pop-up menus abound. Additionally, Fox Software added a number of capabilities to FoxPro, and the company plans to add more capabilities in future versions to make FoxPro the equal of its competitors in functionality. This power, combined with the almost unbelievable ease of use brought from the Macintosh version, makes FoxPro the database program of choice for nearly all PC database needs.

The FoxPro Environment

If this theoretical discussion seems too complicated, don't worry; you will see that FoxPro makes seeing and setting up relations between files a simple matter. As you work through this book, you will learn the basics of working with related files. When you have learned the basics, you will think of more and more ways that FoxPro can save you time and effort by tying files together. More than that, as you use FoxPro, you will find that its unique environment makes it easy to try new things and learn the art of relational databases.

The Apple Macintosh is known for being easy to use. Its user interface depends on multiple windows to present information from the program to you, dialog boxes to get information from you about what you want to do, and a mouse for you to navigate through the windows and dialog boxes. FoxPro has brought this graphical user interface to the PC database world, and you will find that working with it becomes second nature quickly.

Windows

FoxPro presents information in windows. When you tell FoxPro to show you the database, the program does so in the Browse window. When you want to enter or edit data, you use a data-entry window. Many different windows can be present on-screen at one time, and you can resize the windows and move them to make the ones you want to view more visible. Figure 1.4 shows two databases in Browse windows.

Fig. 1.4.
The Browse
window.

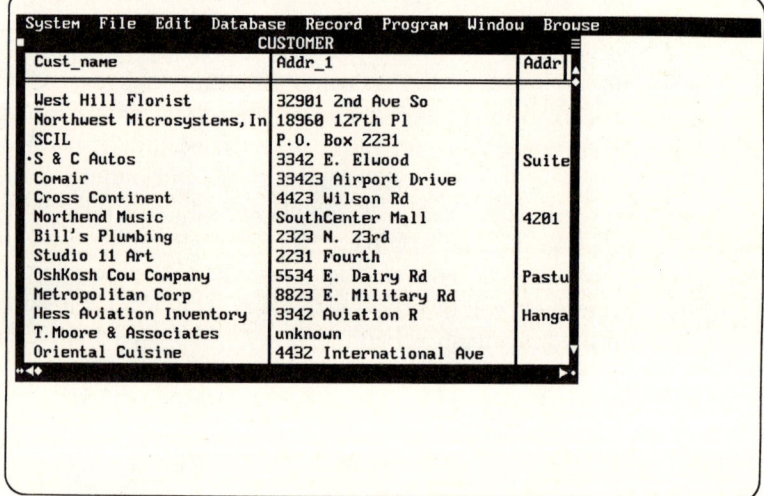

A dialog box is a form of window; FoxPro uses dialogs to get information from you about what you want to do. Figure 1.5 shows the Preferences dialog. A dialog may contain several different types of elements, each representing a different type of choice to be made. These choices, and how to make them, are examined later in this chapter.

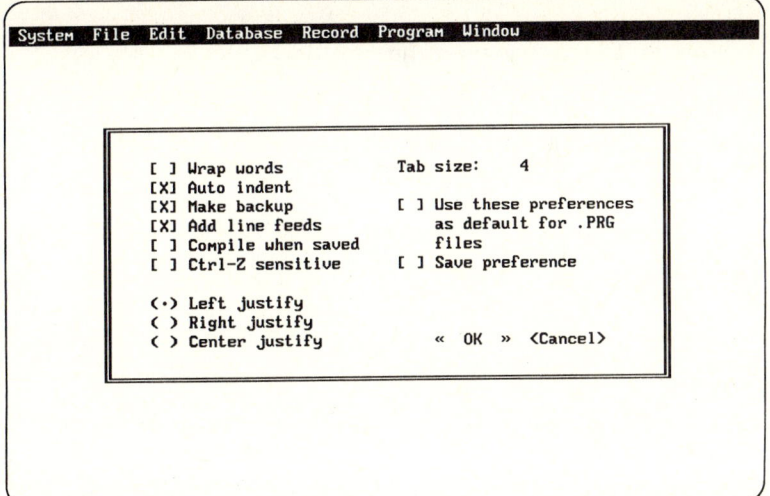

System File Edit Database Record Program Window

```
[ ] Wrap words              Tab size:    4
[X] Auto indent
[X] Make backup             [ ] Use these preferences
[X] Add line feeds              as default for .PRG
[ ] Compile when saved          files
[ ] Ctrl-Z sensitive        [ ] Save preference

(·) Left justify
( ) Right justify
( ) Center justify          «  OK  »  <Cancel>
```

Fig. 1.5.
The Preferences
dialog.

The Mouse

You can use the mouse to accomplish just about everything in FoxPro. As with the Macintosh, the only time you really need to use the keyboard is to enter numbers and text.

Fox Software's first recommendation for speeding up FoxPro is to use a mouse if you're not already doing so. If you're new to using a mouse, you will find that it becomes second nature to you quickly, and you will move without hesitation around FoxPro. If, however, you don't have a mouse or prefer not to use one, all of FoxPro's power is available from the keyboard.

The Keyboard

In many cases, keyboard users of FoxPro will claim that they can do things as fast from the keyboard as mouse users, and often they will be right. Most of FoxPro's commands can be issued with just one or two keystrokes. Even inveterate mouse users will find that the keyboard commands are quick and convenient.

Here is an example of a quick keyboard action equivalent to a mouse selection. The following keystrokes are necessary for you to open the Browse window:

Press   To

Alt-D   Open the File pull-down menu
B   Open the Browse window

For many users, pressing these keys is faster than using the mouse to pull down the File menu and selecting Browse from it. If you're using only the keyboard, you will not feel terribly disadvantaged (although using a mouse *is* faster in many areas). And, if you're a mouse user, you will find that you will want to use the keyboard on many occasions.

The Command Line

FoxBase+ users must rely on the command line, which you use to enter commands to tell FoxBase+ what to do. The command line environment exists in FoxPro, too, in the Command window. Any action FoxPro executes from the menus and windows also can be executed from the Command window. In fact, each action you take in FoxPro is translated to a command line command and appears in the Command window. Figure 1.6 shows the Command window with several lines built by FoxPro from menu actions. As you become more experienced, you will find that you can do some things faster by issuing commands in the Command window.

Fig. 1.6.
The Command
window.

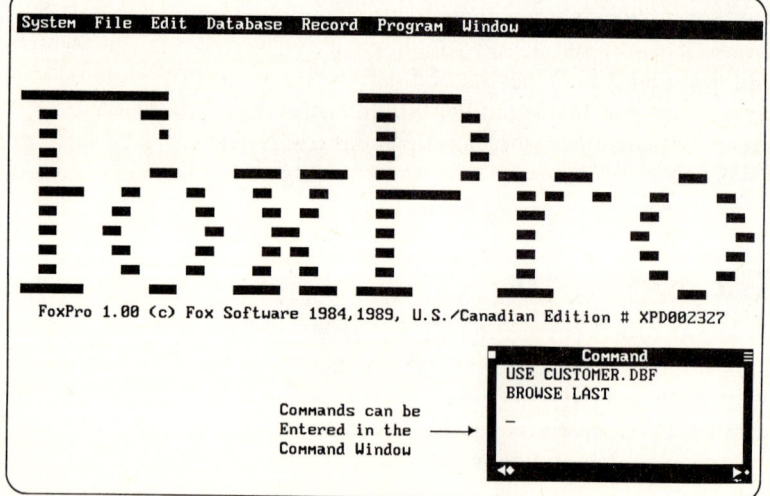

FoxPro Capabilities

What can FoxPro and FoxBase+ do for you? Like any good database manager, FoxPro and FoxBase+ give you the power to manage incredible amounts of data, regardless of its complexity. If you can organize the data at all, FoxPro and FoxBase+ give you data-entry, organizing, and reporting tools to make sense of it. As you become more familiar with these programs, you will find that the FoxPro and FoxBase+ programming language enables you to build more sophisticated applications. If you want, you can use the advanced features of these two programs to develop finished turnkey applications for yourself and other users.

Entering and Editing Data in FoxPro and FoxBase+

At the simplest level, FoxPro and FoxBase+ give you a data-entry screen that allows you to put data into your database quickly and easily. You will find, though, that a custom data-entry screen speeds your data entry and makes it much more accurate. FoxPro and FoxBase+ give you tools to create sophisticated input screens. You can get data for several different databases from the same screen. You can put edit masks in data-entry fields to make sure that the data fits a mold. Numeric fields can have upper and lower limits; FoxPro tells you if you enter a number outside that limit. Text fields can have character "masks," such as dashes or parentheses to make the data fit a mold.

More than anything else, your ability to customize screens makes them easier to use. Compare the default data-entry screen shown in figure 1.7 with the custom screen shown in figure 1.8. Which would you rather use?

Reporting in FoxPro and FoxBase+

The fanciest database in the world is useless if you cannot get information out of it. FoxPro provides an amazingly sophisticated report generator. With it, you can create highly customized reports, with information coming from different databases, with subtotals and totals, and with boxes and lines to make the report easily readable. Figure 1.9 shows a report created with the FoxPro report generator.

Fig. 1.7.
A default data-entry screen.

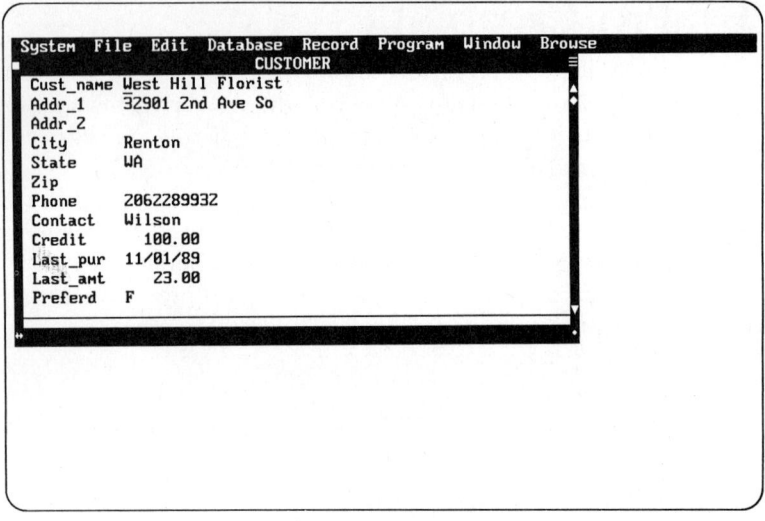

Fig. 1.8.
A custom data-entry screen.

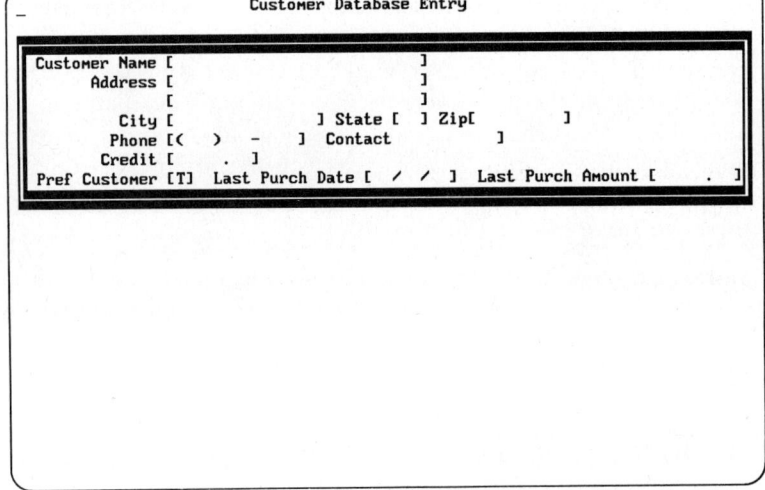

In the area of reporting, FoxBase+ takes a back seat to FoxPro. The FoxBase+ report generator is not as sophisticated as FoxPro's. You will find it capable for basic reports, but more complex reports require some programming ability or an add-on program such as R&R, a report writing program for use with dBASE III, dBASE IV, and FoxBase+.

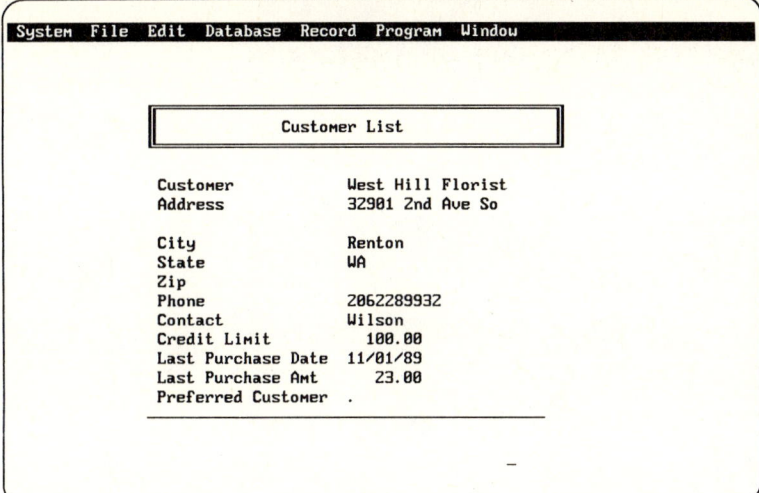

Fig. 1.9.
A FoxPro report.

Programming in FoxPro and FoxBase+

Even if you're not a programmer, you may find uses for the FoxPro and FoxBase+ programming language. When you find yourself doing a sequence of actions over and over again, you may want to automate that sequence so that all you have to do is give FoxPro or FoxBase+ a DO command. At its most basic level, a FoxPro or FoxBase+ program is just a series of commands you enter from the keyboard or with a mouse. Figure 1.10 shows a simple FoxPro program that opens and reindexes a database and then displays it in the Browse window.

You can see that this program, executed with a DO command (from the Program menu or Command window), saves you from executing several commands every time you want to open and look at this database.

Using Advanced Features of FoxPro and FoxBase+

For those of you who develop an in-depth knowledge of FoxPro and Fox-Base+, these programs provide the tools you need to develop complete turn-key systems, with custom menus, pull-down and pop-up menus, data-entry screens, and reports.

Future versions of FoxPro also will support network operations, in which one database can be used by several people at once. FoxPro Version 1.0 does not have this capability.

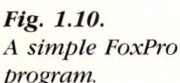

Fig. 1.10.
A simple FoxPro
program.

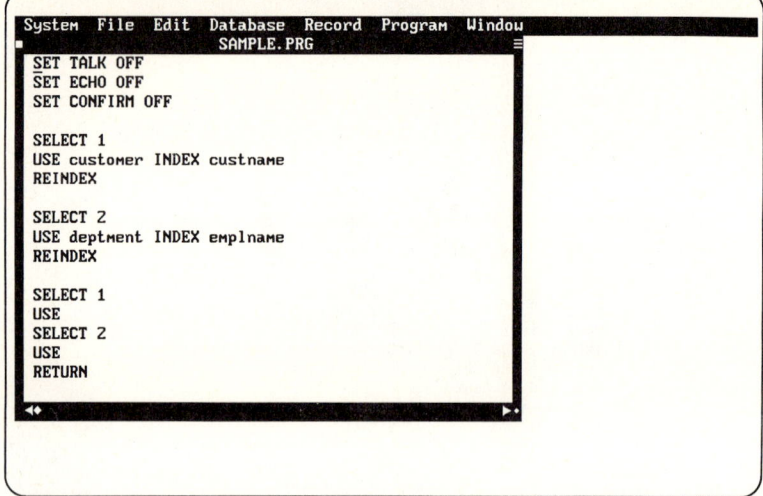

```
System  File  Edit  Database  Record  Program  Window
                    SAMPLE.PRG
SET TALK OFF
SET ECHO OFF
SET CONFIRM OFF

SELECT 1
USE customer INDEX custname
REINDEX

SELECT 2
USE deptment INDEX emplname
REINDEX

SELECT 1
USE
SELECT 2
USE
RETURN
```

The FoxPro Interface

If you're familiar with the Apple Macintosh, you will be familiar with Fox-Pro. FoxPro's interface came directly from the Macintosh world. To use FoxPro, you need to know how to do three things (whether you're using a mouse or the keyboard): make selections from menus, work with windows, and "talk" to FoxPro through dialog boxes.

Choosing from Menus

At all times, FoxPro presents a main menu across the top of the screen (see fig. 1.11). Each word on the menu is called a *pad* and represents a group of actions that FoxPro can perform.

Each of the menu pads has a pull-down menu associated with it, showing all the options for that main menu selection (see fig. 1.12). Not all main menu pads can be selected at all times, and not all options are available at all times. When an option is unavailable, it is dimmed and you cannot select it. For example, if you select the Record menu pad when no database is open, nearly all the options—which do things to a database file—are unavailable.

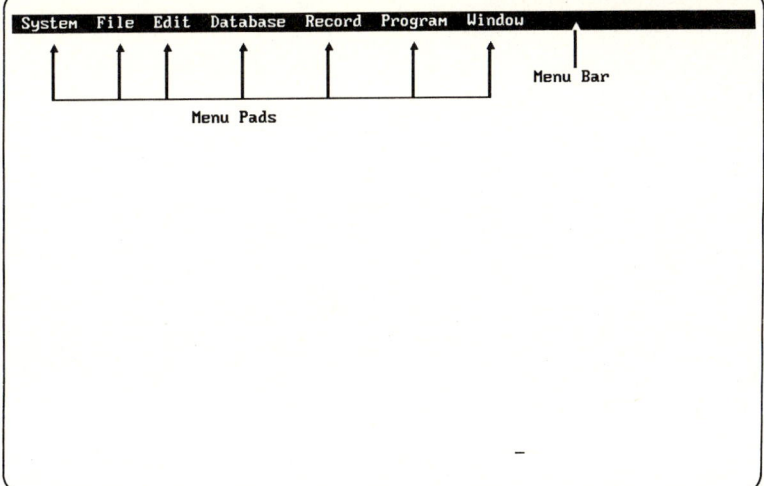

Fig. 1.11.
The FoxPro main menu.

Fig. 1.12.
The File pull-down menu.

To select a main menu pad with a mouse, simply click the pad. To activate the pull-down menu associated with a main menu pad, point to the pad and drag the pointer downward; the pull-down menu appears immediately. To select an item, continue dragging the pointer until the item you want to select is highlighted and then release the mouse button. The pull-down menu disappears, and FoxPro proceeds to do what you asked.

From the keyboard, selecting a main menu item is just as easy. Pressing the Alt key or the F10 key highlights the first main menu pad, System. Now you can use the right- and left-arrow keys to highlight the main menu pad you want, or you can press the key corresponding to the first letter of your menu choice. For example, pressing F highlights the File menu pad. Pressing Enter brings up the pull-down menu associated with that pad. To select from the options, use the up- and down-arrow keys to move the highlight and press Enter when your chosen option is highlighted. The pull-down menu disappears, and FoxPro starts to work.

You also can activate a pull-down menu from the keyboard by pressing simultaneously the Alt key and the key corresponding to the first letter of your menu choice; the pull-down menu appears with the first option highlighted. As an example, pressing Alt-F causes the File pull-down menu to appear.

Using Windows

FoxPro presents everything in windows. Windows can be opened, sized, moved, zoomed, and closed. Some dialog boxes are windows of a sort and also can be moved—but not sized or zoomed. Each of these actions can be done with the mouse and from the keyboard, but they are more easily done with the mouse.

Windows and the Mouse

Windows and the mouse go together easily. Each window contains a number of markers that the mouse uses to move, resize, or close the window. Figure 1.13 shows a window with these mouse markers.

After a window is opened (which occurs when you select a menu choice that calls for a window), you may want to change the window's size or move it. To move a window with a mouse, simply put the pointer in the title bar and drag the window to where you want it. You can drag the window almost off the page, leaving only one border visible.

To resize a window, put the mouse pointer in the lower right corner, where a small dot is located. Now drag that corner until the window is the size and shape you want, releasing the mouse button to set the new size. You also can zoom a window to take up all the screen by clicking the Zoom symbol, the three horizontal lines in the upper left corner of the window; clicking there again returns the window to its original or resized dimensions.

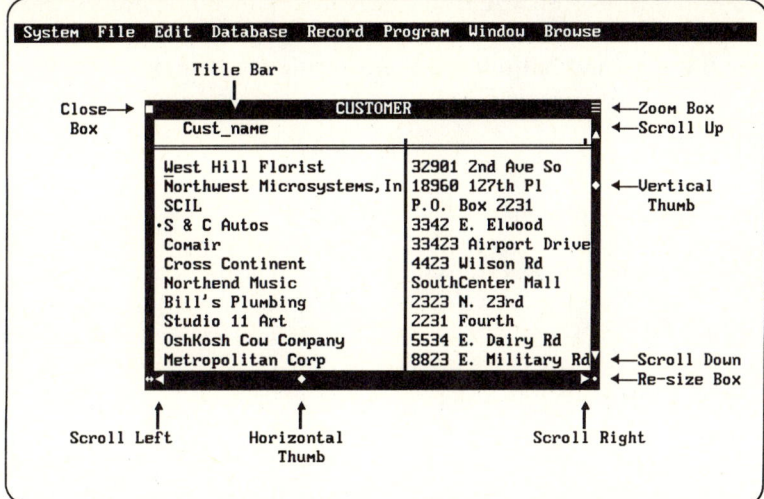

Fig. 1.13.
A FoxPro window with mouse markers.

You can scroll in a window by pointing to the arrows in the Vertical Scroll Bar (the right margin) or the Horizontal Scroll Bar (the bottom margin). Clicking an arrow once scrolls up or down one line, or right or left one field. You also can move in the window by dragging the thumb, which is the diamond shape between the scroll arrows in the scroll bar. Your position in the list being presented will change to reflect where the thumb is located in the scroll bar. If you move the thumb three-quarters of the way along the scroll bar, the window will start listing at three-quarters of the way through the list being shown.

You close the window by clicking the Close Window symbol, which is in the upper left corner of the window, or by choosing Close from the Window menu.

Working with FoxPro windows by using a mouse is quick and easy. If you have a mouse, you will never use the keyboard to move and resize windows.

Windows and the Keyboard

Moving, resizing, and closing windows is easily done from the keyboard. To move a window on-screen, choose Move from the Window menu or press Ctrl-M. The borders of the active window flash, indicating that FoxPro needs to know where you want the window moved to. Use the four arrow keys to move the window to the desired location and press Enter to complete the move.

To resize a window, choose Size from the Window menu or press Ctrl-S. Again, the borders start to flash. Now, however, using the four arrow keys affects only the right and bottom margins, causing the window to change its size. When you have changed the window to the size you want, press Enter to set that size.

You also can zoom a window from the keyboard by pressing Ctrl-Z or choosing Zoom from the Window menu. If the window does not occupy all the screen, FoxPro will expand the window to do so; if you already have zoomed the window, FoxPro will shrink it back to its original size.

Using Dialogs

Dialogs are the primary means of communicating with FoxPro. As with windows, moving around dialogs is easier if you have a mouse, but keyboard users do have all the capabilities available to them.

The elements present in a dialog are examined in the following sections.

Text Buttons

Text buttons are enclosed in angle brackets; examples include <Add...> and <Modify...>. A text button enclosed in double angle brackets is the default; <<OK>> is an example. When chosen, a text button causes FoxPro to take some action. If an ellipsis follows the text button, another dialog will open specific to that action. For space considerations, however, this book omits the angle brackets when referring to one of these buttons.

With a mouse, choose a text button by moving the mouse pointer to the button and clicking. From the keyboard, move the highlight to the text button you want to choose and press Enter.

Check Boxes

A check box is a pair of square brackets next to an option. You use a check box to turn on and off a setting described by the option name. For example, there are check boxes for wrapping words, autoindenting, making backups, adding line feeds, and so on. An X in the check box means that the setting is turned on; no X means that the setting is turned off.

With a mouse, you can turn a check box on and off by pointing to the box and clicking. If you're using the keyboard, move the highlight to the box and press Enter to change the setting. The text for some check boxes has an underlined letter; you can change the setting of these options by pressing the key that is underlined.

Radio Buttons

Radio buttons are a series of choices, each with parentheses next to it; you can select only one of the choices at a given time, just as you can select only one station-selection button on your car radio. When you choose one button, the others go off.

Figure 1.14 shows the Save Current Document As dialog with several elements. The elements present in this dialog are examined in the following sections.

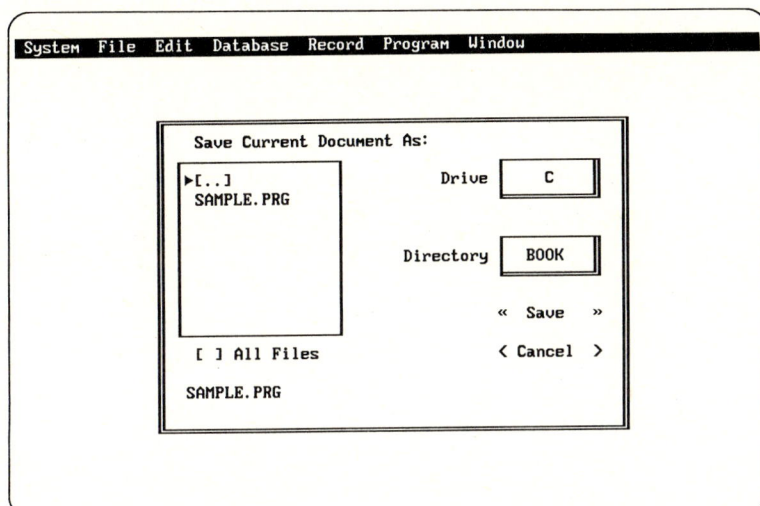

Fig. 1.14.
The Save Current Document As dialog.

Scrollable Lists

The scrollable list appears in the box under the words Save Current Document As. A scrollable list presents a list through which you can move upward and downward to make a selection. With a mouse, use the scroll bar to move through the list, and click on an item to select it. From the keyboard, scroll through the list with the up- and down-arrow keys, and select an item by pressing Enter while that item is highlighted.

Pop-Up Controls

Pop-up controls are boxes that have pop-up menus associated with them. You can identify a pop-up control by the double line on the right and bottom margins of the box. In figure 1.14, you use the Drive pop-up control to choose on which drive you want FoxPro to save the file. To activate the associated pop-up menu, point the mouse to the pop-up control and drag downward to see the menu and make your selection. If you're using the keyboard, tab to the pop-up control and press the space bar; then use the up- and down-arrow keys to highlight your selection and press the space bar again to activate it. Your new selection appears in the pop-up control.

Text Boxes

A text box is simply a field that you use to give FoxPro some textual information, such as a file name. If you're using the keyboard, you can reach the text box by tabbing to it; then enter the text from the keyboard. Mouse users click the mouse in the text box and then enter the text.

Moving Around in a Dialog

A dialog may have many check boxes, radio buttons, scrollable lists, text boxes, and text buttons. Mouse users can select any option by pointing the mouse and clicking. Keyboard users can navigate around the dialog by using the keys listed in table 1.1.

Table 1.1
Keys Used To Move Around in a Dialog

Key	Function
Esc	Exit the dialog without taking any action.
Ctrl-Enter	Choose the default text button and exit.
Tab	Move to the next dialog item.
Shift-Tab	Move to the previous dialog item.
Arrows	Move up and down in a scrollable list.
Home, End	Move to the top and bottom of a scrollable list.
PgUp, PgDn	Move to the previous or next display page in a scrollable list.

Chapter Summary

In this chapter, you learned that FoxPro and FoxBase + can give you control over large and complex data files and that, as you progress, FoxPro and FoxBase + 's power grows with you. By working carefully through the quick starts and the chapters that follow, you will become proficient in the many areas of this powerful and easy-to-use program. You already have become familiar with FoxPro's unique windowing environment. Now you're ready to move on, defining and creating your databases.

Designing and Creating a Database

FoxPro may be the most powerful and easy-to-use database system in the PC world, but it cannot read your thoughts. You must tell FoxPro what information you want to store in your database. And, for all its power, FoxPro can be very inflexible sometimes. When you tell FoxPro about your databases, you must be precise. As nice as it would be, you cannot give FoxPro a command such as,

Create a database with names, addresses, and phone numbers

FoxPro can make a database designer lazy. You can make changes to a FoxPro database so easily that you will be tempted to create your databases "on the fly" and then change them later when you find they're not quite right. You can (sometimes) get away with this on simple databases, but you will not always be creating simple databases. Changes to big, multiple-file databases can be made as quickly, but the changes can ripple through the entire database, affecting screens, reports, and programs. The time to think about your database and understand clearly what you need from it is before you start talking to FoxPro. This is true for even the simplest database. If you follow this practice for all your databases, you will find the complex ones much easier to design and implement.

In this chapter, you learn how to translate what you want from your database system into something that FoxPro can understand and act on. You go from the database idea to the database design to the database definition, which is what you describe to FoxPro. You learn how to define and create indexes that affect the presentation and the processing of your databases.

53

Deciding What Information You Need to Store

FoxPro, like all database managers, is sensitive to its diet; if you stuff it full of useless information, FoxPro will get fat and slow. So it's important that you feed FoxPro only the information it needs to do its job. Your inquiries will run faster, your reports more quickly. The first step in designing your database is deciding what information you need to have in the database files.

Determining Your Objectives

What do you want your database to do? Think through all the things that you want it to do, even far into the future. If you're building a customer file, you eventually may want to track all customer contacts; you may want to store invoices and billings of each customer; you may want to do historical reporting of which customers have bought what products. Now is the time to look at the long term so that, as you build the pieces of the database, you will know you're going in the right direction.

An old management saying goes, "If you don't know where you're going, any road will get you there." That certainly applies to database design; seldom will you build one or two files and find that's all you need. Once you get the database fever, you will think of more and more applications. If you can, at the beginning, give your database a long-term goal.

It is, however, in the short term that you must get that first database up and running. Again, clearly define what you want the first applications to do. Do you want your inventory database to help your salespeople? Or your credit department? You probably have a good idea of what you want this application to do, but you should write down the objectives. These objectives can be the first pieces of documentation in your database dictionary.

Determining Database Output

In a world where the amount of information seems to grow exponentially, it's easy to start designing your database by surveying all the available data applicable to your objective. If you are building a customer database, you may want to include the customer name, address, phone number, contact, president, vice-president, buyer, warehouse address, shipping address, billing address, subsidiaries, parent companies, and so on. But the key to building a clear, concise database design is to start at the other end: what data has to come *out* of the database?

The first thing you should do is design all the reports that you want and all the computer screens that you need. Be as clear and complete as you can. Draw the reports on a piece of paper if that helps; do the same with inquiry screens. Then you can ensure that the necessary data—and only the necessary data—goes into the database. Figures 2.1 and 2.2 show a sample inquiry screen and a sample report for a simple inventory database.

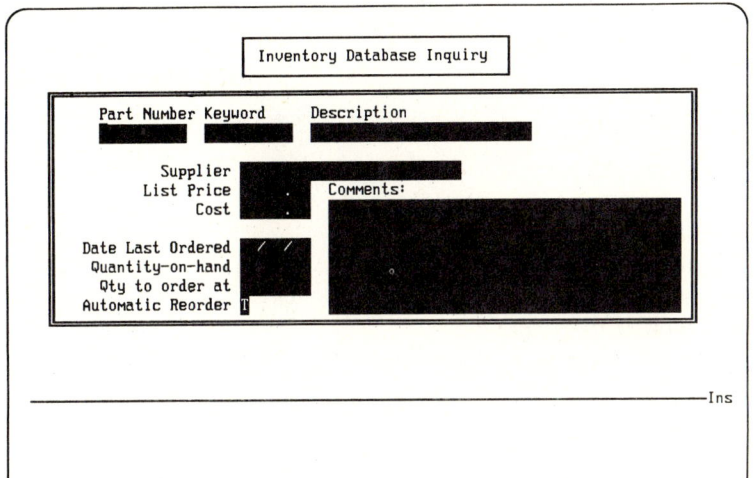

```
           Inventory Database Inquiry


   Part Number Keyword    Description
   ██████████  ██████████  ██████████████████

        Supplier  █████████████████████
      List Price  ████. Comments:
            Cost  ████. ████████████████████
                         ████████████████████
Date Last Ordered  ██/██/██  ████████████████████
Quantity-on-hand   ████  ████████████████████
   Qty to order at ████  ████████████████████
Automatic Reorder  █  ████████████████████


                                            ─Ins
```

Fig. 2.1.
An inquiry screen.

```
                Inventory Database
                Stock Status Report

Date: 01/01/89        Beginning Part Number: 0000000000
Time: 11:32           Ending Part Number   : 9999999999

Part                       Quantity  Re-order  Automatic
Number   Keyword  Description  on hand  Quantity  Reorder   Cost

aaaaaaaaaa  aaaaaaaaaa aaaaaaaaaaaaaaa  nnnn   nnnn      1     $9,999.99
aaaaaaaaaa  aaaaaaaaaa aaaaaaaaaaaaaaa  nnnn   nnnn      1     $9,999.99
aaaaaaaaaa  aaaaaaaaaa aaaaaaaaaaaaaaa  nnnn   nnnn      1     $9,999.99
aaaaaaaaaa  aaaaaaaaaa aaaaaaaaaaaaaaa  nnnn   nnnn      1     $9,999.99

Total Items Processed: nnnn
Items below reorder  : nnnn

End of Report_
```

Fig. 2.2.
An example report.

The second step in designing your database is to identify and name all the pieces of data that you have put on your reports and screens. Because FoxPro databases have a 10-character limit for data names, keep the names short to ease the transition from paper to FoxPro. The data dictionary in table 2.1 lists the data names given to the data for the sample report and screen.

Table 2.1
Data Dictionary for Inventory Database

Report Data Elements

    date
    time
    part _ number
    keyword
    description
    quantity_on _ hand
    reorder_ point
    automatic_ reorder?
    cost
    total_ rpt _ items
    total_ reorder_ items

Inquiry Screen Elements

    part _ number
    keyword
    description
    supplier
    quantity_on _ hand
    reorder_ point
    automatic_ reorder
    cost
    price
    comments

Is it essential to put all this in writing? Yes! One of the great mysteries of the computer system design world is how everyone agrees that documenting a system is absolutely necessary, but no one ever does it. I once inherited responsibility for a huge inventory and purchasing system in which my company had invested over $250,000; the documentation for that system was a few handwritten notes and some comments in the code. We ended up throwing out that system because we couldn't make changes to it.

So start right now to document all systems you create, no matter how simple, by putting things on paper and storing the paper where you will be able to find it. Probably the best investment you can make to ease your database chores is a three-ring notebook and paper.

By defining what information must come out of a database, you also define the information that has to go into it. Look at each piece of data that you have defined as an output of your database. Where will the database get that piece of data? Most of the data will enter your database in the same format as it comes out. The part number that appears on the report and inquiry screens will go into the database and be stored as is. But other information may have to be calculated. If one of the outputs of the system is, for example, the average invoice amount of a customer, the database will not store that value, but it will store each invoice amount and can calculate the average invoice amount.

You should read the database dictionary you are creating and make sure that you understand how each piece of information will be derived. Table 2.2 shows a data dictionary listing the source of each piece of data.

Table 2.2
Data Dictionary for Inventory Database

Report Data Elements

Element Name	Source
date	FoxPro
time	FoxPro
part_number	inventory_record
keyword	inventory_record
description	inventory_record
quantity_on_hand	inventory_record
reorder_point	inventory_record
automatic_reorder?	inventory_record
cost	inventory_record
total_rpt_items	computed
total_reorder_items	computed

Table 2.2—*Continued*

Inquiry Screen Elements

Element Name	Source
part_number	inventory_record
keyword	inventory_record
description	inventory_record
supplier	inventory_record
quantity_on_hand	inventory_record
reorder_point	inventory_record
automatic_reorder	inventory_record
cost	inventory_record
price	inventory_record
comments	inventory_record

Building a Database Structure

Once you know what information you want FoxPro to store in its database, you can see what the structure of the database must be. In a simple one-file database, such as the inventory example, all the information can be stored in one database file.

How do you decide whether you need only one database file or more than one to store your data? This topic is covered in greater depth in Part II, but for now, a quick introduction to database design will help.

In any system, computerized or not, information tends to fall into logical clumps. For instance, in a customer database, a clump of data exists for the customer—name, address, phone number, and so on. In each case, there will be one piece of each type of data for each customer—one address, one phone number, and one city. You gather this data into one file and call it the CUSTOMER file. Another clump of data might be for an order of merchandise—one customer number, one order number, one order date, one total amount. You could then gather this order data into a file called ORDER.

Generally, in designing databases, you identify the clumps of data and put them together into a database file. Then, if you want to tie together those two files to look at all the orders for one customer, for example, you tell FoxPro that a relation exists between the ORDER and CUSTOMER files. FoxPro can provide both customer and order information at the same time, correctly tied together.

If this seems confusing, fear not; by the time you get to Part II of this book, which explores the multiple-file capabilities of FoxPro, your experience at designing and implementing single-file databases will have prepared you well.

FoxPro stores its information in database files. A *database* corresponds to a stack of paper, with each sheet of paper containing information about one clump of data. If you wrote down on a piece of paper all the information you wanted to store about one company, each piece of information would be the same as a database *field* and the whole sheet of paper would be the same as a *record*. If you did this for many companies and stacked all the sheets in a pile, that pile would correspond to a database file. To define a database to FoxPro, you must tell FoxPro about each of the fields in that database.

Now, back to your database. You have defined what data you want out of your database, and you know what fields will store that information. Next, you need to tell FoxPro about these fields. Besides the field names, you must identify the order in which you want the fields in the database and the characteristics of each field. You must lay out the data in the order you want FoxPro to store it. Table 2.3 shows a listing of how you might store an inventory database.

Table 2.3
Storing an Inventory Database

Database Definitions

part_num
keyword
descr
supplier
qty_onhnd
qty_rorder
auto_rordr
cost
price
comments

Understanding FoxPro's Data Types

Having defined the different fields of the database, now you need to decide what types of information these fields are. FoxPro stores seven different types of data (character, numeric, float, logical, date, memo, and picture.) All the data you put into, store, and get out of FoxPro must be one of these types of data.

Character Data

Character data is text data—strings of letters and numbers. Examples of character data include the following:

This sentence could be a (rather long) character field.

AX-4423-ABX

88923.23

Note that a number can be character data. You would, for example, store a Social Security number as a character string, although it contains only numeric digits 0 through 9.

A good rule of thumb in designing your database and its data types is to use character data whenever possible. If you're not going to perform mathematical calculations on a number, store it as character data.

The reason for this rule lies in a database manager's strengths. Nearly all database managers, including FoxPro, are more efficient at working with character strings. Database managers have more functions for character strings, looking up data is faster with character strings, and it is more accurate to store numbers as character strings. You will find your database faster and more efficient, though sometimes slightly bigger, if you use character strings wherever possible. Don't go overboard, though; it is terribly complicated to do mathematical calculations on character data. If you're going to add, subtract, multiply, divide, or perform some other mathematical function on a number, store it as a number.

A character field can hold letters, numbers, and punctuation marks, plus the special graphics characters used to draw boxes and symbols. Essentially, if you can enter something from the keyboard, FoxPro will accept it into a character data field.

You also must tell FoxPro how wide each character field is. Without constraining your database, keep character fields as small as possible. If you need 25 characters for a name field, define it as such. But if you need only 20 and define the field as 25, you will store 5 extra spaces for every record you put into your database. Those spaces add up, wasting disk storage space and slowing down FoxPro.

Numeric Data

A numeric field holds numbers on which you want to do some calculations; this type of field holds numbers, a decimal point, and a leading plus or minus sign. The widest a numeric field can be is 20 characters (but FoxPro maintains only 16 significant digits internally). The plus or minus sign and decimal point each use a space.

If you define a numeric field to be 20 digits long, only the first 16 digits will be accurate; the two digits on the far right of the number may not be accurate due to FoxPro's limitation.

Float Data

A float field, like the numeric type, holds numbers, a decimal point, and a leading plus or minus sign. A float field can be 20 places wide and, like the numeric type, the decimal and plus or minus sign take one place each.

The float and numeric data types may sound identical, but internally, Fox-Pro stores these two types differently. Operations on numeric fields are faster, but sacrifice a small degree of accuracy when many calculations are carried out on one value. Float data requires slightly longer processing time, but maintains a higher level of accuracy. Float data is designed for scientific processing; numeric data will provide an adequate level of accuracy for all but the most demanding calculations.

Logical Data

Logical fields can have one of two values: true or false. When entering data into a logical field, you can enter only an upper- or lowercase T for true, Y for yes, F for false, or N for no. No other values are accepted into a logical field.

Date Data

Date fields hold—you guessed it—date information. The format can be MM/DD/YY or the European DD/MM/YY, but you have to tell FoxPro which date format you want with the SET DATE command.

FoxPro has extensive date manipulation capabilities. You can add to a date a value representing a number of days. FoxPro will calculate the future date representing the original date plus the number of days you added. This feature is sophisticated enough that if you add .25 days to a date field four times, the date field will increment by one day.

Memo Data

Memo fields have always held the promise of extraordinary capabilities, but FoxPro brings that promise to fruition. A memo field enables you to store any amount of textual data in a field that has been defined as only 10 characters wide in your database structure and all the input and output screens.

To enter or see a memo field, you move to that field and press the Ctrl-PgDn key combination. A full-screen text editor opens up the memo field; you then can enter data or edit existing data in the field. The only limit on the amount of information you can put into a memo field is disk size. You can look for strings in a memo field, copy parts of a memo field to other memo fields, or replace one memo field (or part of one) with another.

You will discover many uses for memo fields. One interesting use I have seen is in a FoxBase+ system used for computer system design. The memo fields store descriptions of the processes of the system, of the database structure of the system, and of all the data dictionary information. Some of these memo fields hold many pages of information.

Picture Data

The Picture field type is a vestige of FoxPro's Macintosh heritage. The Macintosh version of Foxbase+ can store graphics in a Picture field type. FoxPro also has a Picture field type, but only to allow a FoxPro database to import directly a Foxbase+ database created in Foxbase+/Mac. Once the database with a Picture type is in FoxPro, you cannot see or work with it. Fox Software says future versions of FoxPro may fully implement the Picture field, but for now, you cannot use it.

Creating a Data Dictionary for All Output Elements

Once you have decided what forms your information will take in FoxPro, it's time to add some information to your database dictionary. Write down in your notebook the database structure, with all the field types and sizes. Add as many comments as you can; you cannot have too many comments in a database dictionary. Table 2.4 shows the database dictionary for the example inventory database. You may recognize that this information is in a form almost identical to what FoxPro will need when you're setting up the database.

Table 2.4
Database Dictionary

Database Definitions

Element Name	Type	Length	Decimal Places
part_num	CHARACTER	15	
keyword	CHARACTER	15	
descr	CHARACTER	25	
supplier	CHARACTER	25	
qty_onhnd	NUMERIC	5	
qty_rorder	NUMERIC	5	
auto_rordr	LOGICAL	1	
cost	NUMERIC	8	2
price	NUMERIC	8	2
comments	MEMO	10	

Now you have defined what information you want to store, but you haven't told FoxPro in what order you want that information presented. If you don't tell FoxPro how to order the database, it presents it in the order in which you entered it. If you enter the XYZ Company, the MNO Company, and the ABC Company, FoxPro will always list them in that order. Although that may suit you for about 10 minutes, you will soon like to see them in alphabetical order in one report, in ZIP code order in another, and maybe in phone number order in a third. Or maybe you would like to see your database sorted by ZIP code and alphabetically by company name within each ZIP code. FoxPro can do it.

You could tell FoxPro to sort the database each time you want to look at it differently. In a sort, FoxPro moves each record to its correct sorted position. Sorts can take an amazingly long time on big database files, so FoxPro provides a better way: indexes.

An index is a separate file that tells FoxPro the order of the database records based on an index expression. Consider the example of the XYZ, MNO, and ABC companies. If you defined an index on company name, the index would tell FoxPro to present the companies alphabetically when showing this database on-screen or processing it in a report. When you have this index file open, any addition, deletion, or change of the database automatically updates the index. Change the XYZ Company to the DEF Company and the index immediately tells FoxPro to present the second record, then the third, then the first, which reflects the new company names. With the power of indexing, there is almost no reason to sort a database. In fact, in five years of working with FoxPro, I have included a sort routine in only one application.

A single-field index is the simplest index and the easiest to define. You use this index when you want your database to be presented in an order based on only one field. If you want the database listed on ZIP codes and don't care about the order of companies within the ZIP code, you define an index on only ZIP codes.

Often, though, you want the database to be presented in an order based on several fields. To accomplish this, you must build an *expression*; an expression that combines several fields. When you define the index, Fox-Pro presents an Expression Builder dialog to ease your job.

To create an index on an expression, open the View window from the Window menu. If the database for which you want to add an index is not opened, open it by clicking one of the work areas in the Work Area box and then choosing Open. Pick the database file from the scrollable list and choose OK. In the View window, choose Setup; in the Setup dialog, choose Add. You will see the Open Index File dialog. Choose New. Then choose Expr from the Index On dialog. FoxPro will open the Expression Builder dialog (see fig. 2.3).

Fig. 2.3.
The Expression
Builder dialog.

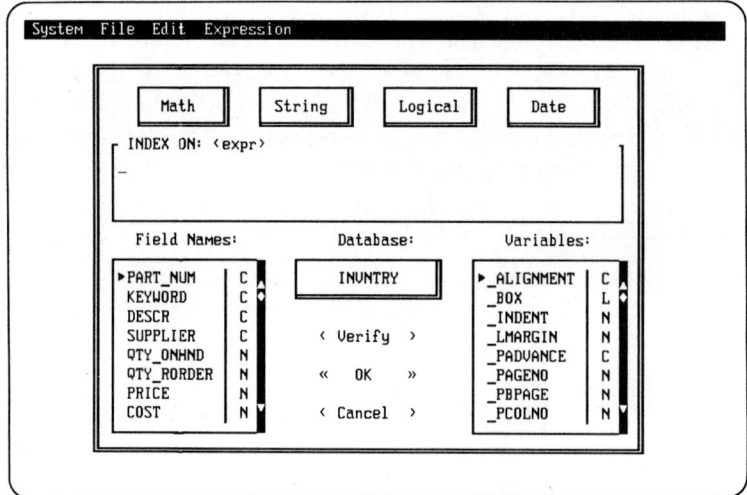

A FoxPro expression is a combination of database field names, memory variable names, FoxPro functions, and text strings. The combination, when processed by FoxPro, creates a value that FoxPro can use for a specific purpose, such as searching or indexing a database. The Expression Builder helps you create an expression by placing database fields and FoxPro functions in a format from which you can pick and choose.

Suppose that you wanted to create an expression to index the CUSTOMER database on the field CUST_NAME. As with all database programs, FoxPro sorts the uppercase letters before the lowercase ones, so the name "HOWARD" will appear before the name "Hobart." To get a true alphabetical sort, you need to build an expression that changes all the characters of the CUST_NAME field to uppercase; FoxPro will then index on the expression, rather than on the actual value in the field. To create this expression, do the following:

1. In the Expression Builder dialog, pull down the menu from the expression box titled `String`. You will see the many FoxPro functions that take action on character strings, whether they are database field values, memory variable values, or text strings you enter. Figure 2.4 shows the String function pop-up menu.

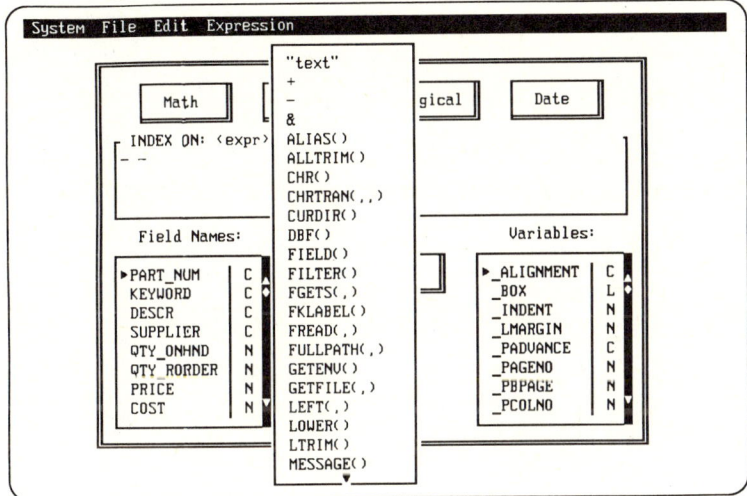

Fig. 2.4.
The String function pop-up menu.

2. Scroll through the string functions and pick the function `Upper()` by double-clicking it with the mouse or selecting it with the up- and down-arrow keys and then pressing Enter. FoxPro places the function `Upper()` in the Expression Builder box. This function causes FoxPro to change all the characters in a character string you place in the parentheses to uppercase characters. Characters already in uppercase are not changed. For example, if you use the expression

   Upper("FoxPro")

FoxPro returns the string "FOXPRO".

If the cursor is not on the closing parenthesis, move it there with the arrow keys, and insert the character string you want converted to uppercase.

3. From the Field Picker scrollable list, choose the field you want indexed, CUST_NAME, in the example. FoxPro places this field in the Expression Builder box.

Your expression is now finished (see fig. 2.5). The expression

Upper(CUST_NAME)

tells FoxPro to index the database on the values in the CUST_NAME field, but only after converting them to uppercase. The actual values in CUST_NAME are not changed.

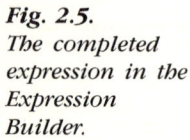
Fig. 2.5.
The completed expression in the Expression Builder.

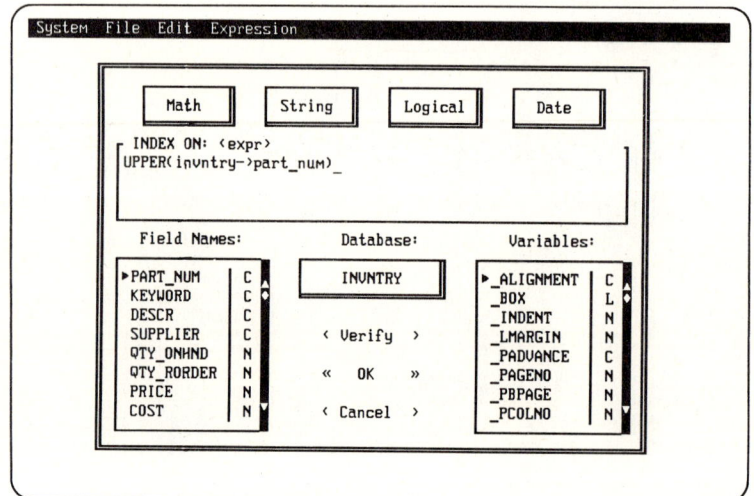

FoxPro expressions can be quite complex, with many fields and functions. Many index expressions will be combinations of fields. In your example inventory database, you might want to list suppliers alphabetically, then by the part numbers that come from that supplier. To do this, you would define an index on the expression

SUPPLIER + PART_NUM

In the Browse window, or in reports using this index, the inventory records would be listed alphabetically by the supplier name. If a supplier provided more than one part number, those part numbers would be listed in order. Figures 2.6 through 2.8 show the results of different index expressions on the example inventory database.

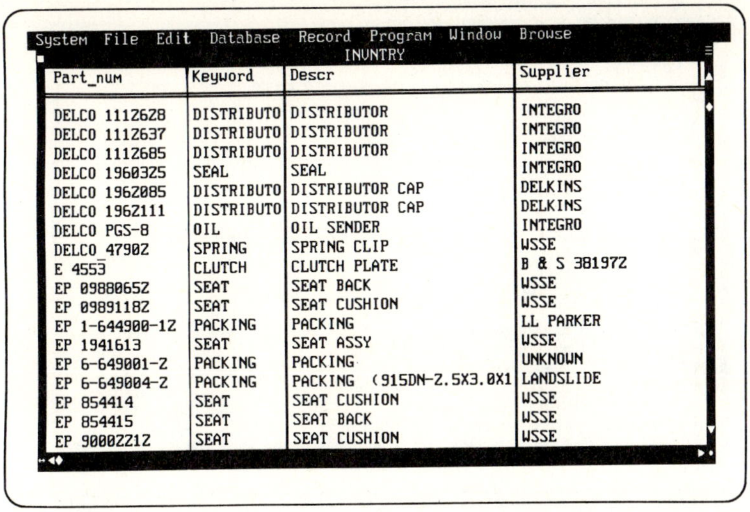

Fig. 2.6.
Using the index
expression Upper
(CUST_NAME).

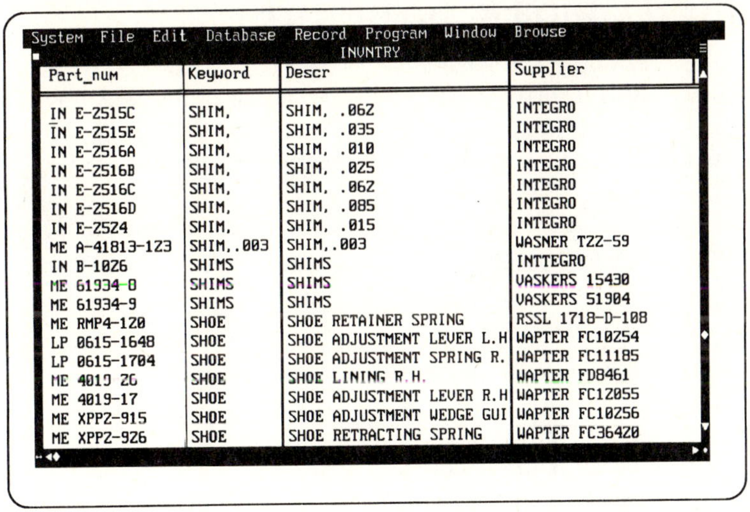

Fig. 2.7.
Using the index
expression Upper
(CUST_NAME) +
ZIP.

Now you have accomplished the hard part of creating a database: you have defined it and designed it. All that remains is to tell FoxPro what you decided.

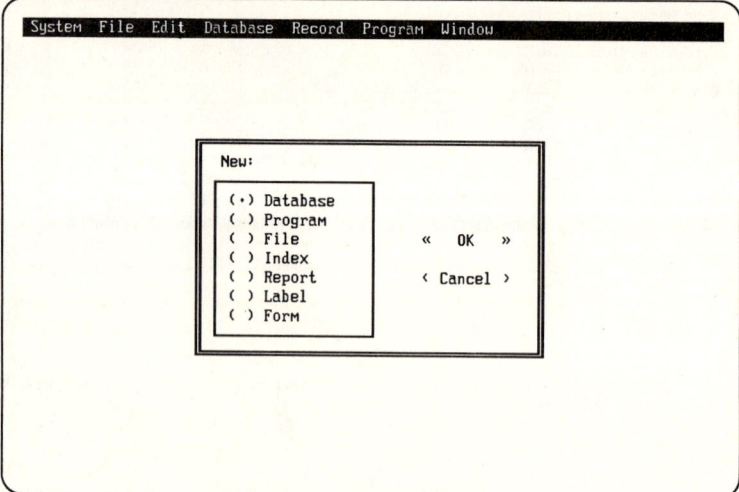

Fig. 2.8.
Using the index
expression Upper
(CUST_NAME) +
DTOC(DATE).

```
System  File  Edit  Database  Record  Program  Window  Browse
                              INUNTRY
  Part_num        Keyword      Descr                      Supplier
  ME 42078        CABLE        CABLE                       IGGY 173MGG-Z-90
  IN LPG-1017     REGULATOR    REGULATOR                   JA ENTR  600
  IN LPG-1005     COVER        COVER                       JA ENTR.  AU6-703
  IN LPG-1006     REPAIR       REPAIR KIT                  JA ENTR. R11-Z8
  IN LPG-1023     VAPORIZER    VAPORIZER ADJ               JA ENTR. 11AZ8
  ME 60344        CHECK        CHECK VALVE 1" SWITCH       JENSON 9ZA
  CL 110139       OIL          OIL SEAL                    JMZ 9397LPD
  CL 110307       SEAL         SEAL                        JMZ 9397LPD
  LP 0133-1050    RING         RING GEAR                   JMZ
  ME 40060-25     BEARING      BEARING                     JOSH
  LP 0208-1013    TORQUE       TORQUE CONVERTER    (REB    JOSH CORPORATION
  IN FD-73474     WHEEL        WHEEL CYLINDER              JOSH IND.   (CL 12189
  IN FE-1476C     MASTER       MASTER CYLINDER             JOSH IND.   (CL 8518Z
  IN FE-1476A     MASTER       MASTER CYLINDER             JOSH IND.   (CL 89949
  IN CL-1188      CONVERTER    CONVERTER                   JOSH INDUSTRIES
  IN CL-1231      CLUTCH       CLUTCH PACK                 JOSH INDUSTRIES
  IN CL-1239      STATOR       STATOR                      JOSH INDUSTRIES
  IN CL-1248      ACCUMULATO   ACCUMULATOR KIT             JOSH INDUSTRIES
```

Defining Database Structure

Because you're creating a new database file, start by choosing New from
the File menu. FoxPro displays the New dialog, shown in figure 2.9. Fox-
Pro assumes that you want to create a new database file and highlights
that choice, so you only have to choose OK, and you're on your way.

Fig. 2.9.
The New dialog.

```
System  File  Edit  Database  Record  Program  Window

  New:

  (·) Database
  ( ) Program
  ( ) File              «   OK   »
  ( ) Index
  ( ) Report          < Cancel >
  ( ) Label
  ( ) Form
```

The Structure dialog, shown in figure 2.10, is the heart of the definition process. In this dialog, you define the fields of the database to FoxPro.

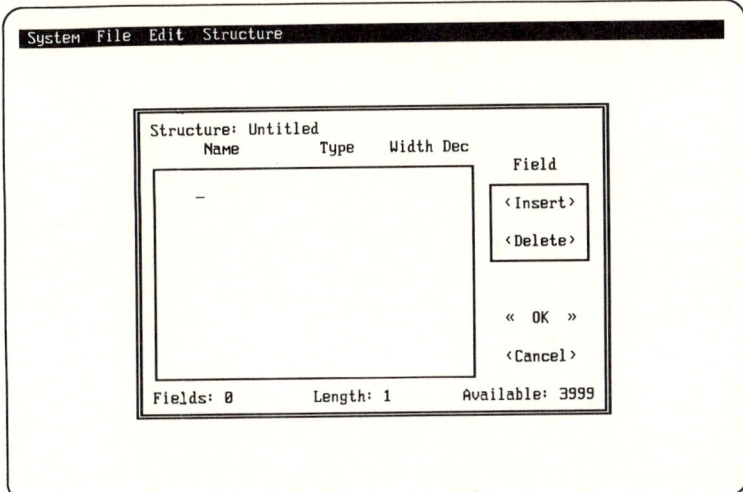

Fig. 2.10.
The Structure
dialog.

Notice that the structure is Untitled. You can save the structure at any time during the definition process. You are asked for a name, which must be a legal MS-DOS name (it must start with a character; contain only characters, digits, or an underscore; and can be no more than eight characters long without spaces). FoxPro automatically appends a DBF extension, indicating that this is a database file, but you will never need to work with the extension.

The number 3999 in the lower right corner represents the maximum length of a FoxPro record. As you add fields to your database definition, this number will be reduced by the length of each field. You can tell how much room you have left in your database definition by referring to this number.

You can insert or delete fields, if you want. Should you realize that you have left out a field (remember, the order you choose is the order in which they initially are displayed in Browse windows), you can highlight the field that the omitted field should follow and choose Insert, which will put a new, empty field before the highlighted field. The order of the field has little effect on FoxPro's performance, but it helps to have the fields you most want to examine at the top; they will always appear in the Browse window.

You also can move fields up and down in the structure. Use the arrow keys to highlight the arrow symbol in the far left column. Press the space bar to choose the field. Now move the up- and down-arrow keys to move the field up and down in the structure. When you have moved the field to the right place, "drop" it by pressing the space bar again.

Defining the fields is, in technical programming language, a "piece of cake." Enter the field name and press Enter or Tab. FoxPro moves to the Type column, which has a default of Char. This column is a scrollable list field, so you can choose a different type from the list, or simply enter the first letter of the type you want: *N* for numeric, *M* for memo, and so on. The valid field types are as follows:

Field Type	Default Length	Decimal Places
Character	8	
Numeric	8	2
Float	8	2
Date	8	
Logical	1	
Memo	10	

The Date, Logical, and Memo lengths cannot be changed.

Press Tab again to move to the Width column, where you enter the width you defined for the field. Memo, logical, and date fields have set lengths that you can't change. If the field is numeric or float, you also must define the number of decimal places. Pressing Enter or Tab again moves to the next empty line. Press Tab from an empty line to move to OK, and you are finished. Figure 2.11 shows a complete customer database structure.

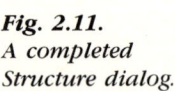
Fig. 2.11.
A completed
Structure dialog.

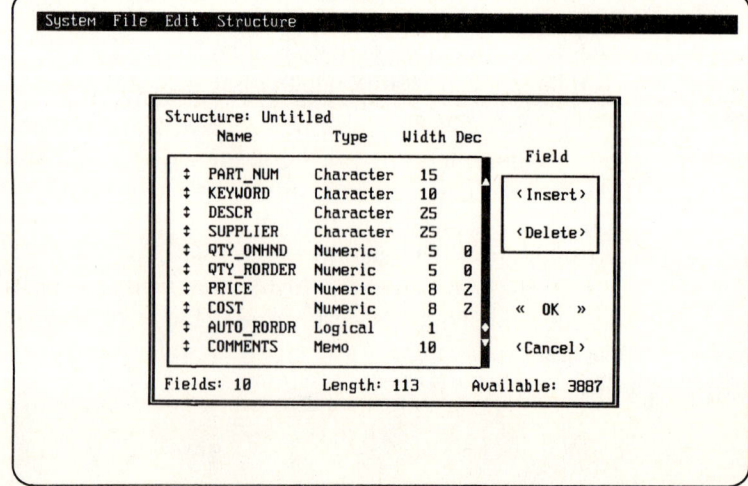

When you click OK, you see the Name File dialog in which you give the database a name. The scrollable list shows database files that already exist, so you know what names not to use for the new one. FoxPro asks whether you want to enter database records. Answer *Yes*, and you see the default data-entry window; answer *No*, and you return to the FoxPro Command window.

FoxBase+ users follow a similar procedure. The command to create a new database file in FoxBase+, which can also be entered in the FoxPro Command window, is as follows:

CREATE *dbf_name*

where *dbf_name* represents the name of the database you're creating.

You see the FoxBase+ input screen in which you enter the field names, types, and sizes (see fig. 2.12). FoxBase+ users don't have the flexibility of moving fields or the scrollable lists of types, but the process is the same otherwise. When you're finished, press Esc to return to the FoxBase+ command line.

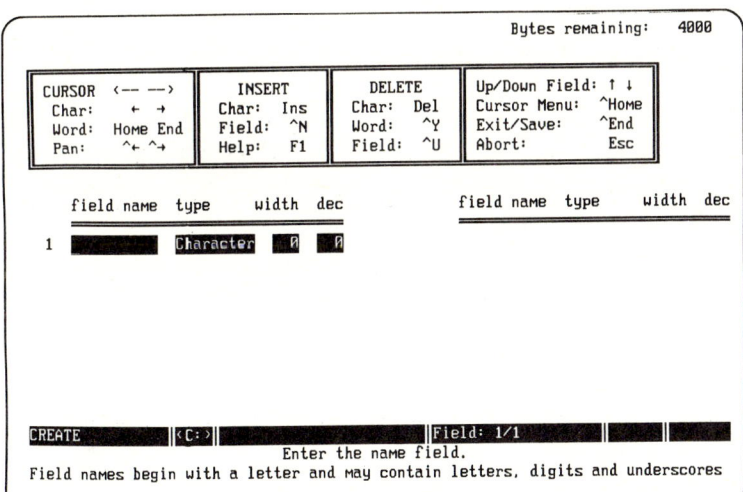

Fig. 2.12.
The Create Database screen in FoxBase+.

If you want to set indexes on this database, now is the time to do so.

Defining Indexes

Just as you defined the database structure to FoxPro, you must define the indexes you want FoxPro to maintain on the database. Do this by first opening the database (if you haven't already done so), and then selecting View from the Window menu. You see the View dialog, shown in figure 2.13. From this dialog, choose Setup, and you see the Setup dialog, shown in figure 2.14.

Fig. 2.13.
The View dialog.

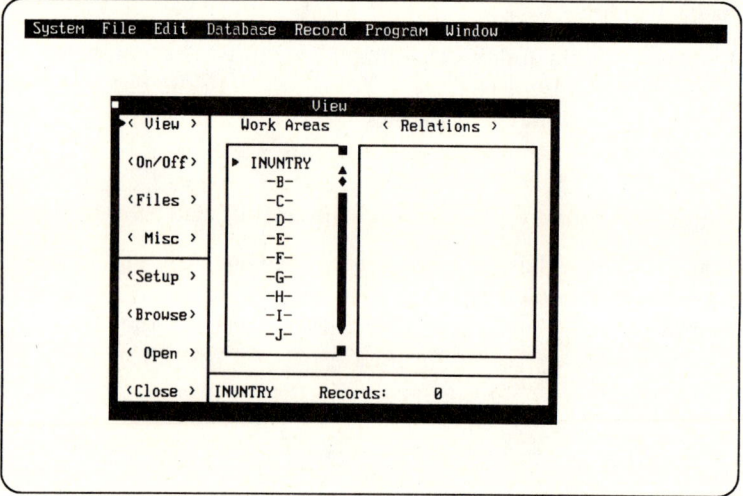

Fig. 2.14.
The Setup dialog.

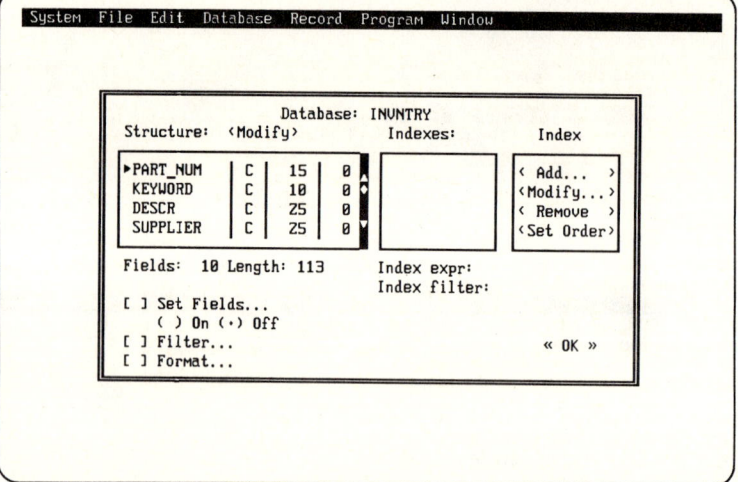

The Setup dialog controls how FoxPro will present your database, either on the screen or in reports. Before you define the indexes, you should look at several other display options.

Setting Filters and Fields

You can tell FoxPro you don't want to see all the fields of the database by using the Fields check box. Setting Fields to On displays the Fields dialog, which asks what fields you want to see. From then on, FoxPro acts as if only those fields exist in your database for display purposes (you can still compute, look up, or delete the hidden fields). In FoxBase+, you set fields with the SET FIELDS *field1, field2, field3* command.

The FILTER command does just that; you tell FoxPro to filter the database records according to a criteria you set and to act as if only those records meeting the criteria exist. If, for example, your filter is

   ZIP = '98058'

FoxPro ignores all records without that ZIP code, acting as if they don't exist. Again, you can set a filter from the FoxPro Command window with the same command FoxBase+ users would enter:

   SET FILTER TO *expression*

The FORMAT command enables you to specify a Form file you have created with FoxView to be used when entering, editing, or displaying records.

Creating Indexes

To define the index, select the work area containing the database, open the Setup dialog, and select Add. You see the Open Index File dialog shown in figure 2.15.

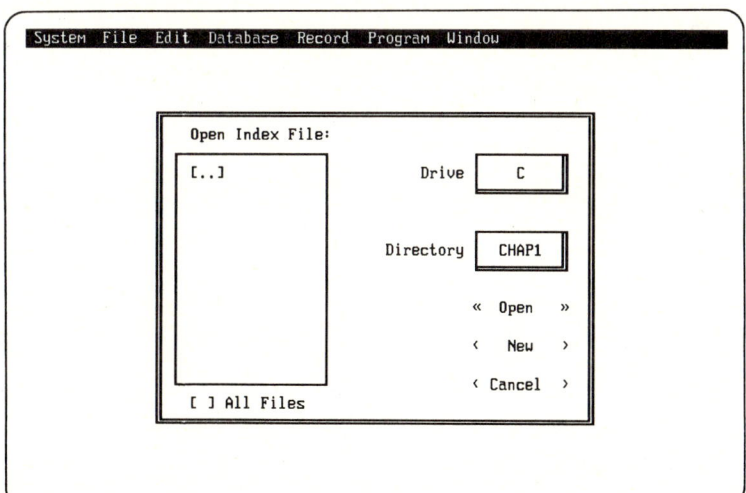

Fig. 2.15.
The Open Index File dialog.

From the Open Index File dialog, select New to tell FoxPro this index file does not already exist. Next, you see the Index On dialog, shown in figure 2.16. If you want to index on a single field name, select that field and press Enter. The field name appears next to the Expr text box, telling you that FoxPro will create an index on that field.

Fig. 2.16.
The Index On
dialog.

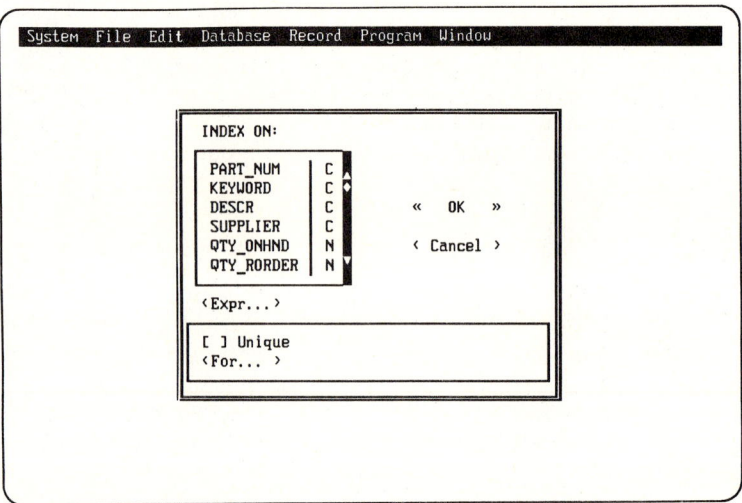

If you need to define an index on several fields or use FoxPro expressions, select the Expr box to display the Expression Builder dialog. In this dialog, you can build index expressions from multiple fields or from expressions involving mathematical or logical operations.

FoxBase+ users, and FoxPro users who like the speed of the command line, can create indexes more quickly from the command line with the command

    INDEX ON *expression* TO *index_name*

where *expression* is a valid FoxPro indexing expression and *index_name* is the name of the index file that FoxPro or FoxBase+ will create.

Attaching Index Files to Database Files

When you define an index file, FoxPro updates and uses that index file for the current session. If you close the database, or quit FoxPro and return later, you must tell FoxPro to associate the proper index files with the database.

In FoxBase+, or in the Command window, you can open a database and indexes with the following command:

OPEN *dbf_name* INDEX *index_name1, index_name2*

FoxPro or FoxBase+ will open the database *dbf_name* and attach the index files *index_name1* and *index_name2*; the first index named will be the controlling index.

In FoxPro you also can use the View Setup dialog to add index files. You also can tell FoxPro at this time which index file will control the database.

Modifying the Controlling Index

If you define only one index for the database, FoxPro uses that one to control how the data is presented and processed. If you define more than one index, you must tell FoxPro which index is controlling; that is, which index FoxPro should use to present and process the database. All open indexes of a database are updated automatically, but only one at a time can control the database.

You can change the controlling index in the Setup dialog of the View window. Where before you chose Add to add indexes to the database, now you use the Control text box to tell FoxPro which index to use. If the indexes aren't open, use Add to open them, then choose the one you want to control the database and select Control. Until you change it again, Fox-Pro will use the selected index to control how it presents and processes the database.

From the FoxPro Command window, or in FoxBase+, you can change the controlling index from the command line. If you have opened the database and index files with the command

OPEN CUST INDEX CUSTNAME, ZIP, PHONE

the database will be controlled by the CUSTNAME index. To change the controlling index to the ZIP index, enter the following command from the command line in FoxBase+ or the Command window in FoxPro:

SET ORDER TO 2

This command tells FoxPro and FoxBase+ to use the index listed second in the original opening index list as the controlling index. To set the controlling index to the PHONE index, you enter

SET ORDER TO 3

In FoxPro, if you have opened the database file and attached the indexes through the View Setup dialog, the way the indexes are listed in the scrollable list index window is the order you refer to in the SET ORDER command syntax.

Deleting or Modifying Indexes

It is easy to delete or modify an index's expression. Go to the Setup dialog of the View window and, in the index corner, select Remove to take an index off the database, or Modify to change its expression. Note that using the Remove option doesn't erase the index; it simply tells FoxPro that, for now, you don't want that index updated as you make changes. Use this option with caution, because if you make changes with an index removed and then later attach that index to the database, the index file will not reflect the state of the database. To you, the result will be puzzling: records you *know* are there will not be found, the Browse window will show records in a funny order, and reports will not work like they did last time. When these symptoms occur, you should reindex the database, which will update the index.

Saving the View

If it seems cumbersome to open a database file and attach indexes each time you want to use them, you can use the View feature of FoxPro and FoxBase+. A view saves information about what databases are open and what indexes are attached to them. You give the view a name and, after that, you open the view from the File menu, and FoxPro and FoxBase+ will set themselves up just as they were when you defined the view.

To define a view, set up your database and index files with the filters, fields, and formats you want in the View window. From that window, select Save from the File menu. You see the Save View As dialog, shown in figure 2.17. When you select Save, all information about which database files are open; which indexes are attached to them; and which filters, fields, and formats are in effect are saved to the View file. To return to that environment, select Open from the File menu, click the View radio button, and select your view.

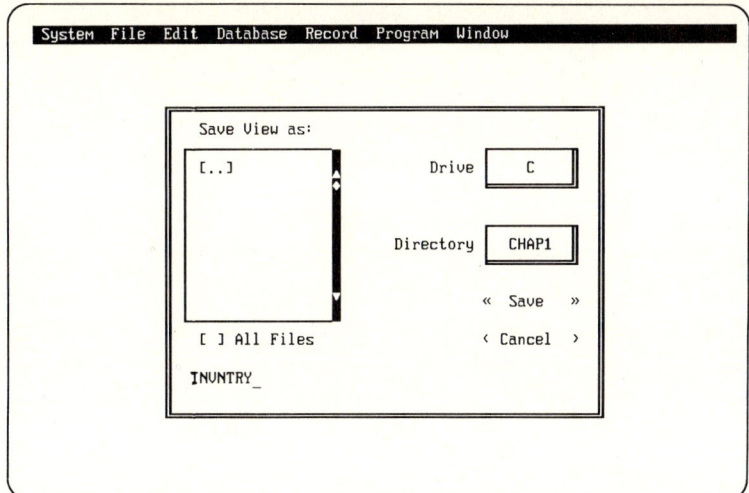

```
 System  File  Edit  Database  Record  Program  Window

        ┌─────────────────────────────────────────────┐
        │  Save View as:                              │
        │  ┌──────────┐┌┐         Drive  ┌─────────┐   │
        │  │ [..]     ││▲│                │    C    │   │
        │  │          ││ │                └─────────┘   │
        │  │          ││ │                             │
        │  │          ││ │       Directory ┌─────────┐ │
        │  │          ││ │                 │  CHAP1  │ │
        │  │          ││ │                 └─────────┘ │
        │  │          ││ │                             │
        │  │          ││▼│          «   Save   »       │
        │  └──────────┘└┘                             │
        │  [ ] All Files            ‹  Cancel  ›       │
        │                                             │
        │  INVNTRY_                                   │
        └─────────────────────────────────────────────┘
```

Fig. 2.17.
The Save View as dialog.

From the FoxPro or FoxBase+ command line, you save a view with the following command:

> SAVE ENVIRONMENT AS *view_name*

and you recall it with

> SET VIEW TO *view_name*

Chapter Summary

Designing and defining your database is the heart of your database system. In this chapter you have learned how to analyze the objectives and requirements of your database, and how to translate those objectives and requirements into a Fox database. This is an important milestone because now you can create one, two, or many databases to suit your needs. Fox-Pro places no limits on how many databases you can create and use.

Entering, Editing, and Viewing Information

As you might imagine, database systems need data. Once you have defined the database structure to FoxPro, it's time to start using the real power of this program: its capability to receive data, store it, and present it in useful ways.

In this chapter, you learn how to enter data into a FoxPro database, how to edit that data, how to look at it in different ways, and how to delete it. If you use only FoxPro's default data-entry screen and the default View window, you will gain much from your database, but if you go a step or two further, learning how to use some of FoxPro's sophistication, your database management system will be much easier to use and much more powerful.

Entering Records into a Database

When you have finished defining a database structure to FoxPro, you are asked if you want to enter data. If you answer *yes*, FoxPro presents you with a simple data-entry window. Whether you're using this default data-entry window or a custom-designed one (it is easy to design elegant cus-

tom data-entry and inquiry screens in FoxPro), each field of the database
has a text field in which you enter information.

Using the Default Data-Entry Window

If, after defining your database structure to FoxPro, you answer *yes* to
FoxPro's question, Do You Want to Enter Data Now?, you are presented with
the default data-entry window (see fig. 3.1). As you can see, each field of
the database has a label, which is the field name, and a data-entry field.
The cursor is in the first field, awaiting your input.

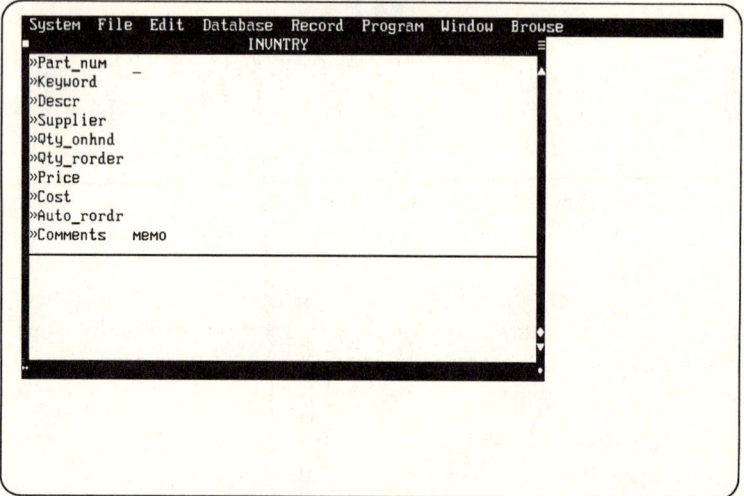

Fig. 3.1.
FoxPro's default
data-entry screen
for INVNTRY.

When you are entering data, if you don't fill a field completely, but are
done with the entry, press Enter to move to the next field. If you fill the
field, FoxPro sounds a beep and moves you to the next field. If you like,
you can change these settings in the View Set-up On/Off dialog. Set Beep
to Off and Confirm to On. When Confirm is On, you must confirm that
you're finished with data entry in a field by pressing Enter.

When you have filled all fields for a record, FoxPro moves to the first field
of the next record (see fig. 3.2). This pattern continues until you press
Esc, to stop, or you choose another window from the Window menu.

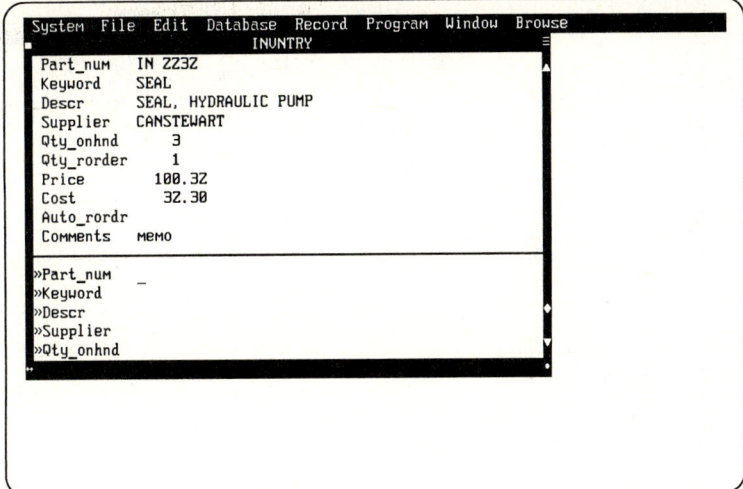

Fig. 3.2.
FoxPro moves to first field of the subsequent data-entry record.

From other places in the FoxPro environment, you can display the data-entry window by choosing Append from the Record menu. The window displays a blank record for you to fill. As before, when you're finished with one record, another is presented.

If you make a mistake but don't realize it until you have left the field, you can use PgUp or PgDn to move to the field with the mistake in it. Then you can use the standard text-editing functions to correct your mistake. You can even move back to previous records to correct errors.

Building a Custom Data-Entry Screen

If you ever have entered large amounts of repetitious information into a computer, you know how tiresome it can be. Any help you can give yourself pays dividends in fewer errors and less mental fatigue. You can create elegant data-entry and viewing screens quickly and easily with FoxView, a stand-alone program. Although there is no comparable program for FoxBase+ users, if you use FoxBase+, you may want to read through this section anyway; FoxView is a powerful incentive to upgrade from FoxBase+ to FoxPro.

FoxView can create very complex and sophisticated screens for entering and viewing data (accessing up to 25 different databases at once), yet it can be used by a beginner to create simple screens. To understand how FoxView works, in this next section you create a screen for the INVNTRY database.

Using FoxView to Create a Quick View

You start FoxView by choosing FoxView from the program menu. You also can start FoxView from the MS-DOS prompt or the Command window by entering

FOXVIEW

FoxView begins with a Logo screen, which you clear by pressing Enter. Next, you see a screen that looks much like an MS-DOS screen (see fig. 3.3).

Fig. 3.3.
The FoxView
command shell.

You can enter many commands from the prompt on the screen, but for now, all you need to do is tell FoxView what database file you want to create a screen for. To do this, enter

USE *file_name*

where *file_name* is the database name. To continue the example from Chapter 2, enter *INVNTRY* for the file name. FoxView responds by telling you the number of fields loaded. Now you are ready to design your form. First, though, some information about FoxView will help you understand what you're doing and form a solid foundation on which you can build your FoxView knowledge.

When you type the USE *file_name* command, FoxView creates a table that contains all the information FoxPro needs to present information about each field. FoxView also creates a default screen. You could use the screen as is, but FoxView's purpose is to enable you to change the screen, making it more pleasing to the eye and easier to use.

To see the default screen FoxView has created, press the F10 key. A new screen opens, and you see a list of your database fields, with an area for data entry for each field (see fig. 3.4). As you can see, this screen is a little primitive. Figure 3.5 shows a more pleasing screen, which you can design and create in FoxView.

Fig. 3.4.
The default form FoxView creates for INVNTRY.

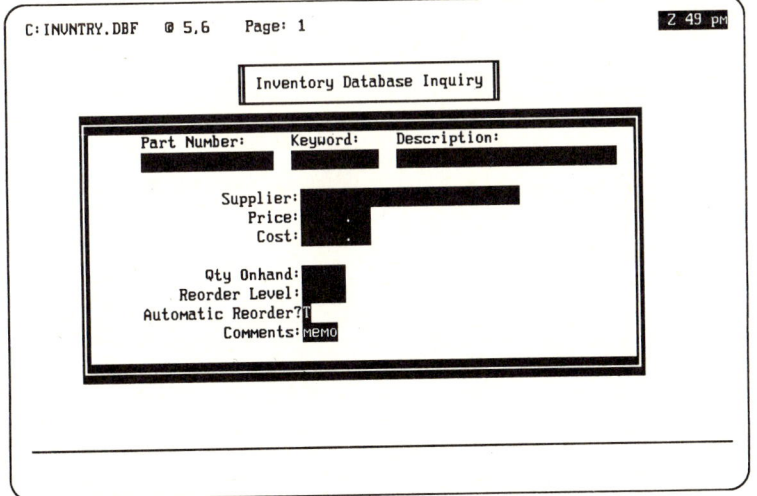

Fig. 3.5.
A custom-designed form for INVNTRY.

In the default screen, a data area exists for each of the fields in your database as does a label associated with the data area. Each of these label/data-area combinations are called *objects*. In FoxView, you can move these objects to new locations and modify how they present data and receive data from the keyboard. You also can add new objects, such as a text string or boxes. Initially, it is easier to accomplish this on-screen, but later you will see how to make changes in the FoxView table of this screen.

If you want to see the table that FoxView has created for this data-entry screen, press F10. You can see that the table, shown in figure 3.6, maintains information about each of the fields, including its location on-screen, what database field information it will accept or display, the label for the field, and other necessary information. As you make changes to the data-entry screen, they are reflected in the table. Likewise, if you make a change to the table, it is reflected in the screen. You can switch between the Screen and Table views by pressing F10 at any time. For screen design, you will find the Screen view easier to work with, because it is a real WYSIWYG (What You See Is What You Get) screen. As you make changes, remember that you cannot undo them; a change is recorded immediately.

Fig. 3.6.
Table view for the default INVNTRY form.

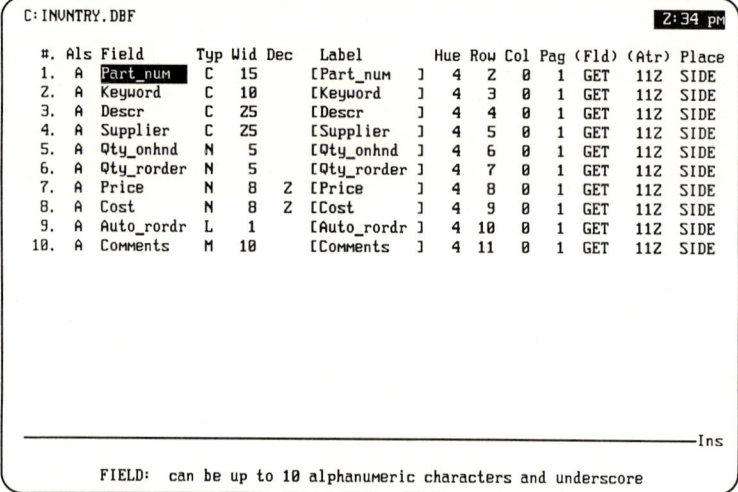

```
C:INVNTRY.DBF                                                        2:34 pm

  #.  Als  Field        Typ Wid Dec    Label        Hue Row Col Pag (Fld) (Atr) Place
  1.   A   Part_num      C   15         [Part_num  ]  4   2   0   1  GET   112  SIDE
  2.   A   Keyword       C   10         [Keyword   ]  4   3   0   1  GET   112  SIDE
  3.   A   Descr         C   25         [Descr     ]  4   4   0   1  GET   112  SIDE
  4.   A   Supplier      C   25         [Supplier  ]  4   5   0   1  GET   112  SIDE
  5.   A   Qty_onhnd     N    5         [Qty_onhnd ]  4   6   0   1  GET   112  SIDE
  6.   A   Qty_rorder    N    5         [Qty_rorder]  4   7   0   1  GET   112  SIDE
  7.   A   Price         N    8   Z     [Price     ]  4   8   0   1  GET   112  SIDE
  8.   A   Cost          N    8   Z     [Cost      ]  4   9   0   1  GET   112  SIDE
  9.   A   Auto_rordr    L    1         [Auto_rordr]  4  10   0   1  GET   112  SIDE
 10.   A   Comments      M   10         [Comments  ]  4  11   0   1  GET   112  SIDE




                                                                           Ins
     FIELD:  can be up to 10 alphanumeric characters and underscore
```

Changing Data-Entry Labels

Each of the data fields has a label attached to it—the text to the left of the field. But as you can see, these labels leave something to be desired. As the database designer, you know what each field means, but if someone else uses this screen, will they know that Auto_rorder defines whether that part should be automatically reordered at a certain point? Probably not, so you need to change the rather cryptic labels to something more understandable.

To do this, move the highlight, using the Tab or arrow keys, to the object whose label you want to change; the selected object will change color. When you reach the object you want to change, press the space bar. The current label appears in the lower left corner of FoxView. You use Fox-Pro's standard text-editing functions to change the label. When you press Enter, FoxPro accepts the change and places it on-screen. As you change the label in the lower left corner text window, it also changes on-screen. You cannot leave this field without recording changes. You can, of course, edit the field back to its original state.

Moving Objects On-Screen

Form design and modification is easiest in Form view. Return to Form view from Table view by pressing F10.

Moving objects on-screen also is easy. Select the object you want to move by highlighting it and pressing F3. You use the arrow keys to move the object to the new location.

To move several objects at once, press F6, use the arrow keys to select the objects, and press Enter to finish the selection. The F3-Move function moves all objects selected.

Many times, certain fields look better if the label for the field is above the field, such as the top row on the INVNTRY screen. To accomplish this, select the field and press Ctrl-T. The data-entry field moves below the label. Figure 3.7 shows the data screen with new labels and a better design. Still, it seems a little stark, but FoxView will help you remedy that problem.

Adding Text to the Screen

You can add text strings to your data screen by pressing Ctrl-N. A new object, labeled text string, appears on-screen. When FoxView creates the object, it also selects the object and presses the F3 key for you so that you can move the object with the arrow keys. Because text object probably doesn't fit into your design for the screen, you can edit it in the lower left corner of FoxView just as you edited the data field labels. In this example, the text object becomes a screen title, centered above the data fields (see fig. 3.8). Once placed, the title becomes like all other objects—it can be selected and moved to a new location.

Fig. 3.7.
*The redesigned
INVNTRY
database form.*

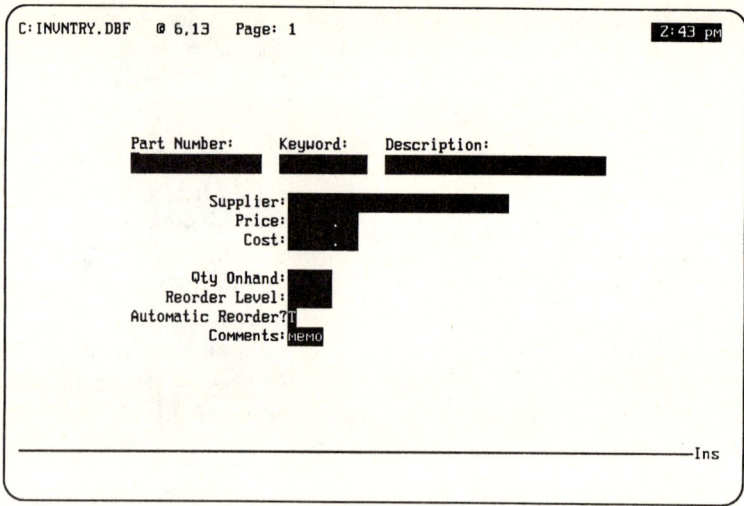

Fig. 3.8.
*A text object
added, and then
edited and
moved to form a
title.*

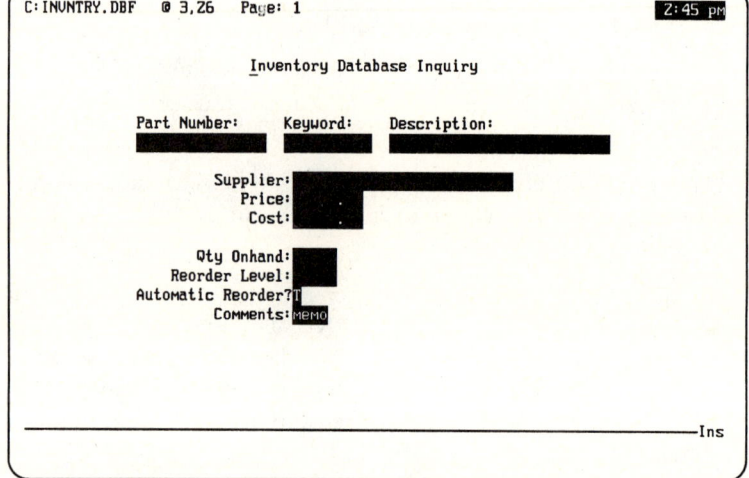

Adding Boxes to the Screen

Boxes can make or break a data screen. If your data screen has logical blocks of data, enclosing them in boxes makes the important areas stand out. Even if you don't need boxes for that reason, a simple box enclosing the screen provides a pleasing border. Uncontrolled use of boxes, however, clutters a screen and makes it confusing. Use boxes sparingly, but do use them.

To add a box, select the Box menu by pressing Ctrl-B. You are presented with a pop-up menu showing the different types of boxes available (see fig. 3.9). Choose the box you want. FoxView returns you to the screen, with a new "box object" in place and selected. Use the arrow keys to move the box on the form. Pressing F4 enables you to size the box. It's easiest first to move the upper left corner of the box to where you want it, and then change the box's size.

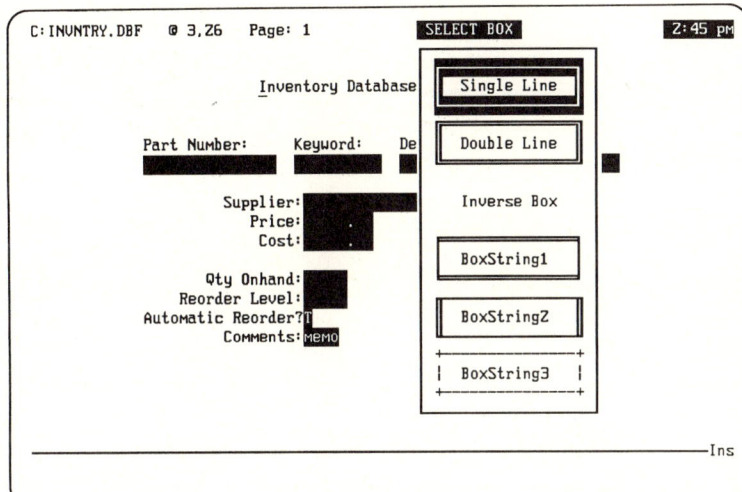

Fig. 3.9.
The Box menu.

Now that you have the FoxPro screen as you want it to look (as shown in figure 3.10), you may want to improve the way the data fields handle their data.

Using Picture and Function Codes

The way the data fields are defined for the default screen, you can put just about any character into any field. The numeric fields will accept only digits, a decimal, and a plus or minus sign, but the other fields are wide open. In many cases, you will want to limit which characters users can enter into a data field and which characters FoxPro will present. You do this by specifying *picture clauses*, which tell FoxPro what to accept and present, and how to format the field.

It is easiest to work from the Table view when specifying how you want fields to look, so if you're in the Form view, press F10 to move to Table view. You can see the table has columns for each object on-screen. In the table, you can change any of the characteristics of each object, including

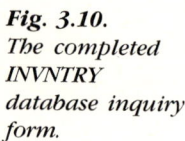

Fig. 3.10.
The completed
INVNTRY
database inquiry
form.

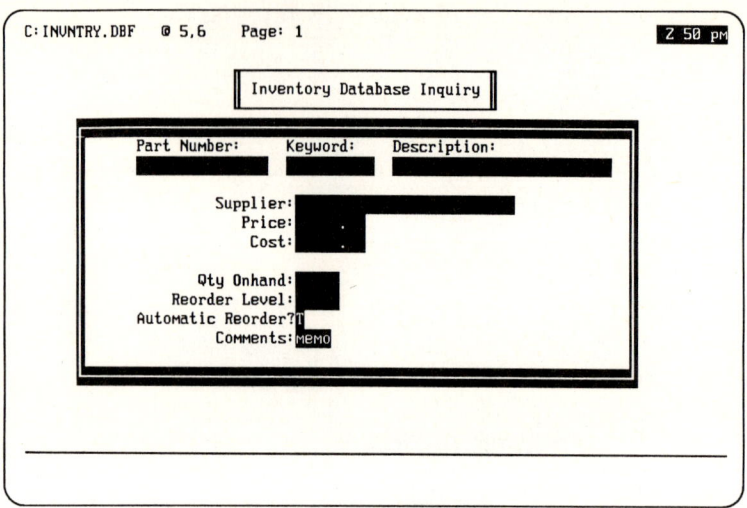

color, size, and appearance. For now, you will be working with the Picture column, which controls the appearance of data in the field. To reach the Picture column in Table view, press Tab until the Table scrolls to the right, bringing into view the Picture, Range, Valid, and Calc columns.

FoxPro and FoxView use two types of codes to determine how data appears in a data field and what data FoxPro accepts into that field. These two codes are called *Function* codes and *Picture Template* codes. Although these codes appear similar and have similar actions, the scope of their actions differs. Function codes apply to the entire field. If you put into the Picture column the code to make characters uppercase (@!), that function applies to all characters in the field—all characters will be forced to uppercase, regardless of what the user enters. To enter a Picture clause or Function code, Tab until the Picture column for the chosen field is highlighted. Then type the Picture clause or Function code wanted.

Picture Template codes apply on a character-by-character basis. If a field is five characters long, you can tell FoxPro you want the first character to be uppercase, the second a digit, the third a decimal point, the fourth any character, and the fifth alphabetic only.

You can combine Function codes and Picture Template codes in one field. You can specify a Function code to apply to the entire field, such as the code to put negative numbers in parentheses, and then specify Picture Template codes to place dollar signs, commas, and decimals in the number.

The format of Function codes and Picture Template codes in FoxPro is as follows:

"@function_code picture_code"

When using these codes in FoxView, leave out the double quotation marks. The @ character identifies the subsequent characters as Function codes. You can place multiple Function codes after the @ ("@!R", for example), but at least one space must separate the last Function code from the first Picture Template code.

Function and Picture Template codes are, at best, confusing for beginning FoxPro and FoxBase+ users. Some examples follow:

Field Type	Picture Clause	Data	Result
CHARACTER	"@A"	abc989dwxyz8a	abcdwxyza

The A Function code allows only alphabetic characters to be entered or displayed.

Field Type	Picture Clause	Data	Result
CHARACTER	"@R 99/99"	1223	12/23

The R Function code specifies that characters other than Picture Template codes exist in this picture. Codes other than Picture Template codes are displayed but not stored when the data is entered. The value for this data field in the database is 1223.

Field Type	Picture Clause	Data	Result
NUMERIC	"$$$,$$9.99"	12332.56	$12,332.56

The $ Picture Template code tells FoxPro to place floating dollar signs before any numbers. The comma and decimal point forces those characters into the appropriate position in the number. (Cobol programmers will recognize this picture clause.)

Experimentation is definitely the best teacher for Function and Picture Template codes. You will find these codes to be useful when you need to ensure that data is in a certain format.

When designing a database, you often will know that the data going into numeric fields should fall into a certain range. You can tell FoxPro not to accept values outside the range; if the user tries to enter such a value, FoxPro will beep and prompt for the data again. FoxPro will continue doing that until the data is in the range or the user leaves the data-entry screen. You set the range using the Range column in FoxView. You are prompted for the upper and lower range limits.

Generating the Format Screen from FoxView

Once you have finished creating your screen and specifying how FoxPro should use its fields, you have one last step before you can use the screen. FoxView has to generate program code that FoxPro can use. When you have become more proficient with FoxPro and FoxView, you will learn how to create entire applications from screens in FoxView; for now, you will generate Format files that FoxPro uses in Append and Edit modes.

To convert your screen design to a Format file, press Esc to access the FoxView menu, and then use the arrow keys to choose Gen. If Select From Template List is not highlighted, use the up- and down-arrow keys to highlight it, and press Enter. From the next window, titled TEMPLATES, choose FORM1 Format File Generator. FoxView asks you to provide a name for your format file. Enter the name (for this example, you enter *INVNTRY*, the same as the database) and press Enter. FoxView creates the FoxPro program code for the Format file. If you want to see this code to learn how FoxPro provides screen input and output, you can open this program file from the FoxPro File menu.

Now, having finished your FoxView chores, choose Quit from the File menu (saving any files FoxView asks you to save) and return to FoxPro.

Using the FoxView Screen

To use the FoxView screen, you first need to tell FoxPro that you want to use the screen for adding, editing, and viewing data. You do this through the View Setup dialog. Choose Format, and all Format files will appear in the scrollable list (see fig. 3.11). Select your Format file, in this example, INVNTRY, and choose Open and OK in the Setup dialog to return to the View window. Close the View window and any other windows that may be open.

Now choose Append from the Record menu. Instead of the dull default screen, your masterpiece appears, ready for your input. The Format file operates on Append and Change commands. You can use all options on the Record menu to find a specific record, and then select Change from the Record menu to edit the record with your custom form. Figure 3.12 shows the custom screen with a record in place for editing with the Change option of the Record menu.

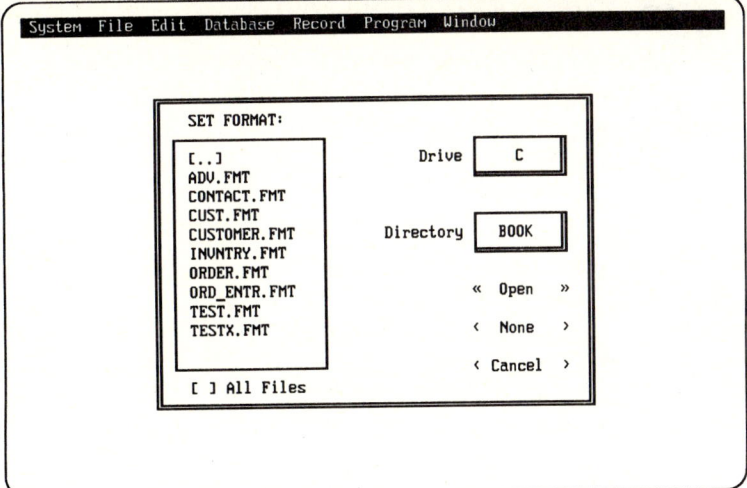

Fig. 3.11.
Selecting a
Format file to
associate with a
database.

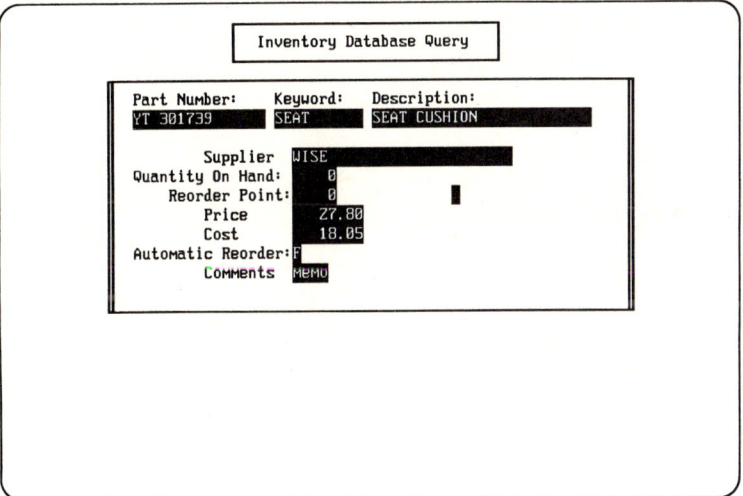

Fig. 3.12.
Editing a record
with the Change
option of the
Record menu.

This brief introduction to FoxView has only touched on its capabilities. With FoxView, you can create polished data-entry screens that are pleasing to the eye and easy to use, even in databases that require access to many different files simultaneously.

Editing in Data-Entry Fields

Just as you can edit your text entry in the dialog text fields of FoxPro, you can edit the data you're entering into your database. When you're in a data-entry field, the following editing functions are available to you:

Key	Function
End	Moves to the end of text in the field
Home	Moves to the start of text in the field
Backspace	Deletes the character to the left
Del	Deletes the character at the cursor
PgUp	Moves to first character of the current field, then to last character of the previous field
PgDn	Moves to last position of the current field, then to first position of the next field
Ins	Toggles insert/overwrite mode

Viewing Information

Now that you have learned how to get data into your database, it is helpful if you also are able to see that data. Reports may be important, but even more important is your capability to look at the data on-screen and to browse through it, reviewing and changing it if necessary. For this type of database work, FoxPro provides the versatile Browse window.

Using the Browse Window

The Browse window is a window into your database. Like any window, it shows you only a small portion of the whole scene at any one time. With your database open, choose Browse from the View window, and the Browse window appears (see fig. 3.13).

As you can see, the Browse window is a standard FoxPro window. It can be moved, sized, and zoomed like any other window, using the keyboard or a mouse. You can move up, down, and sideways in your database by clicking the appropriate mouse markers or using the PgUp, PgDn, and Tab keys. If you want to make a change in the Browse window, move the highlight to the appropriate field and make the change. The Browse window is

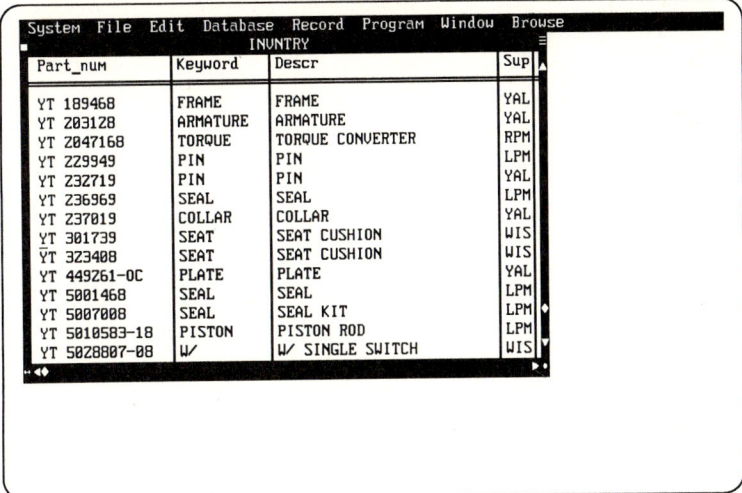

Fig. 3.13.
The Browse
window.

rightly named; you can browse through your database much as you browse through a department store.

The Browse window can make your browsing easy. You can split the window, change the sizes and the order of the fields, show only a subset of the fields and, in general, customize the Browse window to your purposes.

Changing the Browse Window

A number of customizations to the standard Browse window can be made in the View Setup dialog. In this dialog, you can specify which fields you want to appear in the Browse window by selecting the Fields check box. A dialog appears in which you specify the fields FoxPro is to display (see fig. 3.14). Until you specify otherwise, only these fields will appear in the Browse window.

In the Setup dialog you also can specify a *filter* condition. A filter is essentially a database record sieve. To set up a filter, you tell FoxPro, using the Expression Builder dialog that appears when you mark Filter in the Setup window, what condition must be met before a record can be displayed. You can, for example, set the filter to

    ZIP > 90000

and FoxPro will display in the Browse window only those records in which the value in the ZIP field is greater than 90000. Like the fields modifier, the filter is in effect until you turn it off or specify another.

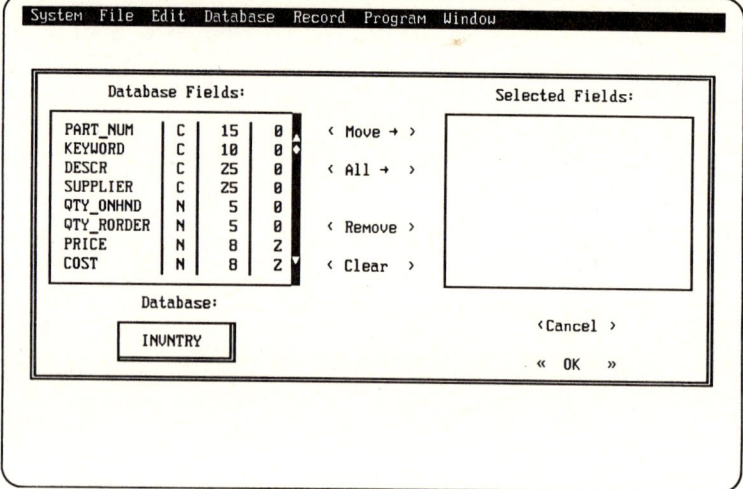

Fig. 3.14.
The dialog to
select fields for
FoxPro to
display.

Often you will want to view several fields that are too far apart to see in the Browse window at the same time. You move fields in the window by selecting the field you want to move and choosing Move Field from the Browse menu. Then you use the left- and right-arrow keys to move the field. Mouse users can accomplish this task even more easily; you grab the heading of the field you want to move and drag it to its new location. Figure 3.15 shows the QTY-ONHND field moved between the PART_NUM and KEYWORD fields.

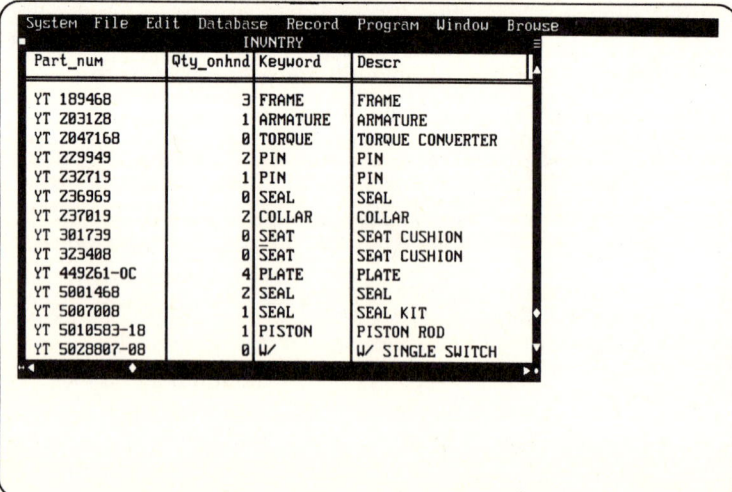

Fig. 3.15.
The QTY_ONHND
field moved
within the
Browse window.

Another common situation in the Browse window occurs when you want to hold one field in the window while scrolling horizontally through other fields. In the INVNTRY database, for example, you might want the PART_NUM field to be visible as you scroll left and right through the other fields.

To do this, choose Resize Partition from the Browse menu. You can use the right-arrow key to move the Browse window to the right, revealing another identical window underneath. (Mouse users can drag the partition marker in the lower left corner to move the top window.) You can move the top window as far as you want (within the bounds of the Browse window). Figure 3.16 shows the partitioned Browse window. You now have two Browse windows in which you can scroll left and right independently. To move from one window to the other, press Ctrl-H.

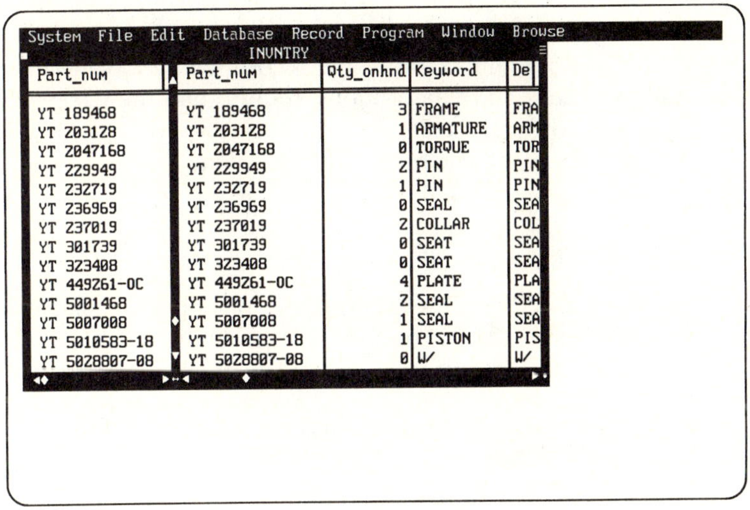

Fig. 3.16.
The partitioned
Browse window.

Notice that the two partitions scroll together vertically as if they are linked together. If you want to unlink them, choose Unlink Partitions from the Browse menu so that the two are independent both horizontally and vertically. When you jump from one partition to the other, however, the second partition will always scroll to make the record currently selected in the first window also active in the second. Suppose that, in a 1,000-record database, you had the first record active in the left partition and were showing the last record in the right. Jumping from the left to the right window would cause the right window to scroll so that the first record would also be active in that partition. If this seems confusing, just try it a time or two.

Using Browse Options

If you enter the BROWSE command from the command line, you can specify many options. You can tell FoxPro not to allow modification of data in the Browse window (NOEDIT), or not to open a data-entry window for appending new records (NOAPPEND), or not to allow deleting a record (NODELETE). You might do this when someone else is going to be using the system, and you want to limit their capability to alter the database. You also can tell FoxPro to use the size and format of the last Browse window of this database (LAST), or to inhibit display of the Browse menu (NOMENU).

Finding Specific Records

If you're looking for a specific record in a FoxPro database, especially a big database, browsing through the database becomes a real chore. Fox-Pro provides several ways to jump right to the record you're looking for. Two of these ways, the Seek and Find options, require that the database be indexed on the field you're searching for; the Locate option will find a record based on any field in the database, indexed or not.

Using Seek and Find

When you want to find a specific record, you are looking for a specific value in one of the database's fields. You may want to find the ABC Company in a customer database, for example, or part number IN 4434 in an inventory file. To use Seek or Find, you must have the database indexed on the field in which your search will take place. In the previous examples, the INVNTRY database must be indexed by PART_NUM and that index must be the controlling index of the database if you want to seek on a part number. If this seems bothersome, consider the advantage: because FoxPro uses the index to find the record you want, the search is almost instantaneous. Even in huge databases, a Seek or Find process seldom takes more than a second.

To seek a record, choose Seek from the Record menu. FoxPro presents the Expression Builder dialog to create the seek expression (see fig. 3.17). The expression must match the indexed expression, which is shown in the border above the Expression Builder window. If your index is a combination of fields or some other valid FoxPro expression, your seek value must be the same, or FoxPro returns an error message. If FoxPro successfully locates the record, use the Browse option to show the field at the top of the Browse window, and use the Edit option to put the found record in the Edit window.

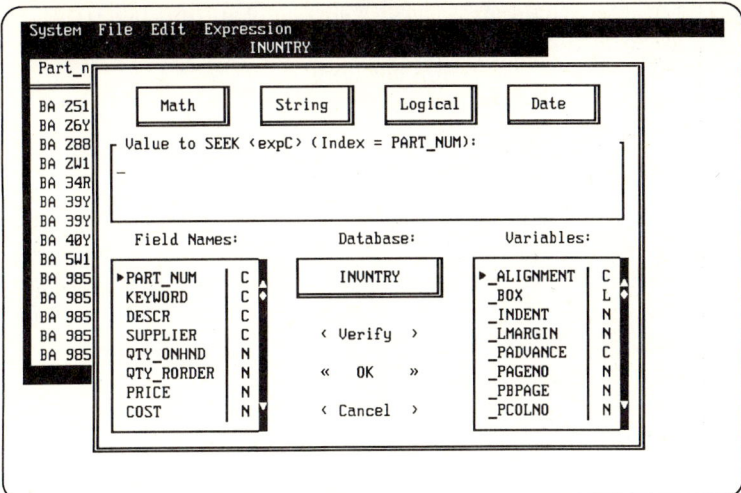

Fig. 3.17.
The Expression
Builder.

If FoxPro cannot find the field you're looking for, it returns a NO FIND message. (Unfortunately, this message may be under the Browse window. If the Browse window returns with the first record highlighted and that isn't the record you're seeking, the seek was unsuccessful.) If the Near setting is on (set in the View On/Off window), the database will be positioned immediately after the closest record. If Near is set to off, the database will be positioned at the first record of the database.

You also can use the Find option to search for character strings, but any experienced FoxPro user will recommend that you use Seek; it is more versatile and reliable.

Using Locate and Continue on Nonindexed Fields

You will encounter situations in which you need to find a record based on a value in a field you haven't indexed. The Locate option enables you to do this. Choose Locate from the Record menu, and you see the Locate dialog.

From this dialog, use the Scope option to tell FoxPro which record numbers to find—all, the next record, a specific record number, or the rest of the records. If you select For or While, you will build an expression in the Expression Builder dialog. You enter the expression you're searching for and the field in which you're searching. If the expression is valid, FoxPro will start at the beginning of the database and look through each record until it finds one matching your locate expression.

Warning: In a large database, a search can take a *long* time. Without an index to help find the record, FoxPro will plod through the database until it finds a record. You will, on average, search through half the database if you're looking for just one record. Even with a high-powered computer, sequential searches take time.

Once you find the first record that matches your locate expression, you can find subsequent ones by choosing Continue from the Record menu. FoxPro resumes the search from the record it just located until it finds the next one matching your locate expression. You can go on until you reach the end of the database file, and you can continue these subsequent searches as long as the Scope, For, or While clauses are valid.

Deleting Data

Although some databases seen to grow eternally, the time always comes when you must delete data. FoxPro makes this an easy process, even giving you the chance to change your mind before it actually throws your data out of the system. Up to a certain point, deleted data can be recalled into the database.

Marking Data

Deleting data in FoxPro is a two-step process. First, you mark a record for deletion, then you pack the database. Packing a database permanently removes all records marked for deletion. Until you pack a database, marked records are not really gone.

You can mark a record for deletion as you browse through the database. When you come to a record that you want to delete, press the Ctrl-T key combination. A mark will appear to the left of the first field in the database, telling you that the record has been marked for deletion. If you make a mistake, press Ctrl-T again, the record's deletion mark disappears, and the record is not deleted.

You also can delete data from the Record menu; when you choose Delete, you see the Delete dialog. The Scope option refers to the number of records, beginning with the current one, that you want to delete. If you choose Scope, the Scope dialog appears to get that information from you.

Deleting with the For option enables you to build an expression to delete every record in the database that meets the expression. If you want to delete all records that have a 0 in the QTY-ONHND field, you would specify the expression

QTY-ONHND = 0

FoxPro then marks for deletion every record in the database whose QTY-ONHND field contains 0.

The While option of the Delete dialog also enables you to build an expression that FoxPro will evaluate to determine whether to mark a record for deletion. Like the For option, you use the Expression Builder dialog to build the expression.

The For option evaluates every record in the database; you are saying to FoxPro, "For every record that meets this expression, delete it." On the other hand, the While option tells FoxPro, "Start at the current record, and step through the database, marking each record for deletion while they meet the expression." With the While option, FoxPro stops marking when it comes to the first record that does not meet the expression; when using For, FoxPro skips over records not meeting the expression and continues until the end of the database.

For all practical purposes, a record marked for deletion is ignored by FoxPro. Reports don't report them, inquiries don't find them. Some Scope commands count records marked for deletion in their actions, but should this become a problem, the SET DELETED ON command causes them to be ignored. Records marked for deletion appear in the Browse window unless you select SET DELETED ON; then they will not appear, though they remain in the database.

Records marked for deletion still take up space in the database, and FoxPro must pass over them in operations. Anytime you can streamline your database by reducing its size, you will improve FoxPro's efficiency. Don't allow your database to be cluttered with deleted records; if you find you're deleting many records, pack the database frequently to remove them.

Recalling a Record

You can bring back a record marked for deletion by using the same set of actions you used to mark it. Ctrl-T unmarks a single record. Choose the Recall option from the Record menu to use the Scope, For, and While commands. When you recall a marked record, it is unmarked, and it rejoins the other records as a full member of the database.

Packing the Database

In some advanced database systems, hundreds of records are added and hundreds marked for deletion each day. Obviously, unless those marked for deletion are discarded, the database will be full of records that are never used. Even in small databases, it is wise to pack the database periodically to remove unused records.

To pack a database, choose Pack from the Database menu. The Pack option discards records marked for deletion and reclaims the space they used. Once you have packed a database, records marked for deletion are gone permanently. If you have index files opened, FoxPro automatically updates the indexes to reflect the deleted records.

Chapter Summary

Entering, editing, viewing, and deleting data in a database are the day-to-day, mundane tasks of data management. These tasks are seldom much fun, yet they are as essential as database design and fancy reports. As you work with FoxPro, you will become experienced at using the tools FoxPro provides to ease the tasks of entering data, and reviewing and deleting it.

Sorting and Summarizing Data

Now that you have learned how to design a database, define it to Fox-Pro, and enter and edit information in it, you're probably ready to get something out of it. The strength of any database system is its capacity to show you summaries of information in new and different ways. With FoxPro, you can view and summarize your database from many new perspectives.

In this chapter, you learn how to tell FoxPro what information you want from your database; how to build FoxPro expressions, which are really nothing more than filters on the database, allowing you to specify explicitly which records and data FoxPro should use when processing your commands; and how to sort and index a database in different ways, providing different perspectives on the information in the database. Memory variables, which you use to store and display summary information, also are introduced. And you will put this information together to learn how to use the Scope, For, and While commands to summarize data on just the parts of the database you specify.

Calculating and Summarizing Information in a Database

The quickest way to summarize information in your database is with the options in the Database menu. To experiment with summary options, open a database with a numeric field (in this example, INVNTRY is open), close all windows except the Command window, and choose Sum from the Database menu. FoxPro brings up the Sum dialog, which gives you four options: Expr, Scope, For, and While. Choose Expr, and the Expression Builder dialog appears (see fig. 4.1). Here you tell FoxPro what you want summed. By selecting the qty_onhnd field and then choosing OK, you tell FoxPro to sum all the values in that field. Make this selection now, return to the Sum dialog, and then choose OK.

Fig. 4.1.
The Expression
Builder dialog.

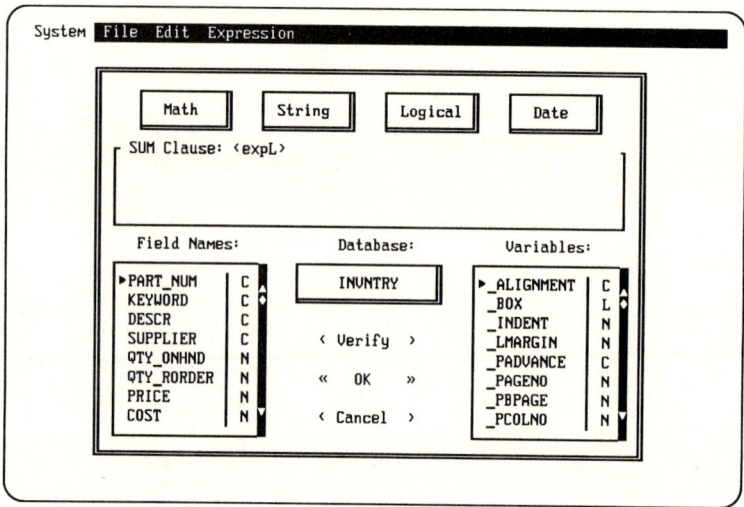

On the screen, FoxPro tells you how many records it has summed and shows the results of the summation (see fig. 4.2). You can use the Sum option when you need to know the total of a numeric field in your database.

If you use the Average option in the Database menu, you get the same dialogs, and FoxPro tells you the average value of a numeric field—the total amount of all the fields divided by the number of records FoxPro summed.

Choosing Count from the Database menu brings up the Count dialog (see fig. 4.3). The Count dialog looks much like the Average and Sum dialogs, but it has no Expr option. Count simply counts records. For now, choose Scope from the Count dialog, and the Scope dialog appears (see fig. 4.4).

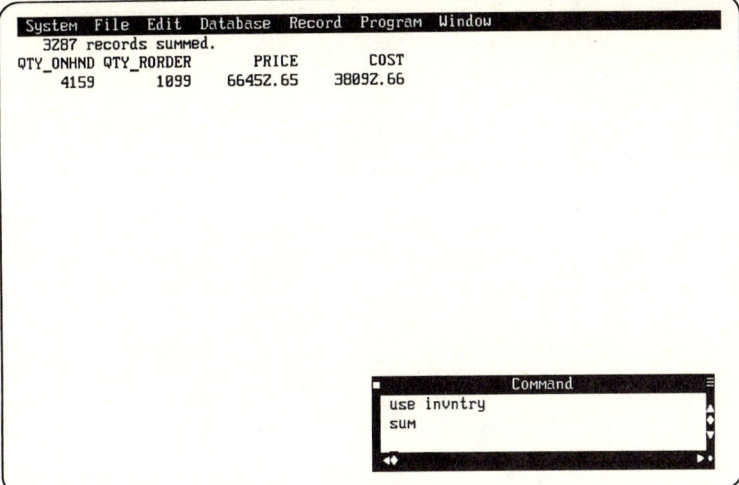

Fig. 4.2.
The results of a
Sum command.

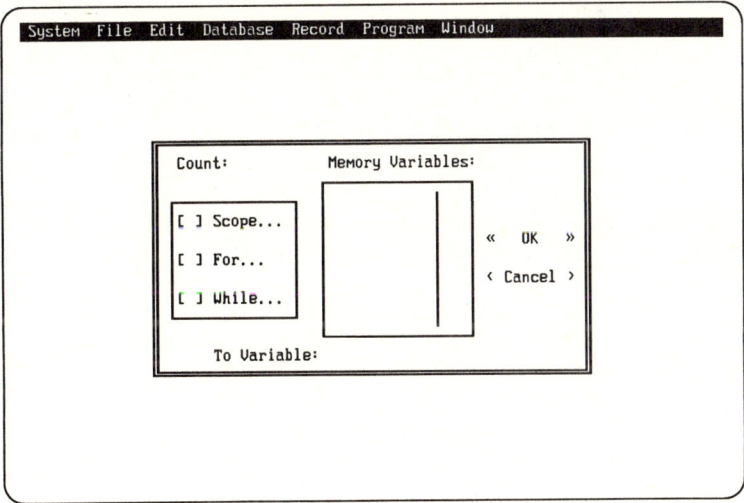

Fig. 4.3.
The Count
dialog.

Scope is FoxPro's way of asking, "Which records should I process, based on their location in the database?" Scope allows you to limit the database search to specific records, based on where the records are in the database. Later, you will learn how to limit FoxPro's searching and processing by using values in the database fields with the For and While clauses. The four Scope radio buttons are as follows:

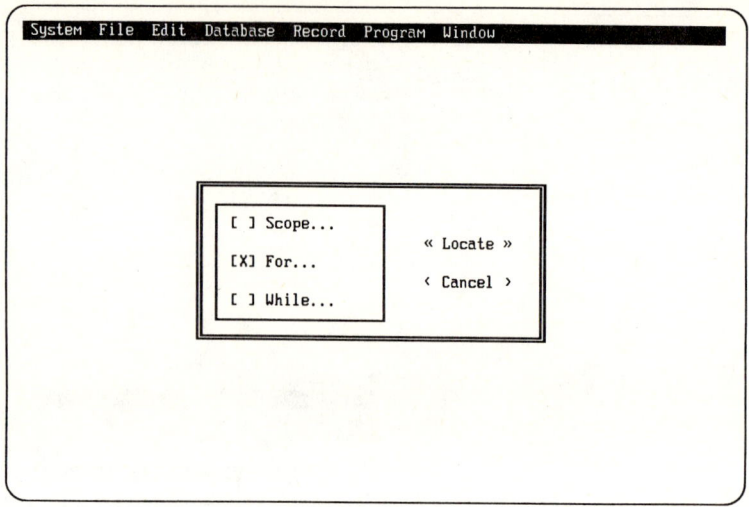

Fig. 4.4.
The Scope dialog.

( ) All   If you select this option, FoxPro searches all records, starting from the beginning of the database.

( ) Next   If you select this option, FoxPro searches the next *n* records, starting from its current position in the database. When you select Next, an input window appears in which you specify the number of records to search.

( ) Record   If you select this option, FoxPro processes only one record. An input window appears when you choose Record to ask what record number you want to process.

( ) Rest   If you select this option, FoxPro processes all records from the current position to the end of the database.

Choosing one of these options tells FoxPro which records to search as it processes the command for which the scope is specified; these limits restrict the search and processing to certain locations in the database without regard to what is in the record. All says, "Process all records," Next says, "Just process a certain number from the current position," Record identifies one specific record number, and Rest says, "Start in the current position and process all records to the end." After you have chosen one of the radio buttons, choose OK. The Count dialog appears; choose OK again. FoxPro then shows the results of its count on-screen.

These three Database menu options—Average, Count, and Sum—can provide information about your database, but they are rather limited. FoxPro is not limited, though; using expressions, you can have FoxPro do sophisticated searches and summaries for you.

Refining Database Searches

Scope allows you to restrict FoxPro searches by the position of records in the database. But what do you do if you want to summarize information from all records in a certain ZIP code range? You can restrict FoxPro's database processing to specific records by using a combination of three capabilities: expressions and the For and While clauses. Using these three features, you can slice your database in different ways to receive the information you need. In this section, you will learn about building expressions and using them in conjunction with the For and While clauses.

Using the Expression Builder

You were introduced to FoxPro expressions in earlier chapters, where you used the Expression Builder dialog to tell FoxPro which data to display and delete. Now you will delve more deeply into expressions, which are the most powerful way—short of programming—to tell FoxPro which database records you want it to search for and process. First, you will look at expressions to limit searches of the database to records with fields containing values you define. When you have mastered that skill, you will apply it to more complex ways of summarizing your data, using For and While restrictions on the search.

If you want to look at or summarize some specific records of your database, you must tell FoxPro how to decide which records to include. You do so by using FoxPro *expressions*. An expression is just an equation; FoxPro evaluates the equation for each record the program encounters in a database search. If the equation evaluates to true, FoxPro includes that record in the process; if the equation evaluates to false, FoxPro skips over it. If you want to see only records where the value in field NAME is JONES, for example, you need to tell FoxPro, "Look at each record; if the name is equal to JONES, list the record to the screen; if not, skip the record." To give this command in a form FoxPro understands, you can use the Expression Builder. The Expression Builder dialog pops up whenever you need it.

Examining Expressions

Perhaps the best way to understand the term *expression* is to see how it is specified on the command line of FoxBase+ or in the Command window of FoxPro. Suppose, for example, that in the INVNTRY database, you want to get the total of the inventory on-hand for all parts with a cost greater than $4. First ensure that the INVNTRY database is open and then issue the command

    SUM QTY_ONHND FOR COST > 4.00

This command is simply a sentence telling FoxPro what to do and how to do it. SUM is the verb of the sentence, telling FoxPro what to do. QTY_ONHND is the object. FoxPro is to sum the QTY_ONHND fields. FOR COST > 4.00 tells FoxPro what records to sum—those in which the value in the cost field is greater than $4.

The expression is

    COST > 4.00

For every record in the database, that expression will be either true (the cost is greater than 4.00) or false (the cost is equal to or less than 4.00). FoxPro will make that comparison for every record it encounters in the database. If the expression is true for a record, FoxPro will add the QTY_ONHND of that record to the total it is keeping. If the expression is false, FoxPro will skip over it.

The preceding expression was a simple one. Now suppose that you want to count how many records exist whose PART_NUM starts with IN and whose QTY_ONHND is zero. The expression is

    COUNT FOR ((LEFT(PART_NUM,2)="IN") AND (QTY_ONHND = 0))

Although this expression is much more complicated, the principle is the same. FoxPro will evaluate the expression to the right of the FOR for every record in the database. If the expression is true for a record, FoxPro will count the record; if the expression is false, FoxPro will skip that record.

Building and Beginning Expressions

Eventually, you will become experienced enough to enter expressions like the preceding from the Command window, but FoxPro provides the Expression Builder dialog to ease the creation of all expressions. To open the Expression Builder dialog, you need to give FoxPro a task that requires an expression. In this section's example, the INVNTRY database is open and the controlling index is on the keyword field. You will perform a Locate operation on this database. Locate requires an expression to tell FoxPro what record to locate. With the INVNTRY database opened and indexed on keyword, choose Locate from the Record menu.

Figure 4.5 shows the Expression Builder dialog that FoxPro uses to get the Locate expression; this dialog appears when you choose For or While from the Scope dialog after you select Locate from the Record menu.

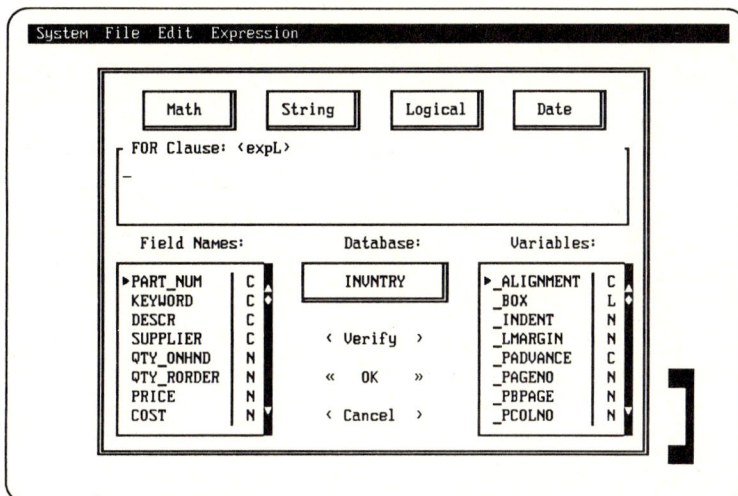

Fig. 4.5.
The Expression
Builder dialog.

In the Title bar of the Expression Builder box, you see the phrase FOR Clause: <expL>. FoxPro is telling you that it needs to construct a logical expression (one that evaluates to either true or false). FoxPro will evaluate the logical expression for each record in INVNTRY, stopping the search when it reaches one for which the logical expression evaluates to true.

To find the first record in the INVNTRY database with a keyword of SEAL, select the field KEYWORD from the field picker. The phrase

    invntry–>keyword

appears in the Expression Builder box. The cursor is at the end of this phrase. Enter

    = "SEAL"

Choose OK and Locate from the Scope dialog to send FoxPro on its Locate mission.

When you have a valid expression, select OK. Immediately, FoxPro starts at the first record in the database to see whether the value in the keyword field is SEAL. As mentioned earlier, expressions are actually logical tests. In this case, for each database record, FoxPro evaluates this equation:

KEYWORD = "SEAL"

If the expression is false, FoxPro goes to the next record. If the expression is true, FoxPro stops and points to the record.

To see that FoxPro has really accomplished its task, browse the INVNTRY database; you will see that the first record with a keyword of SEAL is highlighted.

Obviously, this is a fairly easy example, but it illustrates the power of building expressions. With expressions, you can search databases quickly. To build more complicated expressions that slice the database into finer and finer increments, you need to use some of FoxPro's functions, the topic of the next section.

Using FoxPro Functions

A FoxPro function is much like a "black box"; you put some piece of data into it, the function does something with that data and returns some other piece of data.

AVERAGE() and COUNT() also are functions, and they operate the same way. FoxPro offers many functions, and you can use each to build an expression. To see FoxPro functions, choose Sum from the Database menu and then choose Expr to bring up the Expression Builder. You will see four boxes, labeled Math, String, Logical, and Date. These are the four categories of FoxPro functions. To see each of the functions, open up the scrollable list for each as you review the categories. (Mouse users can click in the box to open the scrollable list; keyboard users need to press Alt-X to pull down the Expression menu and then choose the appropriate function.)

In working with functions, you will encounter the word *argument*. An argument is a value or series of values that the function needs in order to do its job; arguments are placed inside the parentheses after the function name. You will see arguments in the examples that follow.

Math Functions

Math functions return a numeric value, usually taking a numeric value as input. SUM() is a math function, returning as a numeric value the sum of specified fields. The input to a math function is often numeric, but not always. The LEN() function, for example, takes as input a character variable and returns the numeric length of the variable; LEN("This is so much fun!") returns 19, the length of the string argument. Another example of a math function is MIN(<expr1>,<expr2>[, <expr3>...]), which returns the minimum value of the input arguments. The opposite of MIN is MAX. SQRT(<expr*N*>) returns the square root of the numeric argument.

String Functions

String functions return character strings, usually taking character strings as arguments. String functions are valuable tools for modifying strings. If, for example, you want to change all characters in a field to uppercase letters, you can simply specify the expression

> REPLACE ALL *field_name* WITH UPPER(*field_name*)

where *field_name* is the name of the database field you want to convert. With string functions, you also can strip off leading and trailing blank spaces, remove certain parts of a string, or insert one string into another. Some other useful string functions are ALLTRIM(*string expression*), which returns a string stripped of leading and trailing blanks, and RIGHT(*string expression, numeric expression*), which returns the rightmost number of characters in the string. The number of characters is specified in the numeric argument.

Logical Functions

Logical functions always return a true or false value. A logical function used often in FoxPro programming is EOF(), which stands for End Of File. If the database is currently positioned at the end of the file (actually, on the "phantom" record that exists after the last real record), EOF() returns TRUE, telling you that you're at the end of the file. Another logical function is BOF(), which is the converse of EOF(). BOF() returns TRUE if the current position in a database is at the beginning of a file.

Date Functions

FoxPro is proficient at manipulating and working with dates. The date functions return different types of results, but all are related to dates in some way. An example of a date function is DOW(). When you give DOW() a date argument, it returns a number representing the day of the week. Another date function is MONTH(), which returns the number of the month in the date argument.

CDOW(<exprD>) returns a character string with the name of the day of the week for the date specified as an argument. CMON does the same for the name of the month.

Note: You often cannot enter a date value directly from the keyboard. If, for example, you enter the function

? DOW(12/25/90)

FoxPro gives you the error message Invalid function argument value, type or count. The DOW() function requires a date, but because of the 12, FoxPro thinks you have put in a numeric function. To put a date into this function, use the Character To Date function, CTOD(). Give the CTOD function a character string with a valid date; the character string is converted to a real FoxPro date and is fed to DOW():

? DOW(CTOD("12/25/90"))

You get back the answer 3, which means that December 25, 1990, will fall on the third day of the week (Sunday = 1). You will get to know two date functions well, particularly if you advance to writing FoxPro and FoxBase+ programs:

❏ DTOC(*date argument*) returns a string representation of the date. Then you can combine the string date with other strings for printing and searching and indexing.

❏ CTOD(*string argument*) takes a string argument in the form mm/dd/yy and converts it to FoxPro's internal date format, from which you can calculate the day, month, and year differences between dates and all FoxPro's other date capabilities.

Now that you know the basics of functions, you can learn how to put functions to use.

Using the For and While Clauses To Limit Searches

For and While allow you to limit FoxPro's processing of your database based on the value of one or more of the fields in each record. Scope limits the processing based on where records are in the database file, but For and While can include or exclude records based on any expression you can concoct. (You also can combine Scope with For and While expressions, telling FoxPro, "Include only the records that meet both the For and While expression *and* the Scope expression.")

The best way to learn the difference between For and While is with an example. Figure 4.6 shows the Browse window of a simple database with one character field and one numeric field. The database is indexed on Name, so it is in alphabetical order.

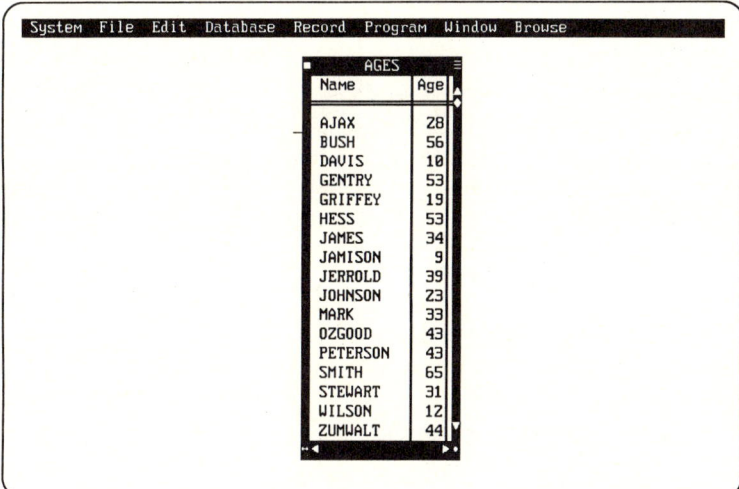

Fig. 4.6.
The AGES database, indexed on Name.

Assuming that no Scope clause is in effect, For tells FoxPro to look at all the records in the database and include those that meet the expression. For example, telling FoxPro to sum on the expression

FOR age < 30

results in the sequence shown in figure 4.7.

On the other hand, While tells FoxPro to start at the current location in the database and process records while the expression is true; in this case, FoxPro will stop as soon as it reaches a record for which the expression is false. Asking FoxPro to sum on the expression

WHILE age < 30

gives you the sequence shown in figure 4.8 and a result of 28.

As you can see, While depends completely on how the database is indexed. If you index the AGE database on the Age field and issue the SUM command on the same

WHILE age < 30

expression, you get the sequence shown in figure 4.9 and a result of 101.

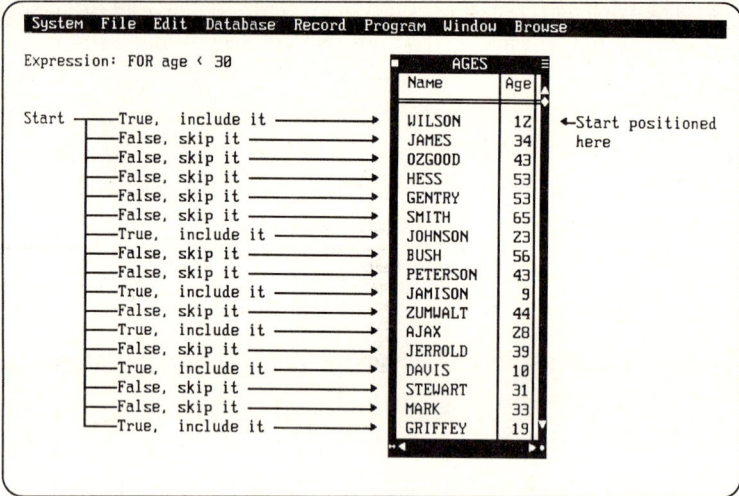

Fig. 4.7.
Processing the
expression FOR
AGE < 30.

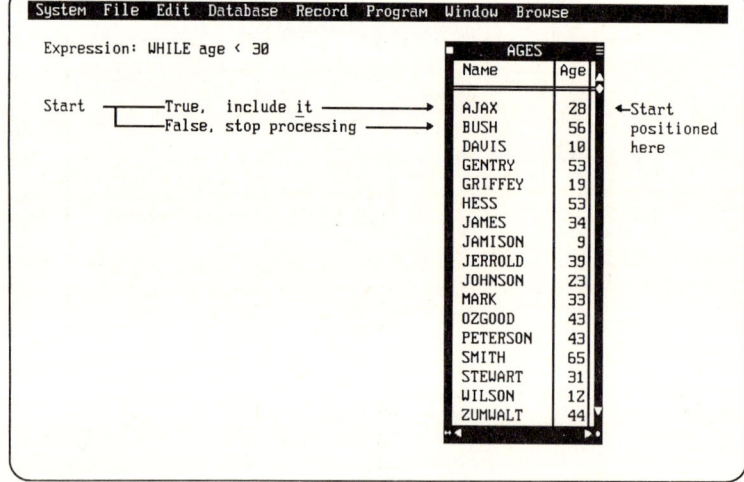

Fig. 4.8.
Processing the
expression
WHILE AGE
< 30.

If you're working with a large database, searching and summarizing with a For clause can take a long time, because FoxPro and FoxBase+ must look at each record and evaluate the expression for it before deciding whether to include the record. Even if only one record in the entire database will pass, every record is checked. If you find yourself in this situation, use the following trick.

First, index the database on the expression you used in the For clause. This action organizes the database so that all the records that pass your

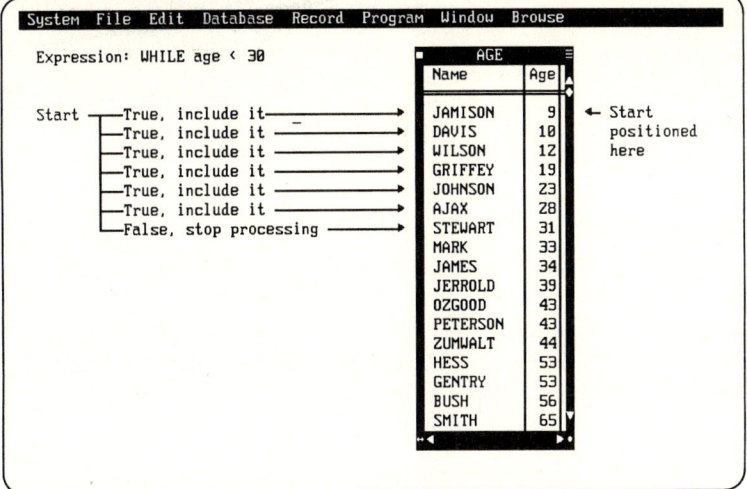

Fig. 4.9.
Using WHILE to process the AGES database, indexed by Age.

evaluation are grouped together. Second, use Seek to find the first of the records that will pass; use the same expression you indexed the database on. Then use While to do your summarizing or searching. Because Seek puts the database pointer at the first record that will evaluate to true on the expression, While steps through the group of valid expressions and stops when it meets the first that fails. If you use this procedure, FoxPro will not have to search the entire database. Figure 4.10 shows how this process works.

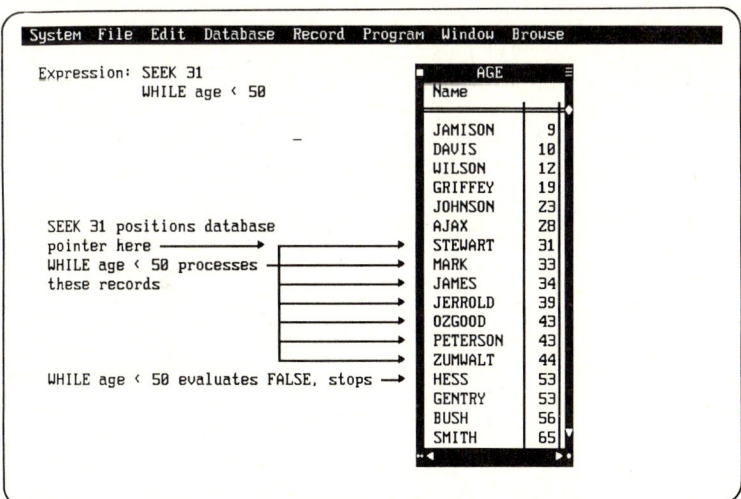

Fig. 4.10.
Using SEEK to change the starting point of WHILE.

Using Memory Variables To Store and Display Information

Often you will find that you want to save the value of a summed field, a count, or an average and use it later. FoxPro provides the means to store values (numeric, logical, date, and string) and reuse those values later. Memory variables are the tools you use for this purpose.

A memory variable is much like a home's mail slot at the post office. It has a name and holds something—in FoxPro's case, a number, string, logical value, or date. You create a memory variable simply by assigning a value to it. Figure 4.11 shows the FoxPro screen as you assign values to memory variables in the Command window. FoxPro shows the results of these actions in the upper left corner of the screen.

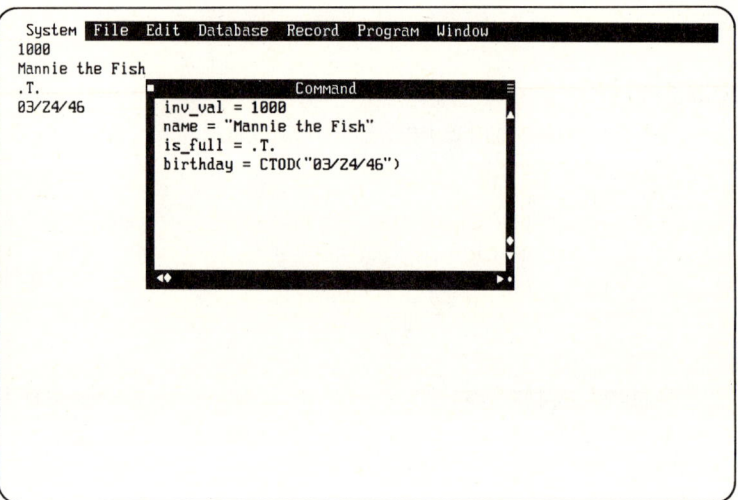

Fig. 4.11.
Assigning values to memory variables.

You also can use memory variables for storing the results of calculations. To store the results of a SUM operation, use this form of the command:

SUM QTY_ONHND FOR COST > 4.00 TO TOT_ONHND

The memory variable TOT_ONHND now contains the value that resulted from the SUM command. You can see this value by using the ? command:

? TOT_ONHND

The result is 34588.

The memory variable types are the same as the field types in a database: character, numeric, logical, and date. You don't have to tell FoxPro what type of memory variable you want to create; assigning the value does that. You can change the types simply by reassigning a new, different value:

INV_VAL = 1000 (creates a numeric variable)
INV_VAL = "Zip" (creates a character variable)

You cannot combine different memory variable types. Figure 4.12 shows a correct way to add memory variables, and figure 4.13 shows an incorrect way to add memory variables.

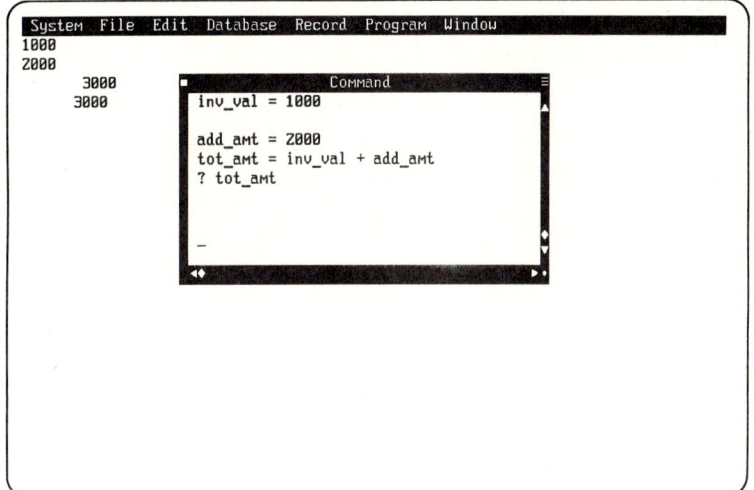

Fig. 4.12.
Adding memory variables.

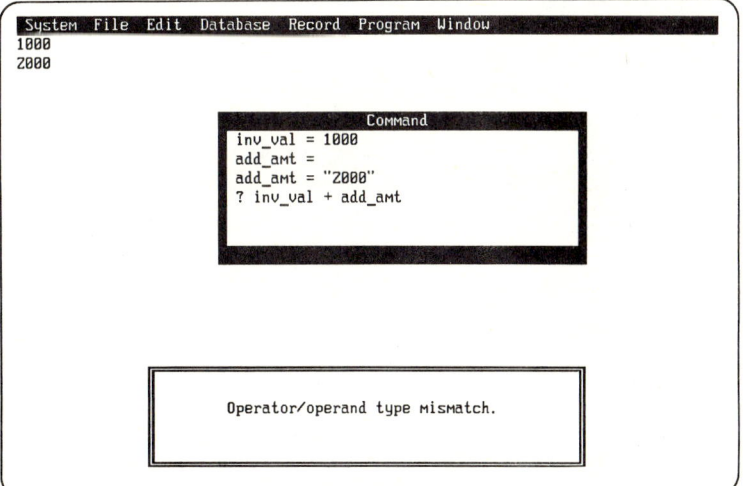

Fig. 4.13.
Adding memory variables of differing types.

Memory variables can be used anywhere you would otherwise use actual values. If you want to count all records in a database that have a cost of more than $4, you can give FoxPro the following expression:

```
TEST_COST = 4.00
COUNT FOR (COST > TEST_COST)
```

Memory variables are absolutely essential for programming in FoxPro (as they are in all computer programming languages), but you will find them useful in all FoxPro and FoxBase+ operations. As soon as you find yourself entering some value repeatedly, think about assigning that value to a memory variable with a shorter name; from then on, you can use the memory variable and be assured that you aren't making a mistake entering the value.

Rearranging the Database

You often will be adding records to and deleting records from your databases. And seldom, if ever, will the database remain in the same logical order after you add and delete records. For example, if you started out entering records alphabetically because that's how you want to see them, the first time you add a record, you will have a problem. FoxPro, like just about all databases, adds new records to the end of the file. When you add the AAAAA Zebra Company to your customer database, however, you need some way to make it the first record—or at least appear to be the first record. FoxPro provides two ways to order your database: sorting and indexing.

Sorting

When FoxPro sorts a database, it copies the records into a new database in an order that you specify. If you want the new database sorted alphabetically based on customer name, FoxPro can do that; if you want the database sorted by ZIP code and then alphabetically by customer name within each ZIP code, FoxPro can do that also. FoxPro can sort a database on any expression you can build.

To create a sorted database, choose Sort from the Database menu. The Sort dialog appears (see fig. 4.14). Use this dialog to tell FoxPro the sort order you want followed.

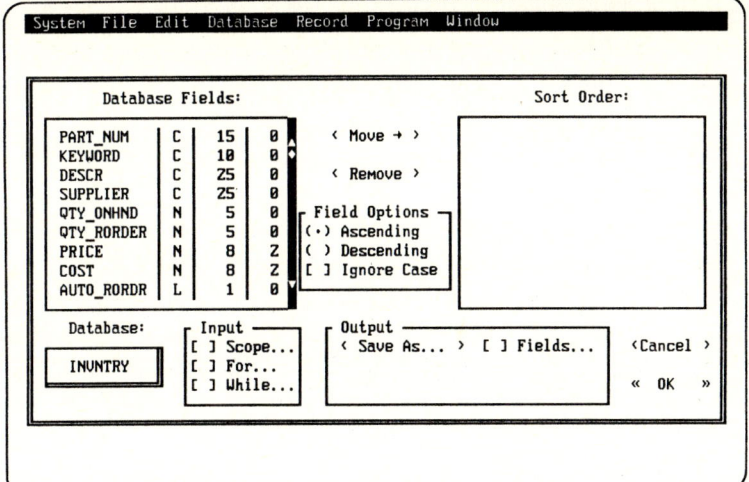

Fig. 4.14.
The Sort dialog.

The first field or expression you specify is the primary sort of the new database; all records are sorted according to that order. If you specify a second sort, FoxPro sorts all records with the same primary sort field in the order of the second sort. If, for example, you choose supplier as your primary sort and PART_NUM as your secondary sort, the new database will have each supplier's records grouped together in alphabetical order, and within each supplier's name, all the supplier's part numbers will be sorted alphabetically. Figure 4.15 shows the Sort dialog with the Sort order identified.

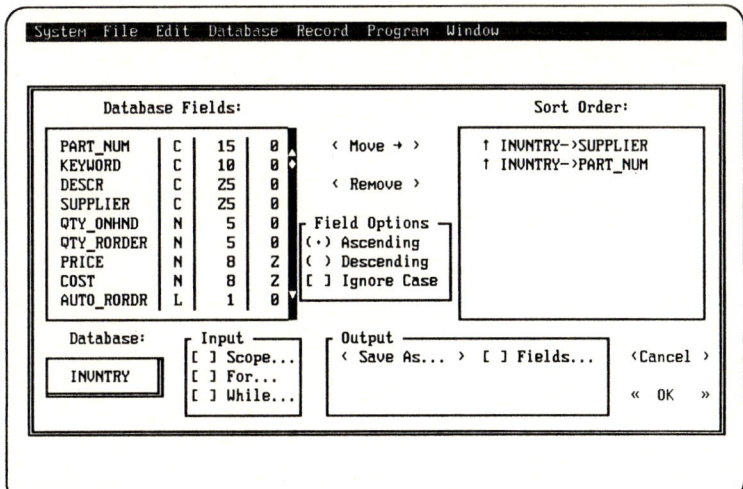

Fig. 4.15.
The completed Sort dialog with a two-field sort.

You can sort just a subset of records in a database. If you want to sort just records for one supplier, you can choose For and build an expression to do that. FoxPro then selects only the records that pass the FOR test and sorts those into the new database.

If you want to sort on an expression, choose Expr and the Expression Builder dialog appears (see fig. 4.16) You can sort on any expression, such as a combination of fields or part of some field. Figure 4.16 shows a sort expression of the two leftmost characters in the PART_NUM field of each record.

Fig. 4.16.
The Expression Builder.

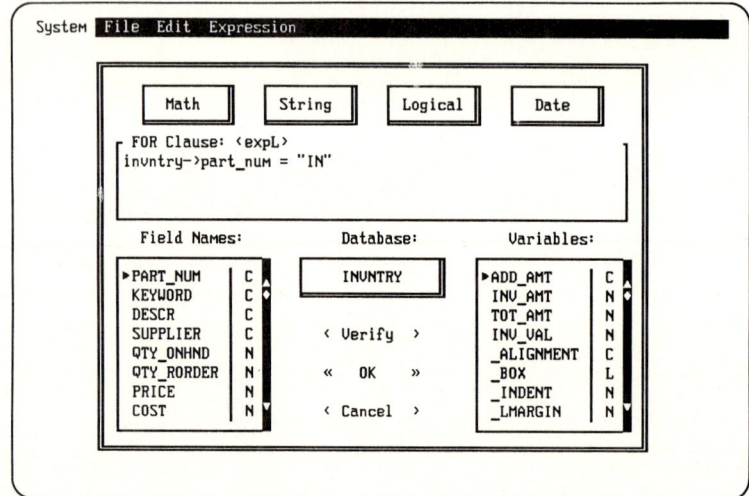

When you have completed describing your sort order to FoxPro, select OK. FoxPro extracts the necessary records and sorts them, giving you information about its progress. When FoxPro is done, the new database is ready for your use.

Warning: Because FoxPro and FoxBase+ physically create the sorted file, plus possibly some intermediate files, a sort can take a great deal of disk space. You need to have free disk space equal to at least the size of the database you're sorting. When the sort is done, you get the free space back, but running short in the middle of the sort causes the process to stop. Also, sorts can take a long time, even for FoxPro and FoxBase+, which have well-deserved reputations for being faster than competitive database programs. The length of the sort depends on how long the sort key is, how long the database records are, and, most of all, how big the database is. The INVNTRY database used as an example in this book is about 19,000 records long; sorting on the PART_NUM field takes FoxPro about 1 minute and 40 seconds on an 80386, 20 MHz computer. Compare that number with about 23 seconds for indexing it on the same field, and you see why sorting is seldom required.

Indexing

Indexing is a different way to order a database, but to the user, the results are often identical. When FoxPro indexes a database, a separate index file is created that tells FoxPro the order it has to access the database records to put them in the right order. Here is a simple example of a database:

1   AAA Company
2   XYZ Company
3   BED Company
4   ZUM Company
5   DED Company
6   ISL Company
7   ACS Company
8   SER Company
9   RSV Company

An example of the index file for such a database, indexed alphabetically, follows:

1   (the first alphabetical record is #1)
7   (the second alphabetical record is #7)
3   (the third is #3)
5   (the fourth is #5)
6   (the fifth is #6)
9   (the sixth is #9)

8 (the seventh is #8)
2 (the eighth is #2)
4 (the ninth is #4)

To present this database in alphabetical order, FoxPro would look at the index file and use the order of the indexes to present the database: database record 1 first, record 7 second, record 3 third, and so on. To the user, the database appears to be in alphabetical order, because there is no appreciable delay in FoxPro getting the index first and then listing the correct record.

Indexing versus Sorting: Which Is Better?

Indexing is almost always the better choice. You can have up to seven different indexes open at one time on a database file, so you can have seven different ways of looking at the database simply by changing which index "controls" the database. If you need more ways, you can simply create the indexes and update them as necessary. While an index is open, whether controlling or not, any changes to its key fields automatically update the index file. In the preceding example, changing the AAA Company to the MMM Company would automatically update the index and rearrange the presentation. Such updating of open index files is almost instantaneous.

Creating a new index is much faster than sorting; FoxPro and FoxBase+ are superior performers in indexing.

Are there advantages to sorting? Arranging an index in descending order is a difficult—but not impossible—task, but arranging a database in descending order is easily done with a sort. Sorted database files don't need index files, but they do need to be sorted each time the sort field changes.

In short, opt for sorting only if you cannot make indexing accomplish what you need. In years of developing FoxBase+ and FoxPro applications, I have included only one sort.

Creating an Index

Creating an index is simple. Open your database and choose Setup from the View window. You will use the right side of the Setup dialog (see fig. 4.17) to add (and later modify) index files. To start, select Add.

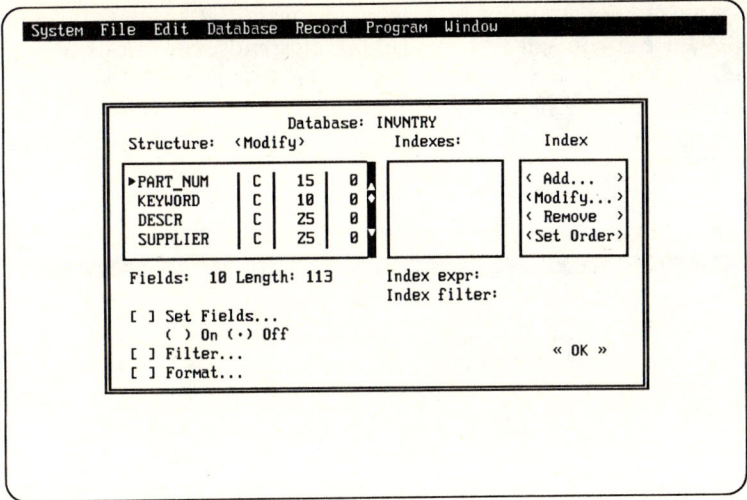

Fig. 4.17.
The Setup dialog.

The Open Index File dialog appears (see fig. 4.18). FoxPro doesn't know at this point that you want to create an index. You have only told the program to add one to the database, and you may simply want to add an existing index. To tell FoxPro that you will be creating a new index, select New.

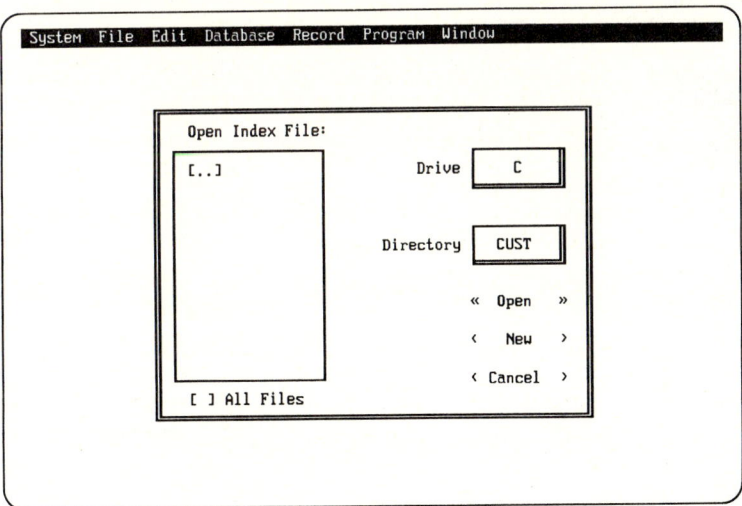

Fig. 4.18.
The Open Index File dialog.

FoxPro responds to your request by bringing forward the Index On dialog (see fig. 4.19). Here you tell FoxPro which fields and expressions to use in creating the index. If you want to simply index on fields in the database, clicking on the fields in the field picker window adds them to the index expression. If you need to define a more complex expression, click on Expr.

Fig. 4.19.
The Index On dialog.

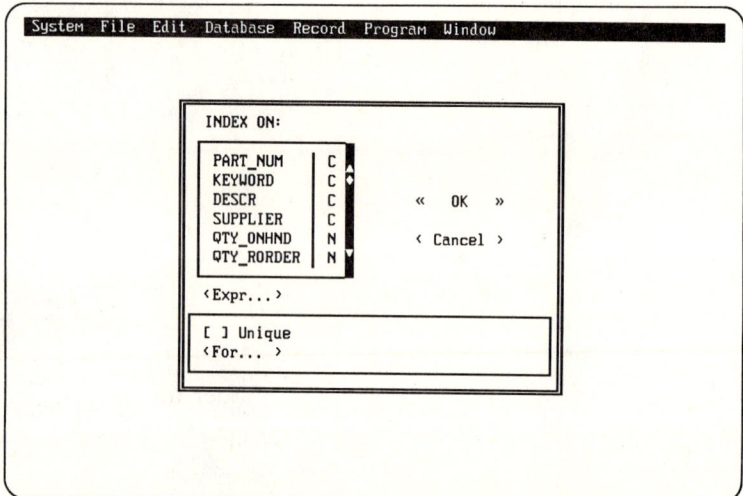

The familiar Expression Builder dialog appears (see fig. 4.20).

Fig. 4.20.
The Index On Expression Builder.

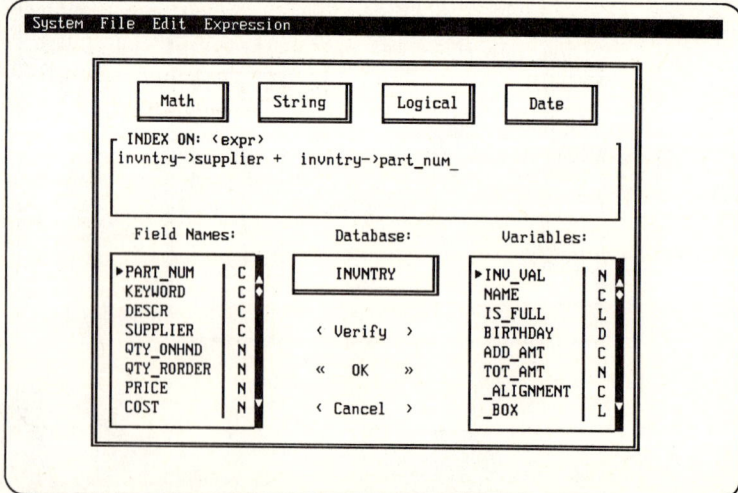

The index expression can be any valid expression. For example, you can build an INVNTRY database index that presents the information in alphabetical order by supplier and within each supplier by PART_NUM by building the expression

SUPPLIER + PART_NUM

When you choose fields from the field names list, FoxPro appends the field name to the database name and the alias symbol (->). The alias and field names will be in lowercase letters. If you type the expression into the Expression Builder, you can omit the database name and the alias symbol. You also can enter uppercase letters; FoxPro expressions are not case-sensitive.

Expressions can be complicated. Suppose that you don't want to have the database in supplier and then PART_NUM order. Instead, you want the database in supplier order and within each supplier by the value of the inventory on-hand for each part. You can use the expression

SUPPLIER + STR(QTY_ONHND * COST)

Here, you convert the inventory value (QTY_ONHND * COST) to a character string by using the STR() function in order to combine it with the character string SUPPLIER. Remember, you cannot combine expressions of different types.

Chapter Summary

All the topics covered in this chapter bear on ways to get different views of your database. You will build expressions to limit searches to records that meet your criteria, you will use Scope to limit how much FoxPro and FoxBase+ search. Sorts and indexes make the database more efficient and show you different ways to look at your database.

Now that you understand how to see different views of your data, you will learn how to retrieve that information in the form of reports, the topic of the next chapter.

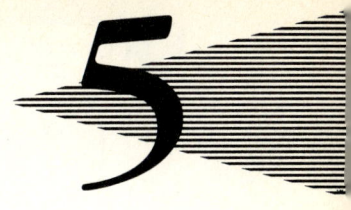

Creating Reports
in FoxPro

Reports are the most visible part of your database, particularly to other people who will use them. If your reports are clear and understandable, your database will be far more usable. On the other hand, if your reports are muddled and difficult to read and understand, the most elegant database design will be for naught. Reports from computer systems have to be good or you might as well not develop the system.

It used to be true that the only thing comparable to the importance of good reports was the tedium of creating them. In the old days, programmers laid out the report format on a sheet of grid paper, and then translated the rows and columns of the report to programming code; if you wanted to change the report, the program code had to be changed. With FoxPro, you can create elegant, understandable reports with a minimum of effort.

In this chapter, you learn how to use FoxPro's Layout window to define and create reports on your databases. First, you will see how simple reports are created using just database fields and some basic titles. Then, you move on to more useful reports, in which you add boxes and lines to emphasize important data, and use FoxPro's built-in functions to provide date and time stamping of reports.

Most important, you learn how to group data, which allows you to calculate subtotals and calculated fields on specific parts of the report. When you're finished with this chapter, you will be an expert at creating the reports you need to show off your database.

The basic process of report writing in FoxPro is designing your report in the Layout window, putting fields and text where you want them on the report, and then running the report from the Database menu.

125

Using the Layout Window

To open a new report, make sure that the database on which you want to report is opened and that the proper index controls it. To continue the example from earlier chapters, make sure that INVNTRY is opened and the PART_NUM index is controlling. This ensures that your report will be in the right order. Choose New from the File menu, and then select Report and OK. FoxPro presents the Layout window, which is the basis for report design (see fig. 5.1).

Fig. 5.1.
The Layout window.

The Layout window is like a blank sheet of paper on which you design your report. You place *objects* on the blank sheet. These objects are database fields you want included in the report, and text fields to make the report more readable. Later, you add lines and boxes (which are objects) to improve the readability of your report.

On the left of the Layout view you see lines labeled PgHead, Detail, and PgFoot. These lines refer to *bands*, which FoxPro uses to create the report. Each band represents a part of the report page. PgHead is an abbreviation for Page Header, which is the top part of each page of the report. Although FoxPro starts by putting four lines in the PgHead, you can change this to any size necessary. PgFoot is the Page Footer, which is the bottom of each report page. Again, you can adjust the four lines to any size you need, including zero lines.

The Detail band is where the action is. In this band you place the fields you want reported for each record of your database. FoxPro creates one

Detail band for each record you want included in the report. A Detail band can be any size necessary, from one line to many. You also can instruct FoxPro to "stretch" character fields vertically, so that there is always enough room to show the entire field.

Next, you will create a report on the Layout screen.

Creating a Simple Report

The first step in creating a report is to put the database fields you want reported into the Detail band. Move the cursor to the Detail band and place the cursor where you want your first field, using the arrow keys or by clicking the band with the mouse. Now, from the Report menu, choose Field or press Ctrl-F. FoxPro displays the Report Expression dialog (see fig. 5.2). In this dialog, you tell FoxPro information about a field you're placing in the Layout window and how to format that field.

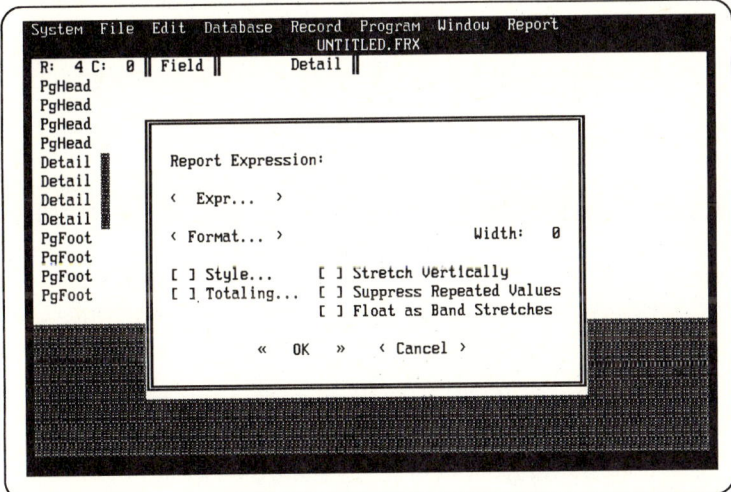

Fig. 5.2.
The Report
Expression
dialog.

If you know what data you want in this field (a database field, for example), you can type the name in the Expr text box. You also can select Expr to display the Expression Builder, from which you can select the database field or build an expression to be displayed. Figure 5.3 shows the Expression Builder with a database field selected.

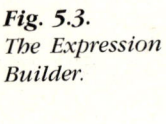

Fig. 5.3.
The Expression
Builder.

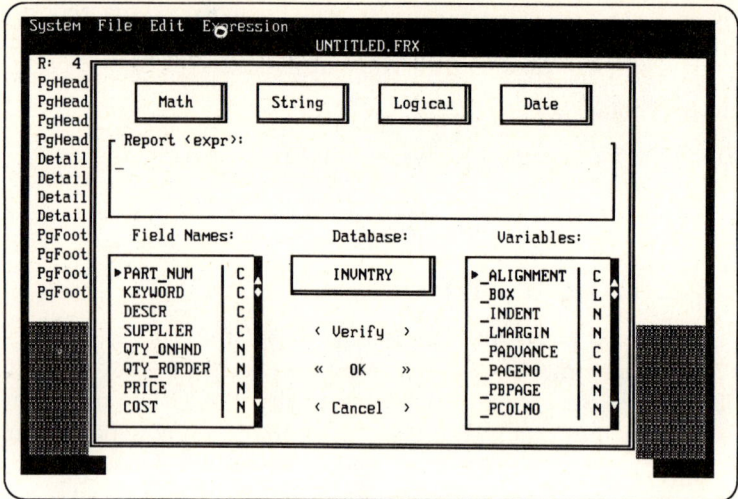

If you select a field from the Field Picker scrollable list, that field (with a prefix identifying the database) is placed in the Expr text box.

Adding Database Fields

Suppose that you want the PART_NUM field to be on the layout; choose PART_NUM from the scrollable list to place the field in the Expression Builder. Select OK to return to the Report Expression dialog. The Expr text box now has the field INVNTRY–>PART_NUM in it. Choose OK again to return to the layout. When you return to the Layout window, you see a field with the PART_NUM identification on-screen where the cursor was located (see fig. 5.4).

You can continue adding database fields until all the fields you want printed in the report are on the Detail band. Figure 5.5 shows the Layout window with the report fields in the Detail band.

Using Objects on the Layout View

FoxPro treats everything you put on the Layout window as an object. You can add objects, delete objects, and move them around. For objects that contain text (database or calculated fields, or text such as titles and labels), you can assign character styles, such as underline, bold, and italic. To change the format of your report, you simply add objects and move objects already created.

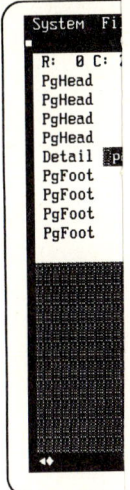

Fig. 5.4.
The Layout window with the first field added.

Adding

You proba
ing a field
the value
(which is
added. Aft
and choos
Expression

In the Ex

    QTY_O

(see fig. 5
been adde
report (se
scroll bar

Adding

To add a
objects in
report, an
page. Late
once at th

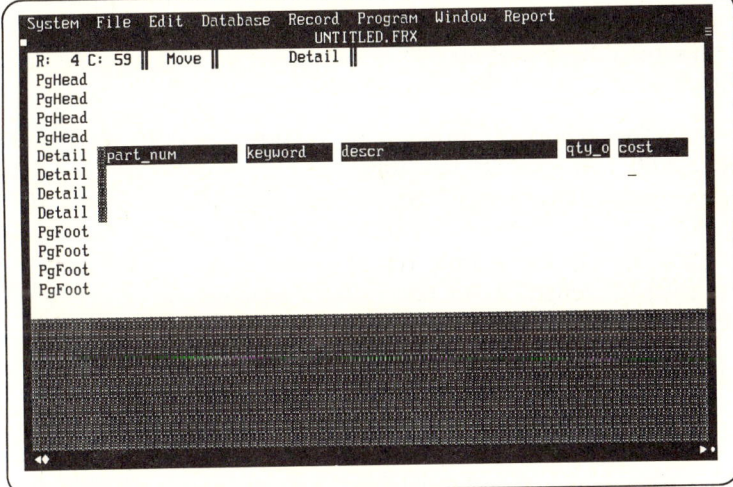

Fig. 5.5.
The Layout window of the basic report.

Using Page Preview

FoxPro's Page Preview feature makes viewing your report creation a snap. Choose Page Preview from the Report menu; FoxPro shows you what your report will look like if you were to save and run it right now. Figure 5.6 shows your example report as it now is defined.

Fig. 5.6.
Page preview of the report as defined.

Fig. 5.8.
Defining a computed field with the Expression Builder.

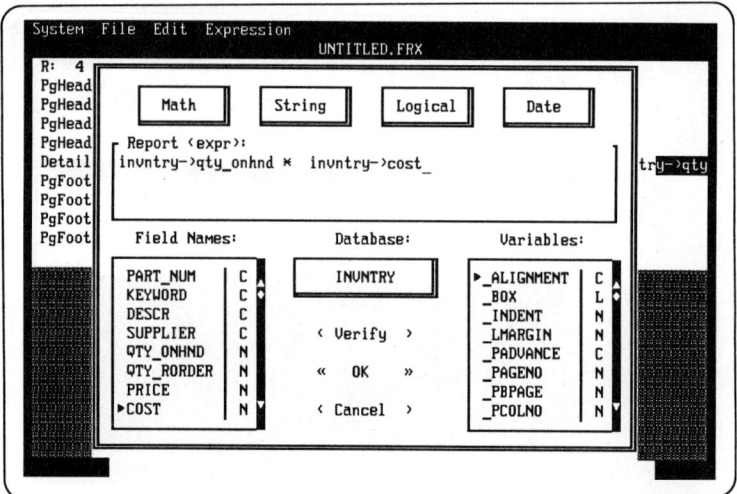

Fig. 5.9.
Page preview of the report with a calculated field.

You can
you can
doesn't
down, ri

Page Pr
and see
right. Fo
run-reco
the price
was used
page hea

Addir

FoxPro
different
change t
Line or
view wit
report m

PgHead
report ou
bands, y

To add a title to your report, place the cursor in the PgHead band and select Text from the Report menu. This time, you don't see a dialog, but FoxPro waits for you to type the text on the Layout. Figure 5.10 shows the screen after a title has been added.

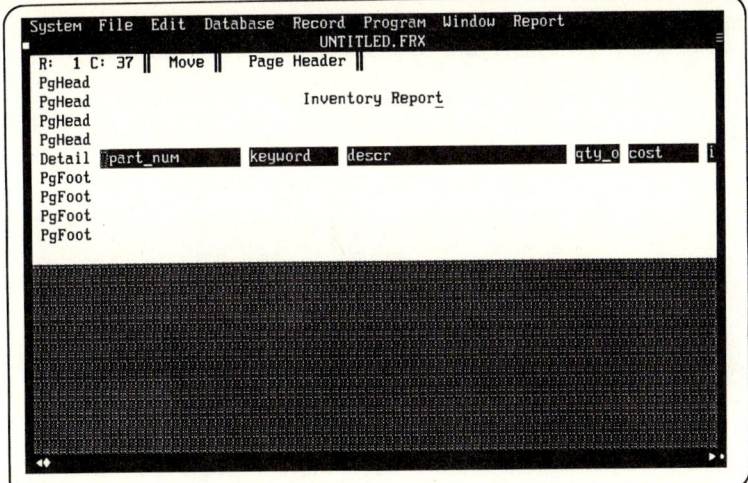

Fig. 5.10.
A title added to
the Layout
window.

Formatting Fields on the Report

Fields can be formatted and styled. Formatting refers to how characters are presented on-screen. To change the formatting of a field, place the cursor on the field and press Enter; mouse users should double-click the field. FoxPro will display the Field dialog. In the Format text box, you can specify Function codes and Picture Template codes, just as you did when creating a data-entry screen. You also can click the Format box, which displays a dialog to help you create formats.

There also is a Style check box in the Field dialog. If you place an X in this box, you will see the Style dialog, shown in figure 5.11. On the Layout window, if you select a text field by double-clicking or pressing Enter, you also will see the Style dialog, in which you can change the style of the characters in the field.

The style options available will vary depending on what your printer is capable of doing. Basic printers have few options; laser printers have many. If an option is available, it will be displayed in bold characters in the Style dialog; those not available are in dimmed characters. Choose the style option for the object selected and select OK to apply the style.

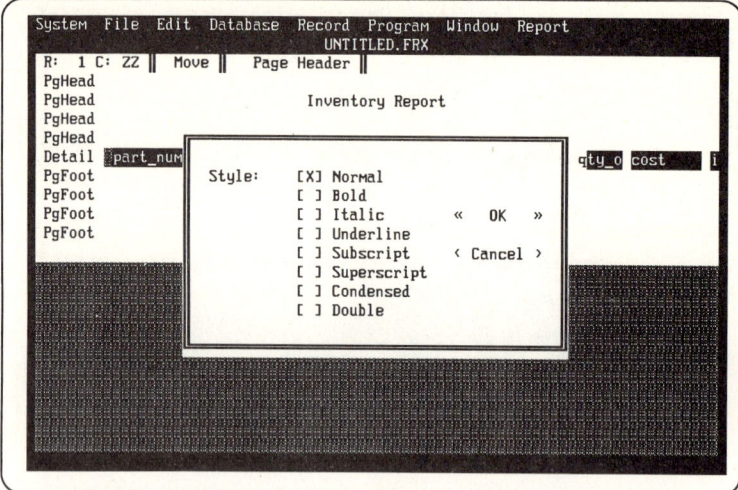

Fig. 5.11.
The Style dialog.

Adding Page Headers and Footers

Another common use of objects in the PgHead band is for column headings. Place text objects, describing each column, in the bottom row of the
PgHead band. Move them as necessary. This causes the column headings
to be printed once on each page, just above the first line of data from
your database. Figure 5.12 shows the column headings after they are
added to the Layout. The resulting page preview is shown in figure 5.13.

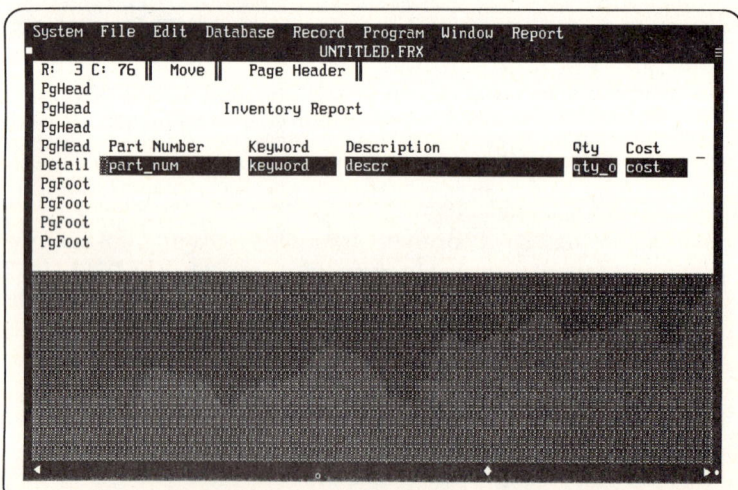

Fig. 5.12.
*The Layout
window with
column headings
added.*

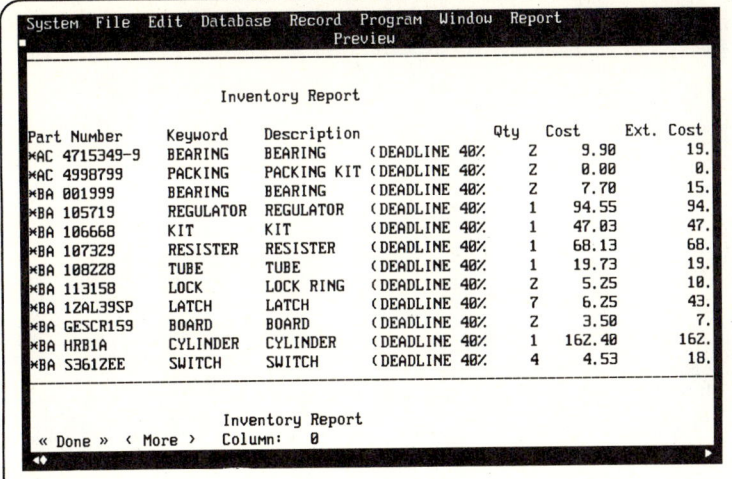

Fig. 5.13.
Page preview
with column
headings.

You add a page footer by following the same process, placing the objects in the PgFoot band. A good use for this feature is the addition of page numbers. To add page numbers, enter

Page:

in the PgFoot band. Place the cursor one column to the right and select Field. Choose Expr to open the Expression Builder. In the lower right corner is a scrollable list titled Variables; these are memory variables that FoxPro keeps track of while it prints a report. To add a page number, select the variable _pageno. Selecting that variable adds it to the expression field (see fig. 5.14).

When you close the Expression Builder and Field dialogs, your page number field will be displayed. Figure 5.15 shows the page header and footer objects on the Layout, and figure 5.16 shows a page preview of your report, with the page number in place. This format is often used for text documents. Many reports have the page number in the page header area, along with date and time stamps, and column headings.

Adding a Title

Although your report now provides the information you wanted about the database, it would be nice to add some other things. For a long report, a title page can provide information about the report, and summary fields at the end of the page can total numeric fields generated during the report. To add a title and summary, you need to add the bands in which they will be printed.

Fig. 5.14.
Adding the
_pageno variable
in the Expression
Builder.

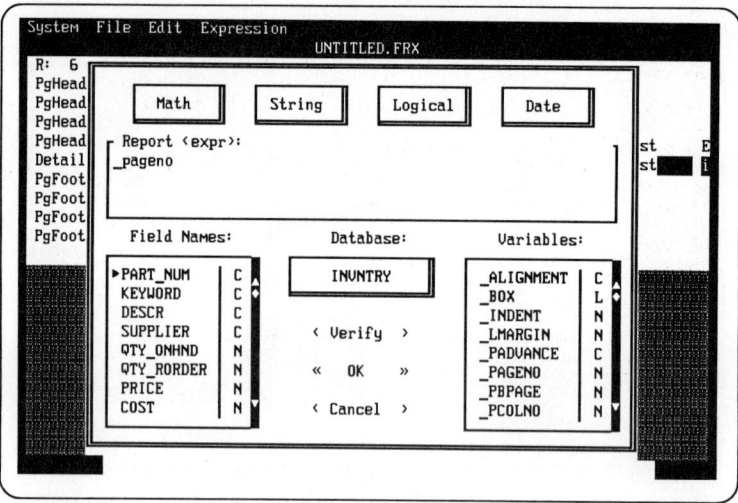

Fig. 5.15.
Adding a page
number to the
report on Layout.

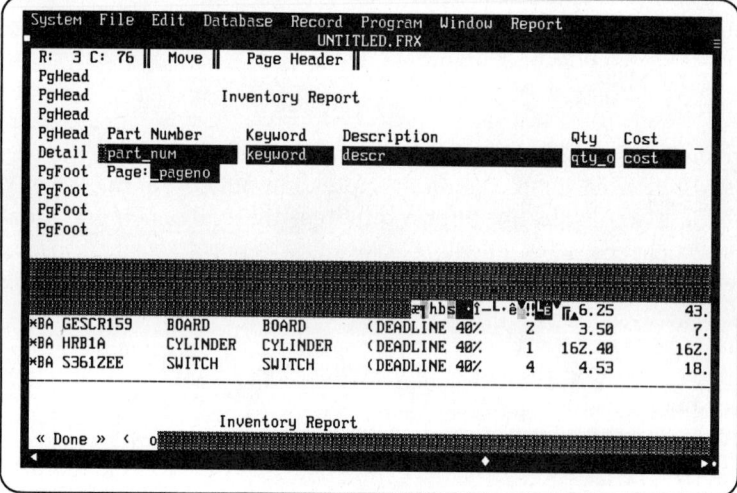

You can add a Title band and Summary band by selecting Title/Summary from the Report menu. You see the Title/Summary dialog, shown in figure 5.17. Mark the Title band or Summary band check boxes to place the appropriate band on the Layout. Associated with each band is a New Page check box. If you check this box for the title, it will appear on a separate page at the beginning of the report. Similarly, checking New Page for the summary places the Summary Band on a separate page at the end of the report. If you also mark the New Page check box, FoxPro places either the Title band or Summary band on a separate page.

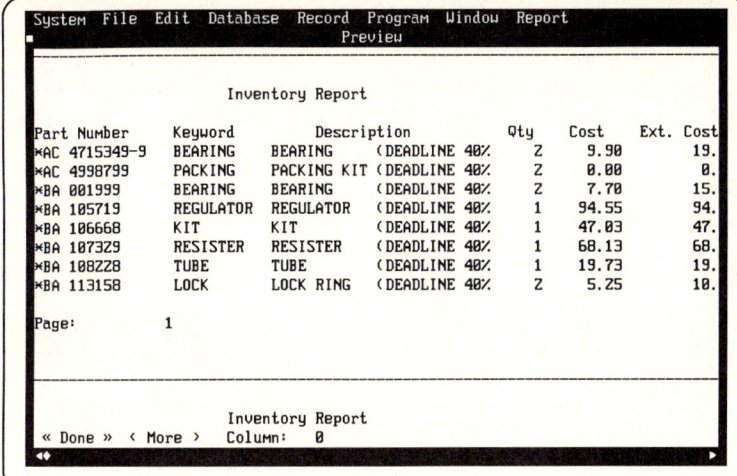

```
 System  File  Edit  Database  Record  Program  Window  Report
                              Preview

                    Inventory Report

   Part Number    Keyword      Description      Qty   Cost   Ext. Cost
  ×AC 4715349-9   BEARING    BEARING    (DEADLINE 40%   Z    9.90      19.
  ×AC 4998799     PACKING    PACKING KIT (DEADLINE 40%  Z    0.00       0.
  ×BA 001999      BEARING    BEARING    (DEADLINE 40%   Z    7.70      15.
  ×BA 105719      REGULATOR  REGULATOR  (DEADLINE 40%   1   94.55      94.
  ×BA 106668      KIT        KIT        (DEADLINE 40%   1   47.03      47.
  ×BA 107329      RESISTER   RESISTER   (DEADLINE 40%   1   68.13      68.
  ×BA 108228      TUBE       TUBE       (DEADLINE 40%   1   19.73      19.
  ×BA 113158      LOCK       LOCK RING  (DEADLINE 40%   Z    5.25      10.

  Page:          1


                         Inventory Report
   « Done »  ‹ More ›  Column:    0
```

Fig. 5.16.
Page Preview of the report.

Once the Title and Summary bands are on the Layout, you can add or move objects as necessary to provide more information and improve the appearance of your report.

Adding Summary Fields in the Summary Band

As you may have guessed, summary fields are simply objects. You place the cursor in the Summary band and choose Field from the Report Menu to bring forward the Report Expression dialog. Place an *X* in the Totaling check box to tell FoxPro that this field will contain information totaled from the report. FoxPro displays the Totaling dialog, in which you enter information about the totaling field (see fig. 5.18).

First, you need to tell FoxPro when to reset the totaled field to zero. In this case, you can have it reset only once, at the beginning of the report, or at the end of each page; these options are selected from a pop-up menu in the Reset box. In cases where you are totaling the whole report, you leave the default value, which tells FoxPro to reset only when the report starts. In this dialog you also tell FoxPro how you want the field calculated. Select the type of calculation you want by clicking the appropriate radio button. When you select OK, you move to the Expression Builder to define what data to sum in the field.

Suppose that you want this field to total the number of items on hand in the inventory—the sum of the QTY_ONHND fields. Choose Sum in the Totaling dialog. In the Report Expression dialog, enter *QTY_ONHND* in

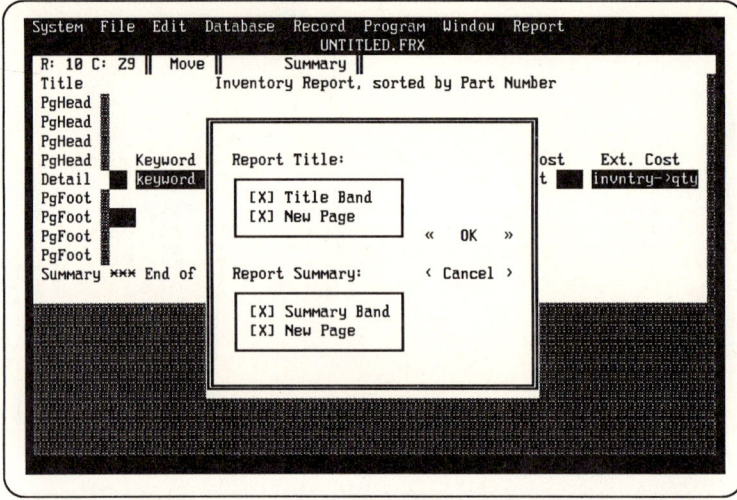

Fig. 5.17.
The Report Title dialog.

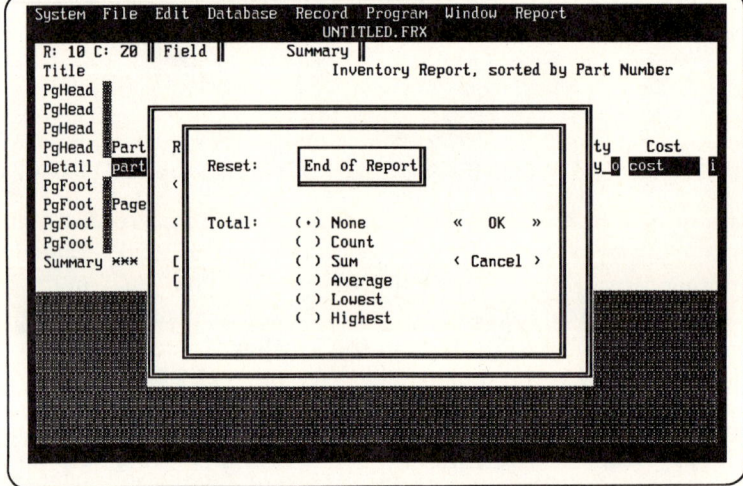

Fig. 5.18.
The Totaling dialog.

the Expr text box. You also can choose Expr to display the Expression Builder dialog. In the Expression Builder dialog, you can enter *qty_onhnd*, or use the Field Picker scrollable list to select the QTY_ONHND field. Because you specified this field to be a summed field, FoxPro knows to sum the QTY_ONHND fields in the report. Figure 5.19 shows the Expression Builder with the field to sum defined.

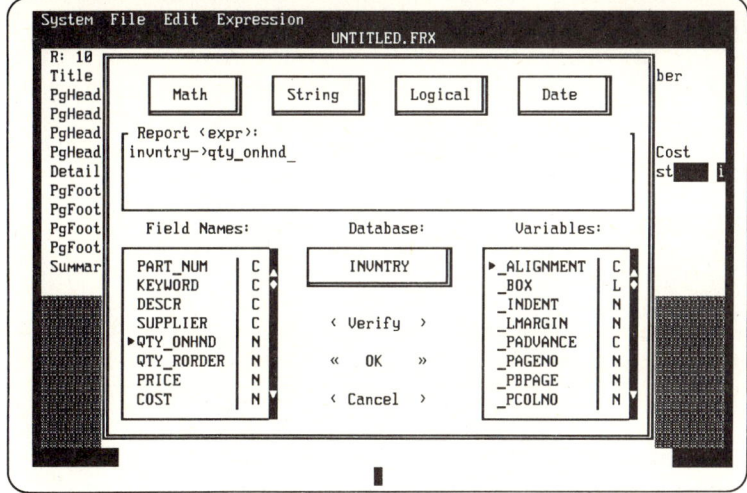

Fig. 5.19.
Using the
Expression
Builder to define
what data will
be summarized.

When you have closed the Expression Builder and Field dialogs by choosing OK, you return to the Layout, and the field is in place. Place a text object to label the summary field, and you're ready to move on.

Add a second field to the Summary band and choose Totaling again. This time, put into the Expression Builder the following computed expression:

QTY_ONHND * COST

This value will be calculated as FoxPro processes the report. Again, add a text object, and your Summary band is done. Using Page Preview you can see the Summary band at the end of the report. Figure 5.20 shows the end of the INVNTRY database.

Although the numbers are right, their formatting leaves something to be desired. You can change the formatting in the Format dialog. You display the Format dialog by double-clicking in the field or by moving the cursor to the field with the arrow keys and pressing Enter. Then select Format in the Report Expression dialog. Figure 5.21 shows the Format dialog for the summed QTY_ONHND field. In the Format text box, place five 9's, which tell FoxPro to use a five-digit number with no decimal places to format this field.

Fig. 5.20.
The end of the report, showing the summed fields.

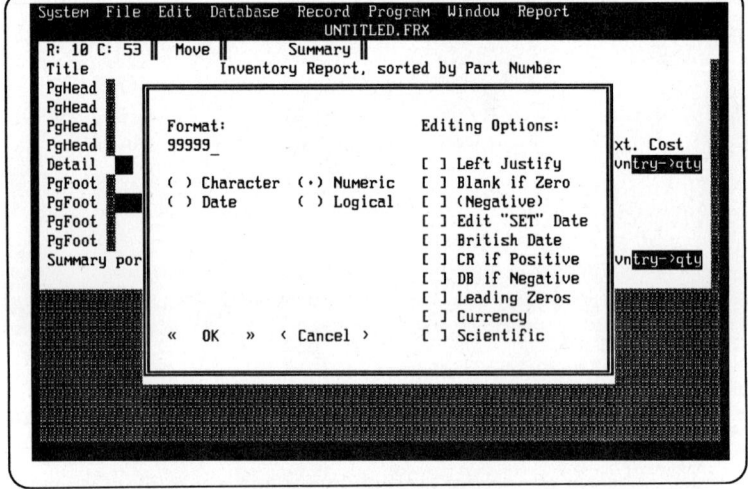

Fig. 5.21.
Formatting the total QTY_ONHND field.

Figure 5.22 shows the same dialog for the summed field of the QTY_ONHND * COST summed field. The Format field 999,999.99 tells FoxPro to put use two decimal places and a comma when formatting the number.

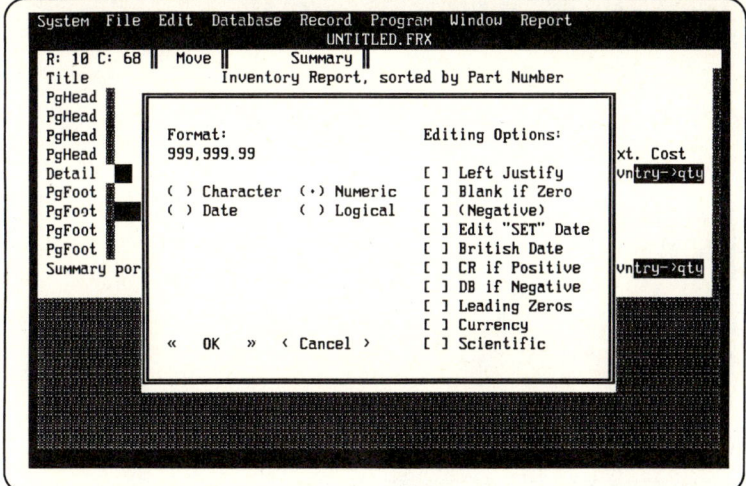

Fig. 5.22.
*Formatting the total QTY_ONHND * COST field.*

You can alternate between Page Preview and formatting from the Layout until the format and placement of the summed fields is right. Figure 5.23 shows the completed report in the Layout window, and figure 5.24 shows the end of the report in a page preview.

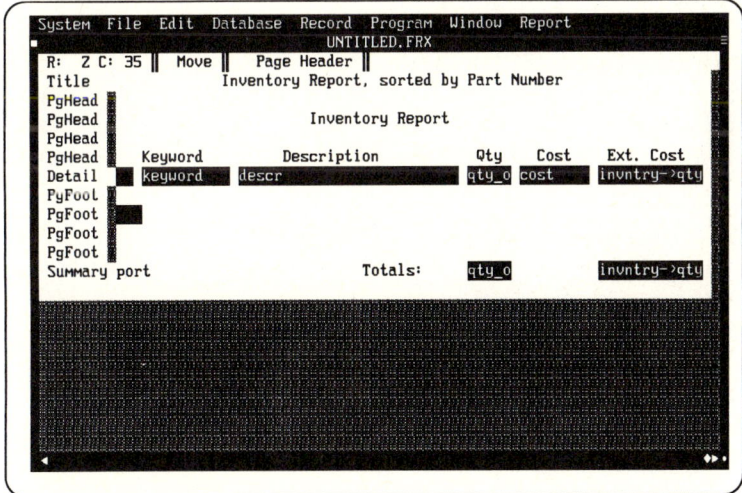

Fig. 5.23.
Layout view of the completed inventory report.

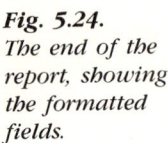

Fig. 5.24.
The end of the
report, showing
the formatted
fields.

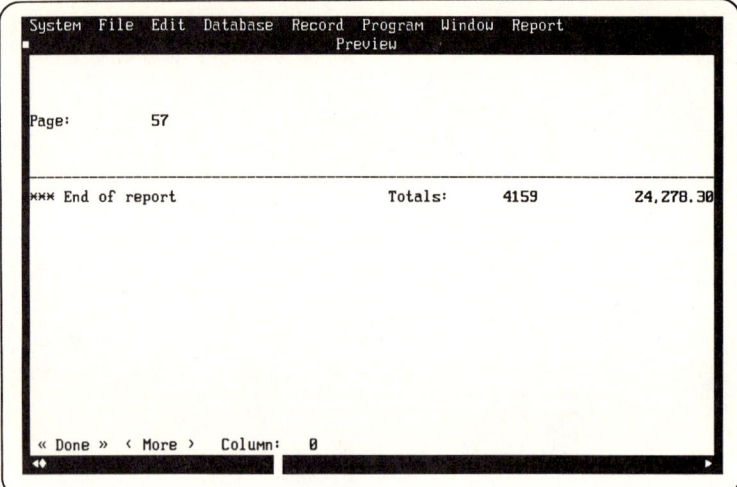

Now your report is completely designed. You have looked at the page preview to make sure that it's a masterpiece, and you're ready to run it. First, however, save the report using the File Save menu.

Running the Report

To run your report, choose Report from the Database menu, and choose from the File Picker scrollable list the name of your report. (You must choose Report in the Type scrollable list to see your report in the File Picker window.) Notice that you can limit what records your report processes with Scope, For, and While options. Figure 5.25 shows the Report dialog you will use to start your report running.

You remember from the previous chapter how to use Scope, For, and While to limit what is processed in a database. These clauses apply to Report processing as well. If you want to limit your report to a certain number of records, based on their location in the database and the current position of the database pointer, use the Scope option. If you want to look at certain records, based on values in the fields, use the For option to limit the report processing to just those records. Use While to limit processing to records with a certain value in a field starting from the current position.

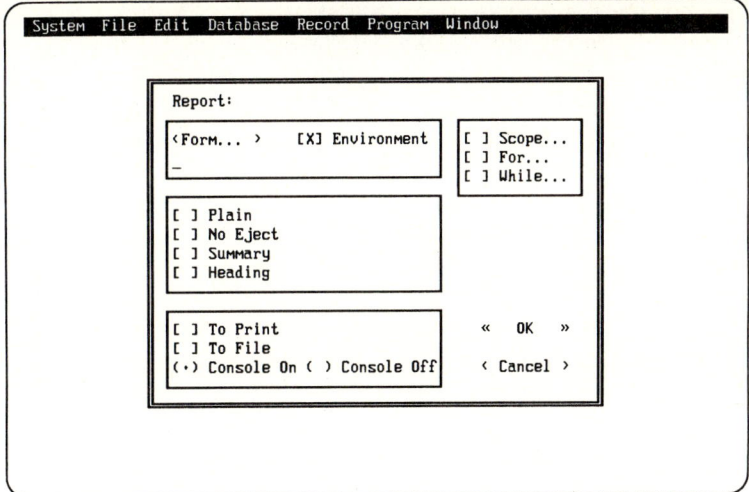

```
System File Edit Database Record Program Window

        ┌──────────────────────────────────────────┐
        │ Report:                                    │
        │ ┌──────────────────────┐ ┌──────────────┐ │
        │ │ ‹Form... ›   [X] Environment │ [ ] Scope... │ │
        │ │ ─                    │ │ [ ] For...   │ │
        │ └──────────────────────┘ │ [ ] While... │ │
        │ ┌──────────────────────┐ └──────────────┘ │
        │ │ [ ] Plain            │                    │
        │ │ [ ] No Eject         │                    │
        │ │ [ ] Summary          │                    │
        │ │ [ ] Heading          │                    │
        │ └──────────────────────┘                    │
        │ ┌──────────────────────┐                    │
        │ │ [ ] To Print         │   «   OK   »       │
        │ │ [ ] To File          │                    │
        │ │ (·) Console On ( ) Console Off│ ‹ Cancel › │
        │ └──────────────────────┘                    │
        └──────────────────────────────────────────┘
```

Fig. 5.25.
The Database
Report dialog.

If you choose the Scope option, you see a dialog asking you to define the scope. Your options are as follows:

All   All records in the database will be processed for the report.

Next   Choosing this option opens a data-entry box, in which you enter a number that represents how many database records you want the report to process, starting from the current record in the database. If the current record in the database pointer is in the middle of the database and you enter 100 in the Next field, your report will process the next 100 records and end.

Record   Choosing this option also opens a data-entry box, in which you enter the record number of the record you want processed. In this case, your report will report only on that one record.

Rest   Choosing this option causes your report to start at the current location in the database and process all the remaining records.

Creating More Advanced Reports

Now that you have created a simple report, you're ready to move on to a more advanced one. In the next report, shown in figure 5.26, you will add boxes and lines to improve the readability, group the data to generate subtotals and make the report easier to understand, and add an object to print out a memo field. When you have mastered these facets of FoxPro reporting, you will be able to create superior reports, becoming a veritable Michelangelo of the Layout window.

Fig. 5.26.
An advanced report.

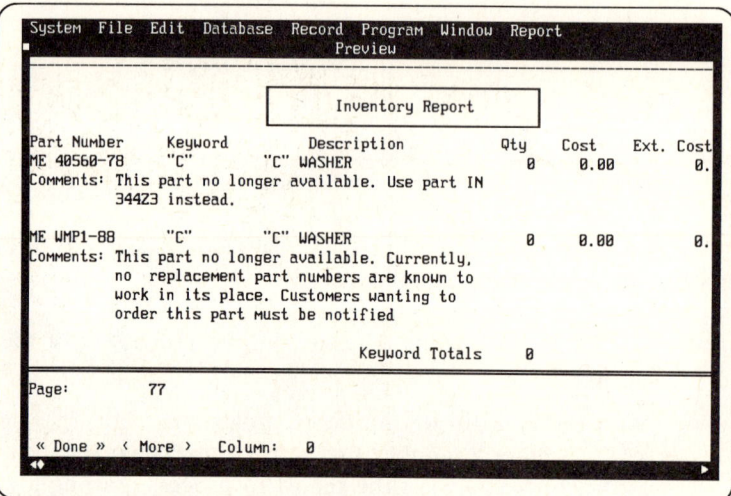

To start, choose Open from the file menu and select the report already created in this chapter. This way, you can modify an existing report layout. Later you can save it with a new name, which preserves your original report, or you can save it with the same name, which replaces the original report with the newly modified one.

Adding Groups and Subtotals

In nearly every database, the records can be grouped logically. In the INVNTRY database, for example, you could group the records by the keyword, contained in the KEYWORD field. When reporting on the INVNTRY database, it would be beneficial to group the records by that keyword, to have a subtotal of the QTY_ONHND fields, and to have a computed subtotal of QTY_ONHND multiplied by cost to show how many of each keyword is in inventory, and what the value of that keyword type's inventory is. Grouping the data by keyword provides a break for the eye when scanning the report, adding to the user's understanding of the data.

To group data and add subtotal fields, choose Data Grouping from the Report menu. In the Group dialog, shown in figure 5.27, you see a scrollable list, which is empty because you have not defined any groups yet.

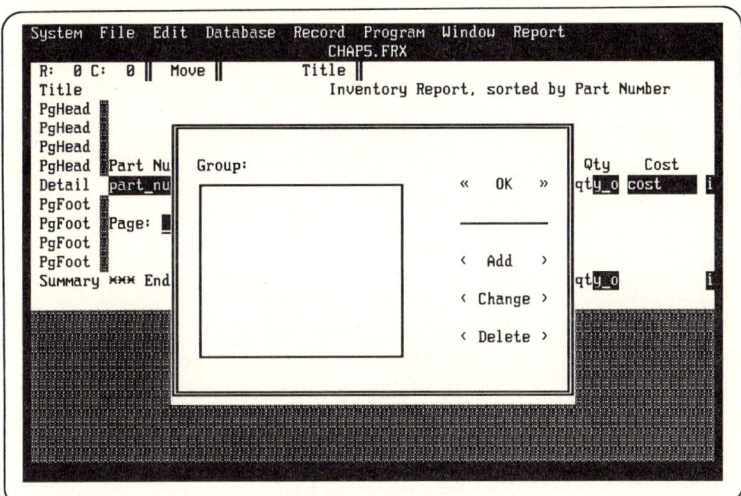

Fig. 5.27.
The Group dialog.

Select Add to add the group you want. FoxPro displays the Group Info dialog, in which you tell FoxPro how to group the report data (see fig. 5.28).

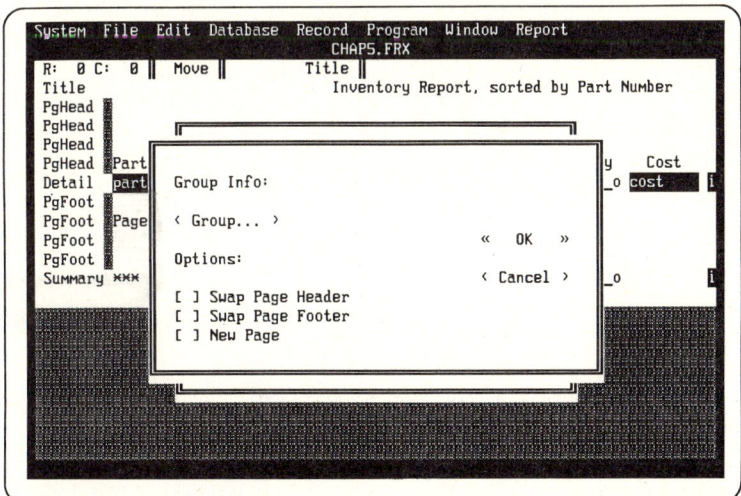

Fig. 5.28.
The Group Info dialog.

The expression you define in the Group Info dialog is the one on which FoxPro will "break" the database into groups. Starting at the beginning of the database (either actually or by an index order), FoxPro processes records, looking at the value of the expression you have identified. When that value changes from one record to another, FoxPro says, "Aha! Time to change groups, which means printing out what's in the Summary band and starting a new group with a group header." Figure 5.29 shows FoxPro grouping where a change in the value of the keyword occurs.

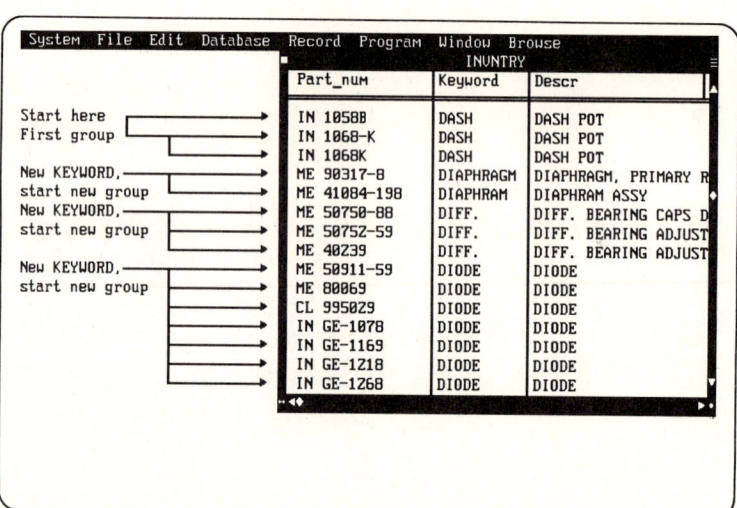

Fig. 5.29.
Progressing
through a
database
grouping on
KEYWORD.

You see, then, that for grouping to work, the database must be sorted or indexed in an order that allows the grouping to be consistent. Consider, for example, what would happen if you defined a group on the KEY-WORD field, but had the database ordered on a PART_NUM index or sort. Each time the value in the KEYWORD field changed, a new group would be generated; if the database is indexed or sorted on PART_NUM, that could happen every record or so, resulting in a bad report. When planning a grouped report, make sure your database is indexed or sorted properly and, if indexed, that the proper index is controlling the order of the database.

In this example, a new index is created, based on the index expression

KEYWORD + PART_NUM

This index will present records by keyword and, within each keyword group, by part number.

If you don't know the expression on which FoxPro will break the report into groups, select the Group field in the Group dialog; FoxPro displays the Expression Builder to assist you. The grouping expression can be any valid FoxPro expression, including one or more database fields, calculated values on the fields, logical values, or anything else you can construct. Close the Expression dialog and you will see the Group dialog with your expression in it (see fig. 5.30).

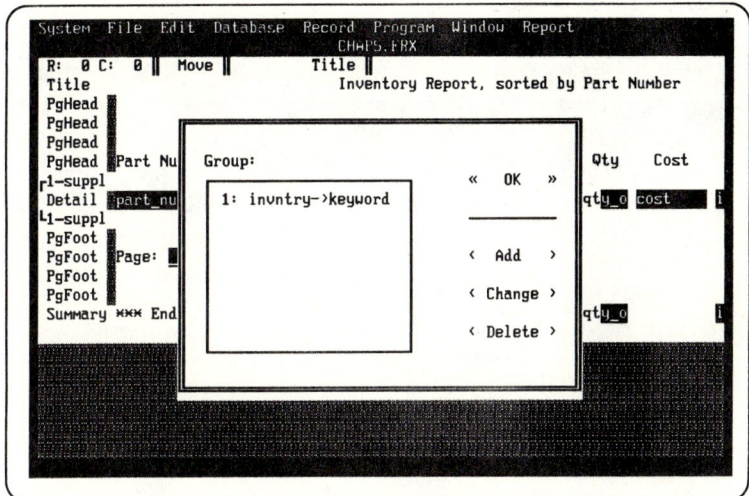

Fig. 5.30. The Group dialog.

Close the Group dialog to return to the Layout, which now displays Group Header and Group Footer bands above and below the Detail Band. This Group Band is identified by the title 1-keywo in the band title column, indicating that this is the first group and that it will break on the expression KEYWORD. If you use Page Preview now, you will see no difference in the report because FoxPro ignores bands that have nothing in them.

To identify the group, you can put fields in the group header giving information about the group just starting. You have added a text object labeling the group and a field object with the value from the keyword field. The Group Header line tells the report reader what is in the next group. You also can add lines to a group for clarity. After you add the Group header in the Layout window, shown in figure 5.31, run a page preview to see how much better the report is with this grouping (see fig. 5.32).

Fig. 5.31.
The Layout view with a group on KEYWORD.

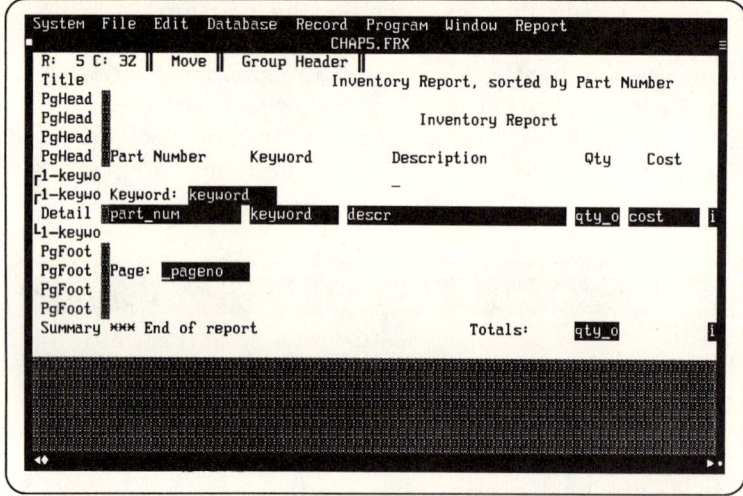

```
System  File  Edit  Database  Record  Program  Window  Report
                         CHAP5.FRX
 R:  5 C: 3Z ‖ Move ‖  Group Header ‖
  Title                          Inventory Report, sorted by Part Number
 PgHead ▌
 PgHead ▌
 PgHead ▌                              Inventory Report
 PgHead ▌Part Number    Keyword        Description          Qty    Cost
┌1-keywo
├1-keywo Keyword: keyword
 Detail ▌part_num      keyword   descr              qty_o cost    i
└1-keywo
 PgFoot ▌
 PgFoot ▌Page: _pageno
 PgFoot ▌
 PgFoot ▌
 Summary ××× End of report                    Totals:   qty_o        i
```

Fig. 5.32.
Page Preview with the report grouped on KEYWORD.

```
System  File  Edit  Database  Record  Program  Window  Report
                         Preview
 ME 50Z59       Z         Z WAY VALVE           0    0.00       0.

 Keyword: Z-FLUID
 MICO 0Z-460-Z38 Z-FLUID  Z-FLUID POWER BRAKE VALVE  0  Z39.68    0.

 Keyword: Z4V
 IN AT-Z4V      Z4V       Z4V HORN              Z   10.50      Z1.
 IN C-1Z3X      Z4V       Z4V COIL              4   11.10      44.
 IN CT-1Z0C     Z4V       Z4V CONTACTOR         0   58.00       0.

 Keyword: ZND
 ME 41813-9A    ZND       ZND COUNTERSHAT & CLUTCH  0  0.00      0.

 Keyword: 3
 ME 6159        3         3 WAY VALVE           0    0.00       0.

 Keyword: 36-48V
 IN C-7Z08      36-48V    36-48V COIL           1   35.00      35.
 IN C-7308      36-48V    36-48V COIL           1   Z8.90      Z8.
 IN C-8Z08      36-48V    36-48V COIL           1   Z6.85      Z6.
« Done »  ‹ More ›  Column:   0
```

Adding a Group Summary Field

Often, you will want to summarize information at the group level, receiving subtotals of numeric fields in the group, or counts of the records printed in the group. Group summary fields are defined and placed in the Group Footer band in the same manner as you defined and placed report summary fields.

When you select Totaling in the Report Expression dialog for the group field, you will see the Totaling dialog. In the Reset scrollable list, choose the data grouping expression as the reset point. This tells FoxPro to reset the Totaling field that you have defined to zero at the start of each new group. Figure 5.33 shows the INVNTRY–>KEYWORD selected as the Reset point.

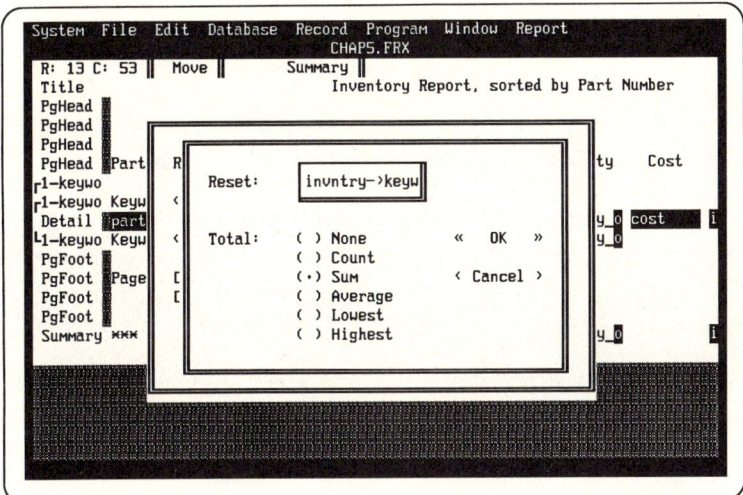

Fig. 5.33.
Setting Reset on a totaling field to the grouping expression.

Figure 5.34 shows the Layout window with summary fields in the Group Footer band; the resulting report is shown in page preview (see fig. 5.35).

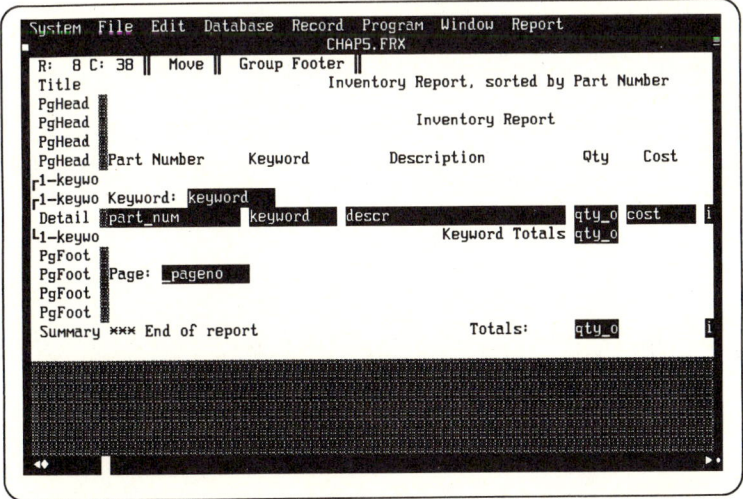

Fig. 5.34.
Layout of the report with a group summary field.

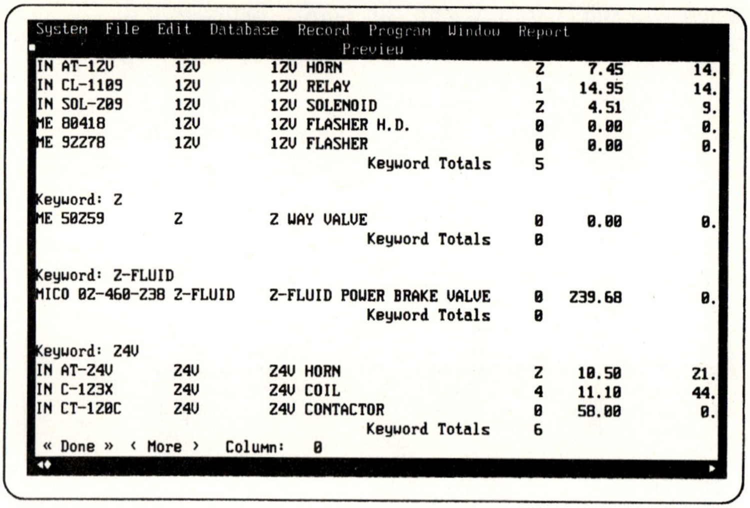

Fig. 5.35.
Page preview of the report with a group summary field.

```
 System  File  Edit  Database  Record  Program  Window  Report
                         Preview
IN AT-12V        12V        12V HORN                    2      7.45     14.
IN CL-1109       12V        12V RELAY                   1     14.95     14.
IN SOL-209       12V        12V SOLENOID                2      4.51      9.
ME 80418         12V        12V FLASHER H.D.            0      0.00      0.
ME 92278         12V        12V FLASHER                 0      0.00      0.
                                    Keyword Totals      5

Keyword: 2
ME 50259         2          2 WAY VALVE                 0      0.00      0.
                                    Keyword Totals      0

Keyword: 2-FLUID
MICO 02-460-238 2-FLUID     2-FLUID POWER BRAKE VALVE   0    239.68      0.
                                    Keyword Totals      0

Keyword: 24V
IN AT-24V        24V        24V HORN                    2     10.50     21.
IN C-123X        24V        24V COIL                    4     11.10     44.
IN CT-120C       24V        24V CONTACTOR               0     58.00      0.
                                    Keyword Totals      6
« Done »  ‹ More ›   Column:    0
```

Adding Graphics

Now your report provides the information you want. One more thing can improve its readability, though—some lines and a box. Lines and boxes are nothing more than objects. You add them by choosing Box from the Report menu, then sizing them and moving them to where you want. A line is a box, sized to have no height. To the example report, you will add a line above and below the data records for each group, and put a box around the title.

Once again, mouse users have the advantage. Choose Box from the Report menu, place the mouse pointer where you want one corner of the box to be and drag the mouse (holding down the button as you move the mouse) to the opposite corner. The box is created as you move the mouse.

From the keyboard, choose Box from the Report menu. Use the arrow keys to place the cursor where you want the line or box to start. Press the space bar to begin creating the line or box. Use the arrow keys to move to where you want the line or box to end. As you move, the line or box appears. When you are finished, press Enter.

In the example, a box has been sized to no height to make a line, and placed in a new Group Header line. A second line has been added to the Page Footer, to put a line at the bottom of each page before the page number. Figure 5.36 shows the Layout with lines and boxes added.

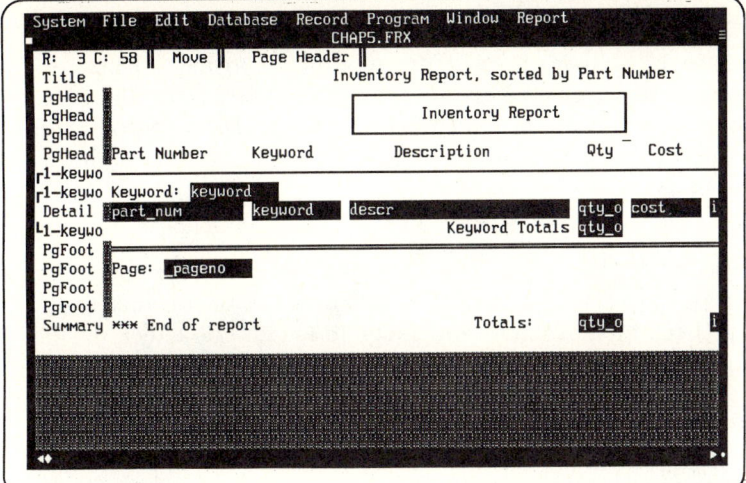

Fig. 5.36.
Layout of the report with lines and boxes added.

Page Preview shows how this lends emphasis to the data groupings you have created. Follow the same process to add a box around the page header, separating it from the report data. Page Preview shows how effective this box and these lines are in improving the readability of the report (see fig. 5.37). (Page length has been set to 19 lines in the Page Layout dialog to allow this figure to show the PgHead and PgFoot bands on one screen.)

```
 System  File  Edit  Database  Record  Program  Window  Report
                               Preview
 ┌─────────────────────────────────────────────────────────────┐
 │               ┌───────────────────────────┐                  │
 │               │      Inventory Report      │                  │
 │               └───────────────────────────┘                  │
 │Part Number    Keyword        Description        Qty   Cost   Ext. Cost│
 │                                                                │
 │Keyword: 9/16-18                                                │
 │ME 5328         9/16-18     9/16-18 THREAD NUT    0    0.00     0.│
 │                                Keyword Totals    0              │
 │                                                                │
 │Keyword: 90                                                     │
 │ME 61389        90          90 DEGREE SWIVEL      0    0.00     0.│
 │ME 61988        90          90 DEGREE STREET ELBOW 0   0.00     0.│
 │ME 62398        90          90 DEGREE ELBOW LONG  0    0.00     0.│
 │ME 63839        90          90 BULKHEAD UNION ELBOW 0  0.00     0.│
 │REGO 69-79      90          90 DEGREE ELBOW       0    0.00     0.│
 │                                                                │
 │Page:          43                                               │
 │                                                                │
 │ « Done »  ‹ More ›   Column:    0                              │
 │◄►                                                             ►│
 └─────────────────────────────────────────────────────────────┘
```

Fig. 5.37.
Page preview of the report with lines and boxes added.

Adding Memo Fields

You also can add a memo field to the report. Memo fields illustrate an important capability of FoxPro reports—their flexibility in handling string fields. A memo field, you will remember, can be as big as 64,000 characters or as small as just a few. FoxPro can handle this wide variation if you stretch the object on-screen to fit the field. Although this capability is used mostly with memo fields, it applies to character fields as well.

Add a memo field object to the Layout, specifying that the memo field COMMENT will be printed. The Report Expression dialog box (see fig 5.38) has a check box, Stretch Vertically To Fit. If you check this box, FoxPro expands the field vertically to as many lines as necessary to print the entire memo field. Within the stretched object, words will be wrapped from line to line, so that no word runs out of the field or is split. Once you have added a memo field, use Page Preview to see its effect (see fig. 5.39). Notice that the memo field stretches vertically, printing as many lines as necessary to accommodate the entire memo field.

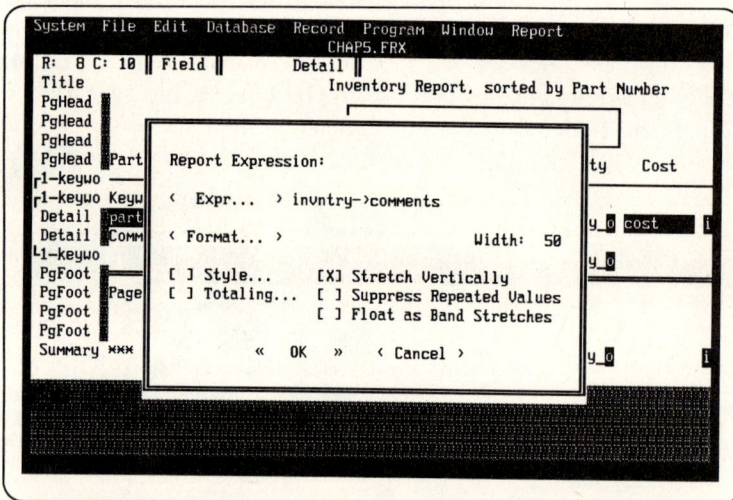

Fig. 5.38.
Choosing Stretch Vertically *to accommodate the memo field.*

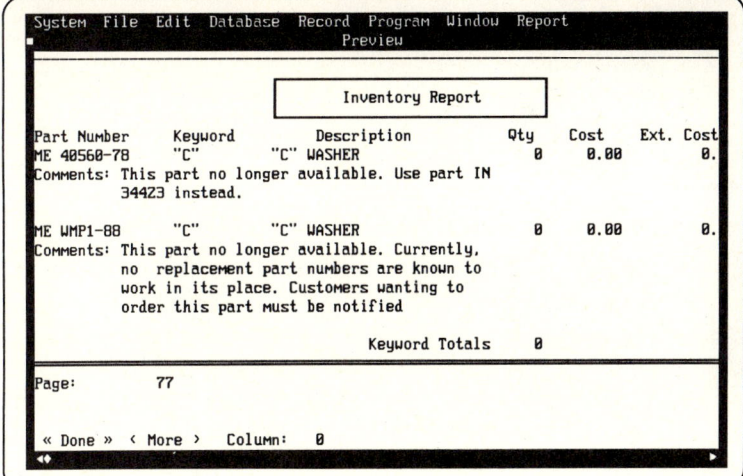

Fig. 5.39.
Page preview of
a report using
Stretch
Vertically.

Chapter Summary

In this chapter, you have learned how to create understandable reports. You have added database fields, text objects, lines, and boxes. To make the data more meaningful and readable, you have learned how to group that data into logical units and how to summarize that data, both at the group level and for the report as a whole. In short, you know enough about FoxPro reporting to extract from your database information in any number of ways.

As you have seen, report writing in FoxPro is quick and easy. FoxPro has turned report writing from pure drudgery into an enjoyable, rewarding process.

Part II

Intermediate FoxPro

Includes

Quick Start 2: Tapping the Power of FoxPro

Designing, Defining, and Creating Relational Databases

Entering Data with FoxView

Managing Multiple-File Databases

Creating Custom Reports

Tapping the Power of FoxPro

So far, you have used FoxPro as a sophisticated file manager, working with only one database file at a time. You have learned the basics of FoxPro—defining databases, creating data-entry screens and reports, and looking at the data in many different ways. Now, it's time to tap FoxPro's power. FoxPro is a relational database system, and this section of *Using FoxPro* teaches you the why's and how's of FoxPro's relational capabilities. When you're finished with Part II, you will understand how the relational power of FoxPro, combined with its extraordinary ease-of-use, makes this program the most powerful and capable database program in the PC world.

Creating Multiple-File, Relational Databases

As you use FoxPro, you will find situations that call for more than one database to store all the information you need. When you need to store and report on information about different types of data, you need a database for each type. FoxPro enables you to create database systems containing two or more databases. You can tie these multiple files together, accessing data from one database while working in the other. Creating multiple-file, related databases is not difficult, and it is in this type of database that FoxPro's power really shows.

This quick start builds on Quick Start 1 by creating another database, one to track contacts a sales force may have with the company's customers. This database will be called the CONTACT database and will be related to the CUSTOMER database, enabling reports and query screens to access information from both databases at the same time. Like the CUSTOMER

157

database, this database will reside in the subdirectory \FOXPRO\CUST, so move to that directory by issuing the MS-DOS command

CD \FOXPRO\CUST

Set the path to the FOXPRO directory

PATH = \FOXPRO

and start FoxPro with the command

FOXPRO

First, you need to define the different databases your system needs. If you have already created one of the databases, define what the second (or third) will contain. If you need to tie the two databases together, include in both a common field, which FoxPro will use to match records in the two database files.

In Quick Start 1, you created a CUSTOMER database, the structure of which is shown in figure QS2.1.

Fig. QS2.1.
The structure of
the CUSTOMER
database.

```
 System  File  Edit  Database  Record  Program  Window
 Structure for database: C:\FOXPRO\CUST\CUSTOMER.DBF
 Number of data records:        15
 Date of last update   : 02/20/90
 Field  Field Name  Type       Width    Dec
     1  CUST_NAME   Character     25
     2  ADDR_1      Character     25
     3  ADDR_2      Character     25
     4  CITY        Character     15
     5  STATE       Character      2
     6  ZIP         Character      9
     7  PHONE       Character     10
     8  CONTACT     Character     10
     9  CREDIT      Numeric        8     2
    10  LAST_PUR    Date           8
    11  LAST_AMT    Numeric        8     2
    12  PREFERD     Logical        1
 ** Total **                     147
```

The CONTACT database is shown in figure QS2.2. Notice that the CONTACT database and the CUSTOMER database both have a field named CUST_NAME. This is called the relational field; when FoxPro is processing records in the CONTACT database, you will be able to access information in CUSTOMER database records as a result of this tie between the two databases (see fig. QS2.2).

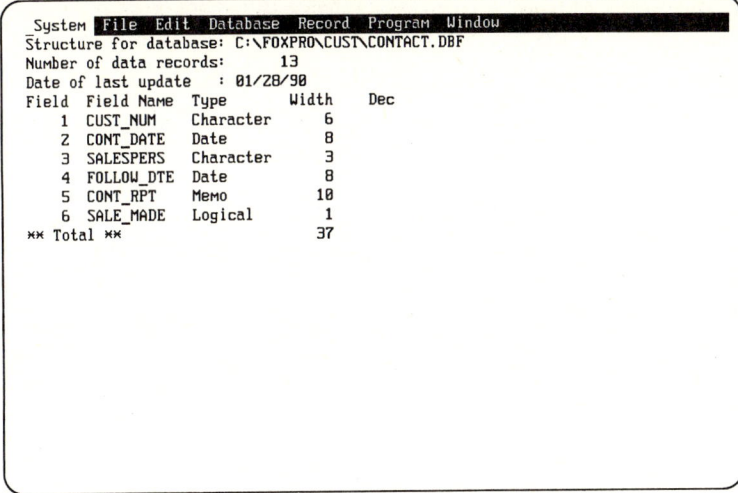

Fig. QS2.2.
The structure of the CONTACT database.

To create multiple file, related databases, follow these steps:

1. To create the CONTACT database, choose New from the File menu. In the New dialog, select Database and OK, and then define the database in the Structure dialog. Figure QS2.3 shows the CONTACT database defined in the Structure dialog. When you're finished, select OK and name the new database CONTACT.

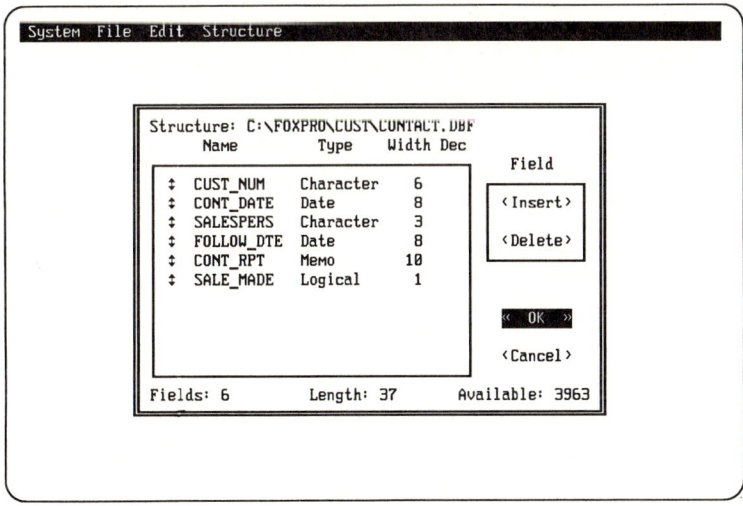

Fig. QS2.3.
The Structure dialog, with the CONTACT database defined.

2. Open the View window. In the first line of the work area box, you see CONTACT, indicating that the CONTACT database is in work area A. If you wanted to add more index files, you would do so here by choosing the Add selection.

Now you have set up the second database for your system. You can work with this database just as you did with the CUSTOMER database in Quick Start 1, entering data into it and creating custom data-entry and query screens with FoxView and reports from the Layout window. However, the power of FoxPro comes from its capability to tie together two different databases, drawing information from both at the same time. As you will see later in this quick start, you can run a report on the CONTACT database and print information from the CUSTOMER database at the same time. FoxPro uses the common CUST_NAME field to tie the two databases together. For now, though, you can use the CUSTOMER database to ensure that you're entering correct information in the CUST_NAME field. To do this, follow these steps:

1. If it's not open already, open the View window by choosing View from the Window menu. The View window should appear as in figure QS2.4.

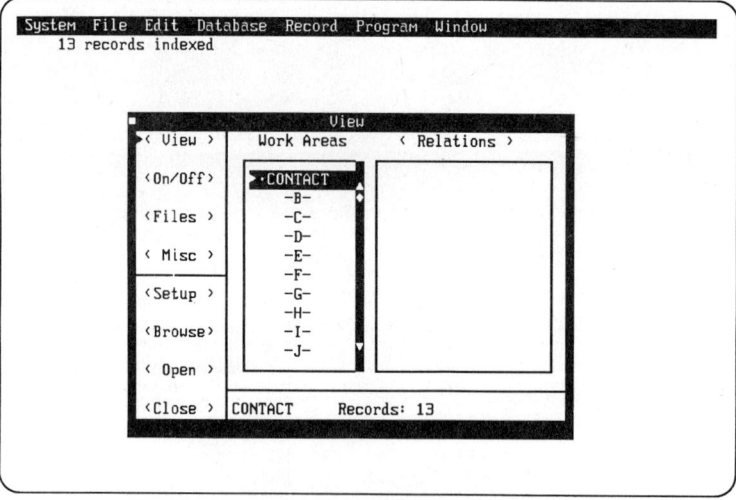

Fig. QS2.4.
The View dialog,
showing the
CONTACT
database in work
area A.

If CONTACT is not in work area A, select work area A, choose Open and pick CONTACT in the File Open dialog that appears. If, for some reason, CONTACT is in a work area other than A, select CONTACT and Close, and then select work area A and reopen CONTACT in that work area with the Open dialog.

2. Select work area B. Because no database is in that work area, the File Open dialog appears; pick the CUSTOMER database you created in Quick Start 1. When you return to the View window, it will look like figure QS2.5.

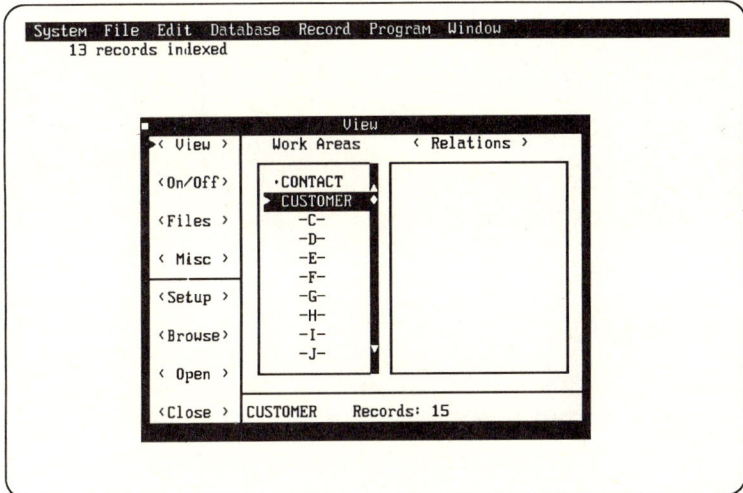

Fig. QS2.5.
The View
window, with the
CONTACT *and*
CUSTOMER
databases open.

3. Open a Browse window on the CUSTOMER database by choosing Browse from the Database menu. Return to the View window (press Ctrl-F1 until the View window appears or select View from the Window menu). Select the CONTACT database to make the CONTACT database the active database, indicated by the active-database symbol. Now, open a data-entry window on the CONTACT database by choosing Append from the Record menu. A data-entry window appears, and the screen looks like figure QS2.6.

4. Clean up your screen by making the View window active and choosing Hide from the Window menu. Next, make the Command window active and do the same. Now, only the CUSTOMER Browse window and the CONTACT data-entry window are on-screen.

   Select the CUSTOMER Browse window, then move and size it until you can see the Browse window and the data-entry window at the same time. Figure QS2.7 shows the screen with both screens visible.

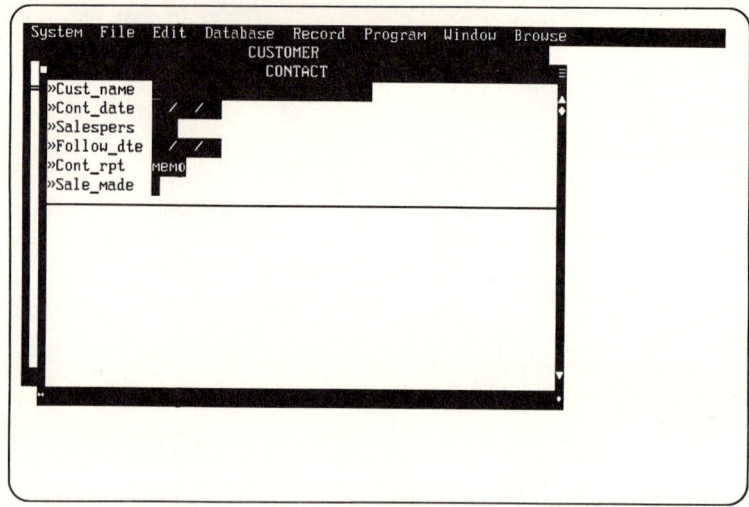

Fig. QS2.6.
The FoxPro
screen with a
Browse window
on the
CUSTOMER
database and a
CONTACT data-
entry window.

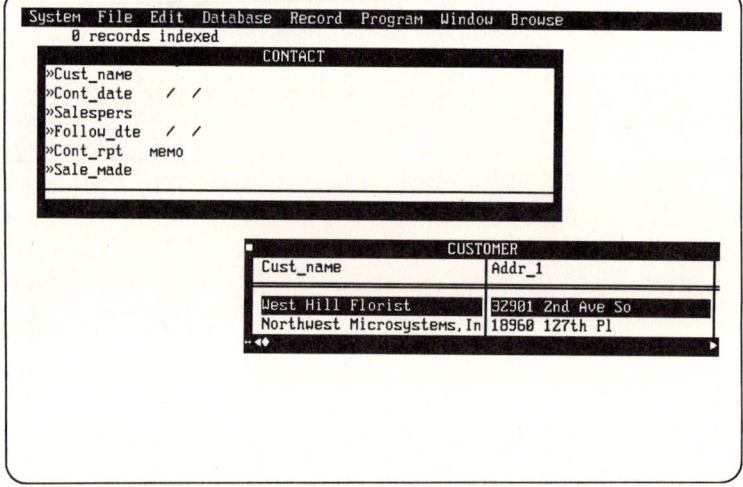

Fig. QS2.7.
Both the
CUSTOMER
Browse window
and the
CONTACT data-
entry window
visible at once.

5. Return to the CONTACT data-entry window by selecting it, and
   enter records into the CONTACT database. To tie the two
   databases together correctly, you must make sure that when
   you're entering a customer's name in the CONTACT database it
   exactly matches the customer name as it exists in the CUSTOMER
   database (differences in upper- and lowercase will not affect the
   relation).

You can move from the CONTACT data-entry window to the CUSTOMER Browse window by clicking in the CUSTOMER window or pressing Ctrl-F1 until the CUSTOMER Browse window is active. You can scroll to the record you want and return to the data-entry window where you can enter the CUST_NAME field, referring to the CUSTOMER Browse window to make sure that the name is correct. Figure QS2.8 shows a record being entered in the CONTACT database with the appropriate CUSTOMER record in view in the CUSTOMER Browse window.

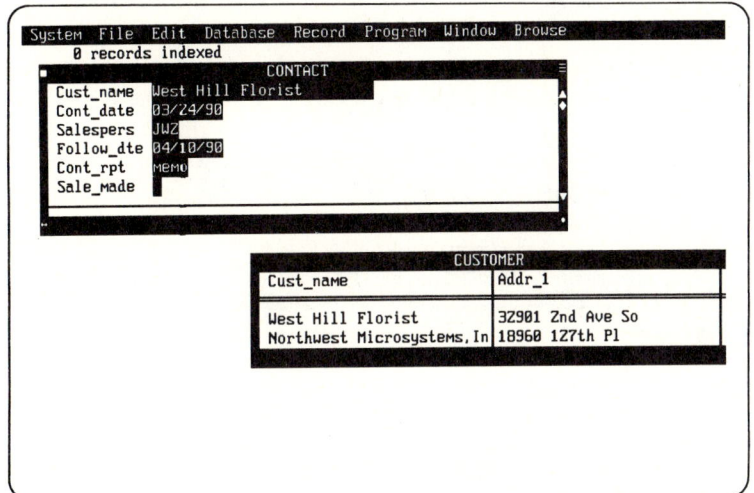

Fig. QS2.8.
Entering a
CONTACT record
while the
CUSTOMER
record is visible.

6. You also can cut and paste the CUST_NAME fields. Move to the CUSTOMER Browse window. Scroll to the record of a customer which you want to enter into the CONTACT database, and then select the text in the CUST_NAME field with either of the following methods:

   ❏ Using a mouse, put the mouse pointer at the first letter of the name in the CUST_NAME field. Drag the mouse to the right while holding down the mouse button. On a color monitor, the characters selected will change color; on a monochrome monitor, the selected characters change from black on white to regular video and are underlined. When you have highlighted the entire name, release the mouse button and select Copy from the Edit menu or press Ctrl-C.

❑ From the keyboard, use the arrow keys to place the cursor at the first character of the CUST_NAME field. Hold down the Shift key while pressing the right-arrow key. Each press of the right-arrow key highlights another character; continue doing this until the entire name in the CUST_NAME field is highlighted. Now choose Copy from the Edit menu or press Ctrl-C.

The Copy command tells FoxPro to make a copy of what you have highlighted and hold that copy in the computer's memory.

7. Return to the CONTACT data-entry window by clicking it or pressing Ctrl-F1. If the cursor is not in the CUST_NAME field, move it there. Choose Paste from the Edit menu or press Ctrl-V (the keyboard shortcut for Paste). FoxPro places in the field a copy of what you highlighted in the CUST_NAME field of the CUSTOMER Browse window. Figure QS2.9 shows this field pasted into the CONTACT database. This is an excellent way to ensure that the two fields match exactly.

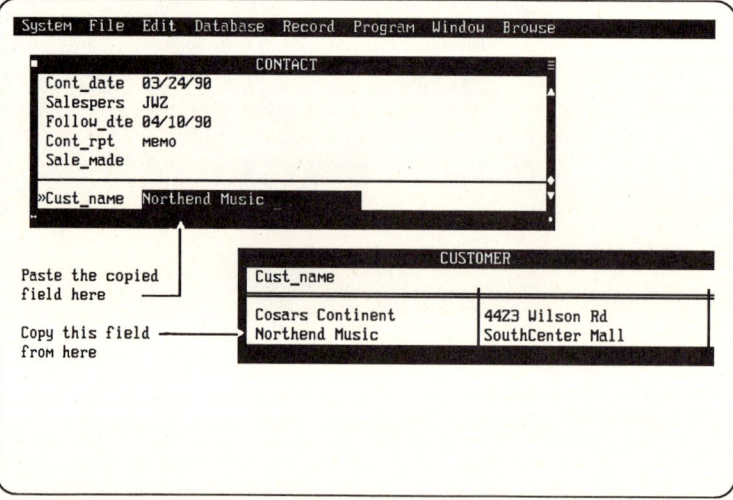

Fig. QS2.9.
Pasting a
CUST_NAME
from CUSTOMER
into CONTACT.

8. Enter information into the CUST_NAME, CONT_DATE, SALESPERS, and FOLLOW_DTE fields. When you reach the CONT_RPT field, press Ctrl-PgDn. This field is a memo field, different from other FoxPro data types in that it is unlimited in how much information you can enter into it. Pressing Ctrl-PgDn opens a text-entry window. In this window, you can enter descriptions that might apply to a sales contact by a customer. Figure QS2.10 shows such a window.

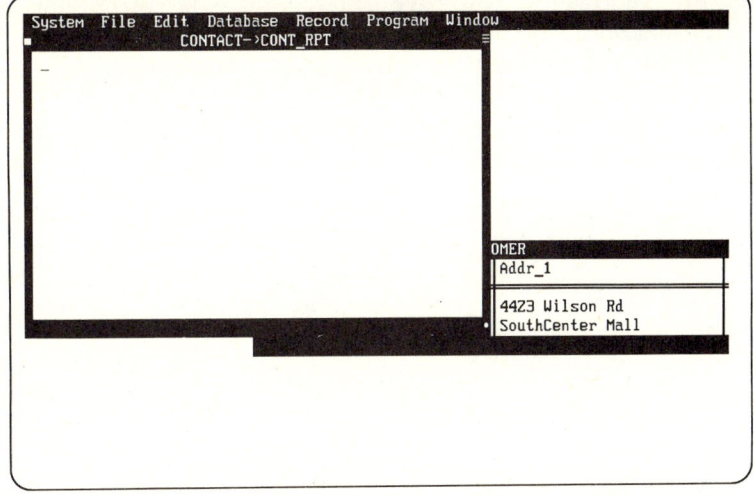

Fig. QS2.10.
A text-entry
window for
entering
information into
the memo field,
CONT_RPT.

9. When you have finished entering information into the text window for the CONT_RPT field, press Ctrl-W, or click the window-close symbol; you return to the data-entry window for the CONTACT database.

10. Continue entering records into the CONTACT database. You should enter CONTACT records for at least several different customers, and more than one CONTACT record for two or three of the customers. Figure QS2.11 shows a Browse window with some records entered.

Cust_name	Cont_date	Salespers	Follow_dte	Cont_rpt	Sale_mad
Cosars Continent	11/30/89	CHZ	01/15/89	Memo	T
Hess Aviation Inventory	10/10/89	DJZ	12/15/90	Memo	F
Metropolitan Corp	12/12/90	DJZ	02/01/90	Memo	F
Northend Music	/ /		/ /	Memo	
OshKosh Cow Company	12/15/89	CHZ	02/01/90	Memo	F
OshKosh Cow Company	03/01/89	CHZ	12/30/89	Memo	F
SCIL	12/21/89	DJZ	01/15/90	Memo	F
SCIL	01/15/90	DJZ	03/15/89	Memo	T
Studio 11 Art	02/15/90	CHZ	03/15/90	Memo	F
T. Moore & Associates	10/31/89	DJZ	01/31/90	Memo	F
West Hill Florist	03/24/90	JWZ	04/10/90	Memo	
West Hill Florist	12/29/89	CHZ	01/05/89	Memo	T

Fig. QS2.11.
The Browse
window showing
records in the
CONTACT
database.

Notice that the information you have entered into the memo field CONT_RPT cannot be seen. To see that information, tab to the CONT_RPT field and press Ctrl-PgDn, just as you did to enter the information. Press Ctrl-W or click the close symbol to exit the memo field. When you have entered 10 to 15 records into CONTACT, press Esc or click the data-entry window-close symbol.

You have now created and entered information into a multiple-file database. So far, it has been much like using a single-file database, as in Quick Start 1. To understand and use the real power of FoxPro, you must tie the two databases together and learn how to draw information from both at the same time.

Tying Together Two Databases

Each of the related databases must have a common field, which FoxPro uses to tie the two together. Both the CONTACT and CUSTOMER databases contain a CUST_NAME field. Once the relation between the two is specified to FoxPro, the active record in the CUSTOMER database will always be the record that has the same CUST_NAME as the active record in the CONTACT database. To set the relation between the two databases and see how this relationship works, do the following:

1. Close any open windows you have on-screen. Open the View window by choosing View from the Window menu. It should appear as in figure QS2.12. If it doesn't, select work area A, then use the Open option to open the CONTACT database in this area.

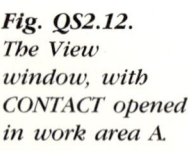

Fig. QS2.12.
The View
window, with
CONTACT opened
in work area A.

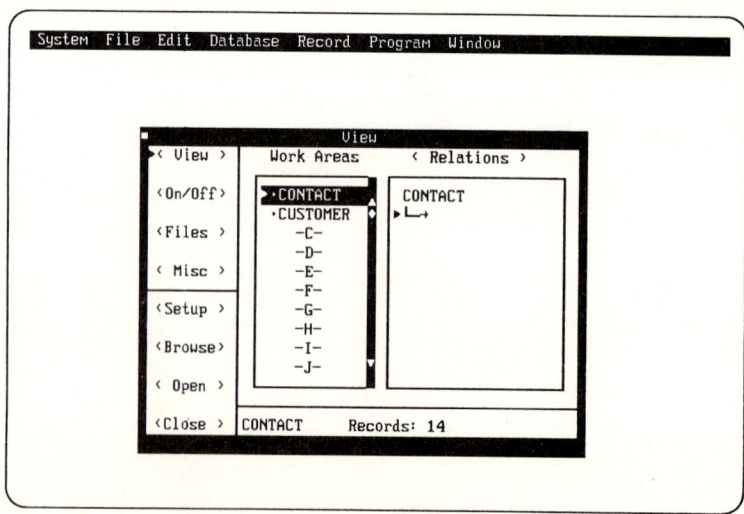

2. Select work area B and open the CUSTOMER database in that work area.

3. With the CUSTOMER database selected, choose Add from the Open Index dialog. The CUSTOMER database must be indexed on the field that ties it to CONTACT, and that index must be controlling the order of the database. From the Open Index dialog, select the CUSTNAME index created in Quick Start 1. If this index does not exist, choose New and create an index on the CUST_NAME field, naming it CUSTNAME.

4. Return to the View window by choosing OK in the Open Index dialog.

5. Select the CONTACT database. A Browse window opens automatically; close this Browse window (you don't need it right now). Click or select Relations. CONTACT appears at the top of the Relations dialog, and an L-shaped arrow appears below it. The View dialog now looks like figure QS2.13.

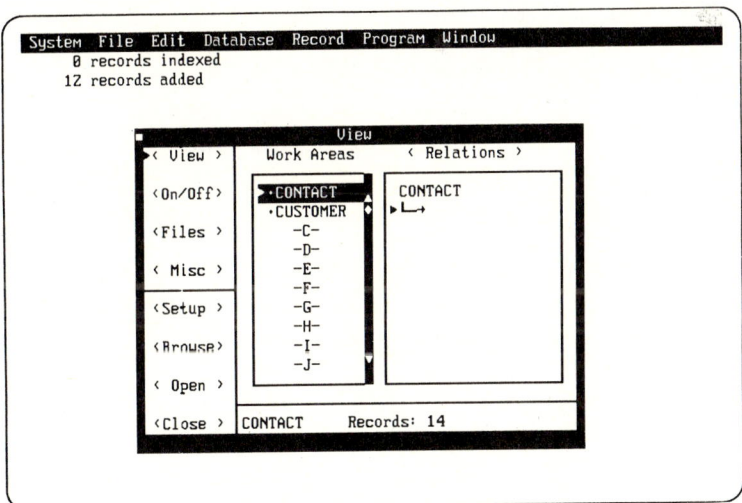

Fig. QS2.13.
Selecting CONTACT as the controlling database in a relation.

6. Move back to the work area box and select CUSTOMER. An Expression Builder dialog opens to receive information on what field will tie CONTACT to CUSTOMER. Choose CUST_NAME. You return to the View window, where CUSTOMER now appears in the Relations box, as shown in figure QS2.14.

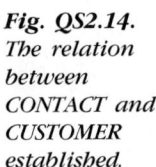

Fig. QS2.14.
The relation
between
CONTACT and
CUSTOMER
established.

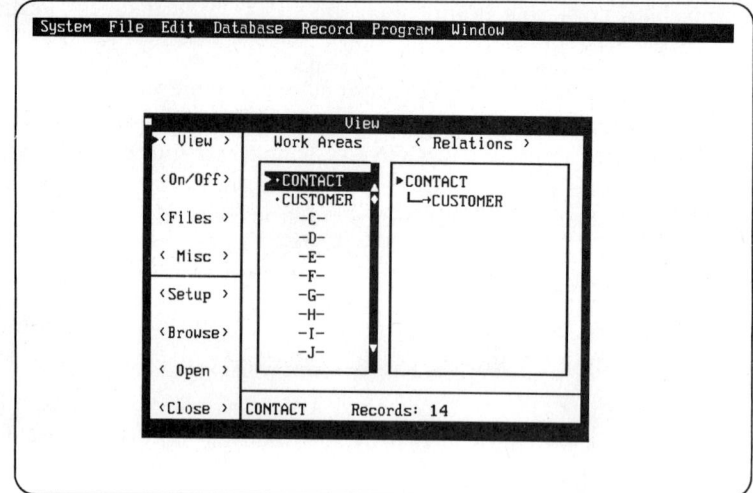

These actions have tied together the databases CONTACT and CUS-TOMER, a process known as "setting the relation." Each database has a "database pointer," an imaginary arrow that points at the active record in the database. With this relation set, when you move the pointer in the CONTACT database, FoxPro automatically moves the CUSTOMER database pointer so that it points to the CUSTOMER record with the same CUST_NAME.

Next, you will want to make use of this relation:

1. Open a Browse window for each database. First, in the View window, select CONTACT in the work area box, and then choose Browse. Return to the View window without closing the CONTACT Browse window. Select CUSTOMER in the work area window and again select Browse. FoxPro opens a Browse window on the CUSTOMER database.

2. To clean up the screen, select the View window and close it. (If the Command window is open, select it and choose Hide from the Window menu.) Move and size the two Browse windows until you can see the CUST_NAME fields for both of them at the same time; for this exercise, it is best if each is only two records high. Figure QS2.15 shows the FoxPro screen with the two Browse windows open.

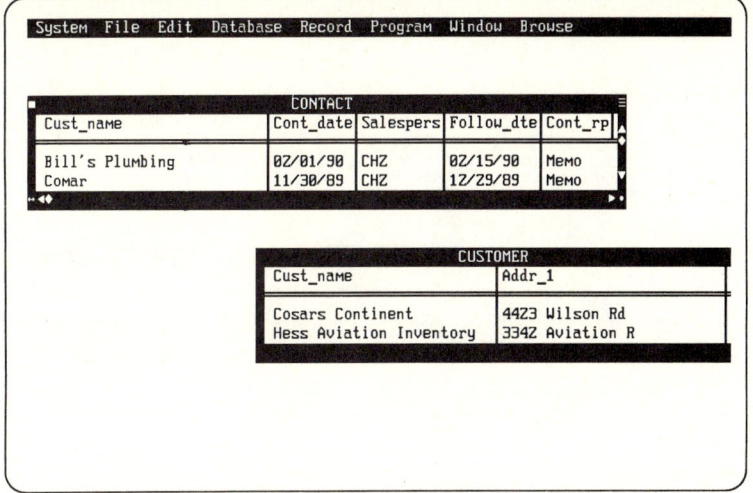

Fig. QS2.15.
Browse windows
on both
CONTACT and
CUSTOMER
databases
opened.

3. Make the CONTACT Browse window active. Select a record in the
   CONTACT database by clicking the record or moving the
   highlight with the up- and down-arrow keys. Now make the
   CUSTOMER Browse window active. You will see that the record
   in the CUSTOMER database has the same CUST_NAME as the
   record you selected in the CONTACT database. FoxPro has moved
   the database pointer of the controlled database, CUSTOMER, so
   that the value in the common field, CUST_NAME, is the same as
   the value in CUST_NAME in the controlling database, CONTACT.
   Figures QS2.16 and QS2.17 show this process in the two Browse
   windows.

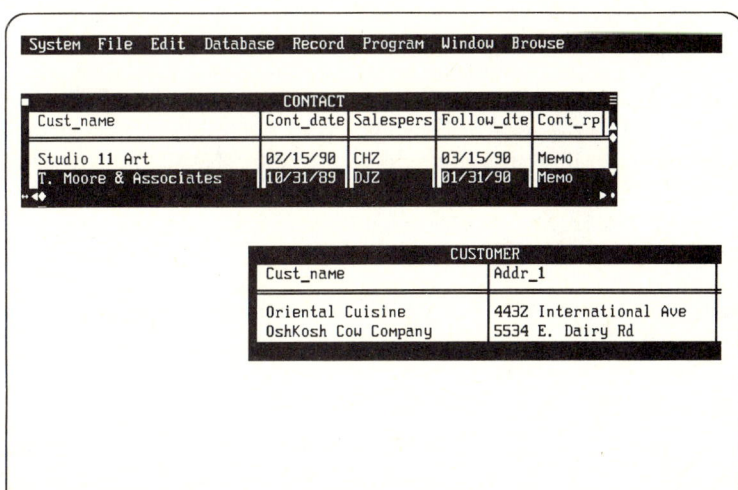

Fig. QS2.16.
Selecting a record
in CONTACT.

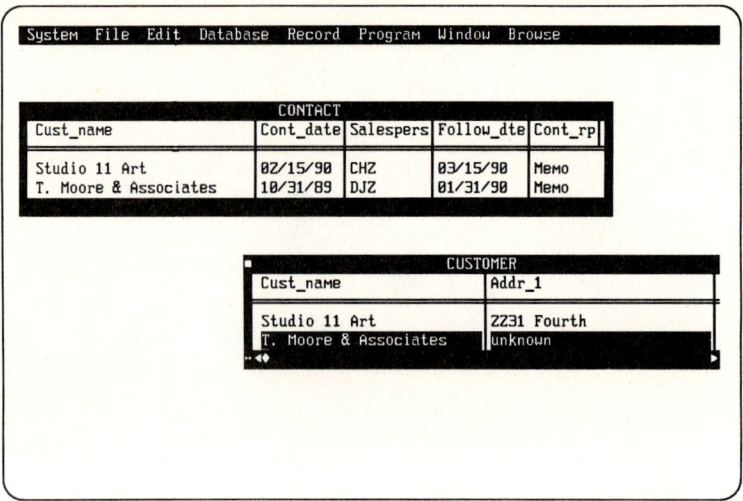

Fig. QS2.17.
The same
CUST_NAME
record selected in
CUSTOMER.

4. Return to the CONTACT browse window and select another record in the database. If you return to the CUSTOMER Browse window, you can see that FoxPro has again matched the records of the two databases.

5. Make the CUSTOMER Browse window active and select a record in that database by clicking it or moving to it with the up- and down-arrow keys. Now move to the CONTACT database. You will see that the active record in this database has not changed. A relationship is a one-way street; CONTACT can control the database pointer in CUSTOMER, but CUSTOMER has no control over CONTACT. (If you wanted CUSTOMER to control CONTACT, you would break the relation from CONTACT to CUSTOMER and make a new one in the other direction.)

To see what happens when FoxPro cannot find a match between CUST_NAME in CONTACT and CUST_NAME in CUSTOMER, return to the CONTACT Browse window and edit one of the CUST_NAME fields. Now return to CONTACT and see what has happened. The active record in CUSTOMER is the first record. FoxPro could not find a match and so gave up, pointing to the first record.

Once you know your databases are set up correctly and the relationship works, you can save this View with a name for later use. To do so, open the View window and choose Save from the File menu. You will see the Save View As dialog, shown in figure QS2.18.

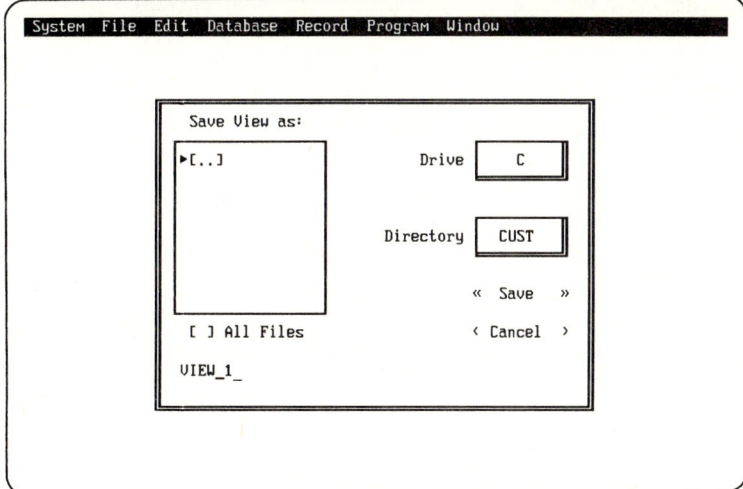

Fig. QS2.18.
The Save View As
dialog.

Save the view as VIEW_1. FoxPro saves information about what databases are open in which work areas, what index files are attached to the databases, and what relations exist between them.

In the future, if you want to reestablish this View, you need only choose Open from the File menu, select View from the Open dialog, and specify VIEW_1 as the view you want to establish. FoxPro will return itself to the exact state it was in when you saved the view, including the sizes of Browse windows.

You have seen how FoxPro relates two database files, keeping them in sync as you move through the controlling database. Doing this enables you to draw information from one database (CUSTOMER), based on the record in another (CONTACT). To see how this can be extremely valuable in your database work, you next create a report that uses this relationship.

Creating Reports on Related Databases

The best database design in the world does little good if you cannot report on it. Fortunately, FoxPro's report writing capabilities are well-suited to creating reports on multiple-file databases. Once you have set up your databases with the correct relations between them, FoxPro can draw information from many databases at one time (up to 25). To create a multiple-file database report, do the following:

1. Open the View window to ensure that the databases are open and the relationship set. When your View window is correct, you can create a report on the two databases. Make sure that the CONTACT database has the "active database" symbol to its left. If it does not, double-click CONTACT to select it, or highlight CONTACT and press Enter to make it the active database.

2. Choose New from the File menu and select `Report` from the New dialog. Select `OK` to open the Layout window. You will create your report on this Layout window.

3. Choose Quick Report from the Report menu. Click `Column Layout`, and then `OK`. You will return to the Layout view, which now looks like figure QS2.19.

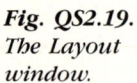

Fig. QS2.19.
The Layout window.

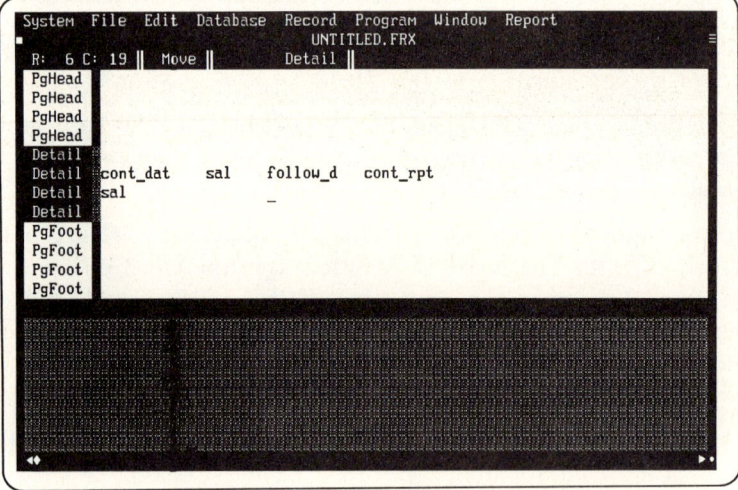

4. Edit the text labels to make them more meaningful. You also should delete the CUST_NAME field, because you don't want the customer name to print on each line of the report. Add a line to the bottom of the Detail Band by placing the cursor in the last line of the Detail Band and choosing Add Line from the Report menu.

5. Next, choose Group Data from the Report menu. In the Group dialog, click `Expr` to display the Expression Builder dialog. In the Expression Builder dialog, change the database to CUSTOMER by pulling down in the `Database` box and selecting `CUSTOMER` from the menu (see fig. QS2.20).

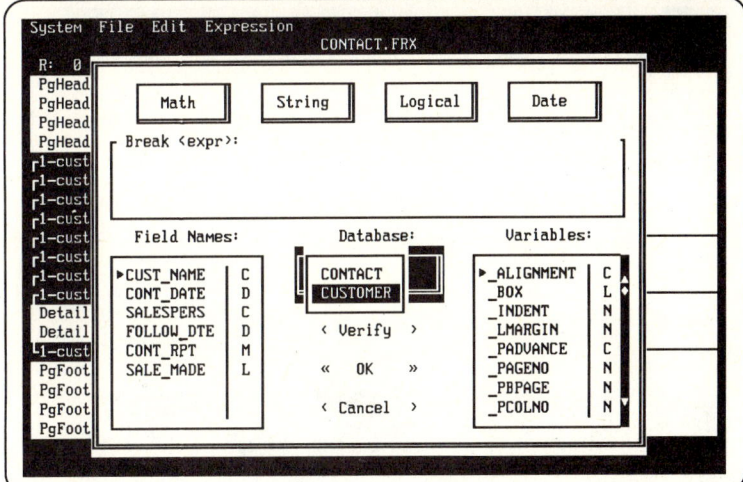

*Fig. QS2.20.
Changing the
database to
CUSTOMER.*

6. Select CUST_NAME from the scrollable list to tell FoxPro that you want your report to group data by the value of CUST_NAME in the CUSTOMER database. When printing the report, FoxPro will move through the CONTACT database, updating the database pointer in CUSTOMER as a result of the relation you have set between the two files. When the value of CUST_NAME in CUSTOMER changes, FoxPro will end one group and start another.

7. When you return to the Layout window, you can see that FoxPro has created a Group Header Band and Group Footer Band. Place the cursor into the Group Header Band and choose Field from the Report menu. In the Field dialog, again change the database to CUSTOMER, and pick CUST_NAME from the list. When you return to the Layout view now, you will see a field labeled customer->cust_name in the Group Header Band.

8. Choose Add Line from the Report menu three times to add three additional lines to the Group Header. In the second line, add a Field for ADDR_1 from the CUSTOMER database. In the third line, add a field for ADDR_2 from the same database, and, in the fourth line, add fields for CITY, STATE, and ZIP from the CUSTOMER database. Your Layout view should look like the one in figure QS2.21.

Fig. QS2.21.
The Layout view.

9. Test your report by choosing Page Preview from the Report menu. FoxPro will run your report and place the output on-screen. Figure QS2.22 shows the output from the report as it now exists.

Fig. QS2.22.
The output of
your report.

You can see that your report works, proving that your databases and the relationships between them are correct. Still, your report is somewhat stark, and with FoxReport's capabilities, there is no reason for a plain-vanilla report. The following steps present some ways to improve the report's appearance:

1. Select the field CONTACT–>COMMENT, which is a memo field in the CONTACT database. Memo fields have special editing functions on the report because they can be any length.

2. Open the Field dialog from the Report menu. You see the Report Expression dialog (see fig. QS2.23). The Stretch Vertically option applies specifically to memo fields and ensures that the field will always be big enough to print the entire memo field. The field will always be the width you specified on the Layout view, but will take up as many lines as necessary. If you want the field to be only one line, make sure that this option is not chosen; the report field will be just as you defined it.

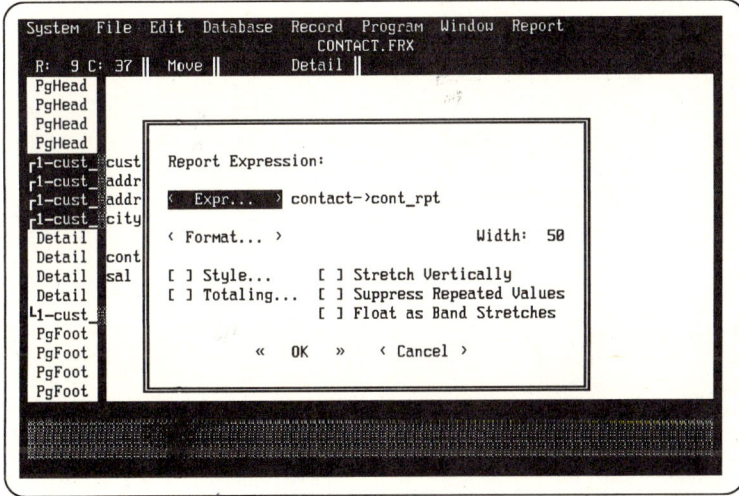

Fig. QS2.23.
The Report
Expression
dialog.

3. Return to the Layout view. Select Page Preview to show the report with the CONTACT–>COMMENT field as defined.

4. Return to the Report Expression dialog for the CONTACT–>COMMENT field and select the Stretch Vertically option.

5. Move the CONTACT–>SALESPERS field to a position below the CONTACT–>COMMENT field. Open the Report Expression dialog on the comment field. When the Report Expression dialog opens, notice the option Float as Band Stretches. Because the field above the CONTACT–>SALESPERS field is a memo field that you have allowed to expand, you must tell FoxPro that fields below that expanding memo field can float on the page, always staying one line below the expanding field. Select the Float as Band Stretches option and OK.

6. Return to the Layout view and choose Page Preview. Your report should look like figure QS2.24, with the CONTACT–>SALESPERS field floating below the comment field.

Fig. QS2.24.
The improved
report.

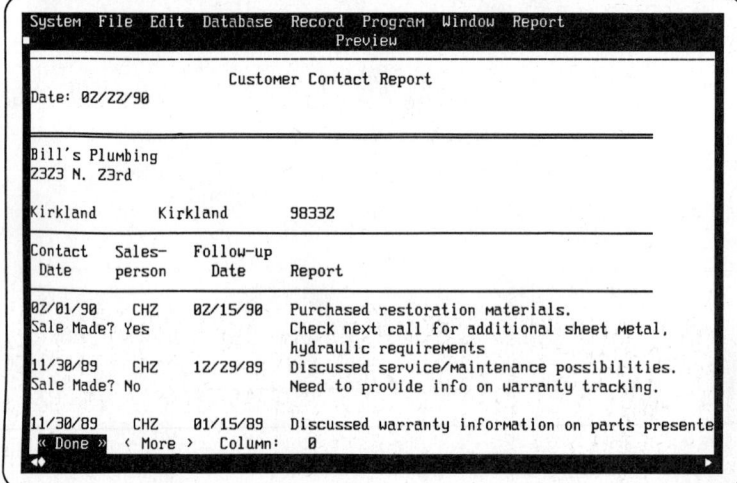

7. Add a line in the Group Footer to mark the end of the report by choosing Box from the Report menu. If you're using a monochrome monitor, you will then choose what type of box you want from the Box dialog.

Now your report is finished. You have succeeded in reporting on the CONTACT database and drawing information from the related CUSTOMER database for the report. This process is the same for databases that contain two, three, or more database files. With FoxPro, reporting on related databases follows the FoxPro philosophy of combining ease-of-use with database power.

Summary

In this quick start, you learned how to create and use multiple database FoxPro systems. You saw how the databases must have a common field so that FoxPro can relate them. Setting up Browse windows on the related databases and moving back and forth between them showed how FoxPro uses the relations you established, making sure that the records of the two databases are in sync and always pointing to the correct record, based on the common, relational field.

Finally, you used the Layout view to create a report that draws information from two different databases at the same time. You can see that this technique is extremely valuable, enabling you to keep different types of data in different databases while viewing and reporting on information from those different types of data. Once you have mastered creating and using two database files at the same time, you will be able to do the same with three, four, or more files.

6

Designing, Defining, and Creating Relational Databases

A lthough you will find that some applications require only one database, most FoxPro applications require two, three, or more databases to represent the different types of data in the application. This is an area in which FoxPro really shines: in its capability to create sophisticated database applications with multiple databases and to tie those databases together in productive ways.

You will want to use more than one database file when the data you need to store falls into more than one logical group. The example in this chapter uses data about customers, the orders those customers place, and the parts ordered. Information about customers is different than information about orders and inventory, so each type of data—customer, order, and inventory—go into separate databases.

In this chapter you learn the essentials of working with multiple-file databases. Defining the databases and how they are to work together is the most important part of creating these applications.

The first part of this chapter discusses the theoretical side of relational databases. The rest of the chapter focuses on defining a multiple-file database system, including the files and the relationships you must tell FoxPro about, and testing the database to make sure that the file structures and relations work as you want them to.

Understanding a Relational Database

The current buzz word in database systems is *relational*. All the latest database systems are relational. Rather than trying to define the why's and wherefore's of relational database systems, first let's look at how data in the real world fits together. From that, you can see how a relational database can represent that data in the computer, making it easier for you to create database systems.

In just about every system you might computerize, the data falls into logical groups. A wholesaler computerizing its operation, for example, would find it has information about each inventory part, each customer, and each order it takes. In database-ese, each of these logical groups of information is called a *data entity*. In this company's database system, each entity would have its own database file to hold that information.

A relationship exists between these data entities, and you want to have your database represent those relationships. In the wholesaler example, a relationship exists between the customer and the orders of the company —each order is placed by a customer. Similarly, there is a relationship between the order database and the inventory database—each order is for some part in the inventory.

Figure 6.1 shows a diagram illustrating the relationships between the wholesaler's data entities.

Fig. 6.1.
Database
relationships.

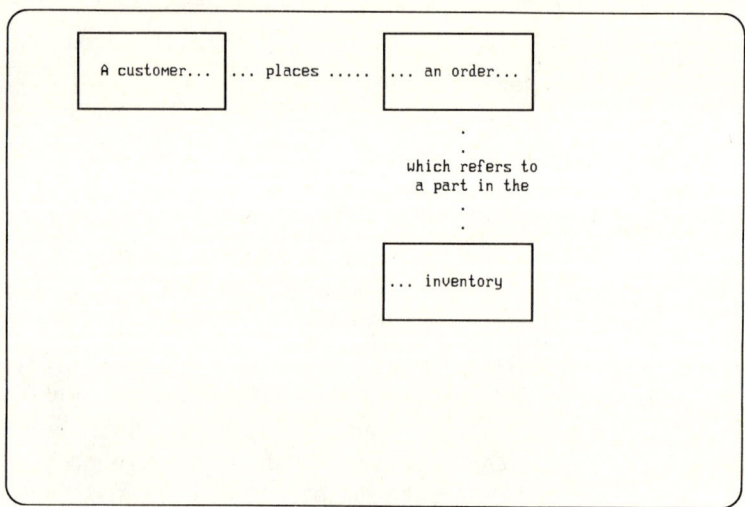

In prerelational database times, the databases and relationships could be defined in a database system, but once defined, were extremely difficult to change. These databases were called *flat-file* databases. When a user wanted to add more types of information and new relationships to the database structure, he was usually greeted with laughter (or tears) and enormous bills for the redesign of the database, not to mention the recoding of many routines. Flexibility was not a part of the flat-file database.

These databases often didn't reflect reality, particularly in the business world where reality is constant change. Today you may want the customer information tied to the ordering system, but tomorrow you also may want it tied to a customer contact system, and the next day you may want it related to something entirely different. Relational databases enable you to define these relationships on the fly, as you need them. In fact, relationships often change many times in just one database application development.

Relational database systems, such as FoxPro, have advantages over other types of systems. FoxPro enables you to make your computerized database system represent the real world more realistically. Relational databases also make that system more consistent and reliable, because there is almost no duplication of information in different database files. Because there is no duplication, a relational database system like FoxPro saves disk space and reduces the effort required for data entry and editing.

Designing a Relational Database

In Part I of this book, you designed a database system that had only one file, a CUSTOMER or INVNTRY file, for example. Designing, defining, and creating a multiple-file, relational database is not much different, but it requires more thought at the beginning and more testing along the way to ensure that everything is all right.

Just as with a single-file system, when you design a relational database system in FoxPro or FoxBase+, you must begin with a clear idea of what you need as output from the system. In nearly all cases, you will be automating a manual system, or improving an existing computerized system, so you have a head start on what the system must do.

As an example, suppose that you want to create a relational system that stores and reports on customers, orders, and inventory. Figures 6.2 through 6.5 show outputs that you have to plan for in this system.

Fig. 6.2.
A Customer report.

```
                        Customer Report

        Date:01/02/90
        Time: 8:34:21
        '''''''''''''''''''''''''''''''''''''''''''''''''''''''''''''
           Number:  1
             Name:  West Hill Florist
          Address:  32901 2nd Ave So

             City:  Renton          State: WA      ZIP:
            Phone:  (206)228-9932

        '''''''''''''''''''''''''''''''''''''''''''''''''''''''''''''
           Number:  10
             Name:  OshKosh Cow Company
          Address:  5534 E. Dairy Rd
                    Pasture 8
             City:  Oshkosh         State: WI      ZIP: 88332
            Phone:  (203)882-1112

        '''''''''''''''''''''''''''''''''''''''''''''''''''''''''''''
```

Fig. 6.3.
An Inventory report.

```
   '''''''''''''''''''''''''''''''''''''''''''''''''''''''''''''
                          Inventory Report
   '''''''''''''''''''''''''''''''''''''''''''''''''''''''''''''
                                           Qty              Ext.
   Part Number    Keyword    Description  On Hand   Cost    Cost
   ''''''''''''''''''''''''''''''''''''''''''''''''''''''''''''
   Keyword: "C"
   ME 4019-1       "C"        "C" WASHER      0      0.00    0.00
   ME 40560-78     "C"        "C" WASHER      0      0.00    0.00
   ME WMP1-156     "C"        "C" WASHER      0      0.00    0.00
   ME 50647-13     "C"        "C" WASHER      0      0.00    0.00
   ME WMP1-88      "C"        "C" WASHER      0      0.00    0.00
   ME 50724-4      "C"        "C" WASHER      0      0.00    0.00
                                              0              0.00
```

Obviously, a full system will have many different reports and inquiry screens, but if the system can supply the basic reports, it also can support just about any inquiries. The goal in designing this system is to make sure that you can access all the data you need for these reports.

Looking at the outputs you need from your system, you can identify the information you must have in the databases. In this example, you see that the information for the Customer and Inventory reports can be taken from the CUSTOMER and INVNTRY databases you created in Part I.

One new database is necessary: ORDER. This database must contain information about the customer placing the order, the date of the order, the salesperson who took it, and what was ordered. For simplicity, assume that an order contains only one item from inventory and that the price is not included.

```
                        Sales Report

Date: 01/02/90
Time:  8:41:13
,,,,,,,,,,,,,,,,,,,,,,,,,,,,,,,,,,,,,,,,,,,,,,,,,,,,,,,,,,,,,,,,,,
Sold To:   10
           OshKosh Cow Company
           5534 E. Dairy Road
           Pasture 8
           Oshkosh          WI  88332
,,,,,,,,,,,,,,,,,,,,,,,,,,,,,,,,,,,,,,,,,,,,,,,,,,,,,,,,,,,,,,,,,,
Order Date: 01/01/90  Salesperson: JWZ
,,,,,,,,,,,,,,,,,,,,,,,,,,,,,,,,,,,,,,,,,,,,,,,,,,,,,,,,,,,,,,,,,,
Part Number  Qty  Keyword    Description      Price
,,,,,,,,,,,,,,,,,,,,,,,,,,,,,,,,,,,,,,,,,,,,,,,,,,,,,,,,,,,,,,,,,,
IN F-17200    1   MASTER     MASTER CYLINDER   58.43



                        Sales Report

Date: 01/02/90
Time:  8:41:14


,,,,,,,,,,,,,,,,,,,,,,,,,,,,,,,,,,,,,,,,,,,,,,,,,,,,,,,,,,,,,,,,,,
Sold To:   1
           West Hill Florist
           32901 2nd Ave So

           Renton           WA
,,,,,,,,,,,,,,,,,,,,,,,,,,,,,,,,,,,,,,,,,,,,,,,,,,,,,,,,,,,,,,,,,,
Order Date: 01/02/90  Salesperson: DJZ
,,,,,,,,,,,,,,,,,,,,,,,,,,,,,,,,,,,,,,,,,,,,,,,,,,,,,,,,,,,,,,,,,,
Part Number  Qty  Keyword    Description      Price
,,,,,,,,,,,,,,,,,,,,,,,,,,,,,,,,,,,,,,,,,,,,,,,,,,,,,,,,,,,,,,,,,,
CASCADE 6045  3   PLUG       PLUG              0.00
```

Fig. 6.4.
A Sales report.

```
                      Inventory Report
                    Part Ordered By Sort
,,,,,,,,,,,,,,,,,,,,,,,,,,,,,,,,,,,,,,,,,,,,,,,,,,,,,,,,,,,,,,,,,
Part No.    Keyword   Description   Ordered by        Date    Qty
,,,,,,,,,,,,,,,,,,,,,,,,,,,,,,,,,,,,,,,,,,,,,,,,,,,,,,,,,,,,,,,,,
BA 988642   BEARING   BEARING       SCIL             03/24/90  10
                                    T.Moore & Assoc. 10/10/89   2
BA SN1467   NUT       NUT           SCIL             02/01/90  10
CL 1303012  OIL       OIL SEAL      Studio 11 Art    01/03/90   9
CL 626115   SPRING    SPRING        Studio 11 Art    01/08/90  10
CL 991867   BREATHER  BREATHER      Studio 11 Art    01/03/90  10
IN E-2138   PULL      PULL ROD, 38" West Hill Florist 01/22/89 100
IN E-2355   RING      RING          Hess Aviation Inv. 01/15/90  1
IN E-2514B  SHIM      SHIM, .025    Hess Aviation Inv. 01/15/90  1
IN E-3060   2ND       2ND RED GEAR  OshKosh Cow Co.  12/15/90   4
                                    Hess Aviation Inv. 12/12/89 10
IN E-3070   WASHER    WASHER        Comair           01/15/90   1
                                    T.Moore & Assoc. 02/02/90   4
IN F-17200  CYLINDER  CYLINDER      OshKosh Cow Co.  01/01/90   1
```

Fig. 6.5.
*An Inventory
Ordered report.*

You could design the ORDER database to contain the customer information (name, address, city, and state) and information about what was ordered (part number, description, and price), but doing that would not be efficient. The customer information is already in the CUSTOMER database, and the inventory information is already in the INVNTRY database. If you duplicate all the customer and inventory information in each ORDER record, you must enter it each time you take an order, and you would have to make sure it was right each time. FoxPro, with its relational capabilities, can tie the ORDER database to the CUSTOMER and INVNTRY databases so that you can access the data stored in them.

Defining Databases and Relationships

Both the CUSTOMER and INVNTRY databases in this multiple-database system were defined in Part I. Using your design work, the structure of the ORDER database can be defined. At this point, you have defined the databases necessary to hold all the data you need in your system. Now you must decide how to define and create the relationships you know exist between the databases. In this system, you need to define the relationship that exists between the CUSTOMER and ORDER databases, and another relationship that exists between the ORDER and INVNTRY databases.

You know that a customer places an order; this is a good definition of the relationship between the CUSTOMER and ORDER databases. Database designers have long used graphical techniques (that is, scribblings on paper) to define database systems, so you should do that here, creating what is known in the database design world as an Entity-Relationship diagram. The E-R diagram is a graphical representation of how your FoxPro database must be set up.

An entity is a logical group of data that you need to store in your system; in FoxPro, then, an entity becomes a database file. In the example system, CUSTOMER is an entity, as are ORDER and INVNTRY. In the Entity-Relationship diagram, an entity is represented by a box, with the name of the entity inside it.

A relationship is what ties two (or more) databases together. In the example, you can define a relationship called IS PLACED BY that ties the CUSTOMER and ORDER databases together; an order IS PLACED BY a customer. If you put this relationship in your FoxPro database, FoxPro will be able to process records in the ORDER database and use the relationship to access information about the customer who placed the order from the CUSTOMER database. Similarly, if you define a relationship between the ORDER database and the INVNTRY database, FoxPro will be able to access information from the INVNTRY database about the part actually ordered.

In the E-R diagram, a relationship is represented by a diamond, with its name inside. Figure 6.6 shows an E-R diagram for the ORDER IS PLACED BY entity-relationship.

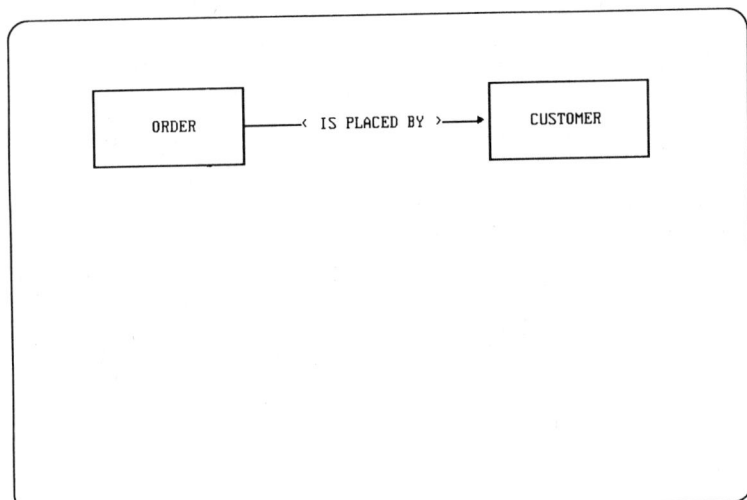

Fig. 6.6.
An Entity-
Relationship
diagram for
ORDER IS
PLACED BY.

Although you have given the relationship a name (IS PLACED BY) in the diagram, you don't use that name to define the relationship to FoxPro; it's used in the E-R diagram for clarity only. To define the relationship to Fox-Pro, you must use indexes.

When you establish a relationship between two FoxPro databases, one database will be the "controlling database" and the other the "controlled database." As FoxPro accesses records in the controlling database, it automatically updates the database pointer in the controlled database. (The database pointer is an imaginary arrow that points at the active record in a database.) In this example, you want the database pointer in CUSTOMER always to point at the record of the customer who placed an order, which is in the ORDER database. You must tell FoxPro how to locate the correct record in CUSTOMER.

Both the ORDER database and the CUSTOMER database have a common field: CUST_NAME. You define this relationship to FoxPro by telling it to tie these two databases together based on the value of the field

CUST_NAME. Then, whenever you choose a record in the ORDER database, FoxPro does the following:

1. Reads the value of the field CUST_NAME in the active record of the ORDER database.

2. Moves to the CUSTOMER database and finds the record in that database that has the same value in CUST_NAME.

3. Sets the database pointer to this record, making it the active record in CUSTOMER.

4. Returns to ORDER to do any processing the user may want to do, such as editing, viewing, or printing data.

Now, if you ask for information from the CUSTOMER database, such as the value of the field ADDR_1, the information retrieved will be that for the customer who placed the order. FoxPro has used the common fields CUST_NAME to relate the ORDER and CUSTOMER databases.

In the Entity-Relationship diagram, you can show how the two databases will be tied together. Under the diamond for the PLACES relationship, put the relational expression for the controlling database toward that database, and for the controlled database toward that database, as seen in figure 6.7.

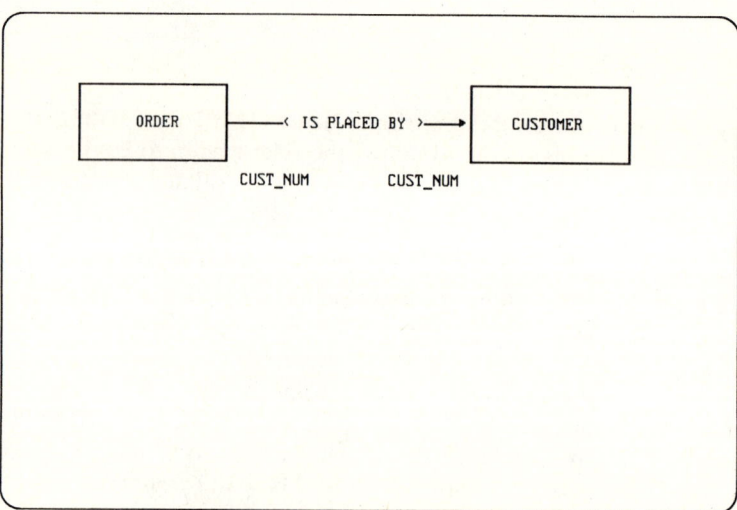

Fig. 6.7.
Adding the relational expressions to the Entity-Relationship diagram.

You also can draw an arrow pointing from the controlling to the controlled entities to remind you which is which.

The controlled database must be indexed on the relational expression or FoxPro will not be able to establish the relationship. So, under the entity, put the index expression that you will need for this database. In this case, it is the field CUST_NAME. The controlling database does not have to be indexed on the relational expression.

Your Entity-Relationship diagram now describes two databases, ORDER and CUSTOMER, the relationship that exists between them (IS PLACED BY), and how that relationship is established. Figure 6.8 shows another E-R diagram with the INVNTRY database added and a relationship, REFERENCES, between ORDER and INVNTRY.

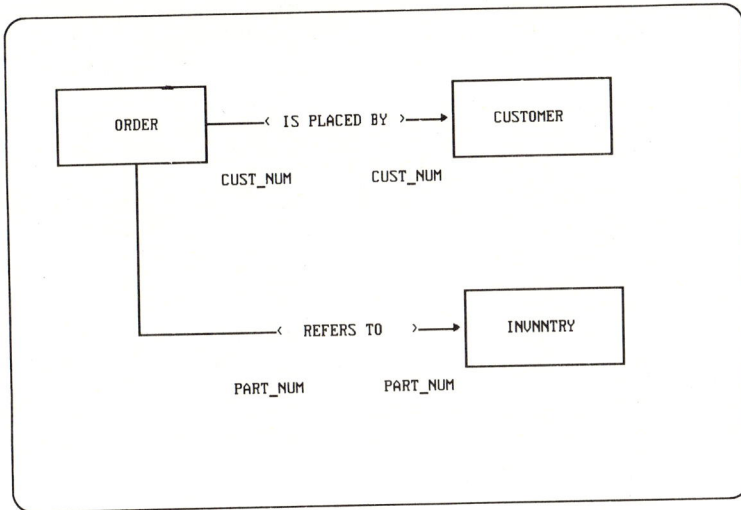

Fig. 6.8.
The completed Entity-Relationship diagram.

Entity-Relationship diagrams are excellent tools to think through your database design before you define it to FoxPro. This introduction to E-R diagramming has been kept simple so that you can see how to use them. As you develop more advanced FoxPro applications, you may want to learn more about E-R diagrams; an excellent discussion of them is contained in *Advanced Structured Analysis and Design*, by Lawrence Peters.

You're probably thinking, "Holy Mackerel. Do I have to go through all this?" No, you don't, but you skip it at your own risk. You easily can make changes to FoxPro databases and, as noted before, flexibility is essential in designing and creating FoxPro databases. Still, the diagramming exercise helps ensure that your databases have the fields needed to tie them together, and that you have a good idea of the structure of your system.

When you have designed your databases and relationships on paper, you must define the system to FoxPro.

Creating Relational Database Systems

The first thing to do when creating relational database systems in FoxPro is define the database files, just as with a single-database file system. The example used in this chapter uses the three database files ORDER, CUSTOMER, and INVNTRY. Table 6.1 shows the structure of these databases.

Table 6.1
Database File Structures

Structure for database : C:\FOXPRO\CUST\ORDER.DBF
Number of data : 17
  records
Date of last update : 01/27/90

Field	Field Name	Type	Width	Dec
1	CUST_NUM	Character	6	
2	ORDR_DATE	Date	8	
3	SALESPERS	Character	3	
4	PART_NUM	Character	15	
5	QTY	Numeric	5	
** Total **			38	

Structure for database : C:\FOXPRO\CUST\CUSTOMER.DBF
Number of data : 15
  records
Date of last update : 02/11/90

Field	Field Name	Type	Width	Dec
1	CUST_NUM	Character	6	
2	CUST_NAME	Character	25	
3	ADDR_1	Character	25	
4	ADDR_2	Character	25	
5	CITY	Character	15	
6	STATE	Character	2	
7	ZIP	Character	9	
8	PHONE	Character	10	
9	CONTACT	Character	10	
10	CREDIT	Numeric	8	2
11	LAST_PUR	Date	8	
12	LAST_AMT	Numeric	8	2
13	PREFERD	Logical	1	
** Total **			153	

Table 6.1—*Continued*

Structure for database :		C:\FOXPRO\CUST\ORDER.DBF		
Number of data records	:	17		
Date of last update	:	01/27/90		

Field	Field Name	Type	Width	Dec
1	PART_NUM	Character	15	
2	KEYWORD	Character	10	
3	DESCR	Character	25	
4	SUPPLIER	Character	25	
5	QTY_ONHND	Numeric	5	
6	QTY_RORDER	Numeric	5	
7	PRICE	Numeric	8	2
8	COST	Numeric	8	2
9	AUTO_RORDR	Logical	1	
10	COMMENTS	Memo	10	
** Total **			113	

Using Work Areas

When you use multiple databases in FoxPro, you use work areas to keep them separate and identifiable. The View window has a box labeled Work Areas. Each work area can hold one database file and all the information associated with that file; index files, formats, field statements, and filters. FoxPro has 25 such work areas, although only 10 can be seen in the Work Area box at any time. You will put each database in your system into a different work area, along with its formats, filters, and index files. All 25 of the work areas can be in use at any time. You will seldom, if ever, use all 25 at once, however.

You must define to FoxPro the databases and the relationships between them. Start by opening all necessary database files, one per work area, using the View window. If any file is open, select and close it to give you a clean start. The View window, with no databases opened, is shown in figure 6.9. You can see work areas A through J.

If you scroll down through the work area, you see that beyond work area J, the areas are numbered rather than lettered. In fact, all work areas are numbered; you can refer to areas A through J as 1 through 10.

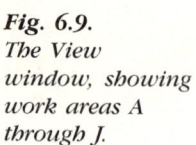

Fig. 6.9.
The View
window, showing
work areas A
through J.

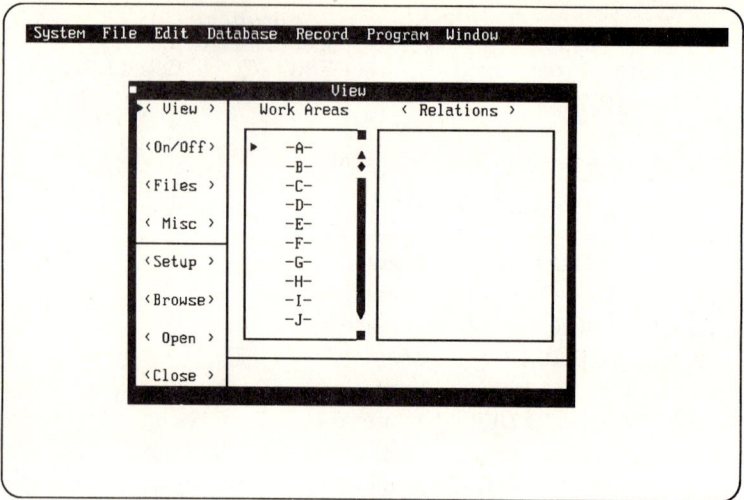

Identifying Work Areas with Aliases

When you have databases open in multiple work areas, you can tell Fox-Pro to access fields by specifying the name of the field, prefixed with an alias to tell FoxPro in what work area the database with that field resides. If, for instance, you have selected a database in work area B and want to access the name field of the CUSTOMER database in work area A, you tell FoxPro to use the value in CUSTOMER>NAME. Alternatively, you can prefix the field with the work area letter, A>NAME or its number, 1>NAME. In all cases, FoxPro knows where to get the name field.

Start by selecting work area A and choosing the Open option. Put your first database file in this work area, then choose Setup to add the index files you need. If you wanted to add a format file and field or filters statements for this file, you would do so in the Setup dialog.

When you return to the View window, it should look like figure 6.10, which has the ORDER database set up as work area A.

To add a second database (the CUSTOMER database in this example), select work area B and follow the same Open and Setup process. When you are finished, your View window should appear as in figure 6.11.

You continue to open databases by selecting subsequent work areas and opening the database and its index files in that work area. After adding a third database, INVNTRY, the View window looks like figure 6.12.

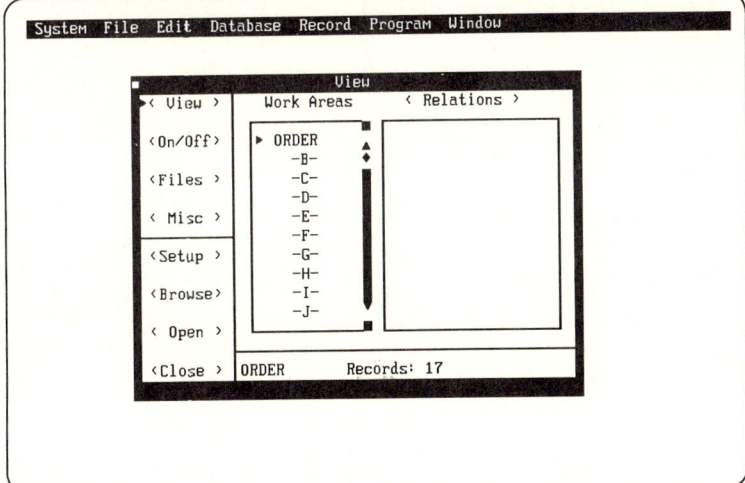

Fig. 6.10.
The View window with CUSTOMER added in work area A.

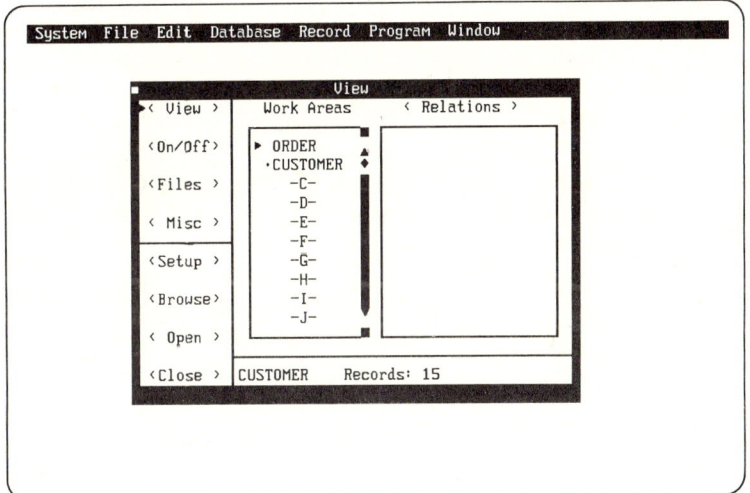

Fig. 6.11.
The View window showing CUSTOMER and ORDER.

If you design and create a system with many database files, you will find that for specific jobs you only need some open at a time, with relationships established between them. You should go through the Open and Setup process for each job-specific setup you need, and then save that "snapshot" of FoxPro for later recall. In this way, you can make FoxPro more efficient and reduce the system's complexity. Saving the view is explained later in this chapter.

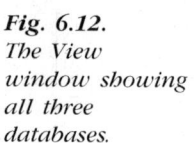

Fig. 6.12.
The View
window showing
all three
databases.

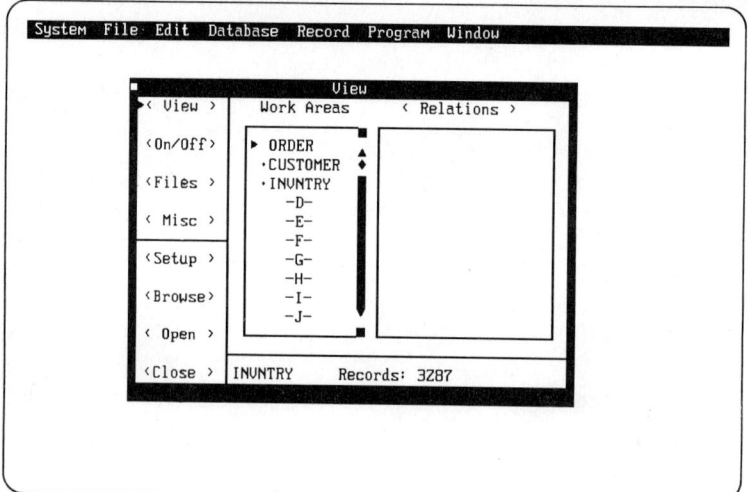

Specifying Relationships in FoxPro

Looking at the Entity-Relation diagram you created in designing your system, you can see what relationships must be set up. In the example used in this chapter, when processing the ORDER database, there must be a relation between ORDER and CUSTOMER, so that when FoxPro processes an ORDER record, it can retrieve information about the customer (CUST_NUM) from CUSTOMER. Because FoxPro will be processing the ORDER database record by record, and retrieving information from CUSTOMER, you know that ORDER is the controlling database and CUSTOMER the controlled one. To set this relationship, select the controlling database (ORDER) and choose Relationships. The controlling database name appears, with an L-shaped indicator (see fig. 6.13).

FoxPro asks you to define the controlled database; select the database at the other end of your relationship, in this example, CUSTOMER. You are presented with the Expression Builder, in which you tell FoxPro what expression, derived from the fields of the controlling database, will be used to find the correct record in the controlled database. In this example, FoxPro wants to know what field in the ORDER database will be used to find the right record in CUSTOMER. Your design dictates that the field will be CUST_NUM, so select that field from the scrollable list, and then choose OK. Now when you return to the View window, it looks like figure 6.14, showing the relationship.

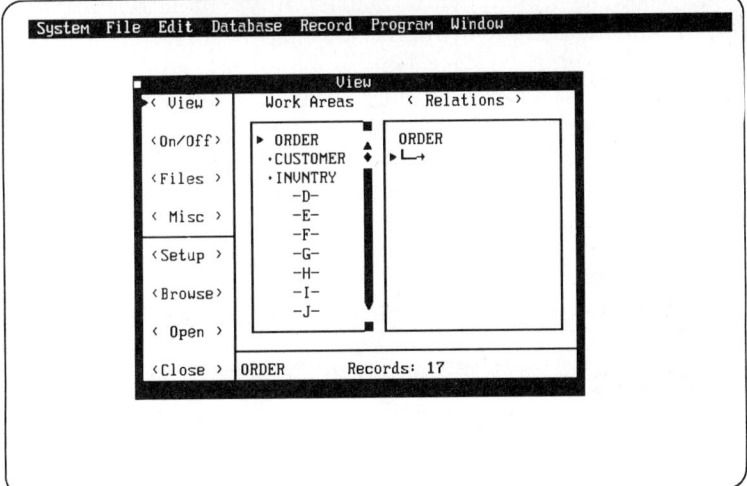

Fig. 6.13.
Specifying the controlling database in a relation.

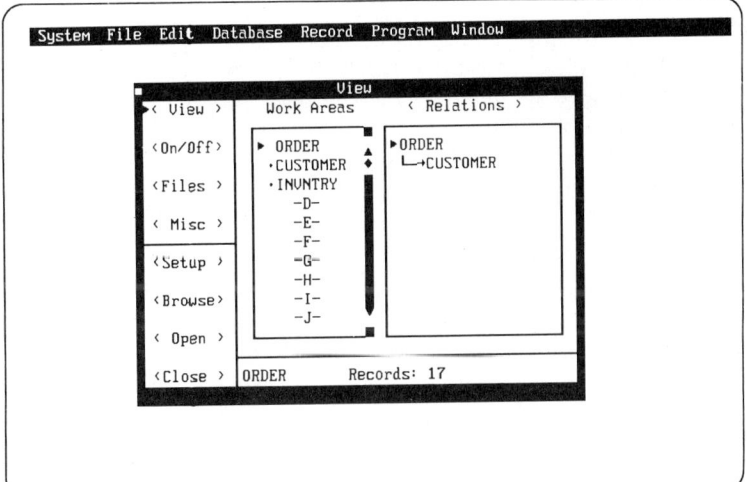

Fig. 6.14.
The View window with the ORDER-CUSTOMER relationship established.

If you're wondering why you didn't have to specify the CUST_NUM field in CUSTOMER, remember that the controlled database must be indexed on the relational expression. FoxPro looks at a record in ORDER, then uses the value of CUST_NUM, which you have specified as the relational expression, and looks for that value in the index controlling CUSTOMER. FoxPro doesn't care what the field name in the controlled database is, as long as it can find the relational expression in the index.

Now you have to do the same thing to establish all the other relationships you defined in your design. Next, the relationship between ORDER and INVNTRY needs to be set. Here the relational expression is PART_NUM in the ORDER database, and again, you must make sure that the index controlling the INVNTRY database is on the field PART_NUM. When you have completed that relationship, you see in the View window a representation of both relationships (see fig. 6.15). Now you're almost ready to see whether your design works.

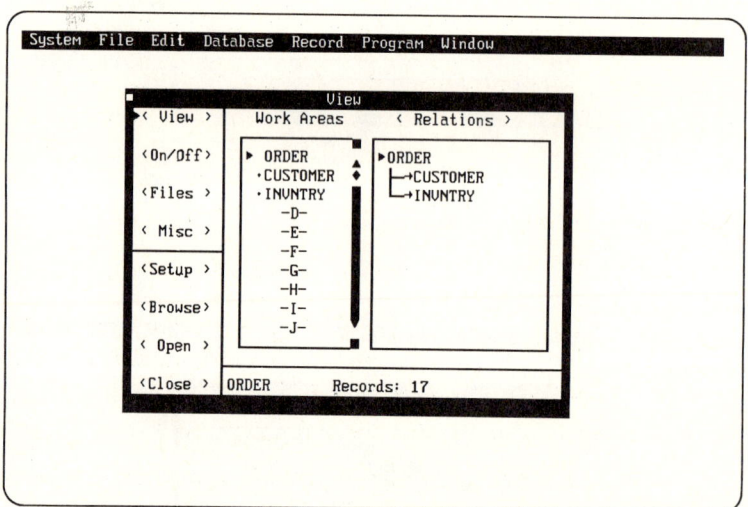

Fig. 6.15.
The View window with all databases and relationships.

Setting Relationships in FoxBase +

The concepts behind defining and designing relationships in FoxBase + are the same as for FoxPro. Defining the relationship differs, though, because FoxBase + does not have FoxPro's window-based user interface. In FoxBase +, you must set up the database files and define the relationships from the command line. In FoxPro, you can use these same commands if you want to work in the Command window.

First, to set the database files and indexes in their correct work areas, you select the work area, then tell FoxBase + what database to use. To set the three example databases into their work areas, enter the following sequence of commands (all text after the && is commentary and is ignored by FoxBase + and FoxPro):

```
SELECT A                    && select work area A
USE CUSTOMER                && open CUSTOMER in this work area
SET INDEX TO CUST_NUM       && open the cust_num index

SELECT B                    && select work area B
USE ORDER                   && open ORDER in this work area
SET INDEX TO ORD_CUST       && open the ord_cust index, which
                            && is on field cust_num in the
                            && ORDER database

SELECT C
USE INVNTRY
SET INDEX TO PART_NUM
```

Now the databases are in their correct areas, with the right index files controlling them. The following sequence sets the relationships:

```
SELECT 2                          && move to controlling database
SET RELATION TO CUST_NUM INTO A
SET RELATION TO PART_NUM INTO C ADDITIVE
```

The ADDITIVE command in the second SET RELATION command tells FoxPro to add this relation to any existing relation for this controlling database. Without this option, FoxPro will replace any existing relationships with the one being specified.

For greater clarity, the sequence just specified used the database names as aliases. The following sequence also works:

```
SET RELATION TO CUST_NUM INTO A
SET RELATION TO PART_NUM INTO C
```

You can see why it is usually preferable to use the database name as an Alias (or whatever Alias you may have assigned the database). Particularly when you need to do some FoxPro programming, the database Name Alias option makes clear which database is in work area A or C.

When this sequence is completed, FoxBase+ (or FoxPro) will look the same as FoxPro set up with the View window. Using the Command window in FoxPro is covered in Chapter 8, but you can see that you often can accomplish FoxPro processes faster through the Command window than by using the windows and dialogs. Using the Command window requires a better knowledge of FoxPro, though.

Saving the Setup

Setting up the databases and relations can be a time-consuming process. You often will find that each thing you want to do in your database system—reports, inquiries, data-entry—requires a different setup of files, indexes, and relationships. FoxPro provides a facility to save a setup and reestablish it later with one command. Because all that is saved can be set up in the View window, these files are called View files.

To save a View, open the View window and make sure that everything is as you want it to be: databases in the correct work area with appropriate index files attached, any filter condition defined, the fields set on or off as necessary, and the right format file included, if you want. Then, select Save from the File menu and give the view a name. Figure 6.16 shows the current view being saved as ORDR_1.

Fig. 6.16.
The Save View
dialog.

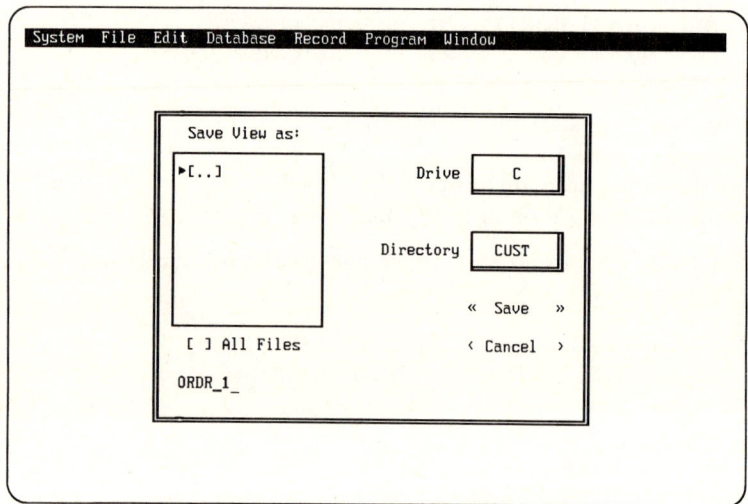

When you want to reestablish that view, select Open from the File menu, change the Type to View, and select the view you want from the File List. When you return to FoxPro, its condition will reflect the saved View.

Saving and Using Views in FoxBase+

FoxBase+ also provides the facility to save and reuse Views. Again, you have to do this from the command line. In FoxBase+, you can save an environment with the command

SAVE VIEW AS ORDR_1

and you can reestablish that environment with the command

SET VIEW TO ORDR_1

As before, FoxPro users can also use these commands in the Command window to accomplish the same purpose.

Testing a Relational Database System

Before you charge off to create the FoxReports and FoxView screens you need for your relational database, you should test the files and relationships to make sure your design works. This can be done easily, and will save you hours of time later on if you find that a relationship was set up incorrectly or essential data not included.

Test the database structure by creating a quick-and-dirty report using fields that show whether the relationships are set up or not. For example, you can test to make sure that the relationships for the Order report are in place.

First, of course, your databases need some data. CUSTOMER and INVNTRY already have data records in them, but ORDER is empty. Make sure that ORDER is the active database (by selecting it in the View window). Then, using the Append option from the Record menu, add a number of records to the ORDER database. Take care that the CUST_NUM you enter exists in the CUSTOMER database and the PART_NUM you use is a valid number in the INVNTRY database. Remember, you're just testing now; for a real system, you would have FoxPro check these values as you enter them to ensure that they're valid.

Once you have entered enough test records in ORDER (at least 20), you can test the relationships by creating a rudimentary report. You need only include enough fields from each database to enable you to see that you have set up the relationships correctly. If, later on, you find you're missing data fields, you can add them, but restructuring the database and relations is more difficult. The following fields will fulfill this testing requirement:

ORDER	CUSTOMER	INVNTRY
CUST_NUM	CUST_NUM	PART_NUM
PART_NUM	NAME	KEYWORD

You can see that, if the relationships are working correctly, each record in the ORDER database will access and print out the right information in the related databases.

Figure 6.17 shows the Layout View of the testing report. You can see that this is a very basic report; you need only a Detail Band to check what fields are accessed as the report progresses through the ORDER database.

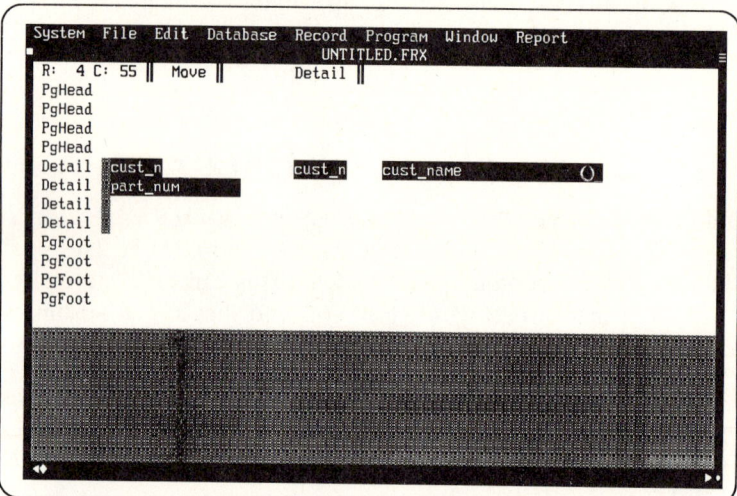

Fig. 6.17.
The test report Layout View.

After saving the report, you can run it by choosing Report from the Database menu. Figure 6.18 shows the results of running this report. You can see that, as FoxPro progressed through the ORDER database, it successfully pulled in the appropriate data from the CUSTOMER and INVN-TRY databases; the relationships worked as planned. You can save this view, knowing that when you want to create the report with all the fancy formatting, you can open this view and it will be correct.

When reviewing test reports, you should make sure not only that FoxPro worked correctly when there was a match between the controlled and controlling database, but that it also handled a no-match situation. In this case, the data from the controlling database (ORDER) should be present, but the controlled database's fields should be blank. When FoxPro cannot make a relational match, it points to a null record in the controlled database. If you find data in a record where you know no match exists, something is wrong with the relation.

This brings up a point of testing: always include test data that should fail. It is too easy to include data you know will work and assume that all is fine when it does work. Systems don't die on common occurrences, but on the once-a-year weird data. So try everything, including data you are sure will never be entered in the system once it's completed.

```
ORDER            CUSTOMER            INVNTRY
5                5                   Comar
IN E-2398        IN E-2398           ROLLER

5                5                   Comar
IN E-2398        IN E-2398           ROLLER

6                6                   Cosars Continent
LP 1400-5509     LP 1400-5509        SEAL

6                6                   Cosars Continent
LP 1425-3378     LP 1425-3378        BEARING

6                6                   Cosars Continent
ME 30129         ME 30129            CHAIN

12               12                  Hess Aviation Inventory
IN E-2398        IN E-2398           ROLLER

12               12                  Hess Aviation Inventory
IN E-2514B       IN E-2514B          SHIM

12               12                  Hess Aviation Inventory
ME 1178          ME 1178             SEAT

2                2                   Northwest Microsystems
BA 992518        BA 992518           RING

10               10                  OshKosh Cow Company
CENTURY 2260E    CENTURY 2260E       CARBURATOR

10               10                  OshKosh Cow Company
CL 1754428       CL 1754428          SHIFT

3                3                   SCIL
CASCADE 662458   CASCADE 662458      SEAL

3                3                   SCIL
F-869            F-869               POLY

13               13                  T. Moore & Associates
BA 988619        BA 988619           BRACKET

13               13                  T. Moore & Associates
LP 1425-3328     LP 1425-3328        BEARING

1                1                   West Hill Florist
CASCADE 6045

1                1                   West Hill Florist
IN E-2138        IN E-2138           PULL
```

Fig. 6.18.
The printed output from the test report.

Chapter Summary

This chapter has contained more theoretical background than any other chapter in *Using FoxPro*. It's essential that you understand the basic theory of relational databases in FoxPro, because it is those relational capabilities that give FoxPro the power for you to tap.

You have learned how to design multiple-file databases, using one database for each data entity. You have learned how to define those databases and, more importantly, the relationships that tie the databases together. Simple tests of the data enable you to make sure that your design is good and that your implementation of the design works.

Now it's time to learn how to put this relational database background to work, entering data into FoxPro and creating inquiry screens that access information from related databases at one time.

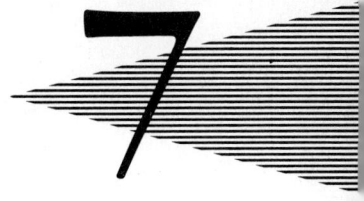

Data Entry and Editing with Multiple Files

In Chapter 6 you learned when a multiple-file, relational database is best, how to define that system, and how to create it. This chapter delves more deeply into entering, editing, and viewing data in such a database.

In this chapter, you learn how to use FoxPro's built-in capabilities to look at more than one related file at a time. You learn how to create a user-defined function to ensure the integrity of the relationship when data is entered.

The power of a relational database is its capability to draw data from different files at the same time. In this chapter, you learn how to create a form file that will enable you to access data in several related files. To do this, you must learn a bit about text editing in FoxPro, about how Fox-View screens are turned into FoxPro format files, and how to change that process just a bit, to your advantage.

This chapter also teaches some "tricks" with FoxPro query and editing screens, such as entering a key value to have FoxPro find the right record and display the fields of that record and all related records. Because this technique requires some FoxPro programming, you also learn the basics of programming.

Editing Text

Because you must do some text editing in this chapter, you need to learn the basics of the FoxPro text editor. If you have worked with memo fields, you already know how to use it; the FoxPro text editor is what you use to enter and edit information in memo fields. To edit a program file in Fox-Pro, choose New from the File menu, select Program, select OK twice, and the Editor window appears (see fig. 7.1). Zoom the window to give you the full screen to work with.

Fig. 7.1.
The Text Editing
window.

```
 System  File  Edit  Database  Record  Program  Window
                        CONTACT.FMT
  × Program.: CONTACT.FMT
  × Author..: John Zumsteg
  × Date....: 01/01/90
  × Notice..: Copyright (c) 1990, Northwest Microsy
  × Version.: FoxBASE+, revision 2.10
  × Notes...: Format file for CONTACT.DBF
  ×
  SET COLOR TO R/N
  @  5,27 SAY "Customer Number: "
  @  6,30 SAY "Contact Date: "
  @  7,31 SAY "Salesperson: "
  @  8,25 SAY "Date to Follow-up: "
  @  9,34 SAY "Comments: "
  @ 10,33 SAY "Sale made? "
```

Unlike the Memo window text editor, long lines do not wrap to the next line in this mode; you must press Enter to end a line. When FoxPro is executing a program file, it processes one line at a time. If you want to continue a long line on the following line, place a semicolon (;) at the end of the first line. Place some text in the text window. Because you're just experimenting, any text will do. Note that as you reach the right margin, the screen scrolls to the right, causing text at the beginning of the line to disappear off the left edge of the screen. Press Enter to end a line and return the cursor to the left edge.

Using a mouse to work in the text editor is easy. To move the cursor anywhere in the file, place the mouse pointer and click. You also can use the scroll bars to get to the part of the file you want. To select a block of text for deleting or moving, for example, drag the mouse from the start of the text to the end. The next command you issue applies to the entire selected block. Figure 7.2 shows a highlighted section of text, ready to be copied or cut.

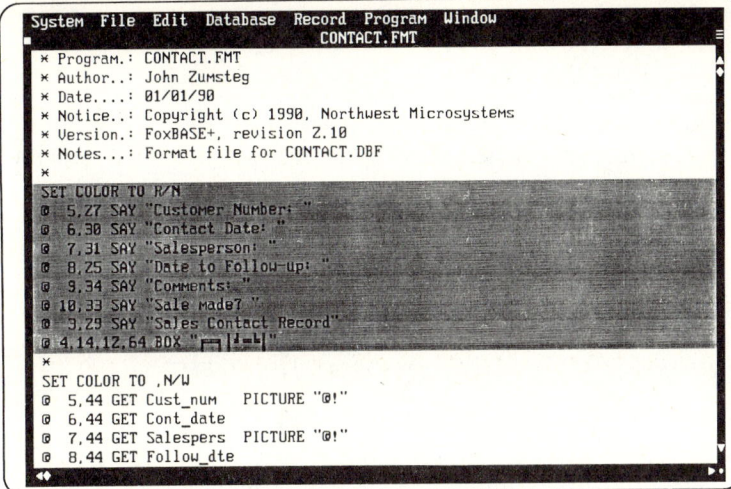

Fig. 7.2.
Text selected,
ready to be cut
or copied.

From the keyboard, you also can navigate in the text window. To move the cursor, use the following keys:

Key	*Action*
Right arrow	Move one character right
Left arrow	Move one character left
Up arrow	Move up one line
Down arrow	Move down one line
Home	Move to start of current line
End	Move to end of current line
PgUp	Move up one window
PgDn	Move down one window
Ctrl-Right Arrow	Move one word right
Ctrl-Left Arrow	Move one word left
Ctrl-Home	Move to beginning of text
Ctrl-End	Move to end of text

To select a range of characters to be copied or deleted, place the cursor to begin selection, then hold down the Shift key and use the arrow keys to move the cursor to the end of the selected text. The selected text is highlighted.

To delete text one character at a time, use either the Del key or the backspace key. You also can highlight the text you want to delete and choose Clear from the Edit window.

To move text, highlight the text you want to move and choose Cut from the Edit menu. Move the cursor to where you want the text copied and choose Paste from the Edit menu.

If you want to copy text, use the same procedure as Cut, except choose Copy from the Edit menu. When you Paste, the text is copied and the original text remains where it was.

Understanding How FoxPro Writes and Reads Screen Fields

FoxPro uses GET and SAY commands to read information from the screen and display information on the screen. The format of the GET and SAY commands, which are used only in Format and Program files, is

> @ *row, col* SAY *field_name*

or

> @ *row, col* GET *field_name*

Row and *col* represent integers that indicate where FoxPro will place the SAY or GET field on-screen. Each of these commands has several options and clauses (some of which were presented in Chapter 2). These two commands are essential for writing to and reading from the FoxPro screen.

Using FoxView To Create a Multiple-File Form

FoxView has extraordinary capabilities for creating elegant data input, editing, and query screens. You can use these capabilities to create a screen that presents data from several related files. To start this process, choose FoxView from the Program menu.

Loading the Database Files

First, set up in FoxView the databases you want to use. You must set them up just as you do in FoxPro. You probably have already saved a View with the databases, so make sure that you know which databases are in which work areas. Load the database files just as you would from the command line in FoxPro or FoxBase, using SELECT and USE. Figure 7.3 shows the FoxView opening screen with the commands for loading three databases. When you have loaded your databases, press F10 to move to FoxView's Form view.

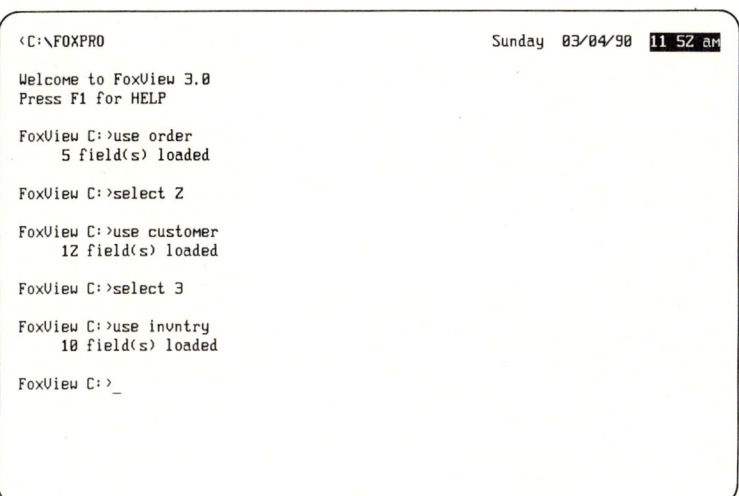

```
<C:\FOXPRO                              Sunday  03/04/90  11 52 am

Welcome to FoxView 3.0
Press F1 for HELP

FoxView C:>use order
      5 field(s) loaded

FoxView C:>select 2

FoxView C:>use customer
     12 field(s) loaded

FoxView C:>select 3

FoxView C:>use invntry
     10 field(s) loaded

FoxView C:>_
```

Fig. 7.3.
Opening multiple databases in the FoxView shell.

As you can see in figure 7.4, FoxView's Form view shows only the fields for the first database file you used. FoxView places each database form on a different page. Press PgDn to see subsequent database files, shown in figures 7.5 and 7.6. Because this format will never do for multiple-file, relational input screens, you must move all the fields onto one screen.

Moving Fields and Pages

First, move through each page and delete fields you don't want on your screen. Seldom do you need to see the fields that form the relationship in all files, so you can delete the fields on all but one page. (In the example, you could delete CUST_NUM from Page 1 or Page 2, and PART_NUM from Page 2 or Page 3.) Any other unneeded fields also should be removed at this time.

The second step is to move the fields on each page to their approximate location on the finished screen. You don't have to be exact, because you can move the fields around later, but you want to avoid overlapping fields when you combine the multiple screens.

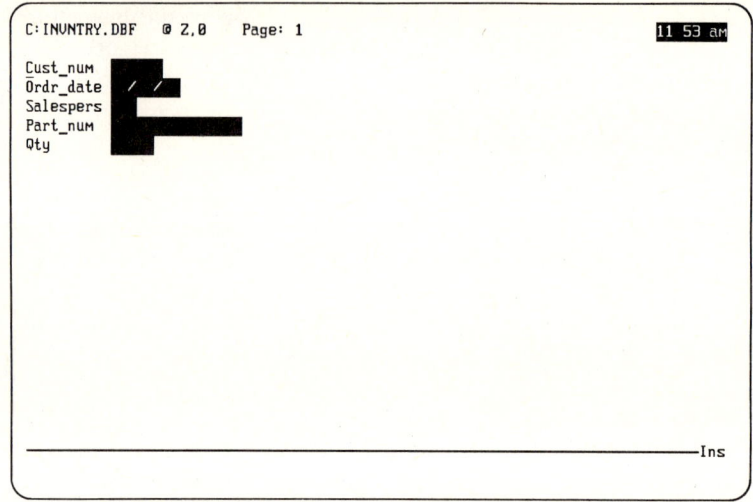

Fig. 7.4.
The first database used in the FoxView shell appears on Page 1 of FoxView.

Fig. 7.5.
The second database is on Page 2.

The next step involves moving all the fields to Page 1 so that they all appear on-screen at once. Use PgDn to move to Page 2, then press F6 and use the Tab and right-arrow keys to select all the fields. Press F3 (Move) and PgUp. All the fields on Page 2 will be moved to Page 1, where you can position them as necessary. Repeat this process with the fields on Page 3, moving them to Page 1 and positioning them there.

Fig. 7.6.
*The third
database is on
Page 3.*

You have combined the two or more screens that FoxView created onto
one screen, combining all fields. Press F10 to return to Form view where
you can see the results of your handiwork (see fig. 7.7).

Fig. 7.7.
*The three
database screens
moved to Page 1.*

Now you can move, size, and change the screen to your heart's content.
FoxView enables you to emphasize data, separate it into logical groups,
and create boxes and labels to give the screen sense and shape. Chapter 3

contains complete instructions for adding titles, text, and boxes to a Fox-View form. Figure 7.8 shows the completed screen for the example database system.

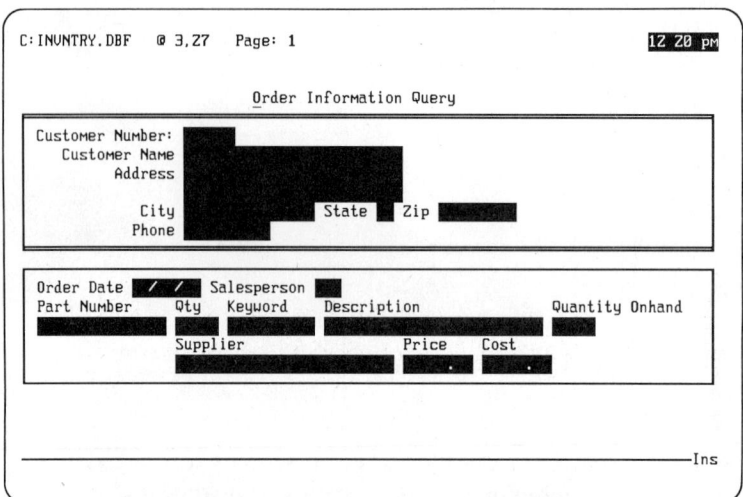

Fig. 7.8.
*The complete
query screen,
using three
related databases.*

Changing GETs to SAYs

You need to make one more change to the Table view before you leave FoxView. Return to Table view by pressing F10. Notice that all the fields have a GET in the (Fld) field. This is because FoxView assumes that you're creating a data-entry screen, and GET tells FoxPro to get some information from the screen. To create a screen to display data, change the GETs to SAYs by placing the highlight on the GET and pressing the space bar. One press changes the value to SAY, a second to HIDE (which means the field disappears), and a third returns to GET. Change all the GETs to SAYs to create a data display screen.

Press Esc to activate the Menu bar, move to the Gen selection (if necessary) and choose Select from the Template List. When the Template menu appears, choose FORM1, Format File Generator, just as you would for a single-database file system. Give the Format file a name and quit FoxView, returning to FoxPro.

In FoxPro, set up your databases as you need them for this form, including indexes and relations. Add the Format file to the controlling database through the View Setup window, or by entering

SET FORMAT TO *fmt_filename*

in the Command window.

You know that when you change a record in the controlling database, the information from the related files also appears on your screen. But if you choose Change from the Record menu, all you see is a screen containing fields from the first database you used in FoxView (see fig. 7.9). What happened? Where did the rest of your form go?

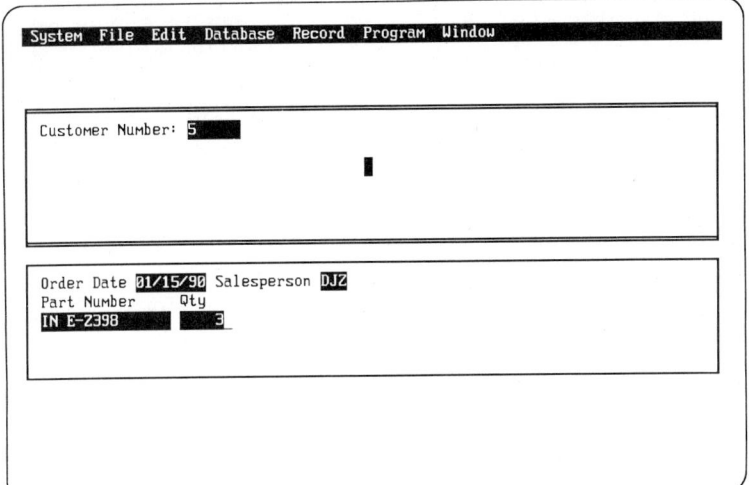

Fig. 7.9.
Using the format file with Change shows fields from only one database.

For some reason, the default form generator creates a form for only the first database file you loaded into FoxView, the one that was on Page 1 originally. It is, fortunately, a fairly simple task to create a new form generator that builds a form file for all databases.

In the process of doing so, you will learn some important information about how FoxView and FoxPro team up with a program called FoxCode to generate form files and complete applications.

Creating a Form Generator for Multiple Files

When you told FoxView to create a Format file from your screen design, it did not simply generate that format file directly from your screen. It actually called a program named FORM1 that read the FoxView table you created, and then FoxView processed the information in the table into a FoxPro Format file. If you want to see what this format file looks like, choose Open from the File menu, place an X in the All Files box and choose the Format file name you specified in FoxView. The Format file name will have an FMT extension (see fig. 7.10). Your Format file is a series of SAY statements with any PICTURE and RANGE clauses you may have specified. There also will be lines that determine the color of the fields (SET COLOR TO BU/N) and commands to create the boxes.

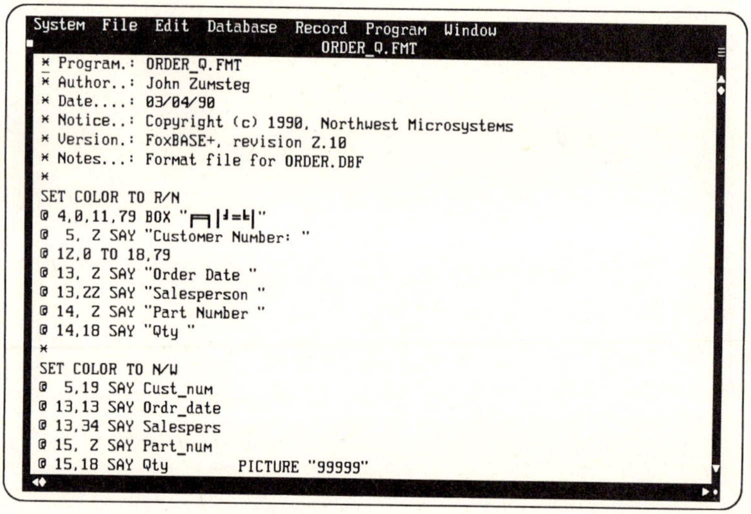

Fig. 7.10.
The Format file created in FoxView.

```
System  File  Edit  Database  Record  Program  Window
                          ORDER_Q.FMT
* Program.: ORDER_Q.FMT
* Author..: John Zumsteg
* Date....: 03/04/90
* Notice..: Copyright (c) 1990, Northwest Microsystems
* Version.: FoxBASE+, revision 2.10
* Notes...: Format file for ORDER.DBF
*
SET COLOR TO R/N
@ 4,0,11,79 BOX "▉|┤=┗|"
@  5, 2 SAY "Customer Number: "
@ 12,0 TO 18,79
@ 13, 2 SAY "Order Date "
@ 13,22 SAY "Salesperson "
@ 14, 2 SAY "Part Number "
@ 14,18 SAY "Qty "
*
SET COLOR TO N/W
@  5,19 SAY Cust_num
@ 13,13 SAY Ordr_date
@ 13,34 SAY Salespers
@ 15, 2 SAY Part_num
@ 15,18 SAY Qty        PICTURE "99999"
```

If the Form has changed FoxPro's screen colors, you can reset them by entering the following commands in the Command window:

SET COLOR TO
CLEAR

Understanding How FoxView and FoxCode Work Together

FoxView does not have a way of directly generating Format files or any other kinds of files. FoxView invokes a Template program, FORM1, to read the FoxView table and create an FMT file from it. If you had chosen FORM2, FoxView would have invoked a Template program named FORM2 to read the table and do different things with that information, resulting in a different output file. You can have any number of these Template files, each of them doing something totally different with the table you created in FoxView.

These Template files are in a language specific to FoxPro, called FoxCode. For now, you don't need to know the specifics of FoxCode or anything about writing programs in it. Just remember that a FoxCode program reads the FoxView table, digests it, and creates a FoxPro program file of some sort.

Unfortunately, the FORM1 template file you used to create your Format file is written in such a way that it processes only the first database it encounters in the FoxView table. Fortunately, it is quite easy to create a new FoxCode program that processes all the databases.

Modifying the Form File Generator

In this section, you modify several FoxCode template language files. You don't need to know anything about the FoxCode template language for this exercise, but if you want to learn more about FoxCode, refer to the FoxView-FoxCode FoxDoc manual.

To modify the FORM1 template file to handle multiple database forms, open the FORM1.GEN file by choosing Open from the File window and selecting Program. Open the directory \FOXPRO\TEMPLGEN, place an X in the All Files check box, and select FORM1.GEN. FoxPro displays that file in the Text Edit window. Immediately save this file with a different name, using the Save As option from the File menu. Save the file as FORMALL.GEN. Now you can edit the file to make the necessary minor changes. When you're finished, you have a new template file, which will appear as FORMALL on the FoxView template list. This new template will create format files that display data from multiple database files in FoxPro.

First, change the title, which is on the first line, from

```
<<title 'Format File Generator'>>
```

to

```
<<title 'Multiple File Format Generator'>>
```

Move through the FORMALL.GEN file to row 18, which contains the line

```
<<#include 'GENFLD.INC'#>>
```

Change GENFLD.INC to GENFLDAL.INC. Move down three lines and change the line that reads

```
<<#include 'GENFMT.INC'#>>
```

to

```
<<#include 'GENFMTAL.INC#>>
```

These lines should now look like those in figure 7.11. By changing these lines, you have instructed FoxCode to look for different include (INC) files when building the FORMALL template. Save the file and press Esc to quit.

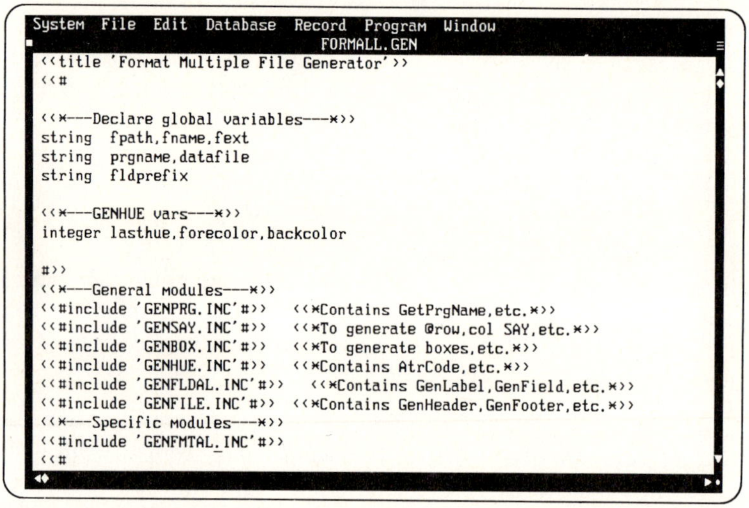

Fig. 7.11.
The modified
FORMALL.GEN
file.

```
  System  File  Edit  Database  Record  Program  Window
                              FORMALL.GEN
  <<title 'Format Multiple File Generator'>>
  <<#

  <<*---Declare global variables---*>>
  string  fpath,fname,fext
  string  prgname,datafile
  string  fldprefix

  <<*---GENHUE vars---*>>
  integer lasthue,forecolor,backcolor

  #>>
  <<*---General modules---*>>
  <<#include 'GENPRG.INC'#>>     <<*Contains GetPrgName,etc.*>>
  <<#include 'GENSAY.INC'#>>     <<*To generate @row,col SAY,etc.*>>
  <<#include 'GENBOX.INC'#>>     <<*To generate boxes,etc.*>>
  <<#include 'GENHUE.INC'#>>     <<*Contains AtrCode,etc.*>>
  <<#include 'GENFLDAL.INC'#>>   <<*Contains GenLabel,GenField,etc.*>>
  <<#include 'GENFILE.INC'#>>    <<*Contains GenHeader,GenFooter,etc.*>>
  <<*---Specific modules---*>>
  <<#include 'GENFMTAL.INC'#>>
  <<#
```

Because you have instructed FoxCode to look for the GENFMTAL.INC and GENFLDA.INC files, you must create them. First, open the GENFLD.INC file from the same directory (TEMPLGEN) and immediately save it as GENFLDAL.INC. Change the first line from

    <<*GENFLD.INC*>>

to

    <<*GENFLDAL.INC*>>

Move through the file until you see the function titled getFIELD. Continue moving through the file until you see the lines shown in figure 7.12.

You need to make only one change. In the line that reads

    if fldvals $ 'AM' <<* PRIMARY and MEMORY workareas *>>

delete the A in 'AM'.

Save the GENFLDAL.INC file and use the File Open menu to open GENFMT.INC. Immediately save the file as GENFMTAL.INC. Again, change the first line to reflect the new file name, from

    <<GENFMT.INC*>>

where *cust* is the name of your directory. In FoxPro, choose FoxView. Because you have already created your FoxView table, you can simply enter the command

LOAD *table_name*

where *table_name* is the name of the table you saved in FoxView. Figure 7.15 shows the FoxView screen as it loads the designed table.

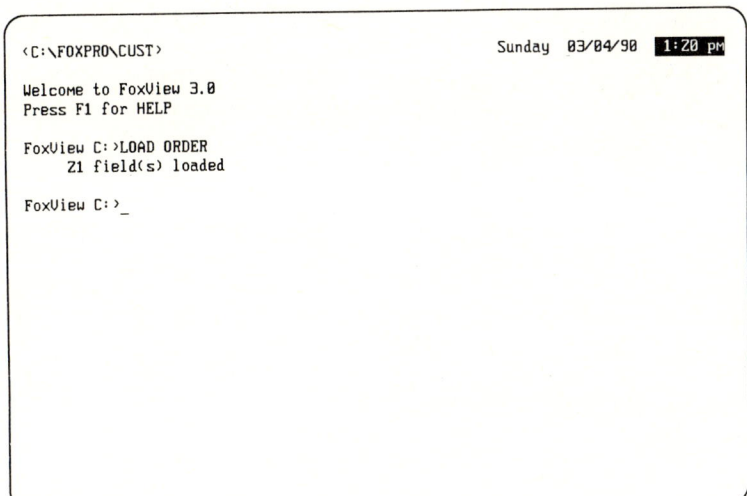

```
<C:\FOXPRO\CUST>                        Sunday  03/04/90  1:20 PM

Welcome to FoxView 3.0
Press F1 for HELP

FoxView C:>LOAD ORDER
       21 field(s) loaded

FoxView C:>_
```

*Fig. 7.15.
Loading the
saved FoxView
table ORDER.*

Now you can generate your new form. Press Esc to display the Gen menu Choose Select from, and you will see the Template screen. The FORMALL template is listed with the title Multiple File Format Generator. Choose FORMALL, give your format file a name (you can use the same name as you did before and overwrite the existing file), and let FoxView invoke your newly created template file. When it is finished, return to FoxPro, set up your databases, and choose Edit from the Record menu. The first record in the controlling database appears and, with it, all the information from the related records in the related databases (see fig. 7.16).

This has been a complicated process to create just one form. Actually, though, most of the work in this section created not one form, but a file that you can use every time you need to display data from different databases on the same screen. Now it's time to learn how to use the form.

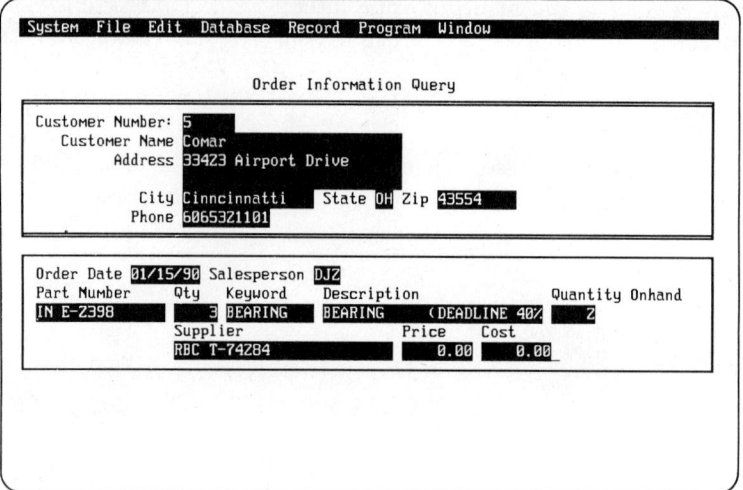

Fig. 7.16.
The multiple-file
format.

Using the Multiple File Form for Data Inquiries

Using a form designed from multiple files is not much different than using single-file forms. You do have to ensure that the current database is the controlling database in your relational setup, otherwise none of the relations will work and your form will display funny answers. In the example, the ORDER database is the controlling database, and the CUSTOMER and INVNTRY databases are controlled by relationships. Using the View window, set up your databases. If you have done this previously and saved the setup as a View file, open that file to bring the setup into FoxPro.

You now can set your format file either with the Format check box in the View Setup dialog, shown in figure 7.17, or by issuing the Command window command

    SET FORMAT TO *fmt_filename*

where *fmt_filename* is the name of the Format file you generated in Fox-View. Now, you can use the Record menu to access and view related records.

Using RANGE and VALID Clauses

A leading cause of database problems is bad data—the old "garbage in, garbage out" syndrome. You should use any method you can to ensure

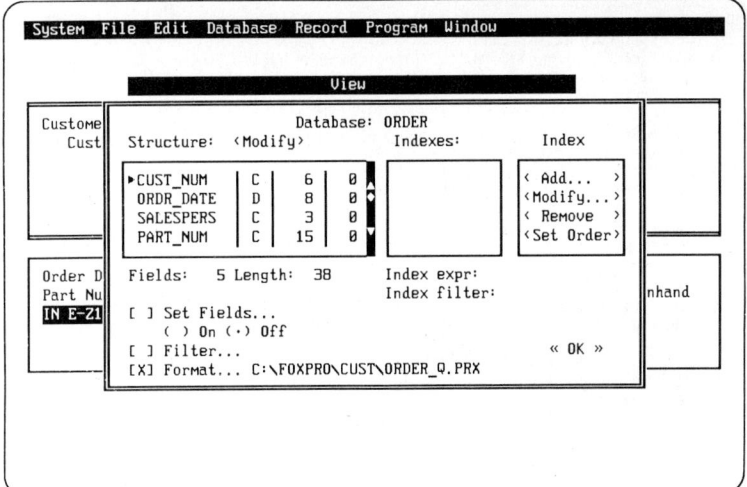

System File Edit Database Record Program Window

```
                               View
                    Database: ORDER
 Structure: <Modify>              Indexes:         Index
 ▶CUST_NUM    | C |   6 | 0                      < Add...   >
  ORDR_DATE   | D |   8 | 0                      <Modify...>
  SALESPERS   | C |   3 | 0                      < Remove   >
  PART_NUM    | C |  15 | 0                      <Set Order>

 Fields:   5 Length:  38      Index expr:
                              Index filter:
 [ ] Set Fields...
      ( ) On (·) Off
 [ ] Filter...                              « OK »
 [X] Format... C:\FOXPRO\CUST\ORDER_Q.PRX
```

Fig. 7.17.
The View Setup
dialog, with the
Format file
specified.

that the user of your database, whether it's you or others, cannot enter data that is inaccurate or invalid. FoxPro provides an excellent way to do this, allowing you to attach to a data-entry field a RANGE or VALID clause.

Using RANGE clauses

A RANGE clause defines the upper and lower limits that FoxPro will accept for a data entry field. You specify a RANGE clause when you are working with the form in FoxView (or you can add it to the Format file that FoxView creates). To add a RANGE clause to a field in FoxView, move to the Table View by pressing F10, then place the cursor in the RANGE column of the field. (On the initial Table View, RANGE cannot be seen; you must Tab right to make the Table View scroll the RANGE clause onto the screen.) Once the field is highlighted, enter the lower limit of the field, then the upper limit of the field, separated by a comma. Figure 7.18 shows the Table View of FoxView, with a RANGE specified for the field CREDIT. With this RANGE clause in place, FoxPro will not, during data entry, accept a value below 0 or above 5,000.

Using a VALID Clause To Check Data Entry

The VALID clause is a FoxPro expression that will be checked against the entered data. If the data passes the test, FoxPro accepts the field; if not, FoxPro rejects the data and puts a message on the screen. Using VALID clauses helps ensure the data is accurate before it gets to the database.

```
C:ORDER.DBF                                                           2:26 PM
    #.  Als  Field      Typ Wid Dec  Picture  Range  Valid  Init  Calc  User
    1.   A   BOXOBJECT   B   79   7  [       ][    ][    ][    ][    ][    ]
    2.   A   Cust_num    C    6      [       ][    ][    ][    ][    ][    ]
    3.   B   Cust_name   C   25      [       ][    ][    ][    ][    ][    ]
    4.   B   Addr_1      C   25      [       ][    ][    ][    ][    ][    ]
    5.   B   Addr_2      C   25      [       ][    ][    ][    ][    ][    ]
    6.   B   City        C   15      [       ][    ][    ][    ][    ][    ]
    7.   B   State       C    2      [       ][    ][    ][    ][    ][    ]
    8.   B   Zip         C    9      [       ][    ][    ][    ][    ][    ]
    9.   B   Phone       C   10      [       ][    ][    ][    ][    ][    ]
   10.   A   BOXOBJECT   B   79   6  [       ][    ][    ][    ][    ][    ]
   11.   A   Ordr_date   D    8      [       ][    ][    ][    ][    ][    ]
   12.   A   Salespers   C    3      [       ][    ][    ][    ][    ][    ]
   13.   A   Part_num    C   15      [       ][    ][    ][    ][    ][    ]
   14.   A   Qty         N    5      [       ][0,5000][    ][    ][    ][    ]
   15.   C   Keyword     C   10      [       ][    ][    ][    ][    ][    ]
   16.   C   Descr       C   25      [       ][    ][    ][    ][    ][    ]
   17.   C   Qty_onhnd   N    5      [       ][    ][    ][    ][    ][    ]
   18.   C   Supplier    C   25      [       ][    ][    ][    ][    ][    ]
   ───────────────────────────────────────────────────────────────────Ins
   0,5000█
          RANGE:  <lower exp>,<upper exp>; press F1 for Help
```

Fig. 7.18.
Adding RANGE limits to a field in FoxView.

Think of a VALID clause as half of an equation, with whatever the user has entered into the field as the other half, as follows:

DATA_ENTERED = the VALID expression

If both sides of the equation are equal, FoxPro accepts the entered data; if they are not equal, FoxPro will reject it. For example, if you have a character field named ZIP, and you only want the user to be able to enter the values "98080", "98081", or "98082", your equation would look like

ZIP = "98080" .OR. "98081" .OR. "98082"

A VALID clause equivalent of this expression would be

VALID("98080" .OR. "98081" .OR. "98082")

To enter this valid clause in the Table View in FoxView, move the highlight to the VALID column for the field ZIP. Enter

"98080" .OR. "98081" .OR. "98082"

Figure 7.19 shows the Table View with this VALID clause entered in the ZIP field.

When you generate the Format file for this screen, FoxView will automatically add the necessary VALID statement and parentheses. When this format file is used in FoxPro, then, the user will only be able to enter these three values; any others will cause FoxPro to place an Invalid Data Entry message on-screen and reject the input.

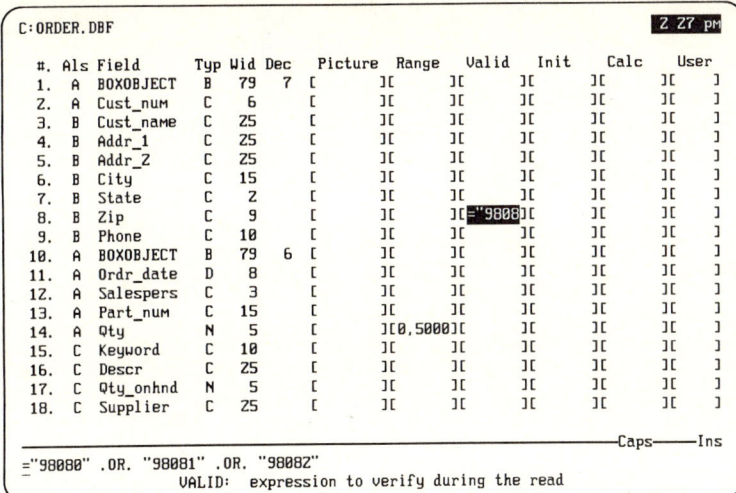

```
C:ORDER.DBF                                                    2 27 PM
  #. Als Field      Typ Wid Dec  Picture  Range  Valid  Init   Calc   User
  1.  A  BOXOBJECT   B   79   7 [       ][     ][     ][     ][     ][     ]
  2.  A  Cust_num    C    6     [       ][     ][     ][     ][     ][     ]
  3.  B  Cust_name   C   25     [       ][     ][     ][     ][     ][     ]
  4.  B  Addr_1      C   25     [       ][     ][     ][     ][     ][     ]
  5.  B  Addr_2      C   25     [       ][     ][     ][     ][     ][     ]
  6.  B  City        C   15     [       ][     ][     ][     ][     ][     ]
  7.  B  State       C    2     [       ][     ][     ][     ][     ][     ]
  8.  B  Zip         C    9     [       ][     ][ ="9808 ][     ][     ][     ]
  9.  B  Phone       C   10     [       ][     ][     ][     ][     ][     ]
 10.  A  BOXOBJECT   B   79   6 [       ][     ][     ][     ][     ][     ]
 11.  A  Ordr_date   D    8     [       ][     ][     ][     ][     ][     ]
 12.  A  Salespers   C    3     [       ][     ][     ][     ][     ][     ]
 13.  A  Part_num    C   15     [       ][     ][     ][     ][     ][     ]
 14.  A  Qty         N    5     [       ][0,5000][     ][     ][     ][     ]
 15.  C  Keyword     C   10     [       ][     ][     ][     ][     ][     ]
 16.  C  Descr       C   25     [       ][     ][     ][     ][     ][     ]
 17.  C  Qty_onhnd   N    5     [       ][     ][     ][     ][     ][     ]
 18.  C  Supplier    C   25     [       ][     ][     ][     ][     ][     ]
                                                         ─Caps────Ins
 ="98080" .OR. "98081" .OR. "98082"
        VALID:  expression to verify during the read
```

Fig. 7.19.
Adding a VALID clause to the ZIP field in FoxView.

Creating More Sophisticated VALID Clauses

There will be times when the test you want to make in a VALID clause is more complex than can be put in one FoxPro expression. For these occasions, you can create a User Defined Function (UDF). Remember, a VALID clause checked the data entered into a field against an expression. If that test returned a TRUE, meaning the entered data met the test, FoxPro accepted the data. A UDF is a mini-FoxPro program which will take the value entered into the data field, process it in some way, and return to the VALID clause a TRUE or FALSE. If the return is TRUE, the VALID clause accepts the data, otherwise it rejects it. This allows you to create some extremely sophisticated tests for your data.

You create a UDF as a FoxPro .PRG program file by choosing New from the File menu and selecting ( ) Program from the radio buttons in the New dialog. A text window opens and you enter your UDF. When you're done, save it using the Save option of the File menu, giving it a name. Then you can add the UDF to the VALID column of the field in FoxView. Sound complicated? It isn't really; follow along as we create a simple UDF that accomplishes the same ZIP test as above.

1. In FoxView's Table view, in the VALID column of the field ZIP, enter

   ZIP_TEST()

   Generate the Format file as usual and return to FoxPro. The format file created has a VALID clause in it for ZIP, so you must create the UDF named ZIP_TEST.PRG.

2. Choose New from the File menu, select Program and OK. A text window opens. Enter the following program text into the window:

```
FUNCTION ZIP_TEST
PARAMETER ZIP
IF (ZIP = "98080") .OR. (ZIP = "98081" .OR. (ZIP = "98082")
   RETURN .F.
ELSE
   RETURN .T.
ENDIF
```

The first line tells FoxPro this is a function named ZIP_TEST. The second line accepts the value from the data-entry field, which will be sent to the function by the VALID clause. That value is assigned to the memory variable ZIP for testing.

If the value equals 98080, 98081, or 98082, the function returns a .T. to the VALID clause, which is FoxPro's shorthand for true. If the data entry value is not one of these three, the function returns an .F., for false.

3. Save this program using the Save option of the File menu, naming it ZIP_TEST. You now have a valid user-defined function. When you use a format file that has this UDF in a VALID clause, FoxPro will take a value for the ZIP field, send it to this UDF and wait for the UDF to "do its thing." When the UDF tests the value and returns a true or false to the VALID clause, FoxPro acts accordingly—rejecting the data with an error message if the VALID clause receives a false, and accepting it if it receives a true.

Testing Relational Values with a User-Defined Function

When entering data into a database that is related to another, it's important that the data in the relational fields (the fields that tie this database to a related one) is accurate. If, for instance, two databases are related on a CUST_NUM field, you want to make sure that the value entered into the CUST_NUM field of the controlled database actually exists in a record in the controlling database. You don't want to enter CUST_NUM "90021" if there is no 90021 in the controlling database. A UDF can accomplish that test.

In pseudo-English, the following is a UDF to accomplish that. The CUST_NUM entered into the data entry field will be passed as the PARAMETER NUM:

FUNCTION CHK_NUM
PARAMETER NUM

move to the controlling database (it must be opened already)
seek on NUM (the value entered)
move back to the original database
if the seek was successful (the number was found)
return a true to the VALID clause
else
return a false to the VALID clause

This UDF would ensure that the user couldn't enter a CUST_NUM value in the controlled database of two related databases unless the CUST_NUM value already existed in the controlling database.

User-Defined Functions can be simple or quite complex. They are an advanced use of FoxPro, but one which can make life much easier by making sure the data entered is valid.

Using the Record Menu To Find Records

Pick Choose from the Record menu (or type *edit* in the Command window) to display the Form with the information from all three databases shown. The relationships that emanate from the controlling database (ORDER in this example) control which records are presented in the controlled databases. If you set all the GETs to SAYs in your form design, you will be unable to change any information. You can, however, use the options offered in the Record menu to access any record in the controlled database and its related databases.

If you use the Seek or Locate options to find specific records, FoxPro does not automatically display them on your form. Seek and Locate only position the database pointer to the correct record. You must select Change from the Record Menu, or Edit in the Command window to activate the form with the information on it.

Once you have selected the Change (or Edit from the Command window) command, you can use the PgUp and PgDn keys to move forward and backward through the database. Again, you move through the controlling database; the related databases follow automatically. When you are finished looking at a data screen, pressing Escape returns control to FoxPro. The FoxPro menu bar is now usable again.

In a large database, you will find yourself using Seek frequently as you look for specific records based on the index expression of that database. With a little bit of FoxPro "twiddling," you can create a file that eases the task.

Creating a Keyed Entry Viewing Program

In working with a multiple-file form, it is easier to find records if you can enter the key fields of the record in the controlling database that you would like to display and have FoxPro automatically do the Seek and Edit to present the field. A fairly simple way to do this is to change the FMT format file to a PRG program file, make a few additions, and then execute the program by choosing Do from the Program menu.

The process you want FoxPro to follow in this program file is as follows:

1. Place the format on the screen without data.

2. Get the key field values from the user.

3. If the user doesn't want to see more, exit from the loop.

4. Seek to find the record with input key field values.

5. Place the values on the screen.

6. Return to the start for another request from the user.

The FMT format file already contains all the SAYs needed, with proper location and PICTURE clauses for formatting. You can edit that file to include the user input of key fields, the test to see if it's time to exit the loop, and the loop itself. By saving the file as a PRG program file, you can execute it with the Do option, rather than using it as a FMT file, which allows no control statements.

Changing the FMT File to a PRG File

First, use the File Open menu, placing an X in the All Files check box to see all FMT and PRG files. Find and open the FMT file you created in FoxView. Use the File Save menu to save it as a PRG file. You must specify the PRG extension or FoxPro will save the file with the FMT extension it was opened with. Figure 7.20 shows the example FMT file being saved as a PRG file.

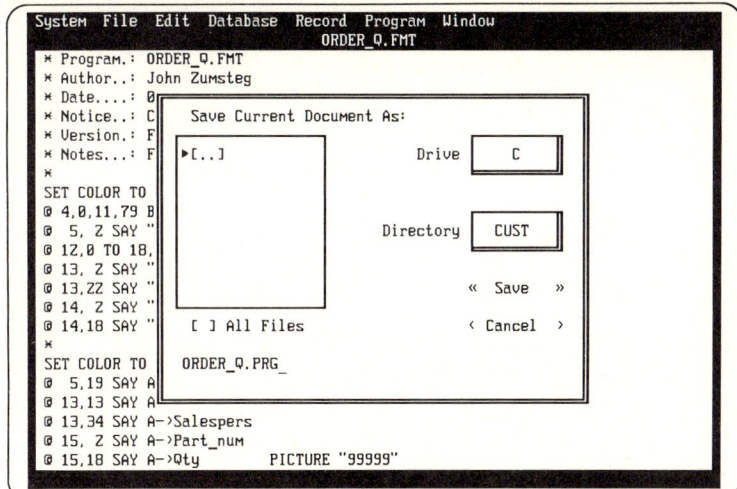

Fig. 7.20.
Saving
ORDER_Q.FMT as
ORDER_Q.PRG.

Adding Memory Variable GETs

The next step is to use the Text editor to add the lines necessary to initialize and read memory variables for the keyed fields of the controlling database. This process can be described as follows:

1. Initialize a memory variable for each key field.

2. GET each memory variable at the same location as the SAY of the form.

3. READ the memory variables.

4. If the memory variables are blank, exit from the routine.

5. Seek on the key fields.

6. SAY all the fields of the controlled and controlling databases.

This procedure is not difficult. In the example, only one key field is in the controlling index, order_num. The lines to insert to read this key field and seek on it are as follows:

```
m_ORD_NUM = "         "      && initialize a memory var to
                                blanks
@ nn, nn GET m_CUST_NUM      && create a GET to get the key
                                field memory variable value
READ                         && read a value into the
                                mem var
IF m_CUST_NUM = "        "    && if nothing was entered
RETURN                       && go back to FoxPro
SEEK m_CUST_NUM              && seek on the key field
```

These lines should go before the SAYs of the data fields in the PRG file. If your key field is made of a FoxPro expression, you must insert another line after the READ and before the SEEK that creates that expression. If, for example, your controlling database was indexed on FIELD1 + FIELD2, the read routine would look like the following:

```
m_FIELD1 = "        "
m_FIELD2 = "        "
@ 1, 0 GET m_FIELD1                    && GETs on screen
@ 2, 0 GET m_FIELD2
READ                                   && read all three GETs
m_key = m_FIELD1 + m_FIELD2
IF m_key = "                    "      && nothing entered
RETURN                                 && back to FoxPro
SEEK m_key
```

Figure 7.21 shows the PRG file, with these lines inserted. The multiple SAYs have been omitted to save room.

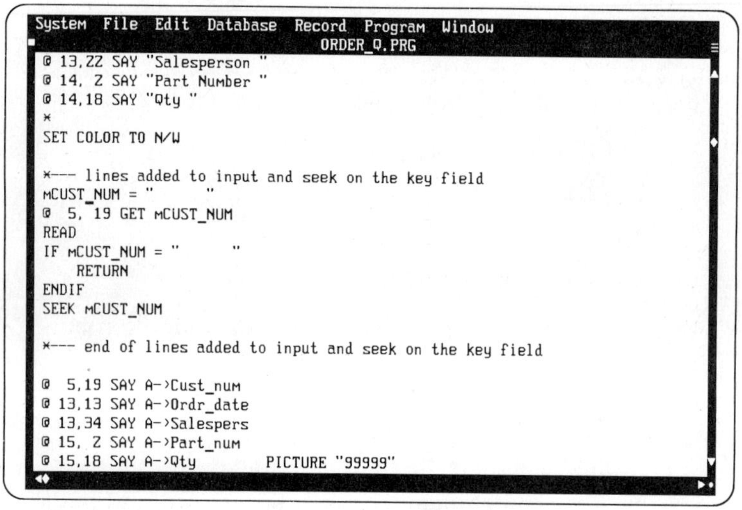

Fig. 7.21.
Lines added to the .PRG file to input and seek on key field values.

```
System  File  Edit  Database  Record  Program  Window
                            ORDER_Q.PRG
@ 13,22 SAY "Salesperson "
@ 14, 2 SAY "Part Number "
@ 14,18 SAY "Qty "
*
SET COLOR TO N/W

*--- lines added to input and seek on the key field
mCUST_NUM = "        "
@ 5, 19 GET mCUST_NUM
READ
IF mCUST_NUM = "        "
    RETURN
ENDIF
SEEK mCUST_NUM

*--- end of lines added to input and seek on the key field

@  5,19 SAY A->Cust_num
@ 13,13 SAY A->Ordr_date
@ 13,34 SAY A->Salespers
@ 15, 2 SAY A->Part_num
@ 15,18 SAY A->Qty          PICTURE "99999"
```

Remember that your view must be set up with the controlling database indexed on the proper extension (in this example, the controlling index, ORDER, is indexed on CUST_NUM). The seek will find the first record that has the key field (CUST_NUM) equal to the value entered. If there is none, all screen fields will be blank.

Your PRG program now has the capability to read from the screen the fields you want to seek on, do that seek, and present the data. Save the

PRG file and try running it. Choose Do from the Program menu and select the newly created file. Assuming that your database files are set up correctly, you are presented with a form that asks for input for the key field. When you enter a value and press Enter, the program continues by seeking on the value and placing the found record on-screen, along with information from related databases. Figures 7.22 through 7.24 show a form awaiting key field input, the entered input, and the results.

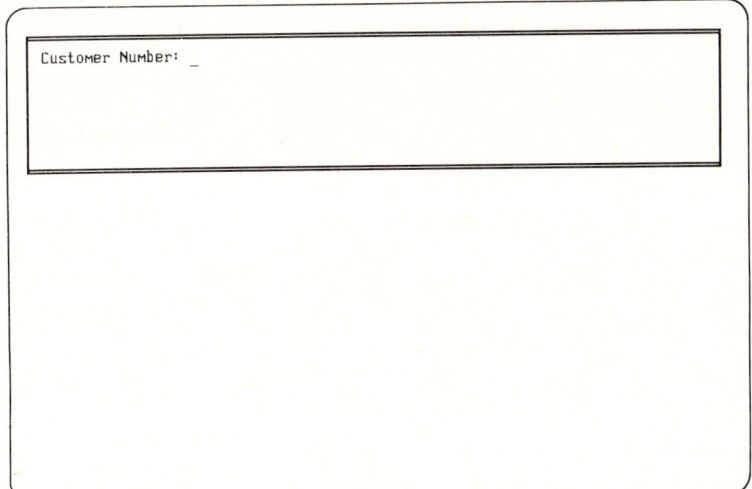

Fig. 7.22.
The form waiting for entry of the key field value.

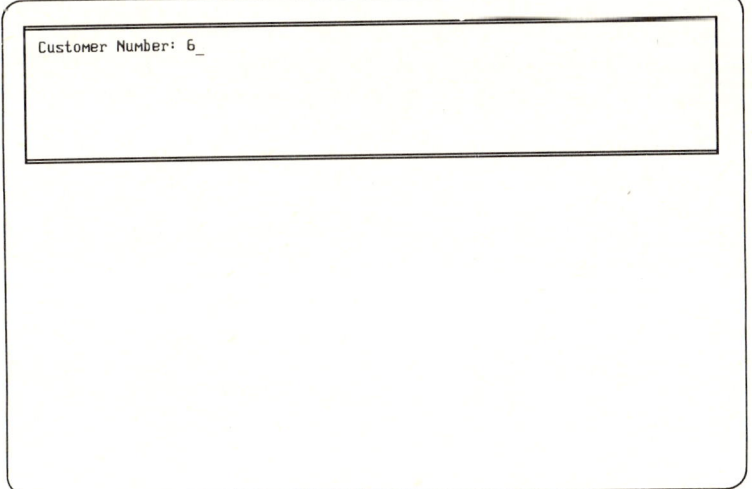

Fig. 7.23.
Entering a CUST_NUM value to find.

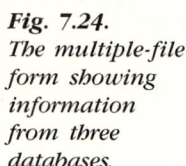

Fig. 7.24.
The multiple-file
form showing
information
from three
databases.

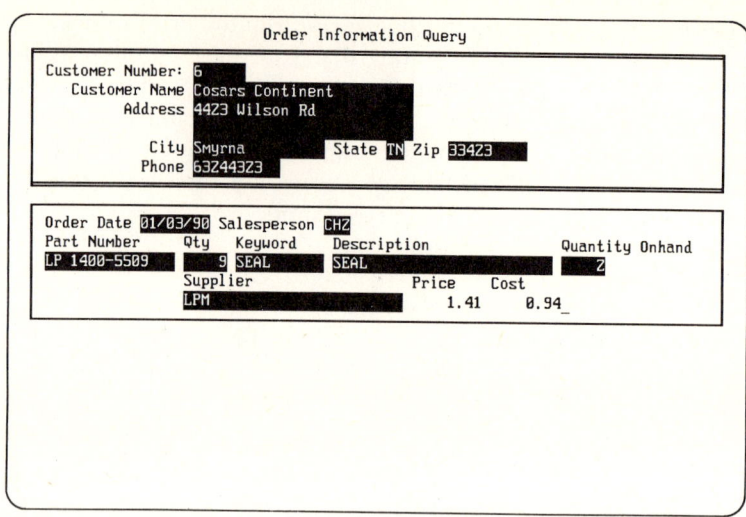

Adding a DO WHILE..ENDDO Loop

When FoxPro presents the correct data, it returns to the Command window for your next command. With just another little change, you can cause your program to loop until you decide to stop. Again, open the PRG file you created. From the Command window, you can enter

MODIFY COMMAND *prg_filename*

to open the file for editing.

Go to the line just above the lines you entered before, in which you initialize the memory variables. Add the command

DO WHILE .T.

Now go to the bottom of the file and, just above the EOF: ORDERQ.FMT statement (which is actually superfluous and can be deleted), add the line

ENDDO

FoxPro will repeat every statement between the DO WHILE .T. and the ENDDO endlessly. The only way to get out of this loop is through the test after the READ statement; if nothing was entered in the GET key field memory variable, your program returns from that test and you are returned to FoxPro.

Adding a WAIT Statement

Because FoxPro loops quickly through the SAYs, returns to the DO
WHILE .T. beginning of the loop, and asks for another input, you will
never see the key value. It will always be blanked out by the next request.
To enable you to look at the entire data record—key field and all—place
commands that cause FoxPro to pause at the end of the SAYs. The best
way to do that is with the following lines above the ENDDO statement
added above the end of the program:

```
SET CONSOLE OFF    && you will not see anything
WAIT               && until you press a key
SET CONSOLE ON     && back to normal
```

Changing the CONSOLE state kills the Press any key to continue message
that WAIT usually issues. If you want to see that message, leave out the
SET CONSOLE commands.

Now your program is complete. The following listing shows what it
should look like. This simple program forms the basis for many data-entry
and query screens. Once you understand this process of changing a FMT
format file to a PRG program file, you will find unlimited ways to use this
knowledge. You could, for instance, eliminate the user input and have
another program call this one, passing the key value to seek.

```
* Program.: ORDER_Q.FMT
* Author..: John Zumsteg
* Date....: 03/04/90
* Notice..: Copyright (c) 1990, Northwest Microsystems
* Version.: FoxBASE+, revision 2.10
* Notes...: Format file for ORDER.DBF
*
SET COLOR TO R/N
@ 4,0,11,79 BOX "UM83>MT3"
@ 5, 2 SAY "Customer Number: "
*-- Lines added to input and seek on the key field

DO WHILE .T.
    mCUST_NUM = "         "
    @ 5, 19 GET mCUST_NUM
    READ
    IF mCUST_NUM = "         "
        RETURN
    ENDIF
    SEEK mCUST_NUM
```

```
@ 12,0 TO 18,79
@ 13, 2 SAY "Order Date "
@ 13,22 SAY "Salesperson "
@ 14, 2 SAY "Part Number "
@ 14,18 SAY "Qty "
*
SET COLOR TO N/W

*-- end of lines added to input and seek on the key field

@  5,19 SAY A->Cust_num
@ 13,13 SAY A->Ordr_date
@ 13,34 SAY A->Salespers
@ 15, 2 SAY A->Part_num
@ 15,18 SAY A->Qty          PICTURE "99999"
SET COLOR TO R/N
@  6, 5 SAY "Customer Name "
@  7,11 SAY "Address "
@  8,15 SAY "    "
@  9,14 SAY "City "
@  9,35 SAY "State "
@  9,44 SAY "Zip "
@ 10,13 SAY "Phone "
*
SET COLOR TO N/W
@  6,19 SAY B->Cust_name
@  7,19 SAY B->Addr_1
@  8,19 SAY B->Addr_2
@  9,19 SAY B->City
@  9,41 SAY B->State
@  9,48 SAY B->Zip
@ 10,19 SAY B->Phone
SET COLOR TO R/N
@ 14,24 SAY "Keyword    "
@ 14,35 SAY "Description"
@ 14,61 SAY "Quantity Onhand "
@ 16,18 SAY "Supplier  "
@ 16,44 SAY "Price     "
@  3,27 SAY "Order Information Query "
@ 16,53 SAY "Cost      "
*
SET COLOR TO N/W
@ 15,24 SAY C->Keyword
@ 15,35 SAY C->Descr
```

```
@ 15,61 SAY C->Qty_onhnd  PICTURE "99999"
@ 17,18 SAY C->Supplier
@ 17,44 SAY C->Price      PICTURE "99999.99"
@ 17,53 SAY C->Cost PICTURE "99999.99"

SET CONSOLE OFF
WAIT
SET CONSOLE ON

ENDDO
*
* EOF: ORDER_Q.PRG
```

Using the Keyed Form Program

Using this PRG file is simple. Again, make sure that your databases are set up properly. Choose DO from the Program menu. You should close all open windows and resize the Command window to be out of the way, because this program file will appear on the FoxPro screen, which is below all other windows. Other windows on the screen will obscure the data screen your program will display.

Using The Form Program
for Data Entry

You also can use your form for editing data in any of the databases. This takes just a few minor changes. First, decide which fields you want to be edited and change the SAYs of those fields to GETs. Include any appropriate RANGE parameters or PICTURE formats. Then, add a second READ at the end of all the SAY and GET statements, replacing the SET CONSOLE OFF, WAIT, and SET CONSOLE ON statements. Figure 7.25 shows where this second READ is added.

Now, after FoxPro has gotten the key field value, performed a seek on it, and displayed the data, the second READ activates the GETs you have just created. You will be able to enter data into those fields you have designated as editable by the GET statements.

A word of caution: I strongly recommend that you not allow a change to the fields in any database that forms part of the relation between the database. You should think of the record in the controlling database and

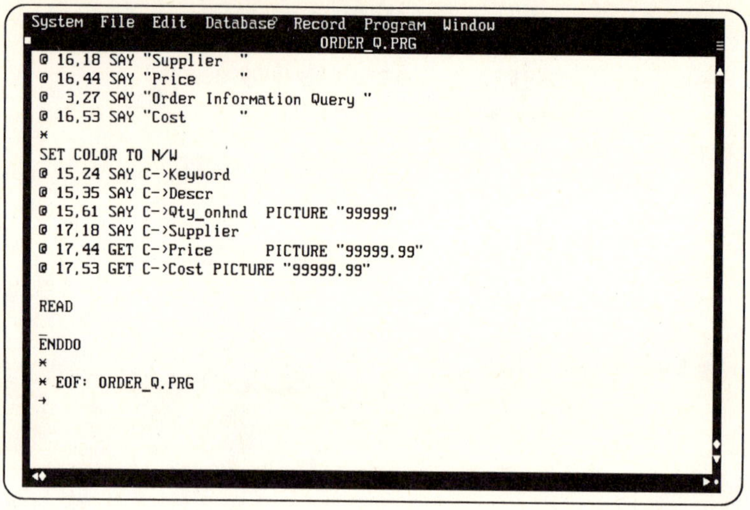

Fig. 7.25.
Adding a second
READ to edit
field data.

```
 System  File  Edit  Database  Record  Program  Window
                         ORDER_Q.PRG
@ 16,18 SAY "Supplier  "
@ 16,44 SAY "Price     "
@  3,27 SAY "Order Information Query "
@ 16,53 SAY "Cost      "
*
SET COLOR TO N/W
@ 15,24 SAY C->Keyword
@ 15,35 SAY C->Descr
@ 15,61 SAY C->Qty_onhnd  PICTURE "99999"
@ 17,18 SAY C->Supplier
@ 17,44 GET C->Price       PICTURE "99999.99"
@ 17,53 GET C->Cost PICTURE "99999.99"

READ

ENDDO
*
* EOF: ORDER_Q.PRG
→
```

those linked to it by the relationships as a unit. If you change something that breaks up that unit, you may end up with records in the controlling database that are not linked to records in the controlled databases or vice versa. In any case, the integrity of the databases' relations will be questionable.

Chapter Summary

This chapter introduced programming, user-defined functions, and Template programs. The examples presented in this chapter will make your FoxPro systems far more reliable and easier to use.

If you master these concepts and realize the potential that FoxPro presents through programming, user-defined functions, and Template programs, you can use these tools to create sophisticated and elegant FoxPro systems that cannot be created in other database systems without huge amounts of programming.

Data entry and inquiry into multiple-database FoxPro systems can be as simple as single-database systems. But with a bit more work and the knowledge of FoxPro that you learned in this chapter, you can make multiple-database FoxPro systems do just what you want them to do, quickly and elegantly.

FoxPro Tips, Tricks, and Techniques

So far, you have absorbed a great deal of information about using Fox-Pro, and you're probably getting a little weary of having new concepts and techniques thrown at you. This chapter will be more enjoyable. This is a potpourri chapter that presents tips and tricks that make FoxPro easier and more fun to use.

A truth about computer programs is that as a program's capabilities increase, its difficulty of use also increases. FoxPro is no exception; although it is far easier to use than its competitors, maneuvering around various windows and dialogs can become tiresome. In this chapter you learn how to set up MS-DOS subdirectories to organize your FoxPro databases and create batch files to ensure that you can access FoxPro from the right directories. You also learn how to use Views to ease the task of setting up different databases and index files.

You learn about two techniques to speed working in FoxPro: keyboard shortcuts and keyboard macros. You are introduced to using the Command window to enter commands, often a faster way to do something than choosing menus and working through dialogs. Finally, you receive a brief introduction to FoxPro programming, which you can use to automate many tasks. In all, this chapter's objective is to ease some of the burden of working with FoxPro and let you take the first steps toward being a FoxPro power user.

Using a Mouse

Fox Software maintains that using a mouse instead of the keyboard is the quickest way of speeding up FoxPro. The mouse makes opening, viewing, sizing, and moving windows unbelievably quick and easy. Working in dialogs with the keyboard requires many key presses to get to the right box and make a selection. With the mouse, it's a simple point-and-click operation. As you learn more about FoxPro, you will find yourself mixing mouse movements and selections with keyboard short-cuts, but even for advanced FoxPro users, the mouse speeds all operations.

With FoxPro comes an offer to purchase an excellent mouse at low cost; if you don't have a mouse, I urge you to take Fox Software up on their offer.

Using Subdirectories and Batch Files

If you know anything about MS-DOS, you're aware of the DOS file structure, and how it stores the program and data files. If you're unfamiliar with this system, this section will serve as a brief introduction, because that file structure really can help or hinder your use of FoxPro. If you want to learn more about MS-DOS and its file directory structure, there are many excellent books on that subject. For now, though, you need to know some basics.

Before MS-DOS 2.0, PC computers stored all their files in one group on the disk. MS-DOS borrowed from the UNIX philosophy and allowed the creation of directories and subdirectories. If, for example, you had files related to an accounting system, you could create a subdirectory named ACCTING and put the program files there. Within ACCTING, you could create a subdirectory for the general ledger, name it GL, and place the general ledger files in it. Then you could create subdirectory for accounts payable and put AP files there, and so forth. Figure 8.1 shows how such a directory structure could be created and used.

Along with directories and subdirectories, you need to understand the concept of the *current directory*. You can move around in the directories, working from different ones, using the MS-DOS CD (Change Directory) command. If you want to work from your ACCTING subdirectory, for example, you issue the DOS command

    CD \ACCTING

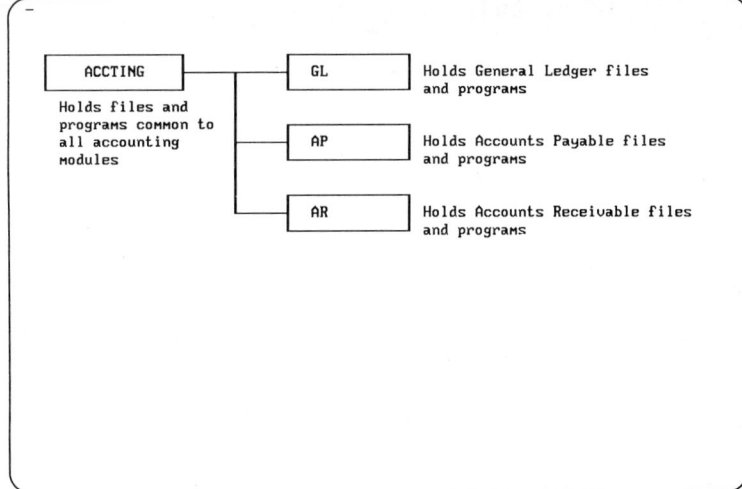

Fig. 8.1.
*An MS-DOS file
directory
structure.*

to move to that subdirectory. After changing to a directory, any commands you issue must refer to programs in that directory, because that is
the current directory.

The last concept to understand is *paths*. You may want DOS to run a program that isn't in the current directory. You can give DOS a path to follow
as it looks for a program. Again, using the accounting example, if you are
in the GL directory and want to run the ACCT program, which is in the
ACCTING directory, you can issue the DOS command

PATH = \ACCTING

Now when you ask DOS to run a program, it first looks in the current
directory (GL). If the program is not there, it starts down the path, looking in each directory named in the path for the program you have asked
for. For example, if your path is set by

PATH = \FOXPRO;\GL;\ACCTING

and you enter the command

FRAMMIS

which tells DOS you want to execute a program named FRAMMIS, DOS
will look for that program in the current directory first. Then if FRAMMIS
is not found there, DOS looks for it in \FOXPRO, \GL, and \ACCTING.
Only if FRAMMIS is not found in any of these directories will DOS issue
the bad command or filename error.

Directories, paths, and batch files can help you organize your FoxPro
applications.

Using Different Subdirectories

When you installed FoxPro, the installation program created a directory in which to put FoxPro (if you used the default, this directory is called C:\FOXPRO on a hard drive) and a number of subdirectories to store the demonstration program, the tutorial, and the template files. Figure 8.2 shows the directory structure created during installation.

Fig. 8.2.
The FoxPro directory structure, created during FoxPro installation.

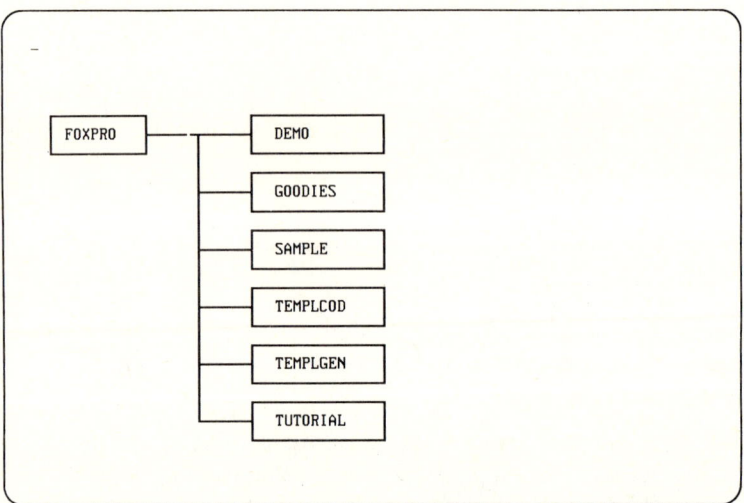

If you have created a FoxPro application, the many database (DBF), index (IDX), report (RPT), and form (FRM or FRX) files are in the same directory as the FoxPro program files. This method works for one application, but if you add a second and a third, things begin to get difficult to manage in that directory. Figuring out which files belong to the application you're working with is difficult. To solve this problem, you can create a subdirectory for each FoxPro application and keep each application's files in its own subdirectory.

A FoxPro application is a complete set of database files, indexes, forms, and reports that form a stand-alone system. For example, you might have an application that tracks customers and contacts, such as the example quick start applications. You also might have a FoxPro accounting application, an inventory application, or other applications, none of which share database files. For each of these applications, you can create a subdirectory and run FoxPro from there. FoxPro then works only with the files and programs in that subdirectory.

Figure 8.3 shows an example of a FoxPro set up that I use. Each of the applications is completely separate. When I run FoxPro from the application subdirectory, FoxPro "knows" about only the files in that directory. As a result, when I open a dialog that gives me a scrollable list of files, I see only the files applicable to the application with which I'm working. I also removed the directories \FOXPRO\SAMPLES, \FOXPRO\FOXVDEMO, and \FOXPRO\TUTORIAL.

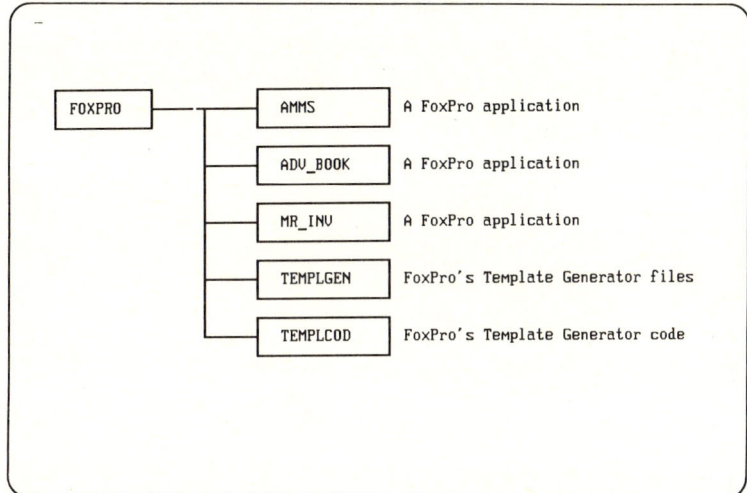

Fig. 8.3.
An example of FoxPro applications in separate directories.

To create subdirectories for FoxPro applications, use the MS-DOS MD (Make Directory) command. Move to the FoxPro directory by entering

    CD \FOXPRO

Then enter

    MD *app1*

where *app1* is the name of the application directory you want to create. MS-DOS directory names have the same rules as MS-DOS file names: you can use up to eight characters or numbers, with no spaces. Directories do not have an MS-DOS file extension.

You can change the current directory while in FoxPro. This enables you to work with different applications without having to exit FoxPro and change the current directory with the MS-DOS CD command. Changing the path tells FoxPro where to look for files when listing scrollable file lists, or when trying to open views that contain file names.

To change the Path in FoxPro, choose Files from the View window. The View Files dialog is shown in figure 8.4. You can change the default drive by selecting the Default Drive box, and you change the path by typing an *X* in the Path check box or by pressing P. You will see the Enter Path Name dialog, shown in figure 8.5. In this dialog, you select the path you want FoxPro to use by highlighting the subdirectory you want and choosing `Select`.

Fig. 8.4.
The View Files dialog, used to change the path FoxPro will use.

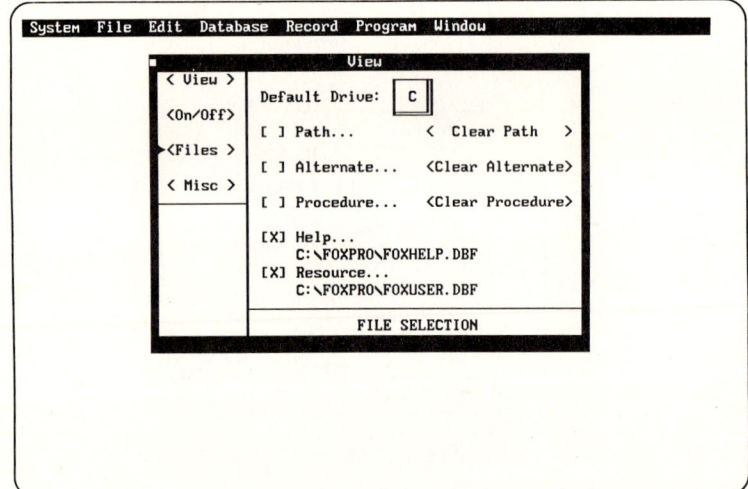

Fig. 8.5.
The Enter Path Name dialog.

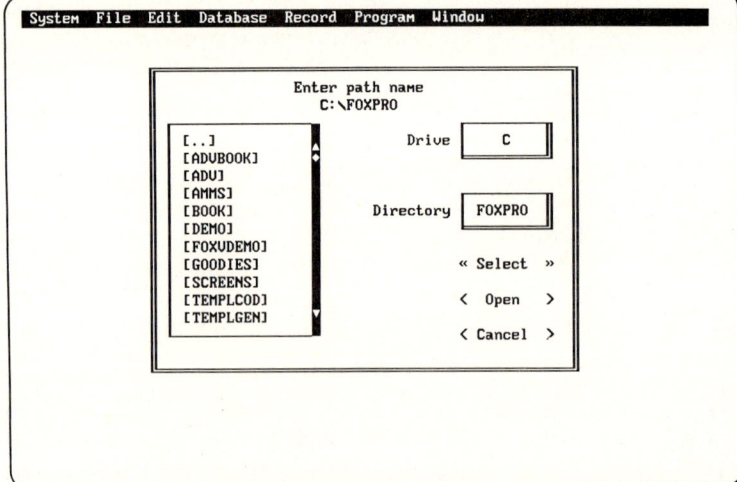

In the scrollable list, you see only subdirectories, which are delimited by square brackets [directory]. The [..] entry, which is always the first entry in the scrollable list, represents a subdirectory's *parent directory*. If, for example, you are in the directory C:\FOXPRO\AMMS and you want to see the subdirectories in the C:\FOXPRO directory, you would choose [..], and FoxPro would show the list of subdirectories in C:\FOXPRO. You can always tell where you are in the directory structure because Fox-Pro lists the directory you have chosen just below the Enter path name line at the top of the window.

You can put any number of directories in the path. If your path is

C:\FOXPRO\AMMS;C:\FOXPRO\ADV

FoxPro will look for needed files in the AMMS subdirectory first, then the ADV subdirectory, issuing an error message only if the needed file is not found in either one. Be cautious with long paths, though, because they can get slow and complicated with many directories and subdirectories. If you set up your subdirectories well, you seldom will need to set long paths in FoxPro.

Eliminating Subdirectory Errors

When you set up the FoxPro directory and subdirectory structures, you can use MS-DOS batch files to ease the chore of setting the path correctly and moving to the right current directory before you start FoxPro. A *batch file* is a file with a series of MS-DOS commands strung together. When you enter the name of the file at the DOS command prompt, DOS reads the files and executes the commands in order. A nice use of a batch file is to move to a directory, set a path, and execute a program. I have a batch file named AMMS.BAT, for example, that contains the following commands:

```
PATH=C:\FOXPRO;C:\DOS;C:\UTILS;C:\BAT;C:\
CD \FOXPRO\AMMS
FOXPRO
```

The first line of this batch file sets the path command, ensuring that Fox-Pro can be run from any subdirectory. The second line changes to the \FOXPRO\AMMS directory, which contains the database, index, report, and form files for a specific application. The last line invokes FoxPro.

Creating a batch file is simple. If your computer has a word processor or text editing program, use it to create the file. If not, you can start FoxPro and issue the command

MODIFY COMMAND C:*filename.bat*

to display the FoxPro text editor and enable you to create the batch files. Assuming that you're working from a hard drive defined as the C: drive, this command creates the batch file in the root directory, from which you can execute the file as you start up your computer.

Although there are many philosophies on hard drive organization, figure 8.6 shows how I set up mine. I'm comfortable with this organization and you may find it an excellent starting point.

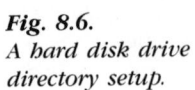

Fig. 8.6.
A hard disk drive
directory setup.

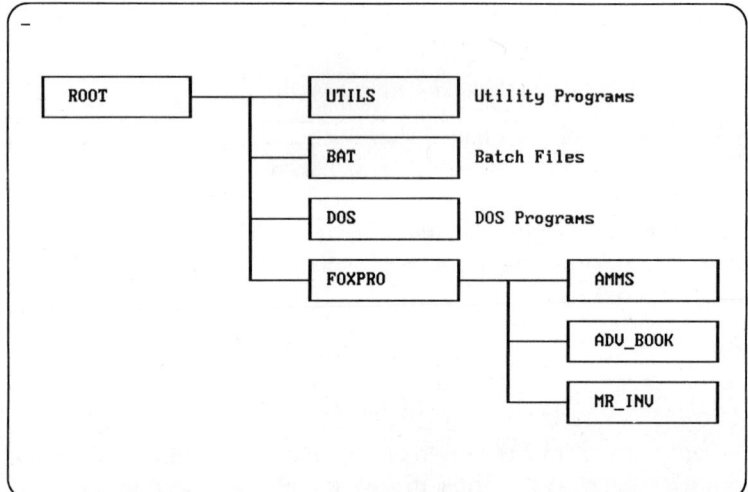

Customizing FoxPro with CONFIG.FP

As you use FoxPro more and more, you will find that you want certain settings to be different from FoxPro's defaults. For instance, I dislike having FoxPro beep at me when I have filled a field, and I prefer my FoxPro systems to require pressing the Enter key to leave a field. FoxPro gives you the capability to customize many things through a file named CONFIG.FP.

The CONFIG.FP (Configuration.FoxPro) file can contain startup defaults for many of the SET commands. These settings include changing the actions of the function keys, different color settings, and the initial View for FoxPro to use, among other things. When you start FoxPro, it looks for a CONFIG.FP file in the current directory. If none exists there, FoxPro looks for the file in the directory in which the FoxPro program itself resides. If none exists, FoxPro uses the default settings.

Because FoxPro searches the current directory first, you can have a different CONFIG.FP file for each FoxPro system you create, as long as you keep each system in a separate subdirectory. You also can have a custom CONFIG.FP in your FoxPro directory for times when you don't need a system-specific one.

Creating a CONFIG.FP file is simple. Invoke FoxPro in the normal way, then create the CONFIG.FP file either from the File Open menu, choosing the Program file type, or from the command line, with the command MODIFY COMMAND CONFIG.FP. FoxPro opens the text editor (see fig. 8.7), which you use to create the CONFIG.FP file. When you're finished, press Ctrl-End, or Ctrl-W to save and close the Text Editor window, naming the file as you go.

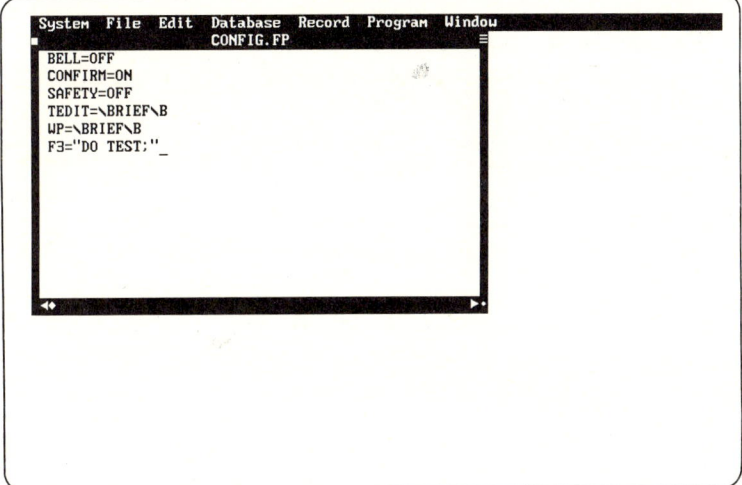

Fig. 8.7.
Entering a
CONFIG.FP file in
the text editing
window.

Following is a list of commands you can put into a CONFIG.FP file, which I think are most helpful. The FoxPro manual has a more detailed description of the many things you can do with this customizing tool. Most of these commands are the equivalent of FoxPro SET commands; in the CONFIG.FP file the SET is omitted. In the following commands, the setting that FoxPro uses as a default is shown in italic.

❏ AUTOSAVE *OFF*/ON—AUTOSAVE tells FoxPro when to save database changes to the disk. If this is set to OFF, FoxPro will saves changes when you close a data-entry or edit window or if you wait five minutes without doing anything. If you set AUTOSAVE to ON, FoxPro saves the changes each time a READ is executed (each time you're finished entering or editing). AUTOSAVE ON is a bit slower, because FoxPro writes the data to the disk more often, but it is safer—you run less risk of losing data that you have entered should the computer's power fail.

❏ BELL *ON*/OFF—This command sets the beeper on or off for error conditions or when an input field is filled. I dislike FoxPro beeping at me, so I turn it off.

❏ CLOCK ON/*OFF*—The CLOCK command turns on or off a clock in the upper right corner of the screen.

❏ CONFIRM ON/*OFF*—If CONFIRM is ON, a FoxPro user must press the Enter key to exit a data-entry field. If CONFIRM is OFF, the cursor will move to the next field when the current one is full. I set CONFIRM ON, which makes data-entry consistent; an Enter is always required. Otherwise, sometimes you will have to press Enter (when you enter a name that is less than the size of the character field, for example) and sometimes you will not (when you fill the field or enter a logical value, for instance).

❏ HEADING *ON*/OFF—With HEADING ON, FoxPro puts the field names at the top of a Browse window. With it OFF, those headings don't appear.

❏ MOUSE <1 to 10>—This command controls the sensitivity of the mouse to movement; the higher the number, the faster the mouse pointer moves. The default is 5.

❏ SAFETY *ON*/OFF—With SAFETY ON, FoxPro asks whether you want to overwrite a file when you save a file with the name of an existing file. With SAFETY OFF, FoxPro assumes that you want to overwrite that file and will not ask. Be careful; you cannot retrieve a file that's been overwritten.

You also can assign character strings to the function keys (except F1). If, for example, you want the F2 key to execute the command DO TEST, you would place into the CONFIG.FP file the following line:

```
F2 = "DO TEST;"
```

The semicolon acts as an Enter, telling FoxPro to execute the command. If you leave it out, you will have to press the Enter after the F2 key. Now, when FoxPro starts, you can execute the DO TEST command simply by pressing the F2 key.

Other possibilities for function key assignments might be to open specific files or views, set format files, or carry out longer strings of commands. If you want to string two or more commands together, separate them by a semicolon. The following line,

F2 = "SET VIEW TO AMMS; SET FORMAT TO AMMS_FMT; APPEND;"

executes three commands just as if you had entered, in the Command window, the following commands:

SET VIEW TO AMMS
SET FORMAT TO AMMS_FMT
APPEND

If you have a favorite text editor, you can use that instead of the built-in FoxPro editor. To tell FoxPro what editor to use, place the following line in your CONFIG.FP file:

TEDIT = "\BRIEF\B"

To define the word processor, which will be used in memo field editing, enter the following line:

WP = "\BRIEF\B"

Note | If your text editor doesn't load, it may be that it requires too much memory. Anything over 384K is too large for FoxPro to load and use on a 512K machine.

The CONFIG.FP file can help you customize FoxPro to your likes, or to the preferences of those who will be using a system you create.

Using Views To Set Up FoxPro

As you have worked through the chapters and examples in this book, you have learned something about views and how they can ease FoxPro's complexity. A view records information about the way FoxPro is set up when the view is created or saved. Once a view is created, you can duplicate that environment by opening the view from the File menu, or by issuing the Command window command SET VIEW TO *view_name*. The following list presents the information that is saved with a view, all of which is set up when you recall the view with the Open or Set command:

❑ All database, index, alternate, and format files currently open in all the work areas.

❑ All fields defined in the set fields list.

❑ All relations you have established in the Relations box of the View Setup window.

❑ All filters for each of the open databases.

❑ The default drive and path settings.

❑ Several other settings used in advanced FoxPro applications.

Creating a View

Creating a view seems simple, but has some complications. To create a view, set up FoxPro the way you want, with database files opened, indexes set, format and field statements as necessary, and the many SET ON/OFF switches set the proper way. Then select Save from the File menu. You will see the Save View As dialog, shown in figure 8.8, which asks for the name you want to assign to this view. The files scrollable list shows any views already defined in the current directory to aid you in choosing a unique name. Once you have given the view a name, you can save it.

Fig. 8.8.
The Save View
As dialog.

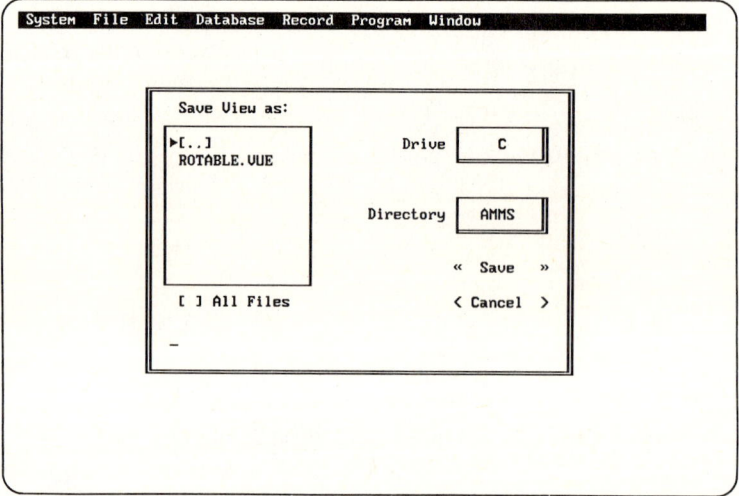

The complication of defining views is you must be certain that everything is set just as you want it. You must make sure that the database files are in the work areas you want them in. Indexes must be set along with the controlling index. Fields and formats must be right, and any relations must be in place (and tested to make sure that they're right). Be very careful that the view is what you want it to be, because if you plan to use that view when running a report or inquiry, and later find you have the wrong relation set up or the wrong controlling index (or the database and work areas reversed, as I often seem to do), your report or inquiry will not work as you expect it to. Using views requires care in setting them up.

Opening and Using Views

Once you have a view defined, you can open that view any time you want FoxPro to use the configuration you specified when you saved the view. Choose Open from the File menu, change Type to View and choose the view you want. FoxPro will assume the configuration of the view.

Views ensure consistency. Without views, you would have to set up Fox-Pro with databases, indexes, and so on, every time you wanted to change things; with views, you can save the configuration and know that every time you want it back, you will have it, with all the details.

Note | When you save a Report Form, you see a Save Environment check box in the Save Report As dialog (see fig. 8.9). If you selected that option, FoxPro created a pseudo-view file with the report's name. If you later run the report, FoxPro opens that view file and sets up itself accordingly. If you have another view in place, it disappears, and you must open it again to reestablish it. Remember this when you run a report and find that your view has changed.

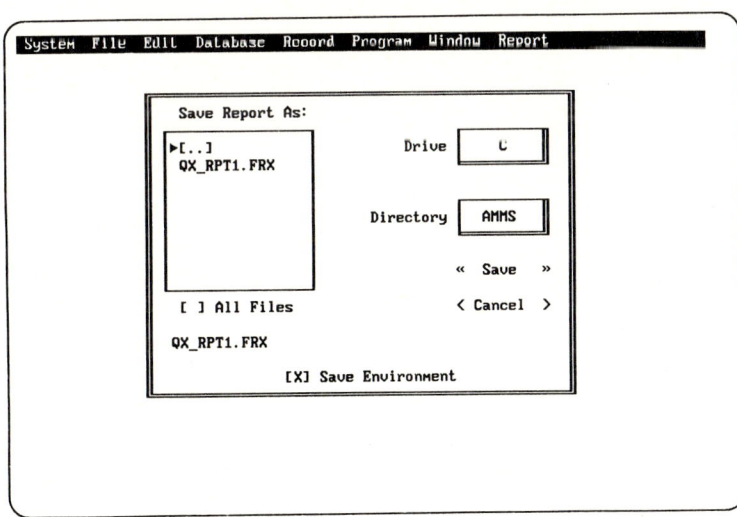

Fig. 8.9.
The Save Report As dialog.

Using Keyboard Shortcuts

Most of the time, you will find that working with the mouse is the fastest way to get something done in FoxPro. But for those FoxPro users working without a mouse, or for the times when you have both hands on the keyboard and don't want to reach for the mouse, FoxPro provides keyboard shortcuts for many commands. The more important keyboard shortcuts are as follows:

Window menu

Ctrl-F7	Initiate the Move Window sequence
Ctrl-F8	Initiate the Size Window sequence
Ctrl-F10	Zoom the window
Ctrl-F1	Cycle through the windows on-screen
Ctrl-F2	Make the Command window active

Browse menu

Ctrl-T	Toggle the delete status of the current record. Each time you press Ctrl-T, the current record changes between marked for deletion and not marked.

Edit menu

Ctrl-F	Find a record
Ctrl-G	Find again, based on the same criteria as the previous Find
Ctrl-A	Select all

When a record has been selected

Ctrl-X	Cut the record's fields
Ctrl-C	Copy the record's fields

Once fields have been cut or copied

Ctrl-V	Paste

Using Macros

A macro is a way of assigning a string of text to a specific key or combination of keys; when you press that particular key-combination, FoxPro "plays back" the string of text as if you entered it from the keyboard. Macros can save you much time and typing if you find yourself typing a particular sequence of keystrokes over and over.

Creating a Macro

The first step in creating a macro is to choose Macros from the System menu. You see the Keyboard Macros dialog shown in figure 8.10.

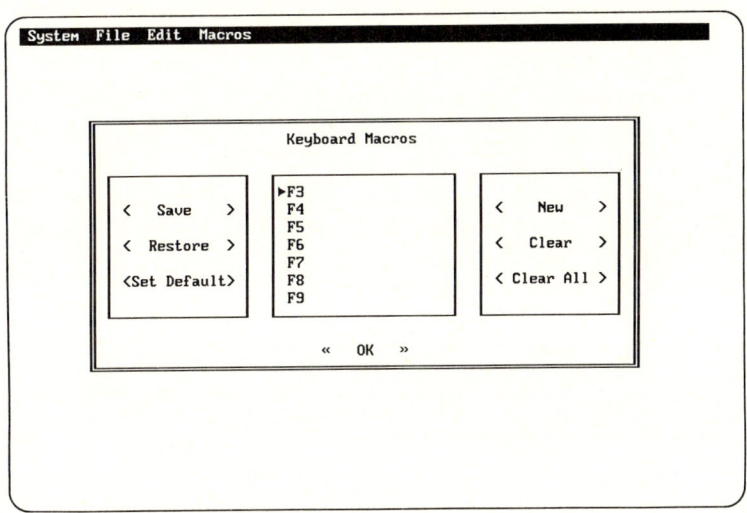

Fig. 8.10.
The Keyboard
Macros dialog.

The scrollable list shows all the keys and key combinations for which a macro has already been defined. Notice that the function keys are listed. These macro assignments are as follows:

F1   Help
F2
F3
F4   Dir (lists the database files in the current directory)
F5   List Structure
F6   Display Status
F7
F8
F9   Append

Any other macro key combinations assigned also are shown.

Storing and Playing Back a Macro

To store a macro, select New in the Keyboard Macros dialog. FoxPro displays the Macro Key Definition dialog, which asks for a key combination to which the keystroke sequence will be assigned. Possible key combinations include:

Function keys
Alt-any key (including function keys)
Ctrl-any key (including function keys)
Shift-Alt-any key
Shift-Ctrl-any key

Once you have entered your key combination, select OK, and FoxPro returns to the Command window, with a message reminder that you're recording a macro. Enter the keystrokes you want; FoxPro executes them as you enter them. When you have finished, press Shift-F10 to stop recording. FoxPro displays the Stop Recording dialog, shown in figure 8.11. Select OK to end the recording process.

Fig. 8.11.
The Stop
Recording dialog.

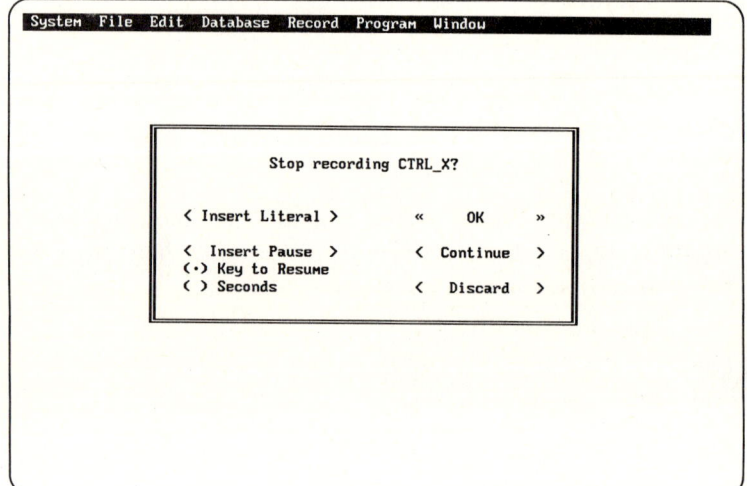

To use the macro, press the key combination you defined. FoxPro enters the commands in the Command window just as if you had entered them from the keyboard. You also could put into the macro text strings that you want entered into a field in a database; pressing the key combination during an Append operation inserts the text string into the fields.

Macros can be a great help when you have a string of commands or text that you find yourself repeating over and over. Any time you find yourself doing this, think about using a macro to save time and tedium, and reducing the possibility of making typing errors.

Using the Command Window

As you have used FoxPro, you have grown accustomed to seeing the Command window, because FoxPro keeps it open most of the time. FoxPro sometimes puts seemingly incomprehensible strings into the Command window (see fig. 8.12). Now is a good time to learn what that window does and how you can use it to be more efficient with FoxPro.

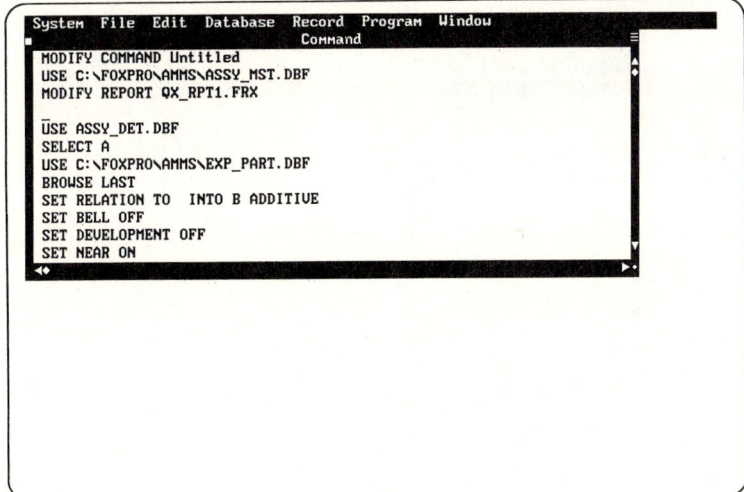

Fig. 8.12.
The Command window, with FoxPro-generated commands.

Before FoxPro, PC database programs operated from a command line— you entered a command string and the program interpreted it and took whatever action you requested. Figure 8.13 shows the FoxBase+ screen, with a command to open a database file and two index files on the command line.

The command shown opens the file designated as CUSTOMER and assigns to it two index files, CUSTNAME and CUST_NUM, making the first file the controlling index. All commands in dBASE III, dBASE III PLUS, dBASE IV, and FoxBase+ are entered this way. Contrasted with FoxPro's window and menu user interface, command-line-driven programs are less friendly and require a more thorough knowledge of the program to do even simple tasks.

Still, the command line has some advantages. As you become more familiar with FoxPro and its commands, you will find that you can enter the command

USE CUSTOMER INDEX CUSTNAME, CUST_NUM

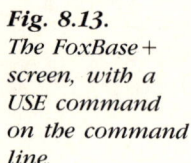

Fig. 8.13.
The FoxBase +
screen, with a
USE command
on the command
line.

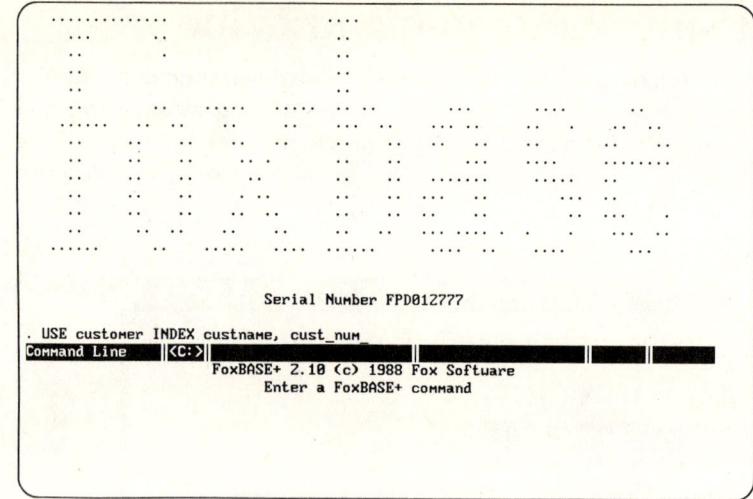

much faster than you can navigate through the File Open window, and then the View Setup window to get everything opened and in place. The Command window can be a high-speed way to get things done in FoxPro, but it does require more familiarity with the system.

Understanding a Command String

Command strings are essentially sentences; they contain a verb and an object. A command string may also contain one or more modifiers or arguments, things that tell FoxPro how to do something. In the command

    USE CUSTOMER INDEX CUSTNAME, CUST_NUM

USE is the verb, telling FoxPro what action to take. Here the command tells FoxPro to set a database into the current work area. CUSTOMER is the object, telling FoxPro what database to associate with the USE command. INDEX is a modifier, which tells FoxPro that the names following are index files to associate with database. The case of the commands, uppercase or lowercase, have no effect on the command. USE, Use, use, or even uSe are all the same thing to FoxPro.

Nearly all FoxPro commands have numerous modifiers, such as the INDEX clause in the USE command, or optional phrases. The only way to learn the nuances of the many FoxPro commands is to spend some time reading the FoxPro *User's Guide*, which lists every command with all its modifiers and options. If you keep it handy while working in FoxPro, you can consult it to learn commands.

Re-using a Previous Command

The Command window has several features you should know. You can use the arrow keys to move back to a previous command. Once the cursor is on the command you want, press Enter to reexecute the command.

Editing and Re-using Previous Commands

Before executing a previous command, you can edit it using standard Fox-Pro editing features. The newly edited command will be put at the end of the command stack in the window, and the original command will be left in place (see fig. 8.14). Notice how the original command is back in its place and the edited command is at the bottom.

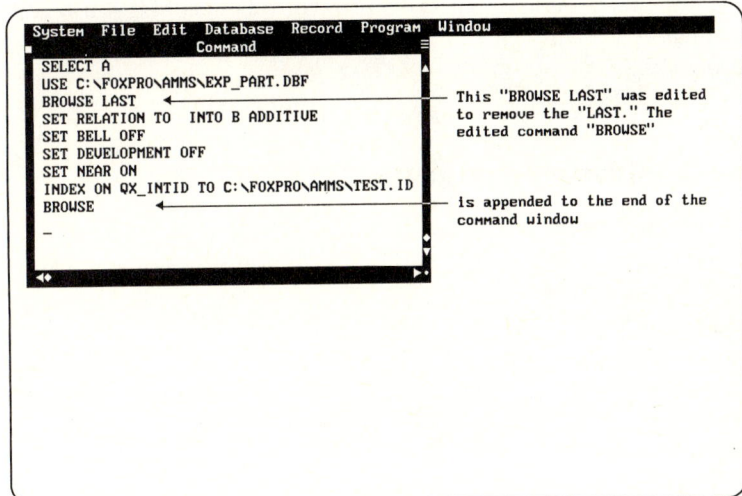

Fig. 8.14.
The Command window, with BROWSE LAST modified to BROWSE.

You also can hide the Command window, using the the Window menu Hide option. This is discomfitting, at best, because you can still enter commands from the keyboard and execute them, although you cannot see them going into the Command window. If this happens—usually by accident—just choose Command from the Window menu to reopen the Command window.

You may find the Command window an annoying presence on the screen. As you become more accomplished, you can watch how FoxPro translates your menu commands into Command window strings before it executes them. Soon, you will be using the Command window to speed up your navigation through FoxPro.

Using the Programming Language

First, you should understand that you don't have to learn to program to use FoxPro. At this point, you're able to use most of FoxPro's power and you haven't had to program yet. However, programming in FoxPro can help you do things quickly and easily.

If you want to gain some programming skills, the FoxPro programming language is a good place to start, because it is quite easy to learn and use. By learning the basics of FoxPro programming, you can automate some FoxPro tasks that views and macros cannot do. So, even if the thought of programming scares you, take a deep breath and read on; you will be glad you did.

FoxPro programs range from a series of simple commands, much like an MS-DOS batch file, to enormously complicated systems. Chapter 11 covers the basics of systems programming in FoxPro; in this chapter, you learn the fundamentals of creating and running a FoxPro program to automate some FoxPro tasks.

Creating a Simple Program

The most basic FoxPro programs are simply series of commands that a user might enter in the Command window. A common series of actions in FoxPro might be as follows:

1. Move to the correct work area.

2. Open a database file and index file in that work area.

3. Edit the file.

4. Close the database.

If you were using the mouse to execute these commands, quite a few point-and-clicks would be required. If you were working in the Command window, you would use the following commands to accomplish this:

```
SELECT 1
USE file INDEX file
EDIT
USE
```

You can create a simple FoxPro program that will execute this sequence of commands when you enter

```
DO AMMS
```

in the Command window. To create this program, open the File menu and choose New. In the File Open dialog, choose Program. A program editing window will open, and you can enter your first FoxPro program.

The editor has essentially the same functions available in memo fields. Enter the four commands shown in figure 8.15, pressing Enter at the end of each line. The && symbols tell FoxPro to ignore everything to the right on a line—the && symbols indicate comments. When you have entered your program, select File Save and give it a name. FoxPro appends the PRG suffix, indicating a program file, and saves the program.

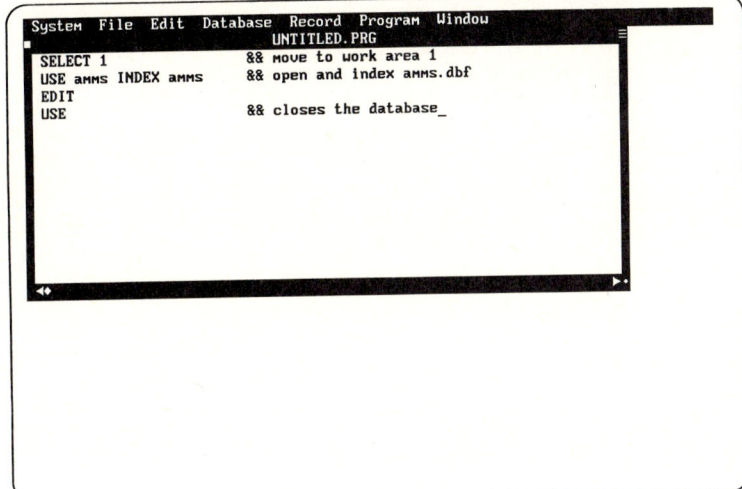

Fig. 8.15.
A simple FoxPro program in the text-editing window.

To execute a FoxPro program, choose Do from the Program menu. Fox-Pro presents the Do dialog, with a list of available PRG files. Select the one you want, and FoxPro will execute it. When the last line of the program is executed, FoxPro returns control to you.

Using the Trace Window

No matter how simple a program seems, it can run into problems. FoxPro helps you find the error by opening a window showing the PRG file that was running, and it highlights the line on which an error was encountered. You can then correct the error, save the file, and try again. Still, there are times when you will encounter an unexplainable error and need more help. The Trace window was made for these times.

The Trace window enables you to "trace" the execution of the program file a line at a time. To use the Trace window, select Step from the Program menu, which tells FoxPro to go through any program file one line at a time. Choose Do from the Program menu. FoxPro executes the first line, and then stops. Now you can open the Trace window from the Window menu. You will see the Trace window, shown in figure 8.16, with the current program in it. Selecting Resume causes the next line to be executed and highlighted. In this way, you can follow what is happening in your program. Obviously, with a four-line command program, Trace is of little help, but when you have a large command file, Trace can show you what FoxPro is doing with your errant program.

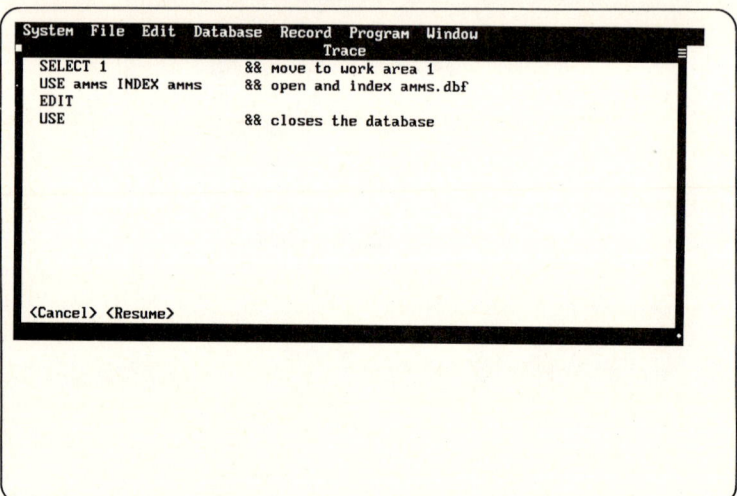

Fig. 8.16.
The Trace
window, tracing
program
execution.

Chapter Summary

For all its ease of use, FoxPro is a complex program. As you become more expert with it, you will find an increasing need to take short-cuts to make your time more productive. This chapter focused on ways to do that.

You have learned how to use views to simplify setting up a specific environment, ensuring it to be consistent from session to session without having to remember every detail and go through the tedious process of setting them. You have seen how the CONFIG.FP file can customize FoxPro to your liking. Macros enable you to store frequently used keystrokes or mouse sequences and play them back, thus saving you time. And finally, you have learned the basics of creating FoxPro program files to execute long sequences of commands automatically. All these techniques make the sophisticated capabilities of FoxPro easier and more productive to use.

Now it's time to move to the next step in using FoxPro's power: creating and running reports on multiple-file, relational databases.

Reporting on Multiple Database Systems

In Chapter 6, you learned basic reporting techniques, working on a one-database file system. FoxPro's report writing capabilities are far more sophisticated than that. This chapter introduces you to reporting on more than one database at a time. You also see how to use some of the sophisticated techniques of the FoxPro report writer.

When you designed your multiple-file relational databases, you did so because you wanted to keep information that logically belonged together in separate databases and be able to reference that information based on related fields. Reporting on these databases is no different; you want to be able to report on one database and draw information from other, related databases to put into the report.

FoxPro's power and flexibility in creating and viewing relational databases is matched by its capability to create clear and concise reports easily. Reporting on a variety of databases, related in many different ways, is not a difficult task. You also learn several advanced techniques of reporting on these multiple-file database systems.

In this chapter, you extend your knowledge of FoxPro's report-writing capability to include working with multiple databases. How you want to report on a relational database system depends on how the databases are related and what you need from the report. You learn what information can go into the Detail Band of the report, and what is best placed in Groups.

Designing Your Report

Because reports are often the most visible result of a FoxPro database system, it's important that your reports be clear and easy to read. Following are some basic guidelines for designing your FoxPro reports:

1. Each page of a report should contain a title, the date, the time the report was printed, a page number, and, if applicable, column headings for the report. This presents the report reader with essential information on each page.

2. Present the information in a logical order. You may choose to print the records in alphabetical order, or you might want to order the records according to the value in a numeric field or by a date in each record. You control the order of a report with the database indexes.

3. If the information in the report has natural groupings, use the Data Grouping facility of the FoxPro Report Writer to group your report. If, for example, you're reporting on orders your company has processed, you might want to group the records by the name of the customer, so that each customer's orders appear together in the report. Or you might want to group on the order date so that all orders received each day are grouped. Grouping data breaks down a large mass of information into smaller, understandable chunks.

4. Use lines and boxes to break up the report and draw attention to data you want to emphasize.

FoxPro takes much of the drudgery out of creating reports. With just a little forethought, your reports can show off your database skills.

Creating Multiple-File Reports

Just as with single-file databases, you use FoxPro's Layout Window to create reports on relational database systems. The first thing you must do is make sure that all your files are set up in the proper work areas, with the necessary indexes controlling them.

Setting Up the Databases for Reporting

As with any FoxPro project, you first must design the report output and plan your approach for making FoxPro do what you want. An example report is shown in figure 9.1. This report is done on an ORDER database, a related CUSTOMER database, and another related INVNTRY database. The structures of these databases are shown in figures 9.2, 9.3, and 9.4, respectively. The relational fields are CUST_NAME between ORDER and CUSTOMER, and PART_NUM between ORDER and PART_NUM. Figure 9.5 shows the View window of these three databases set up to generate the example report.

```
SCIL
P.O. Box 2231
Kent            WA
/////////////////////////////////////////////////////////
  Order    Sales-     Part                      Part      Part
  Date     person     Number      Quantity      Keyword   Price

  01/02/90  DJZ       CASCADE 6045      3                    0.00
  01/22/89  DJZ       IN E-2138       100        PULL      214.00
/////////////////////////////////////////////////////////

S & C Autos
3342 E. Elwood
Phoenix         AZ
/////////////////////////////////////////////////////////
  Order    Sales-     Part                      Part      Part
  Date     person     Number      Quantity      Keyword   Price

  01/01/90  JWZ       CENTURY           1        CARBURETOR 125.25
  12/15/90  DJZ       CL 1754428        4        SHIFT       0.00
/////////////////////////////////////////////////////////

Hess Aviation Inventory
3342 Aviation R
Portland        OR 88423
/////////////////////////////////////////////////////////
  Order    Sales-     Part                      Part      Part
  Date     person     Number      Quantity      Keyword   Price

  01/15/90  CHZ       IN E-2398         1        ROLLER      7.75
  01/15/90  CHZ       IN E-2514B        1        SHIM        1.20
  12/12/89  DJZ       ME 1178          10        FENDER      0.00
/////////////////////////////////////////////////////////
```

Fig. 9.1.
A report on a relational database system.

ORDER is the controlling database, so fields from ORDER go into the Detail Band. ORDER is indexed on CUST_NAME, to ensure that the report is printed alphabetically by customer name.

Generally, you will want to group reports in some order, with appropriate totals on the grouped data. Also, you can use the Group Header to print fields about related databases. You can group on the value of a field in a related database. In this example, you could group on the value of

CUST_NAME in the ORDER field, but for illustrative purposes, this report will group on the CUST_NAME field in CUSTOMER.

Fig. 9.2.
The controlling database in the example report.

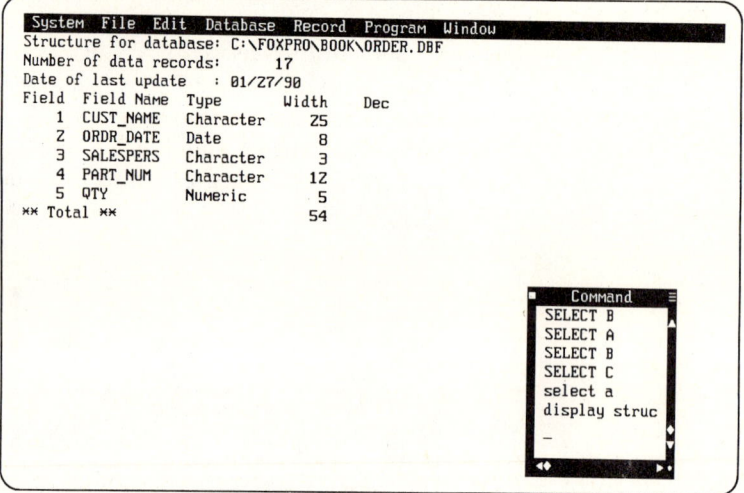

```
 System  File  Edit  Database  Record  Program  Window
Structure for database: C:\FOXPRO\BOOK\ORDER.DBF
Number of data records:       17
Date of last update    : 01/27/90
Field  Field Name  Type        Width    Dec
    1  CUST_NAME   Character      25
    2  ORDR_DATE   Date            8
    3  SALESPERS   Character       3
    4  PART_NUM    Character      12
    5  QTY         Numeric         5
** Total **                      54
```

```
■        Command      ≡
 SELECT B
 SELECT A
 SELECT B
 SELECT C
 select a
 display struc
 _
◄►              ►.◄
```

Fig. 9.3.
One controlled database in the example report.

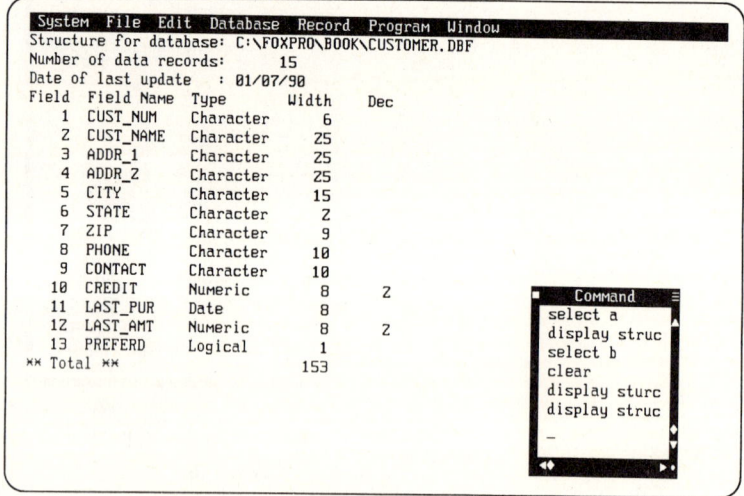

```
 System  File  Edit  Database  Record  Program  Window
Structure for database: C:\FOXPRO\BOOK\CUSTOMER.DBF
Number of data records:       15
Date of last update    : 01/07/90
Field  Field Name  Type        Width    Dec
    1  CUST_NUM    Character       6
    2  CUST_NAME   Character      25
    3  ADDR_1      Character      25
    4  ADDR_2      Character      25
    5  CITY        Character      15
    6  STATE       Character       2
    7  ZIP         Character       9
    8  PHONE       Character      10
    9  CONTACT     Character      10
   10  CREDIT      Numeric         8     2
   11  LAST_PUR    Date            8
   12  LAST_AMT    Numeric         8     2
   13  PREFERD     Logical         1
** Total **                     153
```

```
■        Command      ≡
 select a
 display struc
 select b
 clear
 display sturc
 display struc
 _
◄►              ►.
```

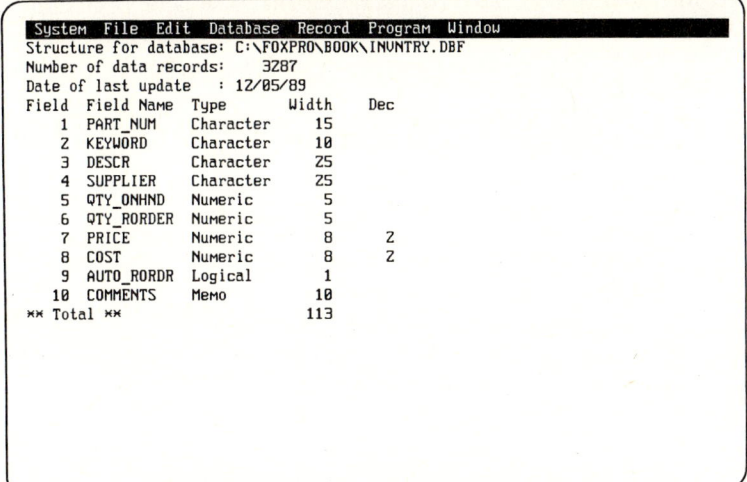

Fig. 9.4.
The second
controlled
database in the
example report.

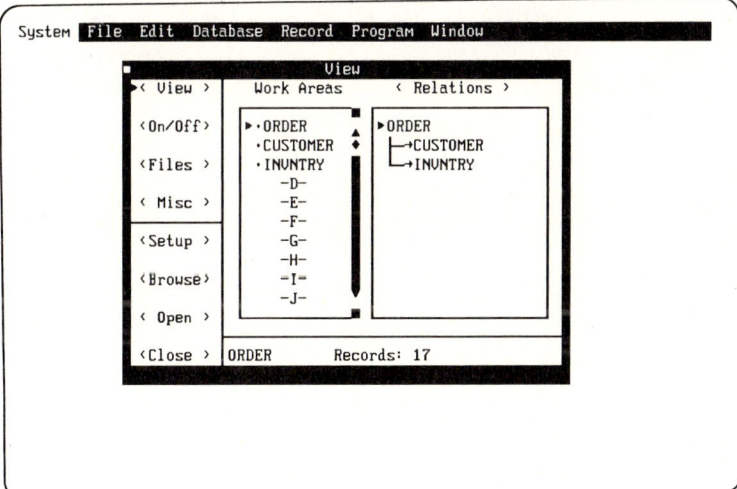

Fig. 9.5.
The View
window for the
databases in the
example report.

Placing Fields in the Detail Band

As with single-file databases, the Detail Band holds fields from the database through which FoxPro proceeds as it generates the report. In a relational database system, this will almost always be the controlling database in a relation. FoxPro starts at the top of the database file according to the controlling index, and steps through each record. If there is a

SCOPE, FOR, or WHILE test, FoxPro executes that test and prints the Detail Band if the record passes the test. Figure 9.6 shows the Detail Band in the Layout Window with fields from the controlling database.

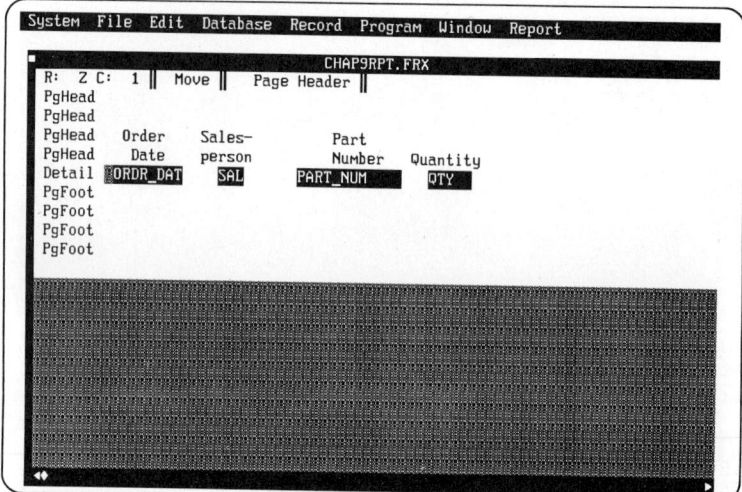

Fig. 9.6.
The Layout view
with fields from
the controlling
database.

Add fields to the Detail Band with the Fields option of the Report menu. If you want to include all or nearly all the fields from the controlling database in the report, use Quick Report to place all fields on the Layout View. Choose Form Layout to make sure that all fields get on the report; in Column Report only as many fields as will fit on the page are placed in the Detail Band. Then move and delete fields as necessary to make the Layout view match your report design.

Adding Fields to the Detail Line

The important advantage of related databases is, of course, to be able to draw information from related files. You will often want to put information on the detail line that comes from a related database. To do this, simply put the field on the line (using Add Field from the Report menu). Select Expr in the Field dialog, and in the Report Expression Builder dialog, select the related database in the database box. Figure 9.7 shows the related INVNTRY database selected, and the KEYWORD field chosen from the scrollable list.

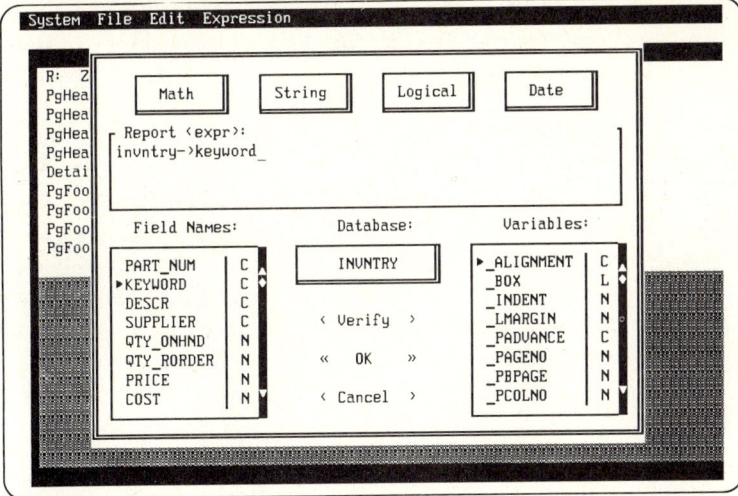

Fig. 9.7.
The Report Expression dialog, adding fields from a related database.

Once the controlling database fields and any necessary related fields are added to the Detail Band, you should use the Page Preview feature to test your layout. If necessary, save and run the report to ensure that all is well so far. Figure 9.8 shows the page preview of the example report. From the page preview, you can tell whether the relationships you have established work as you planned.

```
System  File  Edit  Database  Record  Program  Window  Report
                              Preview

Order    Sales-        Part                 Part      Part
Date     person        Number     Quantity  Keyword   Price
01/03/90  CHZ     LP 1400-5509       9      BEARING     0.00
01/03/90  CHZ     LP 1400-5509       9      PACKING     0.00
01/03/90  CHZ     LP 1400-5509       9      BEARING    16.77
01/03/90  CHZ     LP 1400-5509       9      REGULATOR 141.83
01/03/90  CHZ     LP 1400-5509       9      KIT       105.71
01/03/90  CHZ     LP 1400-5509       9      RESISTER  102.20
01/03/90  CHZ     LP 1400-5509       9      TUBE       29.60
01/03/90  CHZ     LP 1400-5509       9      LOCK        7.88
01/03/90  CHZ     LP 1400-5509       9      LATCH      17.46
01/03/90  CHZ     LP 1400-5509       9      BOARD       5.25
01/03/90  CHZ     LP 1400-5509       9      CYLINDER  220.63
01/03/90  CHZ     LP 1400-5509       9      SWITCH      9.66
01/03/90  CHZ     LP 1400-5509       9      SPRING      9.29
01/03/90  CHZ     LP 1400-5509       9      RING        4.05
01/03/90  CHZ     LP 1400-5509       9      KIT        14.87
« Done »  ‹ More ›   Column:    0
```

Fig. 9.8.
Page preview of the report with the Detail Band defined.

If you run page preview and find the related database fields are blank or contain incorrect values, you can be sure that your relationships are not set correctly.

Grouping on a Related Database

Grouping data lends clarity to your report. Nearly all reports benefit from grouping the data in some form. Data grouping can be done on a related database if the controlling database is indexed or sorted on the link to the related database. In the example, for instance, the report can be grouped on the customer name, with information from the CUSTOMER database in the Group Header, because the ORDER database is indexed on CUST_NAME.

Adding a Data Grouping is the same as with a single-file database, except that here you use a field in the controlled database as the Group expression. Figure 9.9 shows the Group expression on the controlled database field, CUSTOMER−>CUST_NAME.

Fig. 9.9.
Grouping on the value of a related database field.

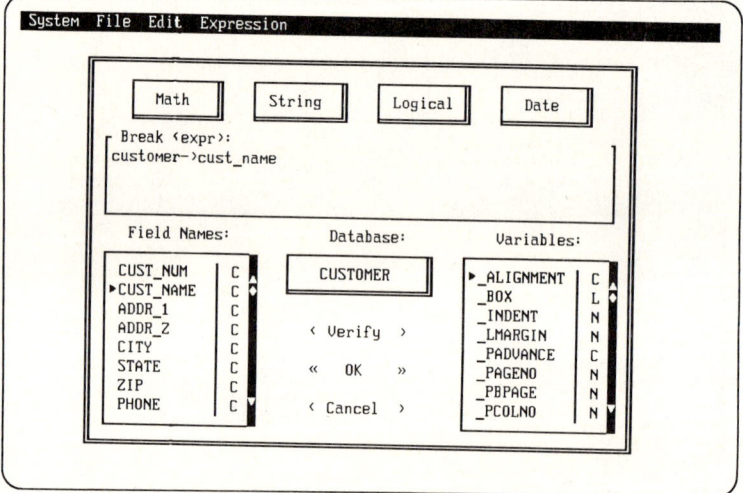

The report will now break whenever the CUST_NAME field in the CUSTOMER database changes. Remember, as it proceeds through the controlling database, FoxPro will maintain the relation to the controlled databases.

Placing Related Database Fields in the Group Header

The Group Header is an excellent place for information drawn from the related database. Increase the number of lines in the Group Header with the Add Line option on the Report menu, and place the necessary fields in the Group Header. As with related database fields in the Detail Band, use the Field Expression Builder dialog to designate the database and field you want. Figure 9.10 shows the Layout View with CUSTOMER information included, and figure 9.11 shows the page preview of this report.

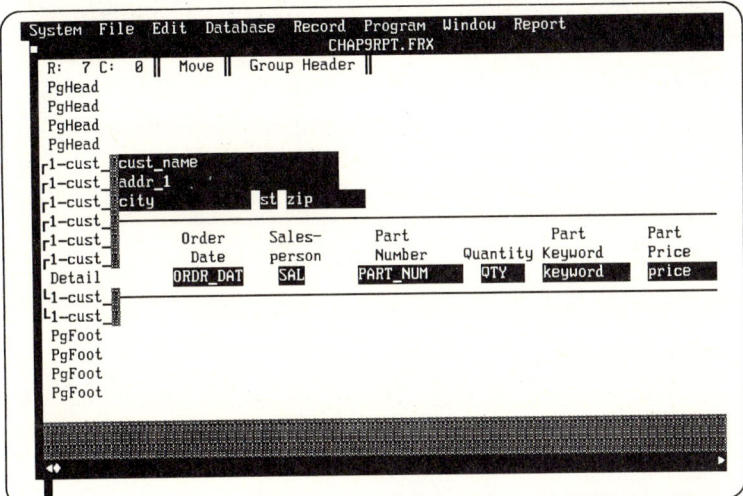

Fig. 9.10.
Layout view with CUSTOMER information in the Group Header.

Fig. 9.11.
Page preview of a relational database report.

As you can see, it's a simple task to place fields from related databases into a report. By setting up these relations, you can ensure that the information in related databases always refers to the current record in the controlling database. You should often use page preview as you design your report on the Layout view to make sure that the body of the report is right. Once you have all the database fields in the report working correctly, you can add the frills, such as a title, date and time stamps, boxes, and lines.

Generating Controlling Database Ordered Reports

In the example just presented, the controlling database had a field, CUST_NAME, on which the report could be properly ordered. Often this is not the case; you will want the report ordered on a field in a controlled database. You must resort to some slightly more sophisticated techniques to achieve your purpose.

Suppose that, instead of having a field CUST_NAME as the relational field between ORDER and CUSTOMER, you have followed my advice and used a customer number to link the two. ORDER and CUSTOMER each have a field named CUST_NUM, and the relation is based on those fields; the controlling database is indexed on the CUST_NUM field. Now, if you use the same report and run it, you get a different result (see fig. 9.12).

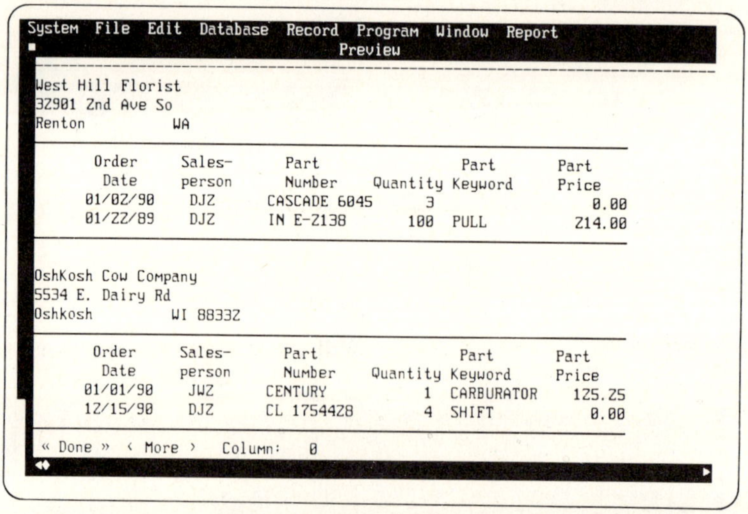

Fig. 9.12.
A relational report based on CUST_NUM instead of CUST_NAME.

```
 System  File  Edit  Database  Record  Program  Window  Report
                              Preview

 West Hill Florist
 3Z901 Znd Ave So
 Renton         WA

      Order    Sales-     Part                   Part       Part
      Date     person     Number    Quantity Keyword      Price
      01/02/90   DJZ      CASCADE 6045    3                  0.00
      01/22/89   DJZ      IN E-Z138     100    PULL        Z14.00


 OshKosh Cow Company
 5534 E. Dairy Rd
 Oshkosh        WI 8833Z

      Order    Sales-     Part                   Part       Part
      Date     person     Number    Quantity Keyword      Price
      01/01/90   JWZ      CENTURY        1    CARBURATOR  1Z5.Z5
      12/15/90   DJZ      CL 1754428     4    SHIFT         0.00

 « Done »  ‹ More ›   Column:    0
```

What has happened? The data grouping still works, but now the report is no longer in alphabetical order by customer name. The customer number, in each of the CUST_NUM fields, does not reflect alphabetical order; customer numbers may be assigned as new customers are obtained, and new customers are not often obtained alphabetically. So as FoxPro proceeds through the ORDER database, it groups the records for CUST_NUM 00001 together, then the records for CUST_NUM 00002, and so on. But because CUST_NUM 00001 is the Zzybob Company and 00002 the Aardvark Company, that's the order in which the report is printed.

One way to solve this problem would be to program a custom report. Though some FoxPro programming can be fun, programming reports seldom falls into that category. To accomplish an alphabetical report, you need to use one of two FoxPro techniques: the JOIN command, or indexing on the related database.

Using JOIN for Reporting

The JOIN command enables you to mesh certain fields of two databases, forming one database that is a combination of the two. You can, for instance, join the ORDER and CUSTOMER databases into one database that has all the order information along with the necessary CUSTOMER information. Then you can create a simple, single-file report on the resulting database, still using a Group to present the CUSTOMER database information.

The format of the JOIN command is

JOIN WITH *alias* TO *new_database_file* FOR *logical_expr* FIELDS *field_list*

First, set up your FoxPro environment by putting each of the databases to be joined in a separate work area. Start the join by moving to the work area of one of the two databases to be joined:

SELECT ORDER

Decide the name of the new file; here it will be ORD_CUST.

Decide which logical expression will cause a record to be written to the new joined database file. Here, you would use

ORDER–>CUST_NUM = CUSTOMER–>CUST_NUM

In other words, you want FoxPro to add, in the new database ORD_CUST, a record each time it finds a match between the CUST_NUM field in ORDER and the CUST_NUM field in CUSTOMER.

FoxPro will look at the first record in ORDER to find the value of CUST_NUM; then, starting from the top of the CUSTOMER database, it looks at each record in that database. If the value of CUST_NUM in the CUSTOMER database matches the value of CUST_NUM in that first ORDER record, a new record in ORD_CUST is created. When FoxPro has looked at each record in CUSTOMER, it returns to the controlling database, ORDER, moves to the second record, and starts again. This continues until all records in ORDER have been matched against all records in CUSTOMER.

Finally, decide which fields will be copied into the new ORD_CUST. This report might require the following fields from ORDER:

CUST_NUM ORD_DATE QTY SALESPERS PART_NUM

and these fields from CUSTOMER:

CUST_NAME ADDR1 ADDR2 CITY STATE ZIP

Now put all this together into the JOIN command, issued in the Command window as follows:

JOIN WITH CUSTOMER TO ORD_CUST FOR CUST_NUM = ;
CUSTOMER->CUST_NUM FIELDS CUSTOMER->CUST_NAME, ;
CUSTOMER->ADDR1; CUSTOMER->ADDR1,;
CUSTOMER->CITY,CUSTOMER->STATE, ;
CUSTOMER->ZIP, ORD_DATE, QTY, SALESPERS, PART_NUM

Note the aliases used for references to the CUSTOMER and INVNTRY databases in the logical expression and field list. Because the ORDER work area is the active work area, no alias is required for references to fields in ORDER.

The result of the JOIN command is shown in a Browse window for the new ORD_CUST database (see fig. 9.13).

The database now has all the information required for the example report. By indexing ORD_CUST on CUST_NAME, you can create a report that accomplishes your purpose. Note that you still need a relation set between PART_NUM and PART_NUM in INVNTRY to obtain the KEYWORD from INVNTRY. Figure 9.14 shows the Layout view of such a report, and figure 9.15 shows the final report.

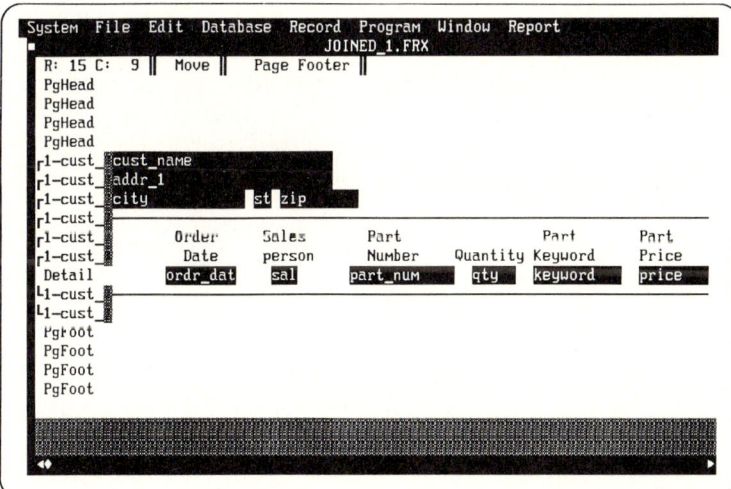

Fig. 9.13.
The Browse window of a joined database.

Fig. 9.14.
The Layout view of a report on a joined database.

Fig. 9.15.
Page preview of the joined database report.

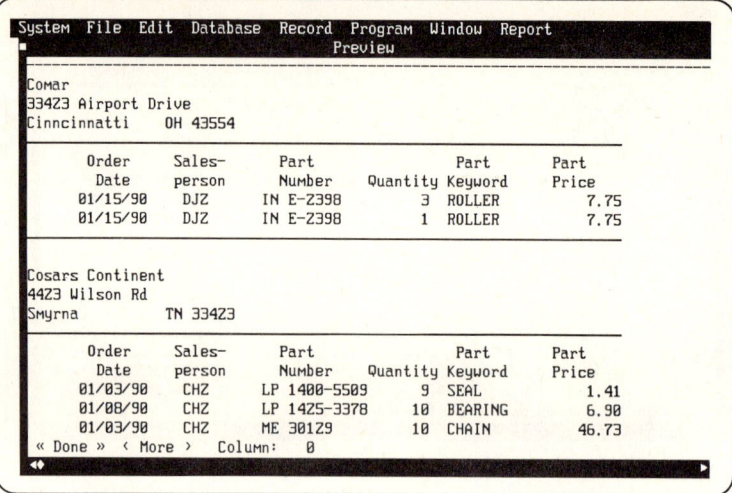

When using JOIN, be careful how you use this command, testing it carefully on a small subset of the database (use SCOPE, FOR, or WHILE to limit the processing). JOIN commands can create huge files if not used properly. The JOIN command starts at the first record and creates a new record for every record in the WITH database that meets the logical expression. If, for instance, you had accidentally used the logical expression

CUST_NUM <> CUSTOMER−>CUST_NUM

the resulting file would have had thousands of records.

Indexing on a Related Database

There is another way to order this report correctly. It is possible, once the databases' relations are set, to index the controlling database on values in the related record of the controlled database. In this way, you can order the ORDER database on the CUST_NAME for each related record.

To do this, make sure that there is a valid relation between the controlling database and the controlled database, in the example, between ORDER and CUSTOMER. That link has been set to CUST_NUM, which means that the controlled database, CUSTOMER, has to be indexed on its field CUST_NUM. Now, indexing ORDER on

CUSTOMER−>CUST_NAME

causes FoxPro to create an index on ORDER that is based on the value in the related CUSTOMER–>CUST_NUM field. Figure 9.16 shows the Browse window of ORDER, with the records in the order of their customer name, even though CUST_NAME is not part of the ORDER database.

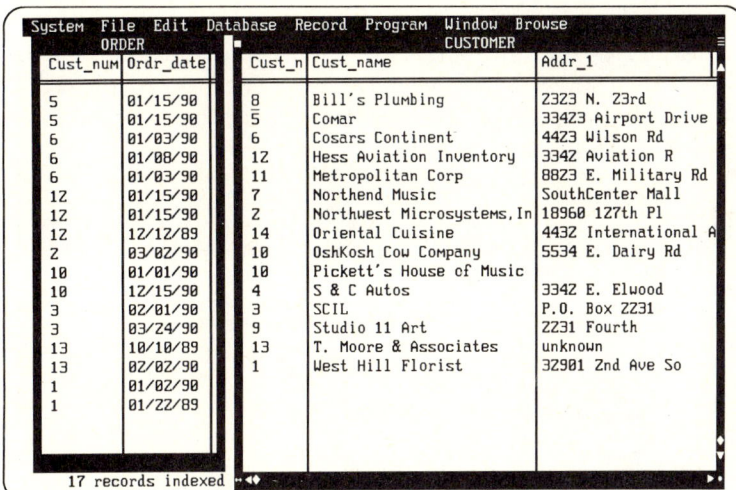

Fig. 9.16.
The Browse
windows of
ORDER and
CUSTOMER.

The CUSTOMER Browse window is also shown so you can match CUST_NUMs to CUST_NAMEs and see the ORDER database is, in fact, ordered alphabetically by the customer name associated with the CUST_NUM relational field. By doing this, you can now process the controlling database using this new index, and know that the records will be presented in alphabetical order, based on their related CUSTOMER–>CUST_NAME field. With this technique, the Layout of the report is the same as the first example; the only thing changed is the index that controls the ORDER database during the report processing.

Caution | You will be unable to use this newly created index for anything but reporting. If you try to make this index control the database without the controlling database being opened and related, you will get an error message. You also will get some interesting error messages when you try to do other standard FoxPro things. When using this method, create the index just before you run the report and discard it (by setting the index to some other index file) as soon as the report is done.

Using Advanced Reporting Techniques

FoxPro provides some advanced reporting techniques, primarily for use on character and memo fields, which may have varying amounts of information in them.

Because Character fields can be large (up to 255 characters), and Memo fields huge (up to 64,000 characters), FoxPro reports require special capabilities to handle them. When you define a field for a Character or Memo field, the option Stretch Vertically is presented in the Report Expression dialog (see fig. 9.17).

Fig. 9.17.
The Report
Expression dialog
showing the
Stretch
Vertically
option.

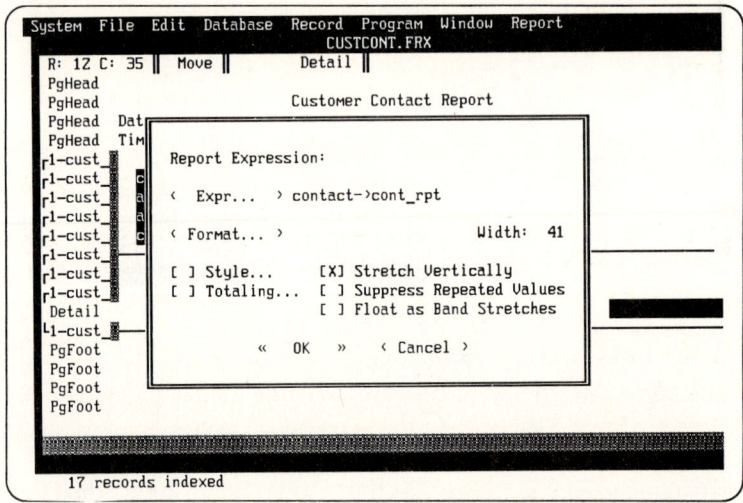

A field with this option will always have the same width (the width you define on the Layout view), but will "stretch" vertically to as many lines as necessary to print the entire field. If you do not select this option, the field will be limited to the width you selected and one line. Figure 9.18 shows a report with a character field not stretched; figure 9.19 shows the same report with the field stretched.

If you place fields below a field that will stretch vertically, you need to tell FoxPro to adjust that field's position, based on the size of the stretching field. When you define the lower field, choose the Float as Band Stretches option; FoxPro will then place the field one line below the last line of the stretched character field. If you don't select this option, the field will be placed on the report as defined on the Layout view; if the character field stretches, it will overwrite the bottom field, making a mess.

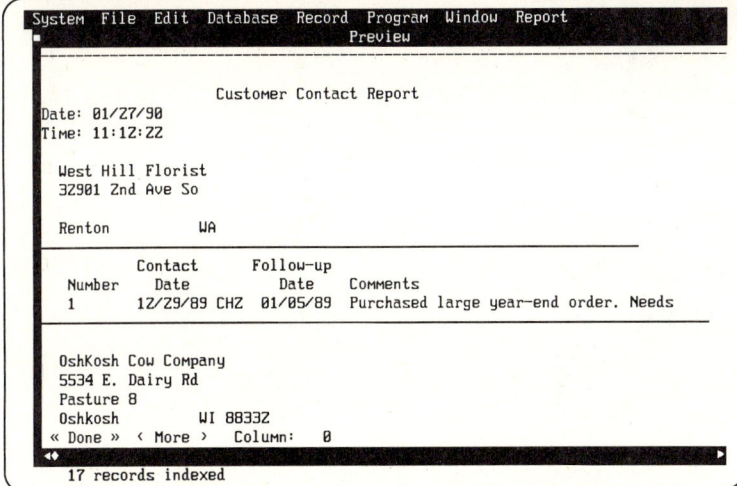

Fig. 9.18.
A Memo field; Stretch Vertically *is not selected.*

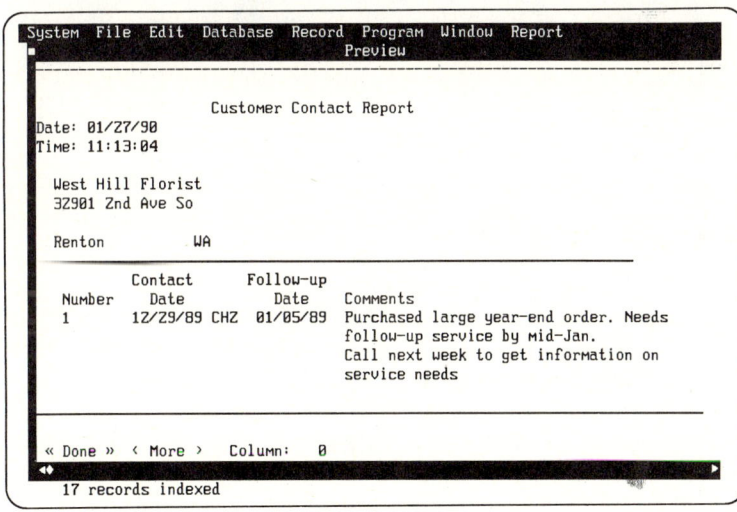

Fig. 9.19.
The same report, with Stretch Vertically *selected.*

Figure 9.20 shows the report with the lower fields floating; figure 9.21 shows what can result if the field is fixed. The "Salesperson" literal field and the SALESPERS database field end up in the middle of the CONT_RPT memo field output.

Fig. 9.20.
Fields floating
below a stretched
field.

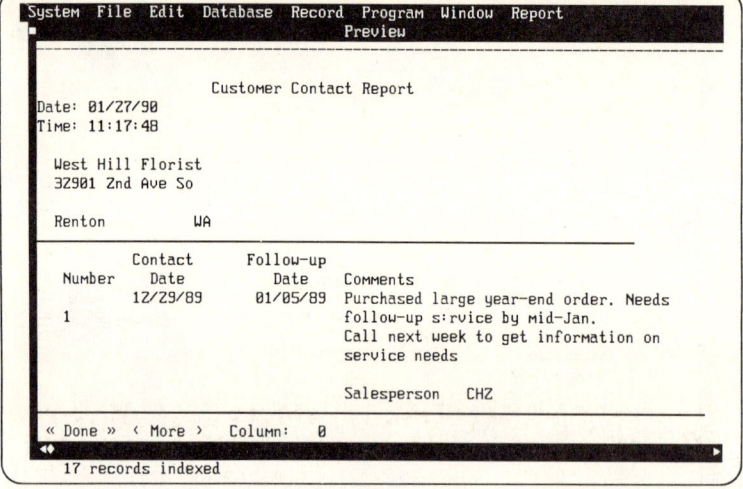

Fig. 9.21.
The same fields,
not floating.

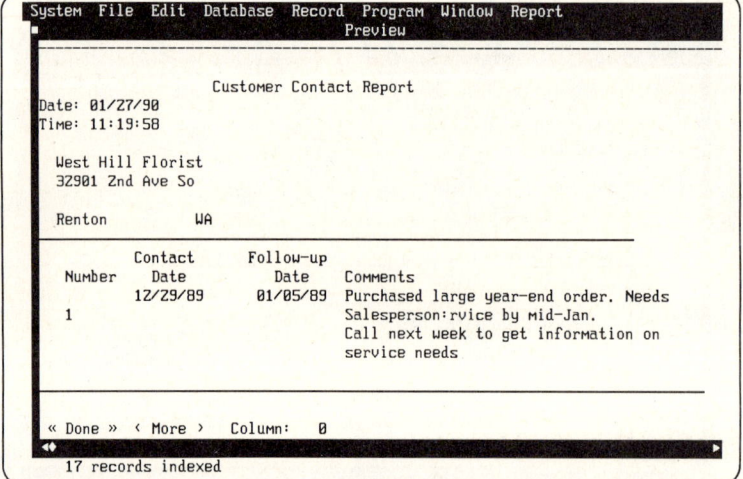

Using Relational Reports

Using relational reports is little different from running a report on a single database system. Reports can be run from the Database Menu with the Report option, or from the Command window. In each case, there are a number of options you should understand.

Using the Database Report Menu

To run a report from the FoxPro menu, choose Report from the Database menu.

In figure 9.22, you see the Report dialog. In this dialog, you can specify the many options that are available to you when you run a report. These options modify settings for the report as well as the report's destination.

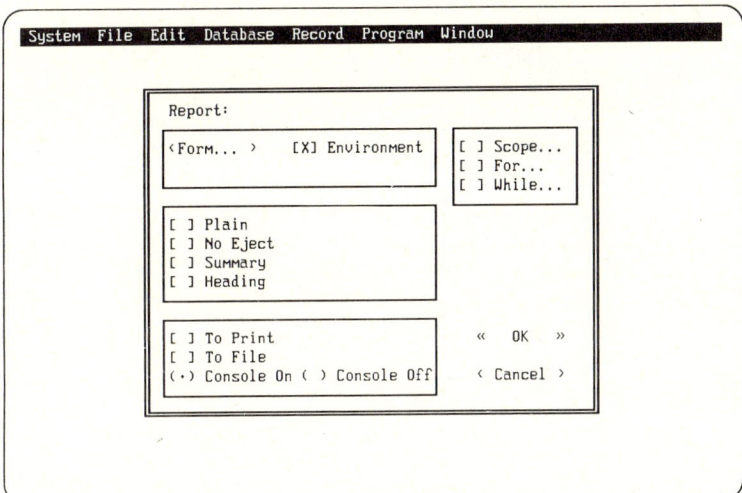

Fig. 9.22.
The Report dialog, with reporting options.

Options available are:

❏ Scope—Allows you to specify a set number of records to be printed, starting from the current position in the database.

❏ For—Allows you to specify a FoxPro expression that will limit the report output to those records matching the expression.

❏ While—Allows you to specify a FoxPro expression that will be matched against each database record encountered. The report will continue as long as the record matches the expression.

❏ Plain—If marked, FoxPro will not print the page number and date at the head of each report page.

❏ No Eject—Tells FoxPro when to go to the top of a new page. A dialog opens in which you can make your choices.

❏ Summary—No lines in the Detail Band are printed; only totals and subtotals.

❏ Heading—The Heading option enables you to add one or more lines of text which will be centered and added to the top of each page of the report. This text is additional to any PgHead and Report Titles you may have placed on the Layout view. When you select Heading, FoxPro presents an Expression Builder that enables you to construct the lines of the Header.

❏ To Print—Tells FoxPro to send the report to the printer. If this is unmarked, the report will appear on the screen only.

❏ To File—Tells FoxPro to print the report to a disk file, rather than the printer. A dialog will open to ask for the name of the file.

❏ Console On and Console Off—FoxPro echoes the report to the screen if the Console On option is marked; otherwise, nothing appears on the screen while the report is printing.

Using the Command Window

If you want to run the report from the Command window (or from a line in a FoxPro program), the format is

REPORT FORM *rpt_name* [*options*]

The *options* correlate to those listed in the Database menu Report option. Options are simply listed after the report name. For instance, this command line

REPORT FORM *test* HEADER NOEJECT

prints a report with a header and no page eject before the report.

Printing reports on complicated, related databases follows the same procedures as for simple, single-file systems. You will use Data Grouping more often and will draw from the related databases, but the basic processes are the same. Still, you will find times that FoxReport just will not do the job. For those needs, FoxPro provides you with programming capabilities for report writing.

Generating PRINTJOB and ENDPRINTJOB Reports

Sometimes, you may encounter situations in which you don't want to use FoxReport and the Layout window to create a report, or you find you cannot. For these situations, FoxPro provides the PRINTJOB and END-PRINTJOB commands, which tell FoxPro to treat everything between them as a report. You tell FoxPro what values to use for page length, right and left margins, and other report parameters by setting System Variables.

To use PRINTJOB and ENDPRINTJOB, you must do a bit of FoxPro programming. The pseudo-English format of such a program is as follows:

```
PRINTJOB
    FOR EACH RECORD IN THE CUSTOMER DATABASE PRINT
    customer information
        MOVE TO ORDER DATABASE FOR EACH RECORD OF
            CURRENT CUSTOMER
        PRINT
    order information
    ENDFOR
ENDPRINTJOB
```

This program could not be done in the Layout view, because it requires looping through the CUSTOMER database and, for each record in that database, looping through the appropriate records in the ORDER database. FoxReport allows looping through only one database. So for a report like this, a program using PRINTJOB and ENDPRINTJOB is perfect. The PRINTJOB and ENDPRINTJOB commands relieve the programmer of keeping track of the number of lines printed, when to go to a new page, what the margins are, and so forth.

The example presented is a bit complex. To learn how to use PRINTJOB and ENDPRINTJOB, you should work through a simpler program; therefore, in the next section you learn how to use this technique with a single database file.

Writing the Report Program

Figure 9.23 shows a simple report generated with PRINTJOB and END-PRINTJOB commands in a program file.

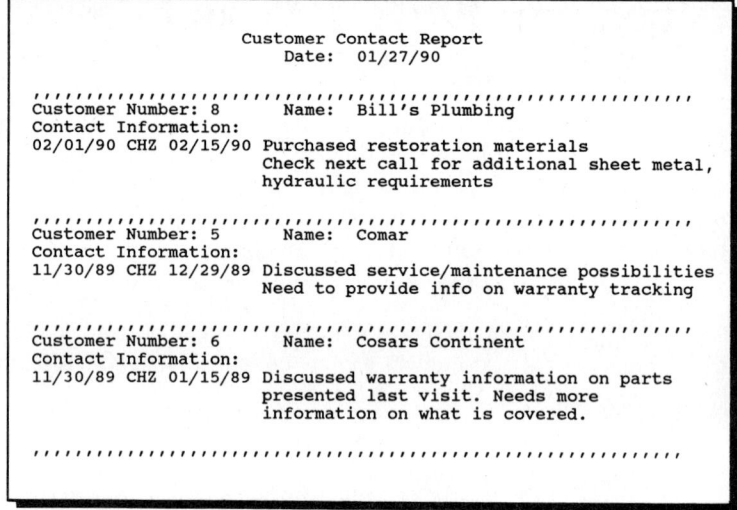

Fig. 9.23.
A simple report generated with a PRINTJOB.. ENDPRINTJOB program.

The program file that generated this report is as follows:

```
SET TALK OFF

* set up the database files and relations
SELECT 1
USE CUSTOMER INDEX CUSTNAME

SELECT 2
USE CONTACT INDEX CUST_NUM

SELECT 1
SET RELATION TO CUST_NUM INTO CONTACT

* set some print job variables
_RMARGIN = 80
_LMARGIN = 0
_WRAP = .T.

* start the printjob
PRINTJOB

    * write a title
    * set the text alignment to be centered between the margins

    _ALIGNMENT = "CENTER"
    ? "Customer Contact Report"
    ? "Date: ", DTOC(DATE())
```

```
* now reset alignment back to LEFT
_ALIGNMENT = "LEFT"

DO WHILE .NOT. EOF()
   ?
   ? REPLICATE(CHR(196),79        && put a line above the record
   ? 'Customer Number:', CUST_NUM, 'Name: ',CUST_NAME
   ? 'Contact Information:'
SELECT CONTACT                    && move to CONTACT database
DO WHILE CUST_NUM = CUSTOMER->CUST_NUM
      ? CONT_DATE, SALESPERS, FOLLOW_DTE, CONT_RPT
     SKIP
   ENDDO
   SET CONSOLE OFF
   WAIT
   SET CONSOLE ON
   SELECT CUSTOMER              && move back to CUSTOMER
   SKIP                         && go to the next record
  ENDDO                         && loop back to start
ENDPRINTJOB

RETURN
*: EOF: PRINTTST.PRG
```

The output for the report is generated by the ? command, which prints the variables listed on the same line. Variables can be database fields, literal texts, or FoxPro expressions. You can use the TRANSFORM clause as you would a PICTURE clause in a FoxReport.

When FoxPro runs a program with the DO command and encounters a PRINTJOB statement, it knows to format output according to the values of system variables. These variables control the number of lines to a page, margins, and so forth. FoxPro continues to format the pages according to these variables until it encounters an ENDPRINTJOB command. At that point, FoxPro reverts to a screen-oriented program. By using PRINTJOB and ENDPRINTJOB, you can create simple or complex reports and not worry about line counts and page breaks.

Setting System Print Variables

The important system variables you use in PRINTJOB..ENDPRINTJOB reports are listed below. You set them with a simple assignment statement, such as

_PLENGTH = 48

which sets the page length to 48 lines. The following assignments can be made from the command line, before running the report program, or as command lines in the program itself:

❏ _ALIGNMENT = <exprC> Used to determine how to justify output on the report. You can assign LEFT, RIGHT, or CENTER to _ALIGNMENT.

❏ _INDENT = <exprN> Sets an indent value. FoxPro will indent lines this number of columns from the left margin.

❏ _LMARGIN = <expnN> Sets the left margin, from 0 to 254 spaces from the physical left margin of the printer.

❏ _PCOPIES = <exprN> Number of copies to print.

❏ _PECODE = <exprC> A string of codes, usually printer codes, that will be sent to the printer at the start of the PRINTJOB. This can be used for printer set up codes that may be necessary. Your printer manual will have more information on this. You can use _PECODE to set the printer to different character sizes, italics, bold letters or other options.

❏ _PLENGTH = <exprN> Sets the page length. FoxPro will move the printer to a new page, and print any header information when it reaches the line defined by _PLENGTH.

❏ _PSPACING = <exprN> Sets the line spacing for the report. You can set line spacing from 1 to 3 lines.

❏ _RMARGIN = <exprN> Sets the right margin.

There are many less-used system print variables described in the FoxPro *Commands & Functions* manual.

Using the Program

To use a PRINTJOB..ENDPRINTJOB program, save the program with a file name and DO that file name. By default, output will go to the screen. If you want output to go to the printer, enter the following command before you do the report file (you also can include it as a line in the report file):

SET PRINTER ON

If you want the output to go to a file, enter these two commands:

SET ALTERNATE TO *file_name*
SET ALTERNATE ON

which tell FoxPro to route a copy of all screen output to the file *file_name*. Remember, though, to stop output to the ALTERNATE file with the command

    SET ALTERNATE OFF

when you're finished. Otherwise, everything that appears in the command window also appears in the report file along with your report.

Writing reports with the PRINTJOB and ENDPRINTJOB commands requires a bit of practice at FoxPro programming. This skill pays off as you create more complex reports that may loop through different databases or do different types of summaries depending on the data. For these reports, you have to do some basic programming. The PRINTJOB and ENDPRINT-JOB commands simplify the bookkeeping aspects of this programming.

Chapter Summary

Report writing is never the high point of database design and development. Yet this phase of your system can really show off your design skills and FoxPro expertise. Using FoxReport and the Layout window gives you a quick and easy way to create most of the reports you will ever need for your databases.

For those times when more complexity is needed, FoxPro gives you its programming capability, tied to the PRINTJOB and ENDPRINTJOB commands, which relieve you of the task of programming for page breaks, indents, right and left margins and the other details of report writing. You will find both these approaches to FoxPro reports valuable and rewarding.

Part III

Advanced FoxPro

Includes

Quick Start 3: Building an Application

Creating Applications with FoxPro

Programming with FoxPro

3

Building an Application

As you become more proficient at using FoxPro, you will find that you grow tired of going through the process of opening database files with the File Open menu, attaching index files with the View Setup dialog, choosing Format files and report files, and so on. Eventually, you will think about using the power of FoxPro to create a ready-to-run application.

You also may find that others want to use your FoxPro systems. For these users who are unfamiliar with the intricacies of FoxPro, you need to provide a turn-key system—one that users can turn on and run without needing to know the details of how FoxPro works. For these users you need to develop a FoxPro application system.

A FoxPro application is a shell of programs that do the things that you, as a FoxPro developer, do with the various FoxPro menus and dialogs. The shell takes care of the details of using FoxPro by opening the proper files, setting up the correct parameters, and so on. A good application also limits the menu items to those necessary for the specific application.

This quick start introduces you to building such an application system. You learn how to create menus for the application, how to put programs and reports you have written into the application or call FoxPro dialogs directly from the shell, and how to test the application to make sure that the application works. When you're finished with this quick start, you will have a basic knowledge of FoxPro application programming.

Creating an Application

If you need to create an application that works with only one database file, you can use FoxView and the FoxPro templates that function in Fox-View. To create a single-file application, follow these steps:

1. Invoke FoxView by selecting FoxView from the Program menu or entering *FoxView* in the Command window.

2. Press Enter when the FoxView opening screen appears to move to the FoxView command line. There, you can tell FoxView what database file to use with the USE database command. If you have already created an input screen for this application and want to use it, use the LOAD *screen_name* command. Figure QS3.1 shows the FoxView command screen with a command to use the database file CUSTOMER.

Fig. QS3.1.
Starting a
FoxView session
by using a
database file.

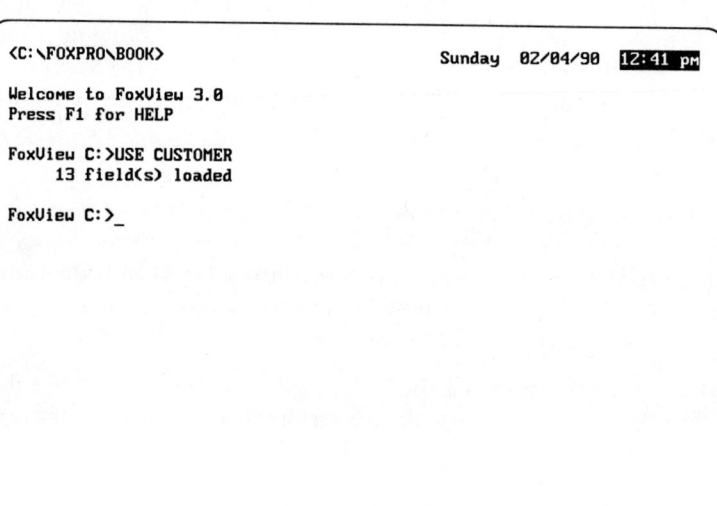

```
<C:\FOXPRO\BOOK>                        Sunday  02/04/90  12:41 PM

Welcome to FoxView 3.0
Press F1 for HELP

FoxView C:>USE CUSTOMER
        13 field(s) loaded

FoxView C:>_
```

3. Press F10 to move to FoxView's Form view, where you can create the screen form. Chapter 2 explains how to create and edit a screen form. You can see a completed screen form for the CUSTOMER database in figure QS3.2.

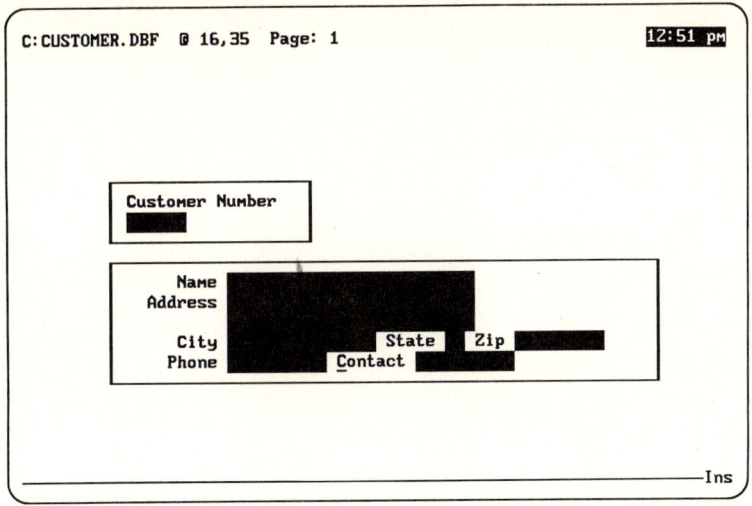

Fig. QS3.2.
The complete
FoxView screen
form for the
CUSTOMER
database.

4. Save the design of your screen by pressing Esc to activate the FoxView menu bar, moving to the Load pad (use the arrow keys) and then moving the menu highlight to Save Table. Pressing the Enter key will place the name of the current FoxView Table (which is how FoxView saves screen forms) in the text editing area at the lower left corner of the screen. Figure QS3.3 shows FoxView waiting for the Table name.

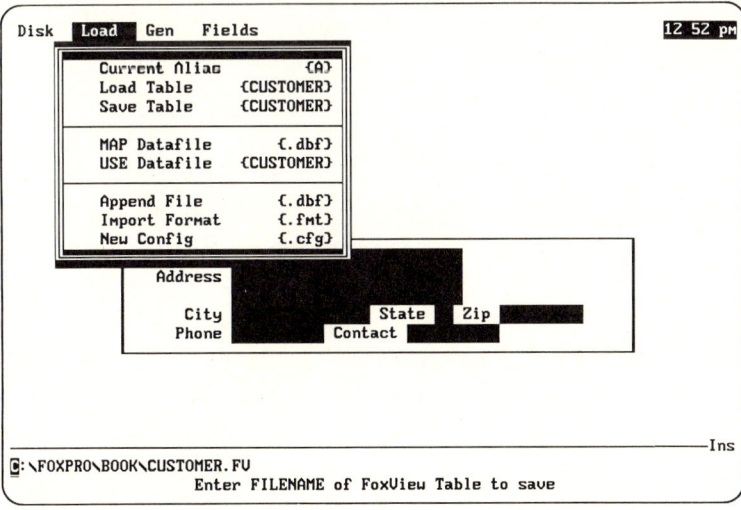

Fig. QS3.3.
Entering a name
for FoxView to
use in saving the
FoxView table.

If you want to save the table with the name shown, press Enter. If you want to give this table a new name, enter the name here. This allows you to save more than one form design for each database. For now, press Enter to save the table.

5. Using the arrow keys, move to the Gen menu pad. The pull-down menu should have highlighted the menu bar Select From Template List. If the pull-down menu does not highlight the correct menu bar, use the up- and down-arrow keys to highlight the Select From Template List bar and press Enter.

6. The bar titled FoxPro Advanced Application should be highlighted (see fig. QS3.4). If it is not, use the up- and down-arrow keys to highlight it and press Enter.

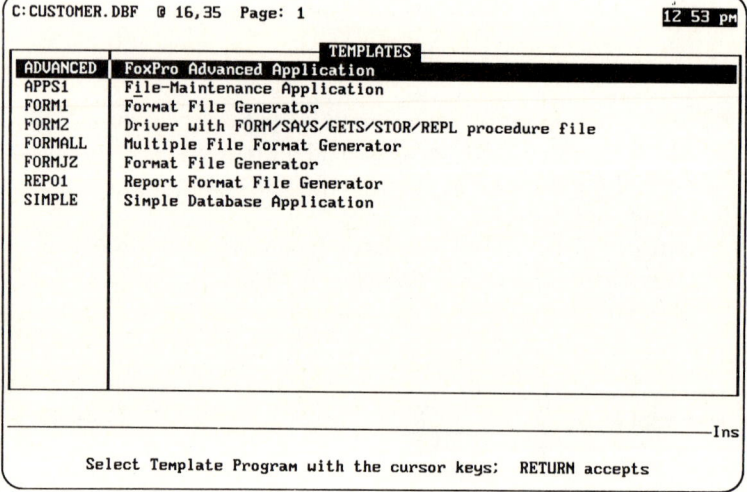

Fig. QS3.4.
Selecting FoxPro
Advanced
Application from
the template list.

```
C:CUSTOMER.DBF  @ 16,35  Page: 1                              12 53 pm
                          ┌─────────TEMPLATES─────────┐
      ┌─────────┬──────────────────────────────────────────────────────┐
      │ ADVANCED│ FoxPro Advanced Application                           │
      │ APPS1   │ File-Maintenance Application                          │
      │ FORM1   │ Format File Generator                                 │
      │ FORM2   │ Driver with FORM/SAYS/GETS/STOR/REPL procedure file   │
      │ FORMALL │ Multiple File Format Generator                        │
      │ FORMJZ  │ Format File Generator                                 │
      │ REPO1   │ Report Format File Generator                          │
      │ SIMPLE  │ Simple Database Application                           │
      │         │                                                       │
      │         │                                                       │
      │         │                                                       │
      │         │                                                       │
      │         │                                                       │
                                                                   ─Ins
           Select Template Program with the cursor keys;  RETURN accepts
```

7. FoxView will place the message

   Enter FILENAME of program to Generate

   at the bottom of the screen and await a file name from you. This is the name of the PRG program file that the Advanced Application Template will generate for you. Enter any valid MS-DOS filename, but don't add an extension; FoxView automatically adds the PRG extension that identifies the generated file as a program file. Figure QS3.5 shows this screen, with the file name CUST entered.

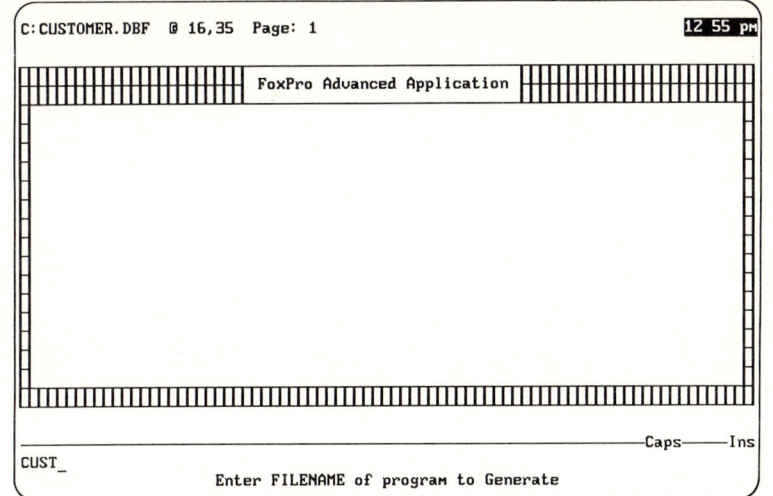

```
C:CUSTOMER.DBF  @ 16,35  Page: 1                          12 55 PM

┌──────────────────── FoxPro Advanced Application ────────────────────┐
│                                                                     │
│                                                                     │
│                                                                     │
│                                                                     │
│                                                                     │
│                                                                     │
│                                                                     │
│                                                                     │
│                                                                     │
│                                                                     │
└─────────────────────────────────────────────────────Caps────Ins────┘
CUST_
              Enter FILENAME of program to Generate
```

Fig. QS3.5.
Entering a name
for FoxView to
use in generating
an application
program.

8. FoxView asks for another name. FoxView is asking for the name of the FoxPro format file that the template will generate. You can use the same name as the application for consistency, or you can give any other valid MS-DOS filename. As with the PRG filename, don't add an extension; FoxView will automatically add the FMT extension FoxPro needs to identify the file as a format file.

9. Now you can sit back and watch the Advanced Application Template generate a host of FoxPro program lines on the screen. When the Advanced Application Template is done, press Enter to return to FoxView. You will also need, in this quick start, a FoxPro FMT format file that has the same screen design. Choose Select from the template list again, then choose FORM1, Format File Generator, from the template list, and give this file the name CUSTOMER. Again, FoxView appends the necessary FMT extension.

10. Press Enter, and then move to the Disk menu pad. From there, pressing Q for Quit will allow you to exit FoxView, after answering the

    Do you really want to QUIT FoxView (y/n)?

    question with a Yes. You may also be asked if you want to save the screen design.

11. You can now return to FoxPro (which will happen automatically if you invoked FoxView from FoxPro). In FoxPro, you can run your application by choosing Do from the Program menu and selecting CUST.PRG from the File Picker list of the Do dialog.

Unfortunately, some releases of the template used to create this application have a bug. Before you can run the program FoxView's template just created, you need to fix a little bug in the generated code. This bug causes the Help file to be constructed incorrectly. If this is the case in your application and you want to fix it, follow the next few steps. Because the bug doesn't affect the operation of the application, you may want to let the bug go.

To fix this bug, open the Program file CUST.PRG from the File Open menu or enter MODIFY COMMAND CUST.PRG in the Command window. When the text editing window with CUST.PRG opens, choose Find from the Goto menu and find the first occurrence of mx (see fig. QS3.6).

Fig. QS3.6.
The CUST.PRG
lines with a bug
in them; change
the mx *to* mx2.

```
 System  File  Edit  Database  Record  Program  Window
                          CUST.PRG

 * --- Removes all non-alpha characters from a string replacing them
 * --- with a space


 FUNCTION alphaonly
 PARAMETER msource
 mlen = LEN(msource)
 mtarget = ''
 FOR mx = 1 TO mlen
     mtarget = mtarget + IIF(ISALPHA(SUBSTR(msource,mx,1)),SUBSTR(msource,mx,
 ENDFOR
 RETURN mtarget
```

Now change the mx on this line and the following line to mx2 (see fig. QS3.7). Save the file with the File Save option and run this simple application by choosing Do from the Program menu. When the Do dialog appears on-screen, choose CUST.PRG and try your application.

The Advanced Application Template you called from FoxView has created a mini-FoxPro system built around the screen you created. The system has four menu pads that provide the basic database functions necessary for you or a user to enter data into the database, inquire or search the database, and create and use reports. Use these menus just as you would use FoxPro menus.

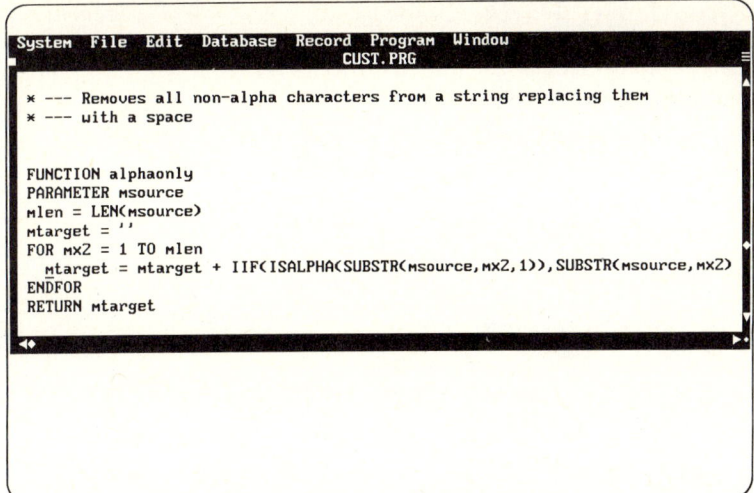

```
System  File  Edit  Database  Record  Program  Window
                            CUST.PRG
 * --- Removes all non-alpha characters from a string replacing them
 * --- with a space


 FUNCTION alphaonly
 PARAMETER msource
 mlen = LEN(msource)
 mtarget = ''
 FOR mx2 = 1 TO mlen
   mtarget = mtarget + IIF(ISALPHA(SUBSTR(msource,mx2,1)),SUBSTR(msource,mx2)
 ENDFOR
 RETURN mtarget
```

Fig. QS3.7.
The fixed lines in
CUST.PRG.

As you can see, this method gives you a quick-and-easy way to create simple applications that you or others can use. The users need not be bothered with the many details of FoxPro. Note, though, that the Report and Label options of the Utility menu call up the FoxPro Report and Label dialogs. If you want to create a true FoxPro "shell" for nonexpert users, you will need to create report and label programs for them. These would then appear in the dialog when the user requests a report or label.

Unfortunately, many FoxPro applications will require greater sophistication, particularly if they use multiple databases. Still, the process to create a more complex application is not terribly difficult. The process does, though, require some knowledge of FoxPro programming, and particularly, of how to create a menu structure in FoxPro. Chapter 11 is devoted to the joys of FoxPro programming. In this quick start, you can enter the program as the program is presented and have a working application when you're done.

Creating Menus for an Application

As you have seen using FoxPro, menus are the heart of the graphical user interface FoxPro uses. Although you could build an old-style command-line driven application or one using "make a choice" menus, FoxPro provides you with all the necessary tools to emulate the menu-driven system. The rest of this quick start shows you how to create an application using FoxPro's menus.

Defining Menu Pads

A FoxPro menu comprises two elements: the menu itself, with a number of pads, and a pop-up menu associated with each pad. In creating a menu-driven system, you need to define each of the menu pads and the options that will be included in the pop-up menus for each pad. Figure QS3.8 shows a menu and a pop-up menu and defines the terms you need to know.

Fig. QS3.8.
A menu and pop-up menu, with their elements defined.

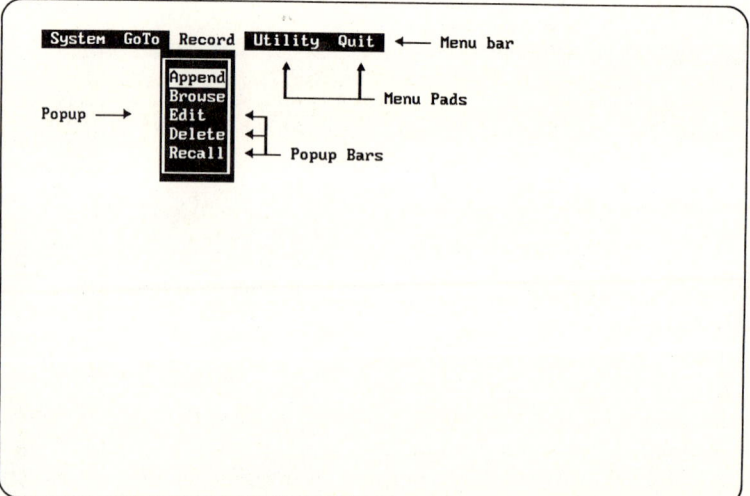

The first thing to do in creating a FoxPro menu application is to decide what pads you want on the main menu. Then, for each pad, decide what options you want to include. To implement the options, you may have to write complete FoxPro programs, or you may be able to have the menu program issue one or two commands. In the rest of this quick start, you will see how to create a menu system similar to the one created with the Advanced Application Generator in the first part of the quick start.

Creating a Menu Program

A menu program in FoxPro is a regular FoxPro PRG program file. Create the program by choosing New from the File menu of FoxPro and specifying Program for the type. A new text-editing window, UNTITLED.PRG, will appear. Give the file a name by choosing Save from the File menu. Now, you're ready to create a menu-driven application program. To create your menu program, follow these steps:

1. Put a CLEAR statement into the program. When you execute the program, the screen clears. FoxPro programs are not case sensitive; upper- and lowercase letters are interpreted the same.

2. Add a HIDE WINDOWS ALL statement to the program. This will hide all the windows on the screen, giving your application a full and clear screen.

3. Define the menu using the DEFINE MENU command. You need to give the menu a name, to which you will refer later when activating the menu. Figure QS3.9 shows the MENU_1.PRG window with the menu defined.

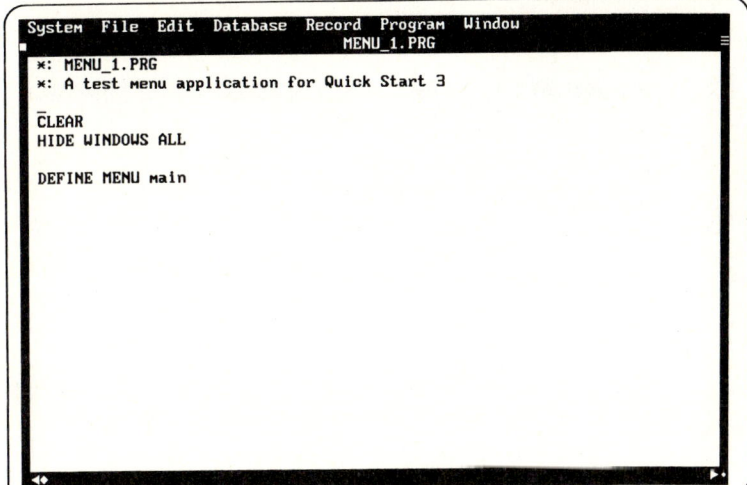

Fig. QS3.9. MENU_1.PRG with the top menu defined.

4. Define each of the pads of the menu, using the DEFINE PAD command. Each pad gets a name along with PROMPT, which is what will form the pad, and a location, specified in FoxPro's row and column format. If you want the prompt to have the first character highlighted, precede the character with the two characters \<. MENU_1.PRG, with its pads defined, is shown in figure QS3.10.

5. Tell FoxPro what to do when a menu pad is selected. This is done with the ON SELECTION PAD command. At this point, have FoxPro execute a subroutine named msg, which writes a message to the screen enabling you to test the menu program. You can see the ON SELECTION PAD commands added to your menu program in figure QS3.11.

Fig. QS3.10. MENU_1.PRG with each of the menu pads defined.

```
System  File  Edit  Database  Record  Program  Window
                              MENU_1.PRG
*: MENU_1.PRG
*: A test menu application for Quick Start 3

CLEAR
HIDE WINDOWS ALL

DEFINE MENU main

DEFINE PAD file    OF main PROMPT "\<System"  AT 00, 00
DEFINE PAD Goto    OF main PROMPT "\<GoTo"    AT 00, 09
DEFINE PAD Record  OF main PROMPT "\<Record"  AT 00, 16
DEFINE PAD Util    OF main PROMPT "\<Utility" AT 00, 24
DEFINE PAD quit    OF main PROMPT "\<Quit"    AT 00, 33
```

Fig. QS3.11. MENU_1.PRG with the ON SELECTION PAD command lines added.

```
System  File  Edit  Database  Record  Program  Window
                              MENU_1.PRG
*: A test menu application for Quick Start 3

CLEAR
HIDE WINDOWS ALL

DEFINE MENU main

DEFINE PAD file    OF main PROMPT "\<System"  AT 00, 00
DEFINE PAD Goto    OF main PROMPT "\<GoTo"    AT 00, 09
DEFINE PAD Record  OF main PROMPT "\<Record"  AT 00, 16
DEFINE PAD Util    OF main PROMPT "\<Utility" AT 00, 24
DEFINE PAD quit    OF main PROMPT "\<Quit"    AT 00, 33

ON SELECTION PAD file   OF main  ACTIVATE POPUP file_pop
ON SELECTION PAD goto   OF main  ACTIVATE POPUP goto_pop
ON SELECTION PAD record OF main  ACTIVATE POPUP rec_pop
ON SELECTION PAD Util   OF main  ACTIVATE POPUP util_pop
ON SELECTION PAD quit   OF main  DO quit_prc
```

6. Enter a line that will cause the menu to be displayed and put into action; this is the ACTIVATE *menu_name* command. At the end of the program, enter the line

   ACTIVATE MENU main.

7. Enter the PROCEDURE msg subroutine. This will write out the message sent to the menu, allowing you to see that the menu is working as it should.

You now have a working menu program, as follows:

```
*: MENU_1.PRG
*: A test menu application for Quick Start 3

CLEAR
HIDE WINDOWS ALL
DEFINE MENU main

DEFINE PAD file    OF main PROMPT "\<System"  AT 00, 00
DEFINE PAD Goto    OF main PROMPT "\<Goto"    AT 00, 09
DEFINE PAD Record  OF main PROMPT "\<Record"  AT 00, 16
DEFINE PAD Util    OF main PROMPT "\<Utility" AT 00, 24
DEFINE PAD quit    OF main PROMPT "\<Quit"    AT 00, 33

ON SELECTION PAD file   OF main DO msg WITH "System"
ON SELECTION PAD goto   OF main DO msg WITH "Goto"
ON SELECTION PAD record OF main DO msg WITH "Record"
ON SELECTION PAD Util   OF main DO msg WITH "Utility"
ON SELECTION PAD quit   OF main DO msg WITH "Quit"

ACTIVATE MENU main

PROCEDURE msg

PARAMETER mchoice

@ 24, 0 CLEAR
@ 24, 0 SAY "Chose " + mchoice
RETURN
```

Now you can test this menu skeleton. Save the file again with the File Save option. Resize the MAIN_1.PRG window to a smaller part of the screen (make sure that the window doesn't cover up line 24, where the PROCEDURE msg will write its message. Choose DO MENU_1.PRG from the Program menu or DO from the Program menu and select MENU_1.PRG from the File Picker list in the DO dialog.

FoxPro will replace the FoxPro menu with the one defined in the MENU_1 program. You can select a pad as you would with FoxPro, using a mouse or the keyboard; your choice will be shown on line 24 by the PROCEDURE msg routine. Figure QS3.12 shows the screen, with the MENU_1.PRG window on-screen, your menu at the top, and a message that results from selecting the File pad. To stop the program, press Esc.

If you get an error message, or your program prints out the wrong message for your choice, review the program carefully to find the error. This part of the program must be correct before you continue with your application development process. The next step is to add pop-up menus to each of the pads.

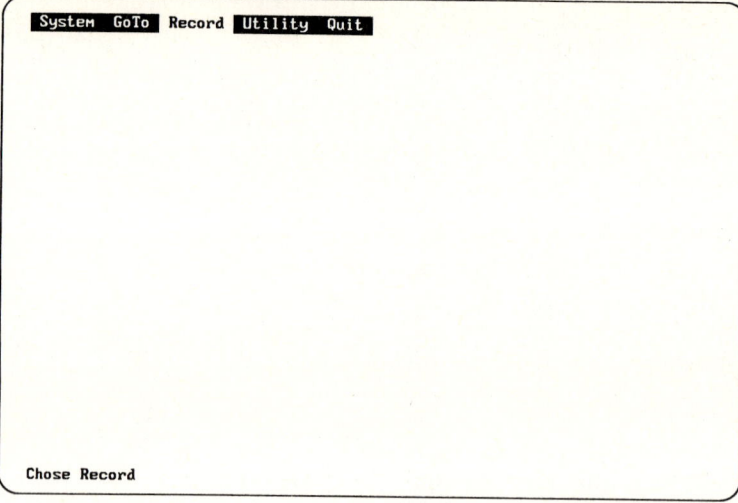

Fig. QS3.12
The MENU_1.PRG
application in
operation.

Defining the Pop-up Menus for Each Pad

Each pad on the Main menu has a pop-up menu associated with the pad. The bars of the pop-up menu reflect actions the user can take. For instance, in the Record menu of the example, the user can add a record by selecting Append or delete a record by choosing Delete. Each of the selections on a pop-up menu correspond to some action you want FoxPro to take when the user selects the bar. Adding pop-up menus to your menus is not difficult—just follow these steps:

1. To add the pop-up menus to your menu program, move the cursor to a blank line between the last DEFINE PAD line and before the first ON SELECTION PAD line. Define the pop-up menu associated with the Record pad using the DEFINE POPUP command. You must give the row and column coordinates of the upper left corner of the pop-up menu. Usually, this will be in line with—or a column or two to the right of—the start of the menu pad with which the pop-up menu is associated. Figure QS3.13 shows MENU_1.PRG with this pop-up menu defined.

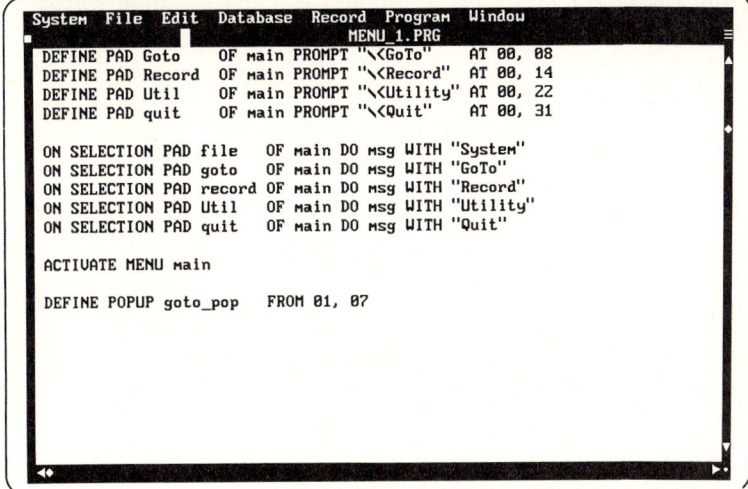

```
System  File  Edit  Database  Record  Program  Window
                           MENU_1.PRG
 DEFINE PAD Goto     OF main PROMPT "\<GoTo"      AT 00, 08
 DEFINE PAD Record   OF main PROMPT "\<Record"    AT 00, 14
 DEFINE PAD Util     OF main PROMPT "\<Utility"   AT 00, 22
 DEFINE PAD quit     OF main PROMPT "\<Quit"      AT 00, 31

 ON SELECTION PAD file    OF main DO msg WITH "System"
 ON SELECTION PAD goto    OF main DO msg WITH "GoTo"
 ON SELECTION PAD record  OF main DO msg WITH "Record"
 ON SELECTION PAD Util    OF main DO msg WITH "Utility"
 ON SELECTION PAD quit    OF main DO msg WITH "Quit"

 ACTIVATE MENU main

 DEFINE POPUP goto_pop     FROM 01, 07
```

Fig. QS3.13.
The first pop-up menu defined in MENU_1.PRG.

2. Define each bar of the pop-up menu, using the DEFINE BAR command. Each bar has a number that defines it. The pop-up menu will be constructed with bar number 1 on the first line, bar number 2 on the second line, and so forth. For each bar, you also must define the PROMPT, which is the character string that will appear as the menu bar. Note the difference between the bar's number and PROMPT; the number will be used by your program for various purposes and will never be known to the user. The PROMPT is what the user sees on the pop-up menu. Figure QS3.14 presents the program with the pop-up menu for the Record pad included.

```
System  File  Edit  Database  Record  Program  Window
                           MENU_1.PRG
 DEFINE PAD Record   OF main PROMPT "\<Record"    AT 00, 14
 DEFINE PAD Util     OF main PROMPT "\<Utility"   AT 00, 22
 DEFINE PAD quit     OF main PROMPT "\<Quit"      AT 00, 31

 ON SELECTION PAD file    OF main DO msg WITH "System"
 ON SELECTION PAD goto    OF main DO msg WITH "GoTo"
 ON SELECTION PAD record  OF main DO msg WITH "Record"
 ON SELECTION PAD Util    OF main DO msg WITH "Utility"
 ON SELECTION PAD quit    OF main DO msg WITH "Quit"

 ACTIVATE MENU main

 DEFINE POPUP goto_pop     FROM 01, 07
 DEFINE BAR 1 OF goto_pop PROMPT "\<Next"
 DEFINE BAR 2 OF goto_pop PROMPT "\<Previous"
 DEFINE BAR 3 OF goto_pop PROMPT "\<Top of file"
 DEFINE BAR 4 OF goto_pop PROMPT "\<Bottom of file"
 _
```

Fig. QS3.14.
Adding define bars with prompts for the pop-up menu.

3. As with the menu, you must program a way to determine what the user has chosen, process the user's choice, and take some action on the choice. This is done with an ON SELECTION POPUP command, which activates a PROCEDURE to take appropriate action; the ON SELECTION POPUP uses the DO command to invoke the PROCEDURE and passes the number of the bar to the PROCEDURE. Figure QS3.15 displays the MAIN_1.PRG with the ON SELECTION POPUP command added, using a DO clause to invoke a procedure.

Fig. QS3.15.
Adding the ON SELECTION..DO command for the Goto pop-up menu.

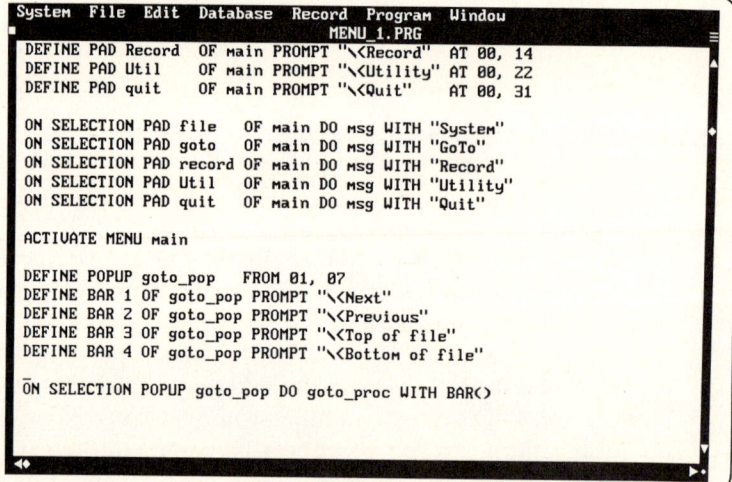

```
System  File  Edit  Database  Record  Program  Window
                         MENU_1.PRG
DEFINE PAD Record    OF main PROMPT "\<Record"    AT 00, 14
DEFINE PAD Util      OF main PROMPT "\<Utility"   AT 00, 22
DEFINE PAD quit      OF main PROMPT "\<Quit"      AT 00, 31

ON SELECTION PAD file    OF main DO msg WITH "System"
ON SELECTION PAD goto    OF main DO msg WITH "GoTo"
ON SELECTION PAD record  OF main DO msg WITH "Record"
ON SELECTION PAD Util    OF main DO msg WITH "Utility"
ON SELECTION PAD quit    OF main DO msg WITH "Quit"

ACTIVATE MENU main

DEFINE POPUP goto_pop    FROM 01, 07
DEFINE BAR 1 OF goto_pop PROMPT "\<Next"
DEFINE BAR 2 OF goto_pop PROMPT "\<Previous"
DEFINE BAR 3 OF goto_pop PROMPT "\<Top of file"
DEFINE BAR 4 OF goto_pop PROMPT "\<Bottom of file"

ON SELECTION POPUP goto_pop DO goto_proc WITH BAR()
```

4. To process the choice made by the user from the pop-up menu, you need a small procedure, which recognizes which pop-up menu was selected and takes appropriate action. You will have to have such a procedure for each pop-up menu defined, so they must be named uniquely. Figure QS3.16 shows the PROCEDURE goto_prc, which processes the choices if the user chooses a bar in the Goto pop-up menu. At this point, the actions are only to display the selected bar for testing purposes.

You should now follow the above steps for each of the menu pads, defining the bars, specifying the action to take with an ON SELECTION... command, and writing a simple procedure to process the action.

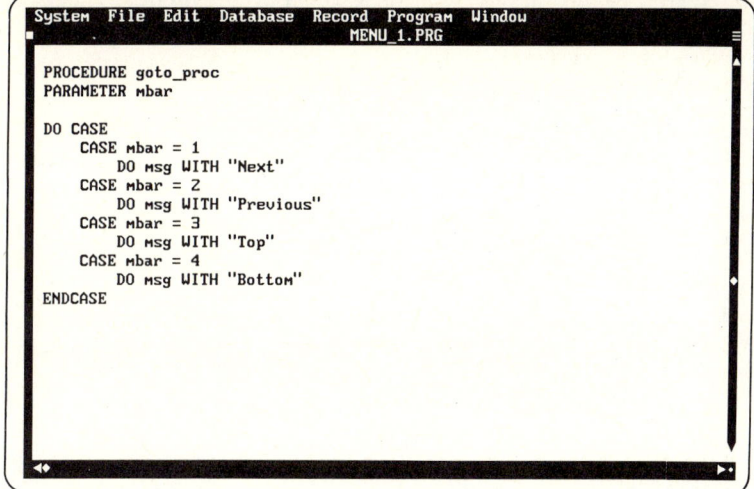

```
System  File  Edit  Database  Record  Program  Window
                         MENU_1.PRG

PROCEDURE goto_proc
PARAMETER mbar

DO CASE
    CASE mbar = 1
        DO msg WITH "Next"
    CASE mbar = 2
        DO msg WITH "Previous"
    CASE mbar = 3
        DO msg WITH "Top"
    CASE mbar = 4
        DO msg WITH "Bottom"
ENDCASE
```

Fig. QS3.16.
The PROCEDURE goto_prc, which processes choices made in the Goto pop-up menu.

5. Because now you want the Main menu to show a pop-up menu when a pad is selected instead of executing the msg procedure, change the ON SELECTION PAD commands to activate the appropriate pop-up menu when a pad is selected. The format for this command is as follows:

    ON PAD pad_name OF menu_name ACTIVATE POPUP popup_name

Figure QS3.17 shows the ON PAD commands, which take the place of the ON SELECTION PAD DO msg WITH commands in MENU_1.PRG.

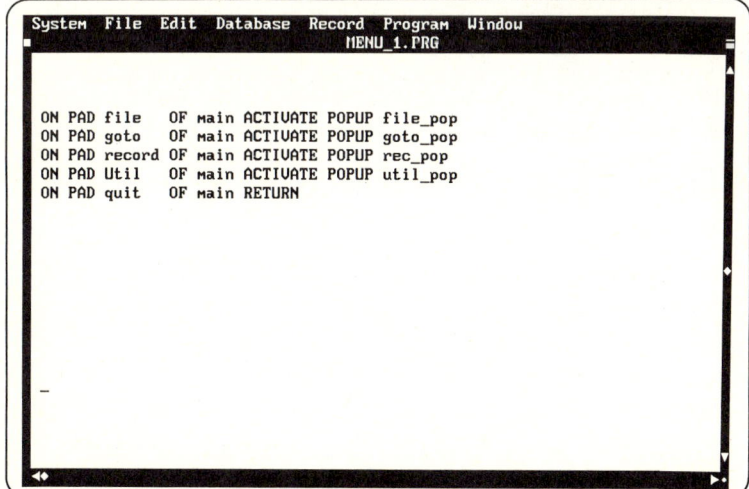

```
System  File  Edit  Database  Record  Program  Window
                         MENU_1.PRG

ON PAD file   OF main ACTIVATE POPUP file_pop
ON PAD goto   OF main ACTIVATE POPUP goto_pop
ON PAD record OF main ACTIVATE POPUP rec_pop
ON PAD Util   OF main ACTIVATE POPUP util_pop
ON PAD quit   OF main RETURN
```

Fig. QS3.17.
The ON PAD..ACTIVATE POPUP commands replace the ON SELECTION PAD commands.

Your new version of the application program, pop-up menus, and processes to handle the selections should look like the following program:

```
*: MENU_1.PRG
*: A test menu application for Quick Start 3

CLEAR
HIDE WINDOWS ALL

* define the Main menu

DEFINE MENU main
DEFINE PAD file    OF main PROMPT "\<System"  AT 00, 00
DEFINE PAD Goto    OF main PROMPT "\<Goto"     AT 00, 08
DEFINE PAD Record  OF main PROMPT "\<Record"   AT 00, 14
DEFINE PAD Util    OF main PROMPT "\<Utility"  AT 00, 22
DEFINE PAD quit    OF main PROMPT "\<Quit"     AT 00, 31

* define the File pop-up menu

DEFINE POPUP file_pop  FROM 01,01
DEFINE BAR 1 OF file_pop PROMPT "\<FoxPro Help"
ON SELECTION POPUP file_pop DO file_proc WITH BAR()

* define the Goto pop-up menu

DEFINE POPUP goto_pop    FROM 01, 07
DEFINE BAR 1 OF goto_pop PROMPT "\<Next"
DEFINE BAR 2 OF goto_pop PROMPT "\<Previous"
DEFINE BAR 3 OF goto_pop PROMPT "\<Top of file"
DEFINE BAR 4 OF goto_pop PROMPT "\<Bottom of file"
ON SELECTION POPUP goto_pop DO goto_proc WITH BAR()

* define the Record pop-up menu

DEFINE POPUP Rec_pop FROM 01,13
DEFINE BAR 1 OF rec_pop PROMPT "\<Append"
DEFINE BAR 2 OF rec_pop PROMPT "\<Browse"
DEFINE BAR 3 OF rec_pop PROMPT "\<Edit"
DEFINE BAR 4 OF rec_pop PROMPT "\<Delete"
DEFINE BAR 5 OF rec_pop PROMPT "\<Recall"
ON SELECTION POPUP rec_pop DO rec_proc WITH BAR()

* define the Utility pop-up menu

DEFINE POPUP util_pop FROM 01, 21
DEFINE BAR 1 OF util_pop PROMPT "\<Report"
DEFINE BAR 2 OF util_pop PROMPT "\<Label"
ON SELECTION POPUP util_pop DO utl_proc WITH BAR()
```

```
* tie pop-up menus to Main menu pads

ON PAD file   OF main ACTIVATE POPUP file_pop
ON PAD goto   OF main ACTIVATE POPUP goto_pop
ON PAD record OF main ACTIVATE POPUP rec_pop
ON PAD Util   OF main ACTIVATE POPUP util_pop
ON PAD quit   OF main RETURN

* start the Main menu

ACTIVATE MENU main
PROCEDURE rec_proc
PROCEDURE file_proc
PARAMETER mbar
DO CASE
    CASE mbar = 1
        DO msg WITH "Help"
    CASE mbar = 2
        DO msg WITH "Open"
ENDCASE
RETURN

PROCEDURE goto_proc
PARAMETER mbar

DO CASE
    CASE mbar = 1
        DO msg WITH "Next"
    CASE mbar = 2
       DO msg WITH "Previous"
    CASE mbar = 3
        DO msg WITH "Top"
    CASE mbar = 4
        DO msg WITH "Bottom"
ENDCASE

PROCEDURE rec_proc
PARAMETER mbar
DO CASE
    CASE mbar = 1
        DO msg WITH "Append"
    CASE mbar = 2
        DO msg WITH "Browse"
    CASE mbar = 3
        DO msg WITH "Edit"
    CASE mbar = 4
        DO msg WITH "Delete"
```

```
        CASE mbar = 5
               DO msg WITH "Recall"
ENDCASE
RETURN

PROCEDURE utl_proc
PARAMETER mbar
DO CASE
     CASE mbar = 1
            DO msg WITH "Report"
     CASE mbar = 2
            DO msg WITH "Label"
ENDCASE
RETURN

PROCEDURE msg
PARAMETER mchoice
@ 24, 0 CLEAR
@ 24, 0 SAY "Chose " + mchoice
RETURN
```

You now can save and test the menu again. Figure QS3.18 shows the menu in action once more, now with the Record pop-up menu activated, and it shows the on-screen results of choosing a bar from the Record pop-up menu.

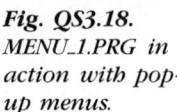

*Fig. QS3.18.
MENU_1.PRG in
action with pop-
up menus.*

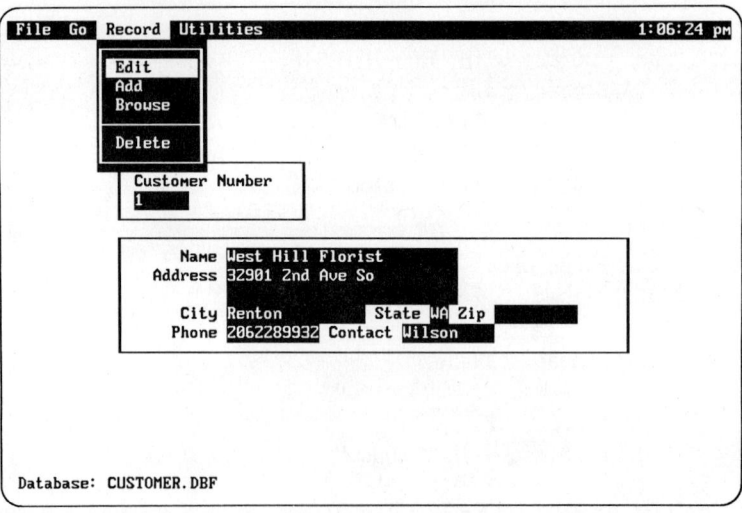

Test the menu program to see that all menu pads and pop-up menu choices work correctly. Once you know they do, it's time to add the program lines that will cause FoxPro to respond to the choices.

Defining FoxPro Actions

To make your menu program work, you now replace the messages your PROCEDUREs send to the screen with actual FoxPro commands that do what the pop-up menu choice requires. In many cases, particularly in simple applications, these can be one or two FoxPro commands. In more complex applications, the pop-up menu choice will activate a FoxPro PROCEDURE or program file. Pop-up choices could also activate yet another pop-up menu or menu.

You also need to add FoxPro commands to open the correct database file and appropriate index files. To make your menu program into a working program, perform the following steps:

1. At the beginning of the program, insert a USE dbf_name INDEX index1 command to open the database file and attach an index file to the database. If your program requires a FORMAT file, insert that line here also. If you have a VIEW file defined that sets up FoxPro as you want FoxPro, you could use a SET VIEW TO vue_file instead. In Figure QS3.19, the commands have been added to the menu program.

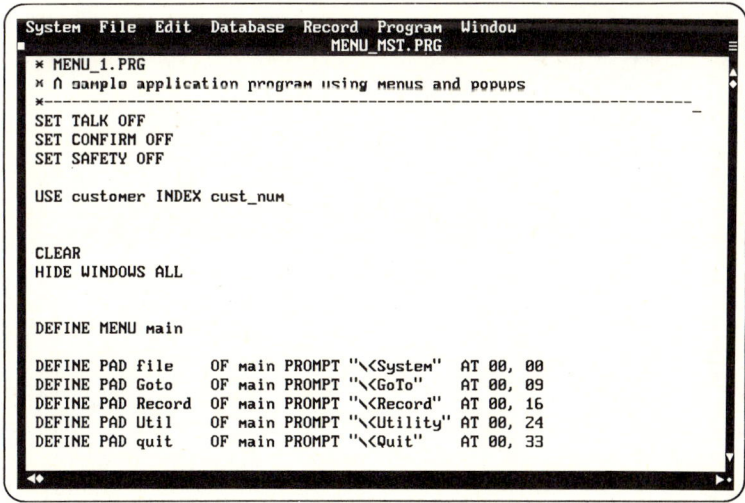

Fig. QS3.19.
Adding comments and SET commands, and opening the database and index files.

2. Put a DO WHILE loop around your ACTIVATE MENU command, to ensure that the program continues until the user chooses Quit.

3. Add the routine to display the records as you work with them. To do this, open another text editing window with the program CUSTOMER.PRG that you created in FoxView. Copy that program into the MENU_1.PRG just after the DO WHILE loop statement.

4. For each CASE statement in the PROCEDUREs that process pop-up menu choices, replace the DO msg command with commands necessary to execute the right FoxPro actions. Figure QS3.20 shows the PROCEDURE for the Records menu, with FoxPro commands replacing the DO msg command.

Fig. QS3.20.
The PROCEDURE
for the Record
pop-up menu,
with commands
replacing the
testing messages.

```
System  File  Edit  Database  Record  Program  Window
                        MENU_MST.PRG
PARAMETER mbar
DO CASE
    CASE mbar = 1
         APPEND BLANK
         DO shou_rec
         READ
    CASE mbar = 2
         BROWSE
    CASE mbar = 3
         DO shou_rec
         READ
    CASE mbar = 4
         DO shou_rec
         IF .NOT. DELETED()
              DELETE
         ENDIF
    CASE mbar = 5
         DO shou_rec
         IF DELETED()
              RECALL
         ENDIF
ENDCASE
```

5. In the case of the Report and Label choices in the Utility pop-up menu, you need to bring up the Report or Label dialog to allow the user to choose which Report or Label format he wants to print. To do this, for the Report choice, you should enter *REPORT* and for the Label option, you should enter *LABEL*.

Note | This doesn't replicate the application created in FoxView with the Advanced Application Template, which allows the user to create or modify reports of labels. Such a program is beyond the scope of this quick start. If you want to include such an option, you can open the CUST.PRG file and cut and paste the appropriate PROCEDUREs from that file into your application.

6. The Quit choice of the System pop-up menu must restore FoxPro's environment to what it was before the program was run. To do so, insert a USE command, which closes the database and index files, a DEACTIVATE MENU command to take your application menu off the screen, and a SHOW WINDOWS ALL command to display the screen windows that were open when you started.

7. Last, you need a PROCEDURE that will put the form you created in FoxView onto the screen. To do this, add the following line:

    PROCEDURE show_rec

    Open a new text window with the program CUSTOMER.FMT in the window by using the File Open menu option. Choose Select All from the Edit menu, and then choose Copy. Close the CUSTOMER.FMT window, place the cursor in MENU_1.PRG just below the PROCEDURE show_rec line, and choose Paste from the Edit menu. The entire CUSTOMER.FMT file will be placed in the procedure show_rec, which allows you to call the file from the MENU_1.PRG.

When you have finished this, your application is complete and ready to test. The entire MENU_1.PRG file is as follows:

```
*: MENU_1.PRG
*: A test menu application for Quick Start 3

CLEAR
HIDE WINDOWS ALL

* define the Main menu

DEFINE MENU main
DEFINE PAD file    OF main PROMPT "\<System"  AT 00, 00
DEFINE PAD Goto    OF main PROMPT "\<Goto"    AT 00, 08
DEFINE PAD Record  OF main PROMPT "\<Record"  AT 00, 14
DEFINE PAD Util    OF main PROMPT "\<Utility" AT 00, 22
DEFINE PAD quit    OF main PROMPT "\<Quit"    AT 00, 31

* define the File pop-up menu

DEFINE POPUP file_pop  FROM 01,01
DEFINE BAR 1 OF file_pop PROMPT "\<FoxPro Help"
ON SELECTION POPUP file_pop DO file_proc WITH BAR()
```

```
* define the Goto pop-up menu

DEFINE POPUP goto_pop    FROM 01, 07
DEFINE BAR 1 OF goto_pop PROMPT "\<Next"
DEFINE BAR 2 OF goto_pop PROMPT "\<Previous"
DEFINE BAR 3 OF goto_pop PROMPT "\<Top of file"
DEFINE BAR 4 OF goto_pop PROMPT "\<Bottom of file"
ON SELECTION POPUP goto_pop DO goto_proc WITH BAR()

* define the Record pop-up menu

DEFINE POPUP Rec_pop FROM 01,13
DEFINE BAR 1 OF rec_pop PROMPT "\<Append"
DEFINE BAR 2 OF rec_pop PROMPT "\<Browse"
DEFINE BAR 3 OF rec_pop PROMPT "\<Edit"
DEFINE BAR 4 OF rec_pop PROMPT "\<Delete"
DEFINE BAR 5 OF rec_pop PROMPT "\<Recall"
ON SELECTION POPUP rec_pop DO rec_proc WITH BAR()

* define the Utility pop-up menu

DEFINE POPUP util_pop FROM 01, 21
DEFINE BAR 1 OF util_pop PROMPT "\<Report"
DEFINE BAR 2 OF util_pop PROMPT "\<Label"
ON SELECTION POPUP util_pop DO utl_proc WITH BAR()

* tie pop-up menus to Main menu pads

ON PAD file   OF main ACTIVATE POPUP file_pop
ON PAD goto   OF main ACTIVATE POPUP goto_pop
ON PAD record OF main ACTIVATE POPUP rec_pop
ON PAD Util   OF main ACTIVATE POPUP util_pop
ON PAD quit   OF main RETURN

* start the Main menu

ACTIVATE MENU main

PROCEDURE rec_proc
PROCEDURE file_proc
PARAMETER mbar
DO CASE
    CASE mbar = 1
        DO msg WITH "Help"
    CASE mbar = 2
        DO msg WITH "Open"
ENDCASE
RETURN
```

```
PROCEDURE goto_proc
PARAMETER mbar

DO CASE
    CASE mbar = 1
        DO msg WITH "Next"
    CASE mbar = 2
        DO msg WITH "Previous"
    CASE mbar = 3
        DO msg WITH "Top"
    CASE mbar = 4
        DO msg WITH "Bottom"
ENDCASE

PROCEDURE rec_proc
PARAMETER mbar
DO CASE
    CASE mbar = 1
        DO msg WITH "Append"
    CASE mbar = 2
        DO msg WITH "Browse"
    CASE mbar = 3
        DO msg WITH "Edit"
    CASE mbar = 4
        DO msg WITH "Delete"
    CASE mbar = 5
        DO msg WITH "Recall"
ENDCASE
RETURN

PROCEDURE utl_proc
PARAMETER mbar
DO CASE
    CASE mbar = 1
        DO msg WITH "Report"
    CASE mbar = 2
        DO msg WITH "Label"
ENDCASE
RETURN

PROCEDURE msg
PARAMETER mchoice
@ 24, 0 CLEAR
@ 24, 0 SAY "Chose " + mchoice
RETURN
```

Now you can test your program. Open the Program menu. If your program is in the active window, the last entry in the Program pop-up menu will be DO MENU_1.PRG (see fig. QS3.21), and you can select the entry to run your program.

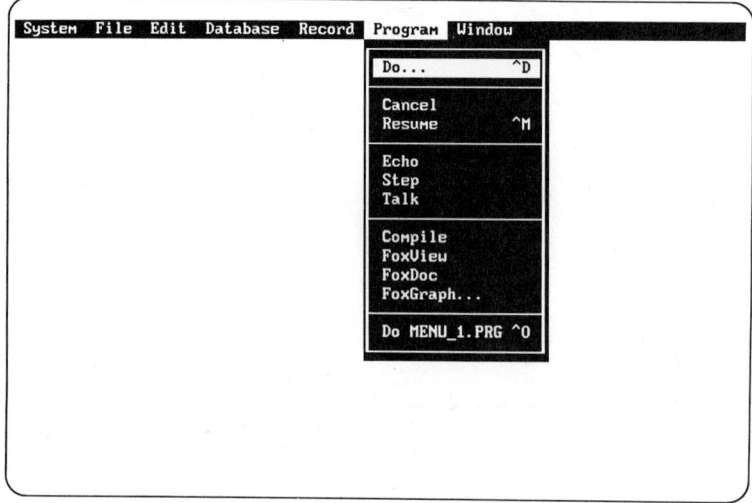

Fig. QS3.21. The Program pop-up menu, with DO MENU_1.PRG added to the bottom.

If the program is not in the active window, you select Do. The Do dialog opens, and you can select your program from the scrollable list (see fig. QS3.22).

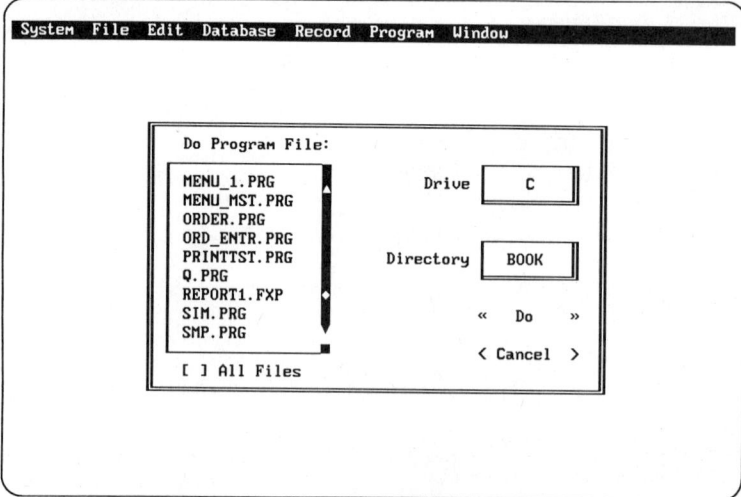

Fig. QS3.22. The Do Program File dialog, with a scrollable list of PRG program files.

Debugging Your Application

Unfortunately, applications don't always run perfectly the first time. In fact, you can get errors when you try to run the program, because at that time FoxPro "compiles" the program lines into a format that FoxPro can execute faster; if FoxPro finds problems with the code, FoxPro will stop and issue an error message (see fig. QS3.23). You must return to the text editing window and correct the error. Fortunately, FoxPro is nice enough to highlight the line in which the error was detected.

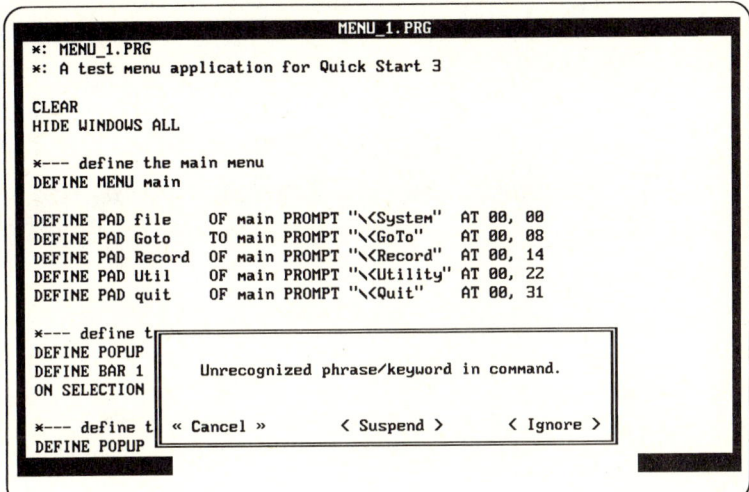

Fig. QS3.23.
An error message.

You may find that a program compiles (which means that FoxPro found nothing syntactically wrong) yet still does not run as you want the program to run. This means that you have made an error of program logic. The best way to find errors is to use the Trace and Debug windows.

Using the Trace Window

The Trace window allows you to see your program in action, step-by-step. To use the Trace window, do the following:

1. Select Step from the Program menu. This causes FoxPro to execute your program one line at a time. Then start your program running, using either the Do choice from the Program pop-up menu or the DO MENU_1.PRG from the same pop-up menu if your program is in the active window.

2. FoxPro will start your program, but execute only the first line. Open the Trace window from the Window pop-up menu and move and resize the window so that it will not block your menus. Figure QS3.24 shows the Trace window opened.

Fig. QS3.24.
The Trace window, with MENU_1.PRG executing in it.

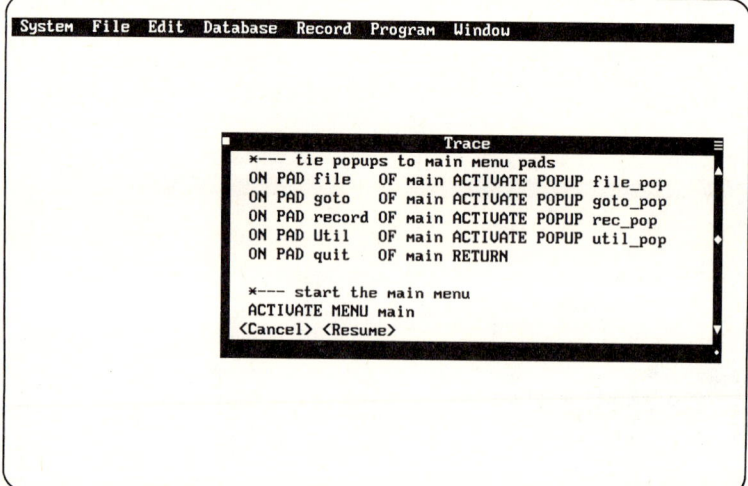

```
 System  File  Edit  Database  Record  Program  Window
```

```
                              Trace
 *--- tie popups to main menu pads
 ON PAD file    OF main ACTIVATE POPUP file_pop
 ON PAD goto    OF main ACTIVATE POPUP goto_pop
 ON PAD record  OF main ACTIVATE POPUP rec_pop
 ON PAD Util    OF main ACTIVATE POPUP util_pop
 ON PAD quit    OF main RETURN

 *--- start the main menu
 ACTIVATE MENU main
 <Cancel> <Resume>
```

3. Click the Resume box of the Trace window to execute the next line of your program. Continue to execute lines one at a time and watch FoxPro place your menu on the screen. At times, you may find that your program causes FoxPro to make a window active on top of the Trace window; in this case, select Trace from the Window menu or press Ctrl-F1 to cycle through windows until the Trace window returns to the top.

4. You also will find times when you want to leap through large hunks of the program rather than going line-by-line. You can set a "breakpoint," that is, a line at which execution will stop, in the Trace window. Scroll to the point at which you want FoxPro to suspend and click on the line with the mouse or press Enter from the keyboard. A diamond will appear to the left of the line, indicating a breakpoint (see fig. QS3.25).

5. Now, from the Program menu, select Step, which will SET STEP OFF. Choose Resume, either from the Program window or the Trace window. FoxPro will execute your program to the breakpoint and stop. Select Step again to SET STEP ON and use the Trace window to execute the rest of the program one line at a time, or until you turn the Step off.

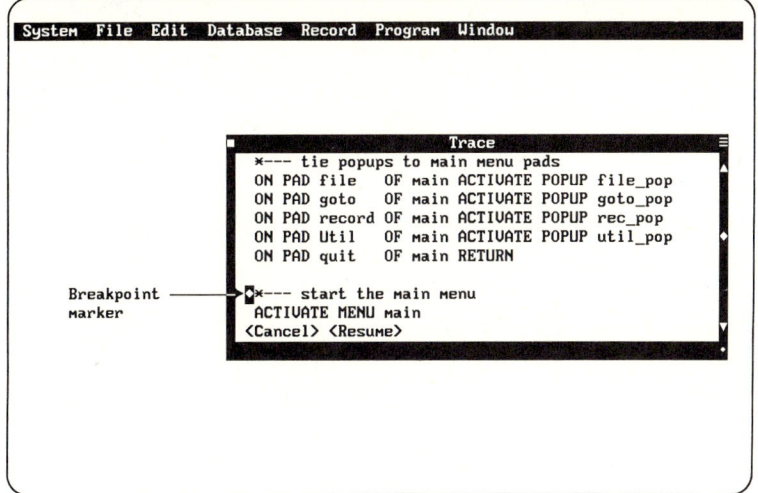

Fig. QS3.25.
The Trace window, with a breakpoint set to stop program execution.

6. If you need to watch the value of variables in your program, the Debug window enables you to do so. Open the Debug window from the Window menu along with the Trace window. In the left side of the Debug window, enter the variable name you want to watch. Then, as you run or Trace your program, the value of that variable will appear in the right side of the window. By clicking in the column between the right and left sides of the Debug window, you tell FoxPro to suspend execution of the program when the value of that variable changes. Figure QS3.26 shows the Debug window, with a variable listed and a breakpoint set.

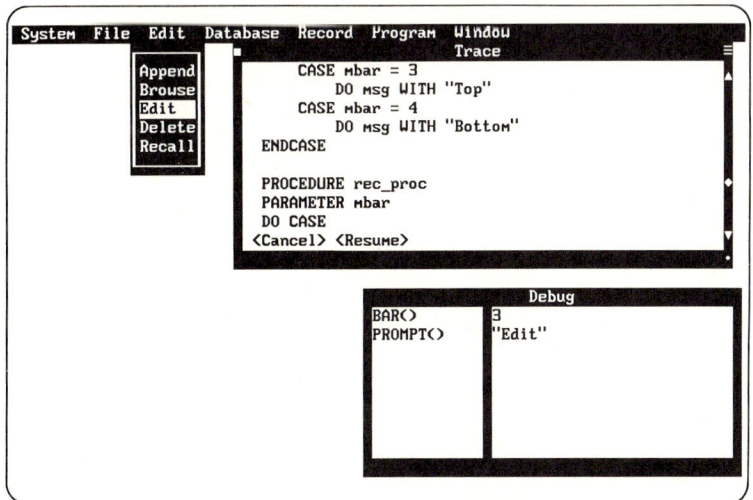

Fig. QS3.26.
The Debug window, showing variables and their values as the program executes.

The application you have just created is quite simple. This application contains no error-checking routines or ways to change the original Fox-Pro environment (colors, window sizes, SET ON/OFF command settings) and return to that environment when the application completes. If you want to see some of these routines, print out the CUST.PRG created with the Advanced Application Template in FoxView. This program (which is actually created by another program!) contains many of these routines, and can be a catalyst for your own creativity in implementing many new ideas in your application.

Summary

This has been a fairly simple example of an application program. Yet the example fully illustrates the basic processes of creating an application. Menus drive the application, just as they do in FoxPro itself. From those menus, you offer the user a series of options from which he selects the one he wants.

In this quick start, you have learned the basics of creating an application that you or others can use. You have created menus and the associated pop-up menus, and seen how to tie FoxPro commands or additional programs to the menus. Complex application programs can have multiple menus and many pop-up menus with hundreds of selections overall, but they are created with the same processes you used in this quick start.

10

Creating Applications with FoxPro

At some point in your FoxPro education, you will need to go beyond FoxPro's interface. You may find that other people need to use the database system you have developed, with its input and inquiry screens, and reports and labels, but they don't want to learn the intricacies of Fox-Pro. Or, you may find that you don't want to use FoxPro's interface all the time. In these cases, you can build an application to run your system.

An application is like a shell that separates the user from FoxPro. An application limits the actions of the user to just those things needed, thus making the system easier to use and understand. FoxPro applications are usually, like FoxPro itself, driven by menus and pop-up menus, from which the user makes choices.

In this chapter, you learn about the tools used to create complete application programs in FoxPro. These include the menu tools, which define, create, and use FoxPro-type menus. Another set of tools implements pop-up menus, which usually are associated with a menu. When the menu item is selected by the user, the pop-up appears with choices about that menu item. Pop-up menus also can be independent of a menu, appearing whenever an application needs to present a list of choices to the user. You learn how to create a complete menu and pop-up system to run your application.

You also learn how to create a help system specific to your application. A help system is essential to those users not familiar with FoxPro or just learning the application.

311

Finally, you learn how to use Windows and different color schemes to give your application system pizzazz. Well-designed windows with colors make an application system easier to use and understand.

Designing an Application

The first step in designing a new application is to identify the necessary functions you want the application to perform. Once the functions have been identified, group them into logical units. Just as FoxPro arranges actions into groups (System, File, Edit, Database, Record, Program, and Window) and then places the actions under menus with these group names, you need to group the actions selected for your application and arrange them under menu names.

Including Functionality in the Application

The functions that make up an application depend, of course, on the application. Some applications can be very simple, providing only basic input and output routines. Other applications can be quite complex, with menus and submenus calling many different FoxPro functions and many custom FoxPro programs to perform specific operations.

Generally, though, your application should include a way to enter, edit, search, and report on each of the databases in the system. If your system has multiple database files with relations between them, you should have a way to report and view the database files.

As with system design, your first question should be, "What information must come out of this system?" Once you have identified the application's outputs—reports and query screens—you can define the routines and options that are necessary to get the required information into the system, and then get the information out.

Defining the Menus Structure

Before you start writing the application system, lay out the menus and pop-up menus you will need to control the system. Doing this enables you to work from a plan, rather than adding and changing on the fly. Figure 10.1 shows the menu and pop-up menu layout for a simple application; figure 10.2 shows a more complicated, multifile layout. In both cases, you can see that, having defined these layouts before you start, your job of creating the menus and pop-up menus in the application will be easier.

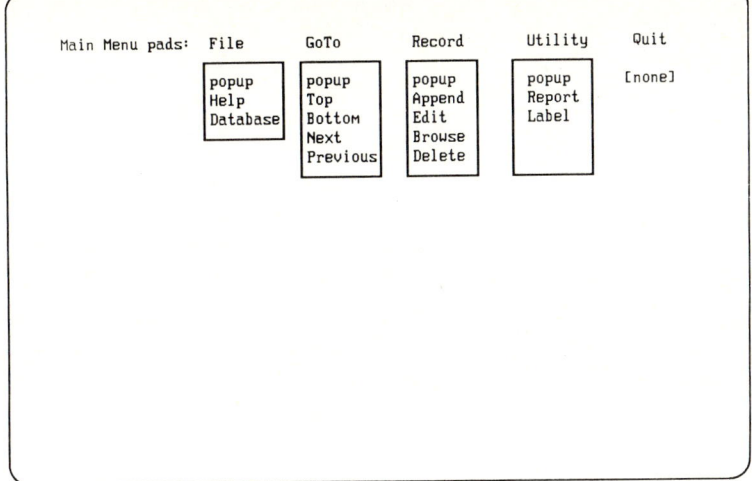

Fig. 10.1.
Menus and pop-up menus for a simple application.

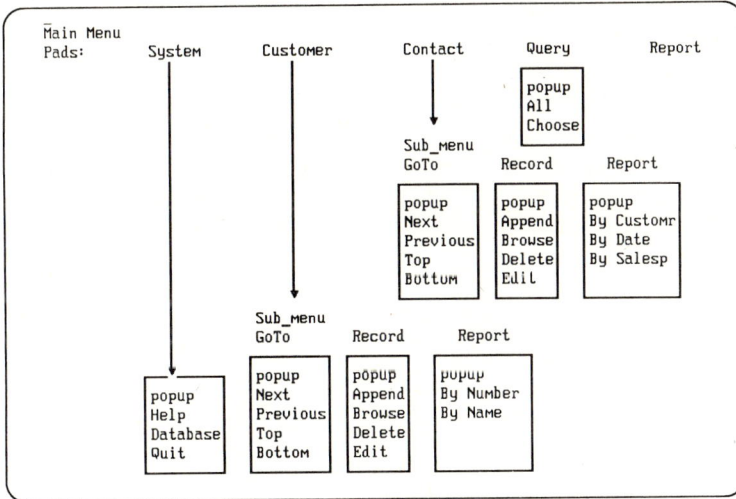

Fig. 10.2.
A more complex application system, with submenus.

Using the Menu and Pop-up Menu Structure

Philosophies about constructing an application are as numerous as application developers; everybody has his own style. Another approach is the top-down approach, in which the highest level of the application menu is written and tested, then the next level is written and tested, and so on until the lowest level utility programs are done.

Another way is the bottom-up method, in which the lowest level programs and functions are written and tested, then the next higher level —which uses the low-level functions—and so on, until the highest level menu can be written and all of the applications on the menu are ready to run.

Yet another way is the inside-out approach. The developer writes and tests the hardest parts of the application to make sure that they can be accomplished. Then the simpler ones can be coded and tested along with necessary menus, utilities, and pop-up menus.

You may find a combination of all three the best approach. If you know a part of your application—say, a particular report or query—will be difficult, write that portion first to make sure that it can be accomplished with your database design. If the report or query cannot be done, you should rethink the design of your databases and application before the application is 95 percent finished and you have to change much of it. Other than that case, I prefer creating the menus and pop-up menus first, because then you can prototype the application.

Prototyping means building the skeleton of the application; the menus and pop-up menus. You can test to see whether you have all the functions your application needs and whether they can be accessed from the correct menus. Prototyping an application ensures that you don't get to the last pop-up menu and realize that you cannot access an important function that was on a menu just deactivated. Once your menus and pop-up menus are complete and tested, and you know the tough programs can be done, you're ready to fill in the application routines.

First, though, you must create the menus and pop-up menus for your application.

Creating and Using Menus

When you define a menu, FoxPro does not put the menu on-screen automatically. The DEFINE statements describe this menu to FoxPro and store the definition in FoxPro's memory. When you activate the menu, FoxPro puts the menu on-screen and enters its menu-processing mode. In this mode, the user presses arrow keys or clicks with the mouse to move in a menu and make choices from pop-up menus. Figure 10.3 shows a FoxPro menu with the menu elements named.

System File Edit Database Record Program Window

Fig. 10.3.
A FoxPro menu,
with its elements
labeled.

Defining the Menu

An application, with all its menus, pop-up menus, and FoxPro statements is a FoxPro PRG program file. The first step is creating an application, and then opening a PRG file. The sample application in this chapter has been created as a program file with the New option of the File menu and saved as CHAP10.PRG.

The next—and easiest—step in creating an application menu is to define the menu. The format of the DEFINE MENU command is

DEFINE MENU *menu_name* [MESSAGE <exprC>]

Each menu has a name, specified in the command as *menu_name*. This name is then used to refer to this specific menu with the ACTIVATE MENU and DEACTIVATE MENU commands. You can add an optional message, which is displayed on line 24 of the screen, or a location specified in a SET MESSAGE TO *row, column* command. The following line defines a menu named TOP_MENU:

DEFINE MENU TOP_MENU MESSAGE "Choose a pad and press Enter"

The DEFINE MENU command tells FoxPro there will be a menu with the name you give it. To add choices to the menu, you must define the menu pads.

Defining the Menu Pads

Each menu pad has four attributes that must be defined. First, the pad has a name, which is used for several menu-processing commands. Second, each pad also has an owner. The owner is the menu of which this pad is a part. Third, each pad has a prompt, which is the string of characters that make up the visible pad on the menu. Finally, each pad has a location, which is specified in FoxPro's standard row, column format. The format of the DEFINE PAD command is as follows:

DEFINE PAD *pad_name* OF *menu_name* PROMPT <exprC> [AT *row, col*],[MESSAGE <exprC>]

You must include the *pad_name*, the *menu_name*, and the PROMPT when defining a menu pad. If you leave out the optional AT row and column location, FoxPro will put the first pad at the left edge of row zero (the top row) of the screen. (The second pad will be to its right, and so on). The following lines define pads for the menu named TOP_MENU:

DEFINE PAD file OF TOP_MENU PROMPT "File" AT 00,00

DEFINE PAD edit OF TOP_MENU PROMPT "Edit" AT 00,06

DEFINE PAD search OF TOP_MENU PROMPT "Search" AT 00,12

DEFINE PAD quit OF TOP_MENU PROMPT "Quit" AT 00,19

Standard FoxPro menus have a character highlighted in each prompt. Pressing that character from the keyboard activates the pad without having to move to the choice with the arrow keys. You can emulate that behavior in your own menus and pop-up menus. In the PROMPT expressions, the two-character combination \< makes the character following it the hot character for that prompt. For example, these commands,

DEFINE PAD report OF TOP_MENU PROMPT "\<Report"

DEFINE PAD record OF TOP_MENU PROMPT "Re\<cord"

create the two pads Report and Record. Press *R* to activate the Report pad, and press *C* to activate the Record pad. When this menu is displayed, the hot characters will be in a different color than the rest of the menu characters to indicate their special nature.

Defining the Action when a Pad Is Selected

When a user moves to a pad and presses Enter or its hot character, some action is expected. You define what that action is with the ON SELECTION PAD command. The format of this command is as follows:

ON SELECT PAD *pad_name* OF *menu_name command*

The *command* can be any FoxPro command, procedure, or program name. Often the *command* will be the name of a pop-up menu that you want to activate. The following are some examples of ON SELECTION PAD commands:

ON SELECTION PAD file OF TOP_MENU ACTIVATE POPUP file_pop

ON SELECTION PAD edit OF TOP_MENU DO EditProc

ON SELECTION PAD quit OF TOP_MENU RETURN

The first selection activates a pop-up menu defined for this pad, the second invokes a FoxPro procedure or PRG program file, and the third issues the FoxPro command RETURN.

Some application developers prefer to have a pop-up menu associated with a menu pad appear whenever the pad is selected. This can be done with the ON PAD command. The format of this command is as follows:

ON PAD *pad_name* OF *menu_name* ACTIVATE POPUP *pop-up_name*

The *pop-up_name* is the name of a defined pop-up menu. If you use ON PAD..ACTIVATE POPUP, the associated pop-up menu appears whenever this menu pad is selected. ON PAD..ACTIVATE POPUP and ON SELECTION PAD are exclusive, you can use one or the other on each menu pad, but not both.

Activating the Menu

Once you have defined the menu and each of the pads on that menu, and specified what action FoxPro should take when a pad is chosen, you can invoke this menu, putting the menu into action with the ACTIVATE MENU command. The format of this command is as follows:

ACTIVATE MENU *menu_name*

FoxPro constructs the menu from the DEFINE MENU and DEFINE PADS commands you have given it, places the menu on-screen, and processes the menu. Until the menu is deactivated, the menu controls FoxPro processing, branching out through pop-up menus and PRG program files or procedures. Unless some part of the programs called by the menu issue a FoxPro QUIT command, control eventually returns to this menu. Only when the user presses Esc or takes an exit path provided by the program, does the menu relinquish control.

Deactivating the Menu

Just as a menu has to be activated to be put on-screen, the application must deactivate the menu when the application is done with the menu. The format of this command is

DEACTIVATE MENU

Because only one menu can be active at a time, no menu name is needed.

Note | Even though only one menu can be active at a time, more than one menu can be on-screen at a time. One menu can activate another menu, which can activate a third menu, all of which are on-screen at the same time (assuming none overlap each other). But only the most recently activated menu is active; the other menus are "out of the action," waiting until the menus they activated are deactivated.

One note of caution about deactivating menus: when a menu is deactivated, control of the program returns to the line following the ACTIVATE MENU command. So, if your program executes one or more PROCEDURE subroutines in response to the menu inputs, don't deactivate the menu in the middle of the processing; everything will stop and you will be back to where you started.

Creating and Using Pop-up Menus

Unlike menus, which are on-screen all the time that they are activated, pop-up menus appear only while a choice needs to be made from them. Pop-up menus can list choices for the user, or can contain lists of programs, files, or databases. In any case, pop-up menus present choices from which the user can select.

Your application programs can determine what choice a user makes from the pop-up menu by using one of two functions. PROMPT() returns the actual prompt string of the user's choice; BAR() returns the number of the pop-up bar assigned in the DEFINE BAR statement.

Defining a Pop-up Menu

As in creating a menu, the first thing to do in creating a pop-up menu is to define it. The format of the DEFINE POPUP command is more complex than that for a menu, because the pop-up menu can take more forms and provide more options. The basic format of the DEFINE POPUP command is as follows:

DEFINE POPUP *pop-up menu_name* FROM *row, column*

The *pop-up menu_name* is a name assigned to this pop-up menu, and the *row, column* defines where the upper left corner will be on-screen. Also like the DEFINE MENU command, the DEFINE POPUP command has options to provide a message on the line 24 of the screen as follows:

DEFINE POPUP *pop-up menu_name* FROM *row, column*
MESSAGE <exprC>

You also can specify the color to assign the pop-up menu with the optional COLOR clause, which can designate the standard and enhanced colors, or select a predefined color scheme.

Once the pop-up menu is defined, you must define which choices will be presented to the user via the pop-up menus. Pop-up menus can contain a list of options, which you define with the DEFINE BAR command, or you can use several other interesting options: PROMPT FIELD, PROMPT FILES, and PROMPT STRUCTURE.

Using The PROMPT FIELD Option

If you define a pop-up menu with the PROMPT FIELD *field_name* option, where *field_name* is the name of a field in the active database, FoxPro places all the values of that field into the pop-up menu for selection by the user. This can be useful when you want the user to choose a value that exists in the database. You present a pop-up menu with the PROMPT FIELD option; the user cannot choose anything but a valid value in the field.

Consider the following DEFINE POPUP command:

DEFINE POPUP *name_pop* PROMPT FIELD CUST_NAME FROM
10,10 TO 30,40

When you use this DEFINE POPUP command while the CUSTOMER database is open and active, it displays the pop-up menu you see in figure 10.4. Each field in the pop-up menu is the value in the field CUST_NAME in one database record. The user chooses a value, and this value is returned by the function PROMPT( ).

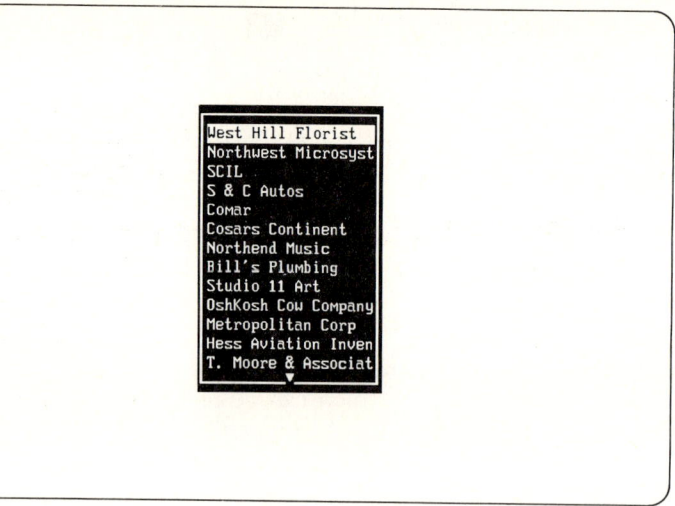

Fig. 10.4.
A pop-up menu
created with the
PROMPT FIELD
command.

Using The PROMPT FILES Option

The PROMPT FILES option of the DEFINE POPUP command does the same thing as the PROMPT FIELD option, except that the pop-up menu is filled with the names of files in the current directory. The format of this variant of the DEFINE POPUP command is as follows:

DEFINE POPUP *pop_name* PROMPT FILES LIKE <*skeleton*> AT *row, col*

The *skeleton* is an MS-DOS file name, with or without the * and ? wild card characters. If you wanted to present a list of PRG program files in a pop-up menu, you could use the following command:

DEFINE POPUP *file_pop* PROMPT FILES LIKE *.PRG FROM 10,10 TO 30,20

This command would create the pop-up menu shown in figure 10.5. As with all pop-up menus, the user's choice will be returned as a string by the PROMPT( ) function.

Using The PROMPT STRUCTURE Option

The last of the three prompt options is PROMPT STRUCTURE. This option places the fields of the active database into the pop-up menu. The format of this option is

DEFINE *pop_name* PROMPT STRUCTURE AT *row, col*

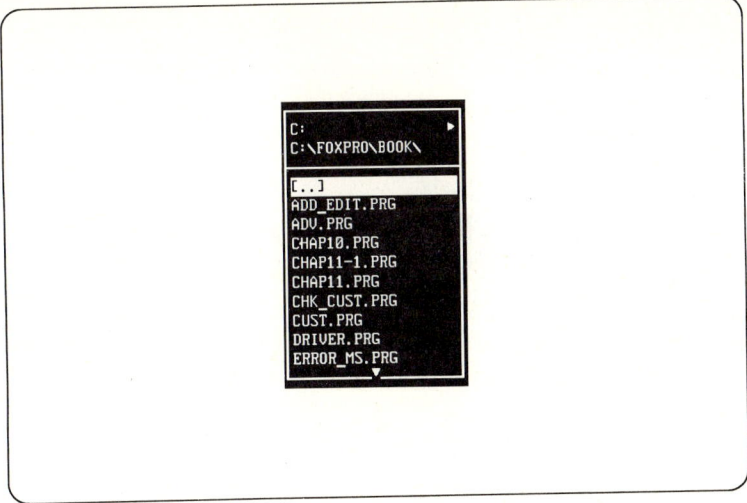

Fig. 10.5.
A pop-up menu created with the PROMPT FILES LIKE command.

Figure 10.6 shows an example of this type of pop-up menu. The example was created with the following command:

DEFINE POPUP STRC_POP PROMPT STRUCTURE AT 10, 10 TO 10, 30

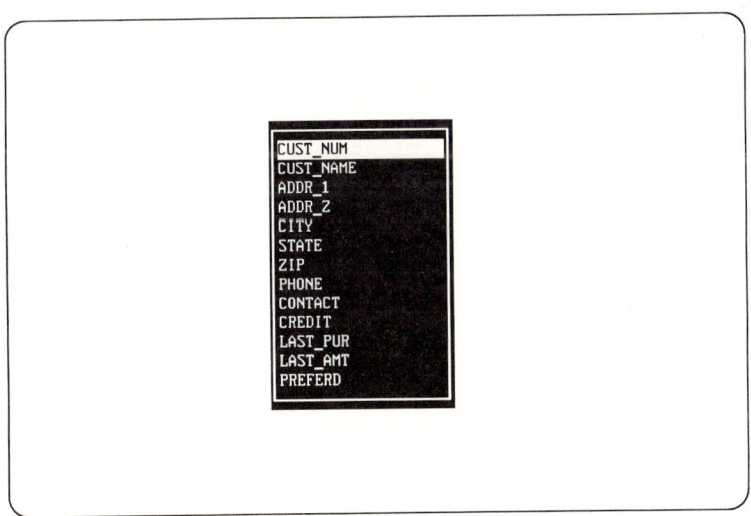

Fig. 10.6.
A pop-up menu created with the PROMPT STRUCTURE command.

Defining Each Bar

For most pop-up menus, you will define each bar individually. To do so, use the DEFINE BAR command. The format of this command is as follows:

DEFINE BAR 1 OF *pop-up menu_name* PROMPT <*exprC*>

where *pop-up menu_name* is the name of a defined pop-up menu and *exprC* is the prompt expression. The number assigned to the bar will be used later to determine which bar a user has chosen. The bars should be numbered consecutively, starting from the top bar.

As with menus, several special facilities are built into the PROMPT character expression. You can define a character of the PROMPT expression as a hot character. A hot character enables the user to press the key corresponding to a bar's hot character to select that bar. To define a hot character, place the two characters \< before the hot character.

If you want to divide the pop-up menu options into subsections with a line between the sections, use the PROMPT option. For example, consider the following DEFINE BAR commands:

DEFINE BAR 1 OF SYS_POP PROMPT "Help"

DEFINE BAR 2 OF SYS_POP PROMPT "Database"

DEFINE BAR 3 OF SYS_POP PROMPT "Open"

DEFINE BAR 4 OF SYS_POP PROMPT "–"

DEFINE BAR 5 OF SYS_POP PROMPT "Quit"

These commands create the pop-up menu shown in figure 10.7. Note that BAR 4 creates a line separating Quit from the other pop-up menu choices.

Once you have defined the pop-up menu and all its options, you must tell FoxPro what action to take when a choice is made from this pop-up menu.

Taking Action on a Pop-up Choice

When a user makes a choice from a pop-up menu, your application must take some action based on that choice. In menus, you used the ON SELECTION PAD to define the action for each pad as part of the menu definition process. With pop-up menus, rather than defining an action for each choice as part of the definition, you define a FoxPro PROCEDURE for the pop-up menu.

Fig. 10.7.
A pop-up menu
created with
DEFINE BAR
commands.

To define what PROCEDURE is to be executed when a pop-up selection is made, use the ON SELECTION POPUP command. The format for this command is

ON SELECTION POPUP *pop-up menu_name command*

Note that the action to be taken is actually any valid FoxPro command. You could put a FoxPro command there, but then that command would be executed no matter what choice was taken from the pop-up menu, which defeats the idea of giving the user a choice. The best way to process the choice is to use a PROCEDURE subroutine, passing to the subroutine the number of the bar that the user selected.

Several FoxPro functions return information that your application can use to decide what action to take. These functions are as follows:

❑ POPUP() returns the name of the pop-up menu from which the user made a choice.

❑ PROMPT() returns the character expression that made up the PROMPT for the choice the user made.

❑ BAR() returns the bar number, from the DEFINE BAR statement, that the user chose.

Each pop-up menu should have a procedure file to process choices made from that pop-up menu. You can pass the choice made as a parameter to the procedure file, for example,

ON SELECTION POPUP SYS-POP DO SYS_PROC WITH BAR()

This statement tells your application that when a user makes a choice from the pop-up menu named SYS_POP, FoxPro should call up the PROCEDURE subroutine named SYS_PROC and pass to it, as a parameter, the bar number that was chosen.

The PROCEDURE should then take action based on which bar was chosen. In pseudo-English, the following is what such a procedure would look like:

```
PROCEDURE  SYS_PROC
 PARAMETER  BAR_NUM
DO CASE
        CASE BAR_NUM  =  1
                statements to execute for choice of bar 1
        CASE BAR_NUM  =  2
                statements to execute for choice of bar 2
        other  case statements for other choices
ENDCASE
RETURN
```

You also could pass, as a parameter, the actual string prompt. In fact, if you have used the PROMPT FIELDS, PROMPT FILES, or PROMPT STRUCTURE options of the DEFINE BAR command, you will have to pass the prompt string, because no bar number is associated with choosing an option from those lists. In that case, the PROCEDURE can look like the following:

```
PROCEDURE file_pop
 PARAMETER file_name
    statements to take action with the file_name chosen
 RETURN
```

Whether you have specified pop-up menu options individually or used the PROMPT FIELDS, FILES, or STRUCTURE options, you must create a PROCEDURE subroutine to process the choice.

Creating a menu system with associated pop-up menus and procedure files can seem complicated. But, in fact, the process is quite straightforward. Following is a quick summary of the steps required:

1. Define the menu, using the DEFINE MENU command.

2. Define each pad of the menu, using the DEFINE PAD command.

3. For each pad in the menu, define what action should be taken when the pad is chosen, using the ON SELECTION PAD command.

4. For each pop-up menu associated with the menu, do the following:

   a. Define the pop-up menu, using the DEFINE POPUP command.

   b. Specify a procedure file to be executed when a choice is made from the pop-up menu, using the ON SELECTION POPUP command. (Cases can occur when you don't use a procedure to process the choice, but these cases will be rare.)

   c. Create the procedure file to process the choice.

See? It's not so hard. The result of working with menus and pop-up menus is a polished, easy-to-use application program. Both you and your users will appreciate your efforts to use menus and pop-up menus to run your application program.

Adding a Help System

Another feature that users have come to expect of any application program is a help system. Your application program should provide one—if for no other reason than to alleviate the number of calls you get asking for help. Fortunately, FoxPro provides a simple and direct means of giving your application a sophisticated help system.

Help systems in FoxPro, even FoxPro's own help system, are standard FoxPro databases. A help database has two fields. One field is a character field named TOPICS that has a length of 16. The other field is a memo field named HELP. The TOPICS field has a string that describes a help topic. The memo field holds the textual information that actually provides the help. When the user presses the F1 key to get help, FoxPro searches the database that is currently defined as the help database and places the TOPICS into a window. From the window, the user can select a topic and FoxPro will place the help information from the memo field for that topic in the same window.

To use a custom help system, you only have to create a new help database, with at least the two fields TOPICS and HELP, and tell FoxPro to use that database for help in your application. Then, when the user presses the F1 Help key, FoxPro will use the custom help database rather than the standard FoxPro one.

Creating the Help Database

A help database for your application is created just as you would create any FoxPro database, using the New option of the File menu. Your help database needs at least two fields, a character field with a length of 30 named TOPICS and a memo field named DETAILS. (You could have other fields as well, which could be used to fine-tune the help system, but that's for pretty advanced applications.)

You should have one database record for each help topic you want to present to the user. Each record in the TOPIC field should be a one- or two-word title for a specific topic, such as Append or Browse. These entries can also be more application-specific, such as Add Customer, Customer Report, or Entering a Contact.

For each record, place the help text in the memo field. Help text can be any length.

Providing a FoxPro-Type Help System

To implement your application help system, place the following line in your application's FoxPro code:

SET HELP TO *help_file_name*

In this line, *help_file_name* is the name of the help file you created.

Your application can have as many help files as you want, with the application switching from one help file to another as necessary. This feature can simplify the help system for anyone using your application, because you can limit the help topics to the area of the application in which the user is working. For instance, if your application has major subsections for the customer, invoice, and inventory databases, you can create a help file for each and use the SET HELP TO command to use the appropriate help file in each database. Then, when a user asks for help in the inventory section, he doesn't have to wade through customer and invoice help topics.

If you want to re-establish the regular FoxPro help system, put the command SET HELP TO FOXHELP in your application.

Creating a Context-Sensitive Help System

Context-sensitive help systems bypass the requirement for the user to choose a help topic. If the application provides context-sensitive help, when the users request help with the F1 key, FoxPro will present a help screen appropriate to what the user is doing at the time. For instance, if the user is entering invoice information and asks for help, the application can present the help screens with the topic of Invoice.

The steps for creating a context-sensitive help system are the same as they are for creating a regular help system. You create the help database and include topics and detail appropriate to specific parts of the application. Then, in your application program, when you want to provide context-sensitive help, you use the following command:

SET TOP TO *topic*

Topic refers to the value in the TOPIC field of the help file record you want to display. For instance, if you want to provide a help screen when a user is entering information into invoices, you could include in the help database the topic Entering Invoices. Figure 10.8 shows the help file INV_HELP with this record.

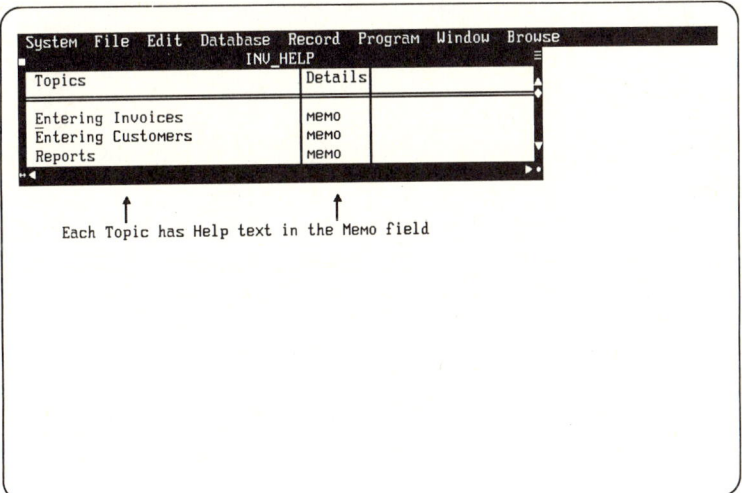

Fig. 10.8.
An INV_HELP file record.

When the application program starts the process used to enter invoices, you should include the following commands:

```
SET HELP TO INV_HELP
        statements in the application program
SET TOPIC TO "Entering Invoices"
```

With these commands in place, when the user presses the F1 help key in this part of the application, FoxPro will display help information associated with entering invoices. FoxPro uses the information from the record you created in the help database (as shown in fig. 10.9) without requiring the user to choose from the list of topics.

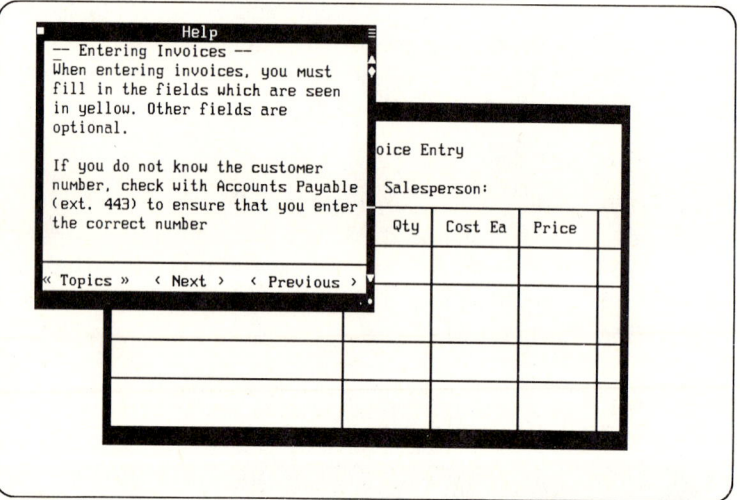

Fig. 10.9.
A context-
sensitive help
screen.

Once the help screen is activated, the user can return to the Topics screen and choose other help topics of interest.

Help systems are essential parts of your applications. Users have rightfully come to expect help systems. Because FoxPro makes creating and implementing a sophisticated help system easy, you have no excuse for failing to provide one.

Defining and Using Windows

As you may have noticed, FoxPro uses windows. You can have your application program use windows as well. Just as with FoxPro's windows, your application program's windows can be opened, moved, sized and closed by the user. If you want, though, you can open a window which cannot be moved or sized or closed. As with FoxPro's windows, you also can specify the colors of each individual window, allowing you to have one color for one part of the application and another color for another part, or one color for one type of window and another color for another type of window. Windows for application programs can be completely controlled by the application developer.

The advantage of using a window over writing to the screen is that a window can be placed on-screen, do its job, and then disappear, leaving all information under the window exactly as it appeared before the window was activated. This makes windows perfect for temporary jobs, such as alerts and error messages, or asking questions of the user.

Defining a Window

Just as you did when you created menus and pop-up menus, you first DEFINE a window to FoxPro. With the definition command, you tell Fox-Pro to build the window in memory, with the various options you specify. Only when you issue an ACTIVATE WINDOW command does FoxPro put the window on-screen.

The basic format of the DEFINE WINDOW command is

DEFINE WINDOW *window_name* FROM *row, col* TO *row, col*

Window_name gives this window a name, which will be used to ACTIVATE, DEACTIVATE, HIDE, and SHOW the window. The first set of *row, col* numbers indicate the location on-screen where the upper left corner will be; the second set defines the lower right corner. If you include a border for the window, the window dimensions include the space taken by the border.

Options for the DEFINE WINDOW command include the following:

❏ TITLE *<exprC>* The character expression will be the title of the window, centered in the top border of the window

❏ DOUBLE

❏ PANEL

❏ NONE

❏ SYSTEM

❏ BORDER_STRING

This last option defines what type of border the window will have. FoxPro defaults to a single line around the window. DOUBLE causes the border line to be a double line. PANEL creates a wide border. NONE specifies no border, and SYSTEM says to use whatever the default for the FoxPro system is.

You also can define your own border string by placing the characters that will be used for the vertical and horizontal lines and each of the corners in a series. The order of this border string is top, bottom, left, right, and then top left corner, top right corner, bottom left corner, and bottom right corner. Each character must be enclosed in quotation marks or expressed as a CHR().

CHR() is a FoxPro function that changes an integer value to its character equivalent. Screen characters are stored in the computer as integers from 0 to 255 (some are not printable to the screen). The CHR() function converts an integer value to a character value.

The following is an example, which gives you the same border as the PANEL option:

DEFINE WINDOW win1 CHR(219), CHR(219), CHR(221),
CHR(221), CHR(219), CHR(219), CHR(219), CHR(219)

Other options for the DEFINE WINDOW command are as follows:

❑ CLOSE or NOCLOSE. If you specify NOCLOSE, the user will not be able to close the window; the window must be closed by your application program. CLOSE allows the user to close the window. CLOSE is the default.

❑ FLOAT or NOFLOAT NOFLOAT. This means that the user will not be able to move the window on-screen. FLOAT is the default, allowing the user to move the window.

❑ GROW or NOGROW. Specifies whether the user will be able to change the size of the screen. NOGROW prevents window re-sizing. NOGROW is the default and allows the user to change the window size.

❑ ZOOM or NOZOOM. Determines whether the user can ZOOM the window to full-screen size. NOZOOM prevents zooming. ZOOM is the default and allows the window to ZOOM to full-screen size.

❑ SHADOW. If SHADOW is specified, the window will have the standard FoxPro shadow on the right and bottom margins. Shadows serve no purpose other than to make the window visually more appealing.

❑ COLOR. You can specify the color of the window. For a more detailed explanation of how to set colors, see the following section.

❑ COLOR SCHEME. Again, refer to the following section for information about color schemes.

Putting the Window On-screen

To put a window on-screen, use the following command:

ACTIVATE WINDOW *window_name*

Window_name is the name you included in the DEFINE WINDOW command. Once you activate a window, all output from your program will go to that window; other windows become inactive.

When you want to remove a window from the screen, use either the DEACTIVATE WINDOW command or the HIDE WINDOW command. Either one removes the named window from the screen. DEACTIVATE WINDOW and HIDE WINDOW are different from each other. HIDE WINDOW removes the window from the screen, but doesn't change the window's active status. If you have hidden the active window, output will still go to the window even though you cannot see the output. If you want to make the screen active again, you can use the SHOW WINDOW command to bring the screen back to the screen. The window will appear with all of the output that went to the window while the window was hidden.

You could also issue an ACTIVATE WINDOW command on a window that you have hidden; the window will return, but the window will return as if it were brand new. That is, the window will have nothing in it.

Many combinations of opening, hiding, showing, and closing windows can be used with the ACTIVATE WINDOW, DEACTIVATE WINDOW, HIDE WINDOW, and SHOW WINDOW commands. Basically, you ACTIVATE a window, HIDE the window to remove the window from the screen temporarily, SHOW the window to return the window to the screen in the same state, and DEACTIVATE the window to remove the window and its contents.

The following program opens a window and writes to it, opens a second window and writes to the second window, hides the second window while continuing to write to the second window, shows the second window with the output taken while the window was hidden, and then returns to the first window to output some more. Although this is not exactly a program you will want to use in your application line-for-line, the program does give a good demonstration of FoxPro's windowing capabilities, and provides a base for your own experimentation.

```
CLEAR
DEFINE WINDOW one FROM 1,0 TO 5, 60 TITLE 'Window One'
DEFINE WINDOW two FROM 7,5 TO 12, 65 TITLE 'Window Two'
```

```
ACTIVATE WINDOW one
? 'Here is a line of output to Window One'
WAIT

ACTIVATE WINDOW two
? 'Here is output to Window Two while it is on the screen'
WAIT

HIDE WINDOW two
? 'Here is output to Window Two while it is off the screen'

ACTIVATE WINDOW one
? 'Just wrote to Window Two while it was hidden'
WAIT

ACTIVATE WINDOW two
WAIT

ACTIVATE WINDOW one
? 'And finally,some output to Window One'
WAIT

DEACTIVATE WINDOW one
DEACTIVATE WINDOW two
```

Using Colors

Just as windows provide your application with a polished look, colors can provide oomph and emphasis to a system. Prudent use of colors in a Fox-Pro application can make the difference between a good system and a great system.

Remember that your application can be used on computers without a color monitor. Therefore, your application should determine what kind of monitor is present, and adjust the colors accordingly. This is, as you have come to expect with FoxPro, not difficult to do. Before explaining this procedure, this section will include a discussion of how to define different colors to FoxPro for use in your application.

A quick summary of FoxPro's color capabilities may be: You can specify a color; 2 colors make a Color Pair; 1 to 10 Color Pairs make a Color Pair List; 10 Color Pairs make a color scheme; and 24 color schemes make a Color Set. Clear as mud, right? Before discussing how to set and change colors, here are definitions of the terms.

Using a Color

FoxPro can put eight different colors on-screen. These eight are represented in FoxPro by codes. The colors and their codes are as follows:

Color	Code
Black	N
Green	G
Blank	X
Magenta	RB
Blue	B
Red	R
Brown	GR
White	W
Cyan	BG
Yellow	GR+

On monochrome monitors, you can specify only four colors: white (W),
black (N), underlined (U), and inverse video (I).

Using a Color Pair

A color pair is two colors, separated by a / mark. The two colors represent
the foreground color and the background color of an object on-screen
(such as a menu, a window, or a data field). For example, in a field containing text, the foreground color is the color of the text and the background color is color of the screen behind the text.

All objects have both a standard mode and an enhanced mode—with colors for each mode. Standard mode is when the object is not selected. For
example, a GET field when the cursor is not in the field will appear in
standard mode. When the cursor moves into a GET field, the field assumes
the colors set for its enhanced mode.

Color pairs are used to change the colors of one object on the screen. The
format of the SET COLOR command is as follows:

SET COLOR OF *object* TO <*standard_color_pair*>,
<*enhanced_color_pair*>

For example, consider the following command:

SET COLOR OF TITLES TO W/B, B/W

This command sets the colors of window titles to white (W) text on a
blue (B) background when the TITLE is in standard mode (the window is
not selected) and blue text on a white background when in enhanced
mode (the window is selected).

You also use color pairs with the SET COLOR TO command. With this command you alter only the colors of user-defined menus and windows. Following is the format for this command:

SET COLOR TO *<standard_color_pair>,<enhanced_color_pair>, <border_color_pair>,<background_color_pair>*

If you arc working with a COMPAQ monochrome monitor, you may find certain standard FoxPro color schemes to be difficult to use, particularly in inverse video fields. I suggest that you try the standard FoxPro color sets COMPQ_COLO and COMPQ_MONO. If you still have problems, experimenting with color sets in the Color option of the Window menu may help.

Using Color Pair Lists and Color Schemes

Color schemes and color pair lists go together. At all times, FoxPro works with a color scheme, which describes the color pairs of 10 objects on-screen. Which 10 objects depends on what FoxPro is doing at the time. For instance, if FoxPro is in its standard operation environment, the 10 objects and the colors assigned to them are as follows:

Pair #	Object	Color
1	SAY field	W+/RB
2	GET field	W+/W
3	Window border	GR+/W
4	An active title	GR+/W
5	An idle title	B/W
6	A selected item	W+/R
7	Hot keys	B+/RB
8	A window's shadow	B
9	An enabled control	B+/RB
10	A disabled control	B/RB

Controls are the items that you can select in a window. An example is the Topic Preceding Next items at the bottom of the Help window. If the control can be chosen the control is enabled; if the control cannot be chosen (for example, Previous when you're at the top of the help list and there is no previous record), the control is disabled.

FoxPro has 10 different color schemes, each of which represents a different part of FoxPro's environment, and each of which contains 10 color pairs to tell FoxPro how to color up to 10 objects in that environment. For instance, there is a Color Scheme for User Windows that tells FoxPro how to color the screen when your application is creating and using windows. Another color scheme tells FoxPro how to color objects in the menu (this one refers to only four objects) and another for dialogs.

Using the Color Picker To Set Colors

The easiest way to work with colors and color schemes is to open FoxPro and choose Colors from the Window menu.

The matrix of foreground and background colors represents all possible combinations of colors FoxPro provides. The upper left corner of the Color Picker shows the objects on a FoxPro screen. In the upper right corner is a scrollable list that contains the color schemes of FoxPro. When you select a color scheme from the scrollable list, the objects in that color scheme are shown in the center of the Color Picker. By selecting one of the radio buttons from that list, you can click the foreground and background combination you would like that object to possess. For this, nothing is better than experimentation.

If you have come up with a complete set of color schemes, or made modifications to only one or two, you can save all those schemes as a color set. Do this by choosing Save. You will see the Color Set dialog, waiting for a name for this color set. Give the new color set a name and select Save /.

Now, when your application starts, you can load the customized color set by issuing the SET COLOR SET TO command. The following is the format for the command:

SET COLOR SET TO <color_set_name>

Color_set_name is the name you assigned your custom color. That set will be loaded and your application will look just as you planned.

Deciding between Color and Monochrome

If you know your application will only run on one type of computer monitor, you can use a color set that is appropriate to that monitor. However, if your application may run on both color and monochrome monitors, you need to provide a way for the application to determine what type of monitor is being used, and load the appropriate color set. By doing so, you will not have to maintain separate versions of your application; one for color, one for monochrome.

A class of FoxPro functions is called System functions. One of these is SYS(2006), which returns the type of graphics card and monitor in use. For instance, if your application is running on a monochrome monitor, the command

   ? SYS(2006)

returns the string `MGA/MONOCHROME`; if the application is running on a VGA color system, the command will return `VGA/COLOR`.

Using this in a program, you can detect the type of monitor and load an appropriate color set using the following routine:

```
        MON_TYPE  =  SYS(2006)
   IF  "color"  $  MON_TYPE
        SET  COLOR  SET  TO  "COLOR"
        ELSE
        SET  COLOR  SET  TO  "MONOCHROME"
   ENDIF
```

By including this small routine, you can ensure that the correct color set will be loaded. The other alternative is to maintain two (or more!) separate versions of your application, one for each type of monitor that the application can run on.

Chapter Summary

Application programming in FoxPro is tremendously rewarding, though at times difficult. Your application can be quite simple, merely allowing others to use your database system without learning FoxPro commands and all of the FoxPro options. Or your application can become quite complex.

In this chapter you learned the basics of creating applications in FoxPro. Like FoxPro itself, most applications will be controlled by menus. Therefore, FoxPro provides sophisticated capabilities for you to include menus in your applications. Also like FoxPro, windows will provide much functionality, and so FoxPro provides extensive windowing capabilities. Colors provide punch and pizzazz to your applications, and FoxPro allows you to completely control colors.

A well-crafted FoxPro application is a pleasure to use. Even for beginning FoxPro users, creating FoxPro applications can be a challenge and a pleasure.

11

Programming with FoxPro

In Chapter 8, FoxPro programming was introduced to overcome some shortcomings. This chapter is a more formal introduction to programming. Even if you're a complete nonprogrammer and you approach this chapter with some dread, you will find that programming can be fun and rewarding. Although I know some artistic people who will argue about it all night (and have), a well-planned, well-crafted program can be a thing of beauty.

In this chapter, you learn the basics of programming in FoxPro. FoxPro includes a complete language, which you can use to instruct FoxPro to do anything you have seen so far: create databases, open windows, accept input, and write output to the screen or printer or files, along with a host of capabilities not available from the screen. You can, for example, develop input routines that test the information you enter and take different actions based on that input—accepting it in some cases, opening another input screen in others, rejecting it with appropriate error messages in yet others.

The most basic aspects of programming include storing information temporarily in memory variables, having FoxPro take different actions depending on the value of an expression, reading information from the screen, writing information to the screen, and creating menus to allow the user to choose what he wants to do. You learn how to do all these things in this chapter. Finally, this chapter includes several basic programs that accomplish tasks your programs will need. From these programs, you can learn some good programming skills; you also can use them as is in your programs or modify them to suit yourself.

The day will come when you realize that FoxPro "out of the box" has some limitations. Compared to its competitors, FoxPro's limitations are less limiting: you can do more with FoxPro than other database programs without resorting to programming, but as you build more advanced applications, you will bump against those limitations more and more.

Eventually you will think of something you want FoxPro to do that you cannot accomplish without programming. It may be adding a custom menu to make your database system easier for others to use, or an input or output screen that just cannot be done in FoxView. When you find yourself frustrated because FoxPro cannot do what you want it to do, it's time to turn to programming.

Creating a FoxPro Program

You have seen FoxPro put into the Command window a translation of your mouse or keyboard actions into a command. A FoxPro program is simply a series of those commands, which FoxPro executes one after the other or according to commands that change the order of command execution. You can use these commands to do anything you can do with the mouse or keyboard, and much more.

FoxPro programs are made up of three basic building blocks: FoxPro commands; memory variables, which hold data of some sort for later action; and programming constructs, which tell FoxPro to loop through a series of commands or jump to a different area of the program or make a decision based on the value of a variable or database field. With these three building blocks, you can create complex database systems.

To create a FoxPro program, you can use the File Open menu, choosing Program from the Radio Button choices of the File Open menu. A Text Editing window, with the title Untitled.prg will open. In this window you create your program. In the Command window, enter the command

MODIFY COMMAND *file_name*

where *file_name* is the name of your program file. In either case, the Text Editing window will open, ready to take your program. If you have a favorite text editor you would rather use, you can have FoxPro open the text editing window with that editor by adding a

TP = *editor_name*

command to the CONFIG.FPX file (see Chapter 8).

Using FoxPro Commands in Programs

You may have already started using FoxPro commands in the Command window. In a FoxPro program, these commands are used exactly as you would enter them in the Command window. The following is a FoxPro program made up of nothing but FoxPro commands:

```
SET TALK OFF
SET ECHO OFF
SET CONFIRM ON
SET SAFETY OFF

    ...
SELECT 1
USE CUSTOMER INDEX CUST_NAME
SELECT 2
USE ORDER INDEX ORD_NAME
SET RELATION TO CUST_NAME INTO CUSTOMER
BROWSE NOMODIFY
RETURN
```

FoxPro starts at the first line of a program and moves through the commands one line at a time. Later you will see ways to modify this flow of control.

Adding Comments to a FoxPro Program

Comments are an indispensable part of all FoxPro programs. No matter how good your program is, the day will come when you need to change it; then you will be glad you included comments.

Comments should explain parts of the program that may otherwise be unclear. Following is a code fragment that is well-commented:

```
* Loop through input routine until user presses Esc to quit
DO WHILE .NOT. done
    ....
    input program lines
    ....
    READ
```

```
* readkey() will return 12 if user presses Esc
   IF READKEY() = 12
   DONE = .T.                && set loop test to indicate Esc
   ENDIF
ENDDO
```

```
* user has terminated; close files and return
USE
```

This fragment shows the two ways to add comments to a FoxPro program. When a line begins with an asterisk (*), FoxPro ignores everything on the line. Note that the asterisk does not have to be in the first column, but it does have to be the first character on the line. The second way to comment in FoxPro is with &&, which tells FoxPro to ignore everything on the line to the right of the &&. This is used to put a comment on a line that also has FoxPro code.

Make sure that your comments tell you something valuable. It does no good to comment something that is clear simply by reading the code. A well-commented program is easier to debug and easier to change.

Using Memory Variables

A fundamental aspect of all computer languages is their capability to store a piece of data with a name tag and later refer to that data and use it simply by using the name tag. In FoxPro, memory variables give you this capability. Memory variables are a way to store data and refer to it by name.

Assigning Values to Memory Variables

You assign a value to a memory variable with the = assignment; then you can use that value simply by referring to the name you have given it. For example, the code

```
CURR_REC = 100
...program statements
GOTO CURR_REC
```

assigns the value 100 to a memory variable named CURR_REC. At a later point in the program, the memory variable CURR_REC is used in a GOTO statement. FoxPro will read this statement, know that CURR_REC has the value 100, and execute a GOTO 100 command.

Memory variables can take the same characteristics as database fields, but there is no MEMO memory variable type. Thus, memory variables can be of the types character, numeric, float, date, and logical. A memory variable's type is defined by what is assigned to it. The expression,

CURR_REC = 100

assigns 100 to CURR_REC and makes CURR_REC a numeric type variable. If, later in the program, FoxPro encounters the line

CURR_REC = "This is the current record"

it redefines CURR_REC as a character variable.

You can assign to a memory variable the value from any valid FoxPro expression. For example, the expression

BIG_NUM = ORDER–>AMOUNT >= 100000

sets the variable BIG_NUM to a logical type and assigns to it FoxPro's representation of true, .T., if the AMOUNT field of the current record in the ORDER database is equal to or greater than 100,000.

Once a memory variable has been defined by an assignment statement, you can substitute it anywhere you could put the actual value—in expressions, for example:

CURR_REC = 100
SKIP
CURR_REC = CURR_REC + 1

Here, CURR_REC has been assigned the value of 100 and a SKIP statement is executed. Afterward, CURR_REC is set to the value of itself plus 1 (CURR_REC + 1). In the assignment statement, the CURR_REC on the right side of the equation has substituted for the value 100.

Combining Memory Variables

Because memory variables act according to their types, you can build expressions that use two or more types as if they were simply values:

STRING1 = "Here is string one "
STRING2 = "and here is string two"
STRING3 = STRING1 + STRING2
? STRING3

Here is string one and here is string two

(The ? in the example is a FoxPro command that prints to the screen the expressions following it. The ? and ?? commands are explained later in this chapter.)

However, if you execute an expression with the wrong type, such as the following:

```
NUM1 = 100
STRING1 = "Here is string one"
STRING2 = STRING1 + NUM1
```

you see the output and the error message in figure 11.1.

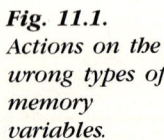

Fig. 11.1.
Actions on the wrong types of memory variables.

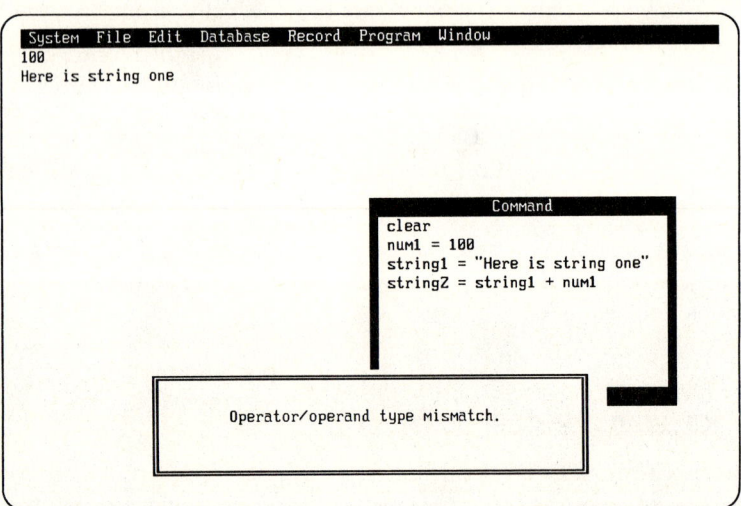

```
 System  File  Edit  Database  Record  Program  Window
100
Here is string one




                                    Command
                        clear
                        num1 = 100
                        string1 = "Here is string one"
                        string2 = string1 + num1




              Operator/operand type mismatch.
```

When you need to combine a character memory variable and a numeric memory variable, change the numeric variable to a character with the STR( ) function:

```
STRING3 = STRING1 + STR(num1)
```

There are limits on the number of memory variables you can have active at one time in FoxPro, but they are so great that you will probably never bump against them. If you do, you can consult the FoxPro manual to learn how to fine-tune FoxPro to allow more memory variables.

Memory variables are an essential part of FoxPro programming, just as they are an essential part of any computer language.

Controlling the Flow of Execution

The real power of computer programs is their capability to execute differently, depending on conditions they recognize. Computer programs can decide how to run based on the value of a piece of data. In pseudo-English here is how a computer program might make such a decision:

```
IF ORDER->AMOUNT is greater than 10,000
    process statements that apply to big orders
ELSE
    process statements that apply to small orders
ENDIF
```

This fragment of a program would execute different statements depending on the value in the AMOUNT field of the current record of the ORDER database. Statements that dictate how the program will execute are called *flow-of-control* statements or *constructs*; they change the flow of the program based on some value or expression. FoxPro has several flow-of-control statements, all of which you will use.

Using Logical Expressions

Each flow of control construct has a logical expression; how the construct acts depends on whether that logical expression evaluates to true or false. You discover how the flow of control statements use the logical expression in the following sections.

The logical expression can be any valid FoxPro expression that FoxPro can evaluate to true or false. As such, the expression must compare two values, one on each side of a logical test. The format for logical expressions is

expression_1 condition expression_2

The conditions can be any of the following:

❑ = Equal. If *expression_1* and *expression_2* evaluate to the same value, the result of the logical expression is true; otherwise it is false.

❑ > Greater than. If *expression_1* is greater than *expression_2*, the logical expression is true, otherwise it is false.

❑ < Less than. The opposite of >. If *expression_1* is less than *expression_2*, the logical expression is true; otherwise it is false.

❑ >= Greater than or equal to. If *expression_1* is the same as expression_2 or greater than it, the logical expression is true. If expression_1 is less than *expression_2*, the logical expression is false.

❑ <= Less than or equal to. The opposite of greater than or equal to.

❑ <> Not equal. If *expression_1* is not equal to *expression_2*, the logical expression evaluates to true; if they are equal, the logical expression evaluates to false.

You can combine one or more logical expressions using AND and OR. The format for this is

logical_expression_1 .AND. *logical_expression_2*

logical_expression_1 .OR. *logical_expression_2*

FoxPro evaluates *logical_expression_1* and *logical_expression_2* separately. In the case of the AND logical test, only if *logical_expression_1* and *logical_expression_2* are both true will FoxPro evaluate the whole expression to be true.

In the case of the OR construction, if either *logical_expression_1* or *logical_expression_2* are true, FoxPro will return a true for the whole expression. Only if both are false will FoxPro make the whole expression false.

This is less confusing than it sounds. With a bit of practice, you will understand these logical expressions and compound logical expressions.

There also are a number of standard, built-in FoxPro expressions that return a logical value, such as EOF( ), FOUND( ), and UPDATE( ). These also can be used in flow of control constructs.

Using IF..ELSE..ENDIF

As you saw, the IF..ELSE..ENDIF construct gives you a way to execute one set of statements if a condition is true and to skip those statements, optionally executing another set, if the condition is false. The format of the IF..ELSE..ENDIF construct is as follows:

```
IF logical_expression = TRUE
    execute these statements
ENDIF
```

Optionally you can add an ELSE set of statements:

```
IF logical_expression = TRUE
    execute these statements
ELSE
    execute these statements
ENDIF
```

You don't have to include the ELSE; if you don't and the logical expression evaluates to false, FoxPro skips to the statement immediately following the ENDIF. In any case, you must end with the ENDIF; otherwise, FoxPro will not know when to start executing statements again.

Following is a fragment of code using an IF..ELSE..ENDIF construct:

```
IF EOF()                && if at end of file
    CLOSE DATABASES
ELSE
    SKIP
    ? "Record Number: ", RECNO()
ENDIF
```

Using DO WHILE..ENDDO

Many times you will want FoxPro to execute the same block of statements more than once. You use the DO WHILE..ENDDO construct in this case. The format of this is

```
DO WHILE logical_expression = TRUE
    statements to execute
ENDDO
```

FoxPro evaluates *logical_expression*. If it is true, FoxPro executes all the statements between the DO WHILE and the ENDDO. When it reaches the ENDDO, FoxPro jumps back to the DO WHILE and evaluates the logical expression again. As long as that expression remains true, FoxPro keeps executing the block and jumping back to the DO WHILE. As soon as the logical expression becomes false, FoxPro jumps to the first statement after the ENDDO and continues on its merry way.

Following is a fragment of a program using the DO WHILE..ENDDO construct:

```
COUNT = 0
TOT_AMT = 0
DO WHILE COUNT < 1000
   COUNT = COUNT + 1
   TOT_AMT = TOT_AM + AMOUNT
   SKIP
ENDDO
```

After initializing the COUNT and TOT_AMT memory variables (if you don't, you will get a error message the first time you try to use them in the COUNT = COUNT + 1 statement), FoxPro evaluates the logical expression COUNT < 1000. Because the first time through, COUNT equals zero, FoxPro executes the statements between the DO WHILE and ENDDO commands. Then it jumps back to the DO WHILE and evaluates the logical expression again. This continues for 1,000 records, until COUNT, which is incremented by one each time the program loops, is no longer less than 1,000. FoxPro evaluates the logical expression, which returns false, and jumps to the statement after the ENDDO.

A word of caution: somewhere in the loop you must include a statement that causes the logical expression to change. In this example, it is the statement

```
COUNT = COUNT + 1
```

If that statement were omitted, COUNT would never change, and the DO WHILE logical expression would never evaluate to false. This is the endless loop that programmers know and hate. Only an interrupt (pressing the Esc key) will break the loop, and that stops the whole program. Remember: inside the body of the DO WHILE..ENDDO, there must be a statement that changes the logical expression.

DO WHILE..ENDDO commands can be for a set number of iterations, as in the example, or for a variable number. The code fragment also could be written as follows:

```
TOT_AMT = 0
DO WHILE TOT_AMT < 10000
   TOT_AMT = TOT_AMT + AMOUNT
      SKIP
ENDDO
? "TOT_AMT" = ", TOT_AMT
```

In this case, the number of loops is not predefined. FoxPro continues to loop through the database, adding the value of the AMOUNT field to the memory variable TOT_AMT, until TOT_AMT exceeds 10,000. At that point, the logical expression evaluates to false and FoxPro jumps to the ? statement following the ENDDO.

Using FOR..ENDFOR

In the first DO WHILE..ENDDO example, the loop ended when the variable count reached 1,000. Another way to set up a loop for a specific number of iterations is with the FOR..ENDFOR programming construct, in which a memory variable is used as part of the FOR statement:

```
FOR MEM_VAR = 1 TO 100
    statements to execute
ENDFOR
```

The memory variable MEM_VAR is set to 1 at the start of the FOR loop. FoxPro executes the statements between the FOR and the ENDFOR. When it reaches the ENDFOR, FoxPro increments MEM_VAR by one (or, if STEP is specified, by the amount specified after STEP) and tests whether MEM_VAR has exceeded the limit (in the example, 100). If it has, FoxPro jumps to the statement following the ENDFOR and continues.

If you want the memory variable to be incremented by something other than the default 1, use the STEP clause:

```
FOR MEM_VAR = 1 TO 100 STEP 2
    statements to be executed
ENDFOR
```

In this example, FoxPro increments MEM_VAR by two at the end of each loop and then tests to see whether it has exceeded the maximum.

FOR..ENDFOR loops are useful when you have a set number of iterations. Note that you also can use memory variables for the FOR limits:

```
START = 1
END = 100
FOR
MEM_VAR = START TO END
    statements to execute
ENDFOR
```

Using SCAN..ENDSCAN

When your loop involves looking through a database, SCAN..ENDSCAN may be the programming construct you need. When FoxPro encounters a SCAN statement, it starts at the beginning of the current database file and executes each statement between the SCAN and the ENDSCAN for each record in the file. You can use SCOPE, FOR, and WHILE clauses to limit the scan process.

```
SCAN FOR ORDER->AMOUNT > 1000
    statements to be executed
ENDSCAN
```

This SCAN..ENDSCAN example is equivalent to the following code:

```
DO WHILE .NOT. EOF()
  IF ORDER->AMOUNT < 1000
     LOOP
ENDIF
    statements to execute IF ORDER->AMOUNT > 1000
    SKIP
ENDDO
```

Using DO CASE..ENDCASE

The IF..ELSE..ENDIF construct enables you to define the direction your FoxPro program takes on an either/or basis. Depending on the value of the logical expression, the program either does one thing or another. Often times you will want to give your program more than one alternative route; the DO CASE..ENDCASE construct is designed for these cases. DO CASE..ENDCASE enables you to specify any number of routes, depending on the value of variables.

The format of the DO CASE..ENDCASE is

```
DO CASE
   CASE logical_expression_1
      statements to execute if logical_expression_1 = TRUE
   CASE logical_expression_2
      statements to execute if logical_expression_2 = TRUE
   CASE logical_expression_3
      statements to execute if logical_expression_3 = TRUE
   OTHERWISE            && optional OTHERWISE clause
      statements to execute if none of the CASE logical expressions
         are true
ENDCASE
```

When FoxPro encounters a DO CASE statement, it moves to the first CASE statement and evaluates the logical expression. If that logical expression is true, FoxPro executes the statements between that CASE statement and the next CASE statement. When those statements have completed, FoxPro jumps to the statement after the ENDCASE and continues.

If the first CASE logical expression is false, FoxPro moves to the second and evaluates that CASE statement's logical expression. This continues until one of the expressions is true, or until FoxPro encounters the optional OTHERWISE statement. If an OTHERWISE statement is included, the commands in that block will be executed. If there is no OTHERWISE, and none of the logical expressions evaluated to true, FoxPro jumps to the statement following the ENDCASE and continues.

You can see that the DO CASE..ENDCASE construct can take any number of alternative routes through your program. An excellent example of DO CASE..ENDCASE statement usage is to process a menu choice:

```
get a choice from a menu
DO CASE
   CASE CHOICE = "A"
      SET PROCEDURE TO PROC_1
      DO PROG_1
   CASE CHOICE = "B"
      SET PROCEDURE TO PROC_2
      DO PROG_2
   CASE CHOICE = "C"
      SET PROCEDURE TO PROC_3
      DO PROG_3
   OTHERWISE
      ? "That is not a valid menu choice."
ENDCASE
```

This fragment sets procedure files and executes a program based on whether the user entered A, B, or C in response to a menu. If the response was something other than A, B, or C, an error message is issued.

Note that it is not required that the logical expressions have anything in common. It is entirely possible to have a DO CASE..ENDCASE fragment that looks like the following, in which all the logical expressions are completely different:

```
DO CASE
   CASE AMT > 100
      ? "The total amount is greater than $100"
```

```
CASE EOF()
    ? "You're at the end of the file"
CASE MONTH(DATE()) <> "JAN"
    ? "This isn't January!"
CASE RECNO() > 100
    ? "Record number = ", RECNO()
ENDCASE
```

No other computer language I know allows this; the CASE statements must be on the same variable. Although FoxPro does allow such logical expression mixing, I recommend avoiding this programming practice. It makes for confusing programs, and confusion is the last thing you need when you're programming.

Using Screen Input and Output

Sooner or later, you must get some information from the user or write something to the screen. FoxPro provides several ways to read data from the user and write information to the screen from a program.

Using INPUT and WAIT

The simplest way of getting information from the user is with the INPUT and WAIT statements. These statements stop program execution and wait for the user to enter something from the keyboard.

The difference between INPUT and WAIT is that INPUT will always put the user's input into a memory variable; you must specify the memory variable in the INPUT statement as follows:

```
INPUT "Enter your last name: " TO LAST_NAME
```

In this example, the user's input is assigned to the variable LAST_NAME. If you use WAIT, you can optionally assign the user's response to a memory variable, but it is not necessary. The following expression,

```
WAIT "Error encountered"
```

causes FoxPro to stop, issue the Error encountered string and wait until the user enters something. Pressing Enter causes FoxPro to discard the input and continue processing the program.

The two statements also differ in the character string that can be used as a prompt. If you omit this prompt string with INPUT, nothing appears on-screen. With WAIT, omitting the character string prompt causes FoxPro to issue the message Press any key to continue, and then wait for the user's input.

Using the ? and ?? Statements

You use the ? and ?? statements to place information on the screen in Fox-Pro. You place one or more expressions after the ? or ?? statements, and FoxPro writes those expressions out to the screen. If you use the ? statement, FoxPro issues a carriage return/linefeed combination so the list starts on the next line; using the ?? statement suppresses the movement to the next line, so the list is printed on the current line, starting at the cursor position. For example, the expression

    ? 'This is line 1'
    ?? 'This is line 2'

results in

    This is line 1This is line 2

In this example, the ? statement causes the line 1 string to be printed on a new line; the ?? statement simply prints the line 2 character string on the same line, starting where the first string ended.

You can list a series of expressions with the ? and ?? statements as follows:

    ORDER–>AMOUNT = 100.00
    ? "Amount: " , ORDER–>AMOUNT, " plus or minus a few bucks."

results in

    Amount: 100.00 plus or minus a few bucks.

Each expression in a ? or ?? list can have several optional clauses for formatting and positioning on the line. A PICTURE or FUNCTION clause, described in the Chapter 3 discussion of FoxView and the Chapter 5 section on Report Writing (and more thoroughly in the @ SAY..GET section later in this chapter) can be included, as can an AT clause, which places the expression at a specific column on the output line:

    AMT = 123.45
    TOT_AMT = 12,990.34
    ? AMT FUNCTION "$9" AT 5, TOT_AMT PICTURE "99,999.99" AT 20

results in

$123.44   12,990.34

The ? and ?? statements also are useful for writing reports, when used in conjunction with the PRINTJOB..ENDPRINTJOB commands. For screen output, they are limited in that they write only to the current line on-screen. For full-screen data entry and output, FoxPro provides the amazing capabilities of the @ SAY..GET statements.

Using @ SAY..GET

Full-screen data entry and display screens are an essential part of a full FoxPro database system. You have seen how with FoxView you can create input and inquiry screens that ensure the accuracy of input data and enhance the presentation of the output. When programming in FoxPro, knowledge of the FoxPro commands @ SAY and @ GET will give you great flexibility in this area.

@ SAY and @ GET are shorthand for the FoxPro commands that place information at specific places on-screen. The actual format of the commands is as follows:

@ *row_num, col_num* SAY *expr [options]*
@ *row_num, col_num* GET *data [options]*

The *row_num* specifies the row number on-screen, from 0 to 24 where you want the SAY or GET statement to appear; the *col_num* represents the column, from 0 to 79, at which you want the SAY or GET to start. In the SAY command, the *expr* represents a FoxPro expression. That expression may be any memory variable or database field or any valid FoxPro expression. In the GET command, the *data* represents a memory variable or database field. The *[options]* modify the expression or data.

Using SAY To Put Information On-Screen

The SAY statement in a program tells FoxPro to place the SAY expression on-screen at the location you specify. The following is an example of several SAY statements in a program:

```
FNAME = "John"
LNAME = "Pickett"
@ 0, 0 CLEAR              && clear the screen
@ 1, 10 SAY "Last Name : " + LNAME
@ 2, 10 SAY "First Name: " + FNAME
```

When FoxPro encounters these lines in a program, it first clears the screen, then, at row 2 and column 10, places the string

First Name: + FNAME

which concatenates the memory variable to the end of a literal string, First Name:. The result of this code fragment is seen in figure 11.2.

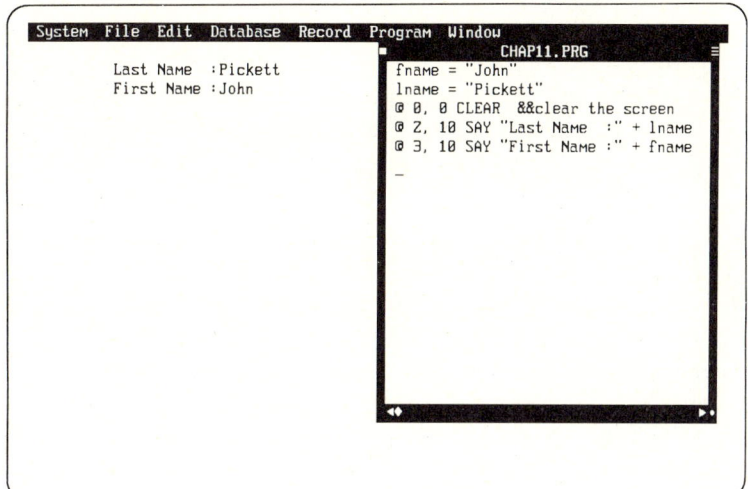

Fig. 11.2.
SAY statements
with character
strings
concatenated for
output.

The CLEAR command clears only the bottom FoxPro screen. Windows that are on top of the FoxPro window remain on-screen. For these examples, the window remains on-screen so that you can see the program and the result of the program at the same time.

There are many formatting options available for the SAY statement, but because they also are valid for the GET statement, the next section looks at that statement first.

Using GET and READ To Get Information

When you issue an @GET statement in a program, FoxPro sets a field at the row number and column number you have specified. You can use a PICTURE clause to specify the field's length; otherwise FoxPro will set the length to be the length of the database field, if your GET is for a database field, or the current length of the memory variable, if the field is for a memory variable.

Issuing the GET statement in a program does not actually cause FoxPro to read data from the screen. To activate GET, you must issue a READ statement. When you do that, FoxPro steps through all the active GETs on-screen, in the order you placed them there, until each has been read, or the user has pressed a key indicating to end data entry (Esc, PgUp, or PgDn). The following is an example of using GET statements to read from the screen in a program:

```
FNAME = "John"
LNAME = "Pickett"
@ 0, 0 CLEAR          && clears the entire screen
@ 1, 10 GET LNAME     && place a field on-screen
@ 1, 10 GET FNAME     && and another
READ
```

Only when the READ is executed in the program does FoxPro take information from the GET fields. When the GETs are placed on-screen, the current value of the memory variable or database field is placed in the GET field. Figure 11.3 shows the screen when the code fragment is executed. FoxPro has reached the READ statement and is awaiting input from the user. The values assigned to the memory variables are displayed and may be accepted by simply returning through the fields.

Fig. 11.3.
FoxPro waiting at a READ statement for input.

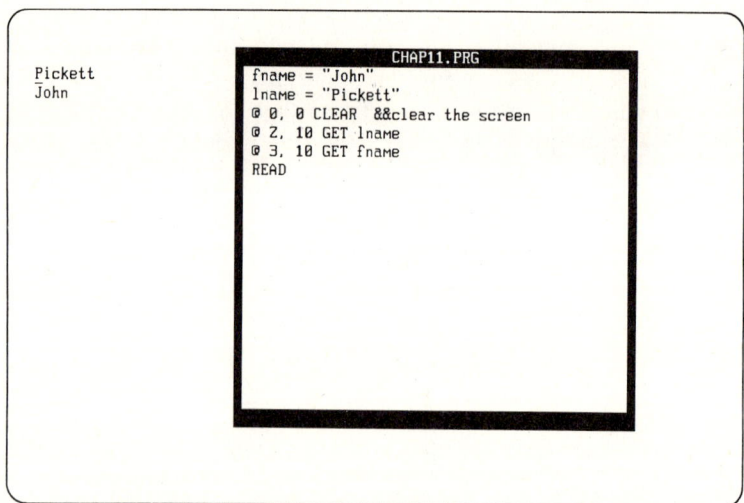

Combining the SAY and GET Commands

Often you will want your GET field to have a literal string before it; in FoxView these are called *labels*. To format your data-entry screen in this manner, combine the SAY and GET statements into one statement as follows:

@ *row_num, col_num* SAY *expr* GET *data*

The GET field will be placed with one space between the end of the SAY expression and the start of the GET field. Again, an example shows this best. Combining the code samples for the SAY and GET statements, you can write the program as follows:

```
@ 0, 0 CLEAR              && clear the screen
@ 1, 10 SAY "Last Name: " GET LNAME
@ 2, 10 SAY "First Name:" GET FNAME
READ
```

The results in the data-entry screen are shown in figure 11.4.

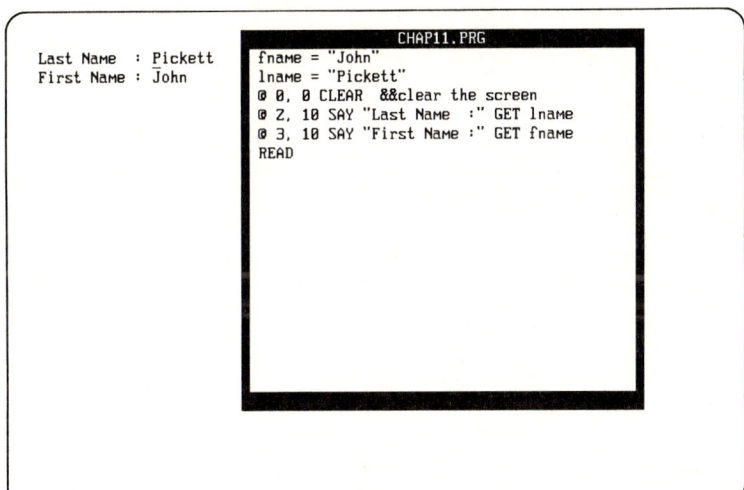

Fig. 11.4.
The screen using SAY..GET combination statements.

You can get quite sophisticated with data-entry and display screens using SAY and GET statements. You can see many examples of these in action by creating screens with FoxView and using the MODIFY COMMAND file to look at the FMT files generated. But you will find as you program more that FoxView has some limits that you can overcome by programming things yourself.

Using FUNCTION Clauses To Format a Data Field

With FUNCTION and PICTURE clauses, you can improve your screens and the accuracy of the data on them.

FUNCTION clauses contain codes that format an entire field of data. A FUNCTION clause is a string of characters, so it must begin and end with double-quotation marks. The first character in a FUNCTION code string must be an @. Some examples of FUNCTION clauses are as follows:

FUNCTION "@!" This function forces all characters in the field to be uppercase.

FUNCTION "@A" The function displays and accepts only alphabetic characters.

Following is a list of valid FUNCTION codes:

A Allows alphabetic characters only.

B Left-justifies numeric output in an output field.

C Puts a CR (credit) after a positive number in a numeric field.

I Centers output text.

J Right-justifies output text in the field.

L Displays leading zeros. This causes a numeric field to be completely full. For instance, in a numeric field with length of 8, the number 5 will be displayed as 00000005.

M Allows you to specify a list of items that will appear in a pull-down window. You could, for example, specify:

   M Foxbase, Foxbase+, FoxPro

which would then allow the user to choose from only these three choices when inputting to the field.

R Tells FoxPro that the format string contains characters other than standard PICTURE codes and that these characters are to be placed in the field as edit masks. For instance, @R (999)999-999 causes a field to appear as (   )   -   and accepts only the characters 1 through 9. This is useful for creating edit masks for your data.

S<n> Limits the field to n characters wide, but allows scrolling if the input variable is wider.

T Trims the leading and trailing edge blanks from the data in the field.

X Places a DB (debit) symbol after a negative number.

Z The field will be blank if its value is zero; otherwise FoxPro displays a 0. Used only with numeric fields.

(Enclose negative numbers in parentheses.

! Accepts any number, but converts lowercase alphabetic characters to uppercase.

^ Displays numeric data in scientific notation.

$ Displays numeric data in currency format.

Using PICTURE Clauses To Format a Data Field

Unlike FUNCTION codes, which format all the characters of a data-entry or display field, PICTURE clauses format each character of that field individually; they are pictures of the way you want the field formatted. For instance, if you want a numeric field to be formatted with a leading dollar sign, with commas, and to have four digits before the decimal point and two after, you would use the following command:

@ 0, 10 SAY DOL_AMT PICTURE "$9,999.99"

The valid PICTURE formatting codes are as follows:

A Allows only an alphabetic character to be entered.

L Allows only logical characters, which are T, t, F f, Y, y, N, n.

N Allows only a letter or a digit.

X Allows any character.

Y Allows only logical Y, y, N, or n to be entered. Lowercase is converted to uppercase.

9 Allows only a digit to be entered if the field is character. If the field is numeric, allows digits and the plus (+) or minus (−) signs.

Allows digits, blanks, and signs.

! Converts a lowercase character to uppercase.

$ Displays the currency symbol (usually the dollar sign, $).

* Displays asterisks in front of a numeric value; useful for check protection.

. The period specifies the decimal position.

, A comma is used to separate digits to the left of the decimal point.

Using Other GET Options

Many other useful options are available to work with SAY and GET programming. These include the following:

RANGE *low_limit, high_limits* Allows you to specify the range of a numeric GET statement. FoxPro will beep and display an error message if the user tries to enter a number outside this range.

VALID ‹*exprLogical*› Allows you to test the input data, using a FoxPro expression or a user-defined function. In either case, if the result is FALSE, FoxPro will reject the input with an error message.

WHEN ‹*exprL*› The field will be READ only when the value of the logical expression is TRUE. This allows you to skip fields under some conditions and READ them under others.

DEFAULT ‹*expr*› Places the expression in the field as a default value.

MESSAGE ‹*exprC*› Defines a character string to be a message which will be displayed on the last line of the screen during data entry. This is a good way to have a mini-help system for your data entry screens.

Creating Structured Programs

Any programmer worth his salt knows about structured programming. FoxPro provides excellent programming capabilities to create your programs in a structured, maintainable way. Structure programming simply refers to breaking your programs down into manageable hunks of code, each of which does one thing and only one thing. Because FoxPro enables you to call one program from another, you can create well-structured programs easily.

When designing a FoxPro program, think about how you will actually program the beast. You will find that your program does some things many times, such as issue error messages, or read data from one database file, or ask for information from the user. When you find sections of code that

will be repeated often in your program, break them out into separate programs. You could, for example, have a program that looks like the
following:

    issue error message to screen
    wait for response to error message
    . . . .
    put a series of GET statements on-screen
    READ the GET statements
    process the information in the GET statements; if some information
        was not right, issue error message to screen; wait for response
        to error message
    . . . .
    put the GET statements back on-screen
    READ the GET statements
    process the information again

Although this all may work just fine, consider what happens if you decide
that you want your error message to appear in a different place on-screen.
You must go through your program, find each place the error message is
written and change the program to reflect the new location. In a large
program, I can guarantee you will miss at least one.

The solution is to place the error message in a separate program file and
execute that file from the main program:

    DO *error_msg*
    put a series of GET statements on-screen
    READ the GET statements
    process the information in the GET statements; if some information
        was not right,
    DO *error_msg*
    put the GET statements back on-screen
    READ the GET statements
    process the information again

Now, if you want to change the error message location, you do so in only
one place, the error message program. Likewise, you can place any routine that you call more than once in a separate file.

The key to structured programming is to have each subprogram do one
programming process. Then, when something goes wrong with that process or you want to change it, you have to change only that one program.
Large FoxPro systems may contain hundreds of program files, each of
which follows this rule.

Using Subprograms

When one program calls another, you will often want the calling program to pass some data to the subprogram and receive some data back. FoxPro gives you the ability to do this with the DO..WITH option.

To send data to a called subprogram (called passing a parameter), the subprogram has to know what data is going to be sent to it. The first line of a subprogram that will receive data should be a PARAMETER statement, which lists what information the subprogram can expect. In the last example, you saw a subprogram called ERROR_MSG, which might print an error message on-screen and wait for the user to press the Enter key to go on. Such a routine could be used for many error messages if it could be set up to receive the error message from the calling program. Here's how to do that:

```
* ERROR_MSG procedure
PARAMETER E_MSG

@ 23, 1 SAY E_MSG
@ 24, 1 SAY "Press any key to continue..."
SET CONSOLE OFF
WAIT
SET CONSOLE ON
RETURN
```

Now, when you execute ERROR_MSG, you must pass the error message string as follows:

```
DO ERROR_MSG WITH "Invalid Last Name Entered"
```

or

```
DO ERROR_MSG WITH "Date must be later than 01/01/80"
```

When the ERROR_MSG routine is called with the DO command, FoxPro passes the character string after the WITH option to the subprogram. ERROR_MSG knows it will get a string to use as the message.

You can see the advantage of the PARAMETER statement. It lets you use one routine in many different places, with different data going to it at each of those different places. Your alternative—not a very good one at all—is to write the routine each place you need it, with the correct data for that specific place. Subprograms are an absolutely essential capability of all programming languages, and FoxPro is no exception.

Using Procedure Files

One disadvantage of using small, segmented programs is that it slows down FoxPro. Each time FoxPro encounters a DO statement, it must load the program into memory and execute it. In a large system, in which Fox-Pro must search a long directory and then load what may be some rather large programs, this can add up to long pauses in execution. If you use procedure files, you can alleviate this delay.

A procedure file is simply a file that contains many FoxPro programs. Using the SET PROCEDURE TO *procedure_file_name* command, you tell FoxPro that it should first look in the procedure file for any programs called with the DO statement. When FoxPro encounters the SET PRO-CEDURE TO statement, it loads the procedure file into memory if there is enough room. (If not, FoxPro does some fancy footwork that will dramatically speed up calls to programs in the procedure file.)

Now, when your program calls another with the DO command, FoxPro does not go looking on the disk for the program; it already has it in memory. You will not believe how fast executing a program in a procedure file can be.

To place PRG program files into a procedure file, use your favorite text editor to merge the individual programs into one file. The only change you must make is to add, as the first line of each procedure, the line

PROCEDURE *proc_name*

where *proc_name* is the name of the program to be called. If, for example, you have created a file called ERROR_MS.PRG and want to put it into a procedure file called UTILS.PRG, you would place the line

PROCEDURE ERROR_MS

as the first line of this procedure in the program file. When you have more than one procedure in UTILS.PRG, it will look like the following:

PROCEDURE *add_line*

. . . .

program lines of the *add_line* procedure

. . . .

PROCEDURE *edit_line*

. . . .

program lines of the *edit_line* procedure

. . . .

PROCEDURE *error_ms*

. . . .

program lines of the *error_msg* procedure

A helpful trick to creating program files that may be used in a procedure file is to include the PROCEDURE *proc_name* as the first line of every program file you create, with an asterisk (*) as the first character. That makes the line a comment, ignored by FoxPro if the program file is executed with a DO command. Then, when and if you include this program in a procedure file, you only have to delete the asterisks to make the program a valid procedure.

You can create a procedure file with the FoxPro text editor. First, open a new program file from the File New menu option. Secondly, use the File Open option to create a second text editing window with the file you want to include in the procedure file. Figure 11.5 shows two windows open, one for the UTILS.PRG procedure file and a second for the program ERROR_MS.PRG.

Fig. 11.5.
Two program files open at the same time in different windows.

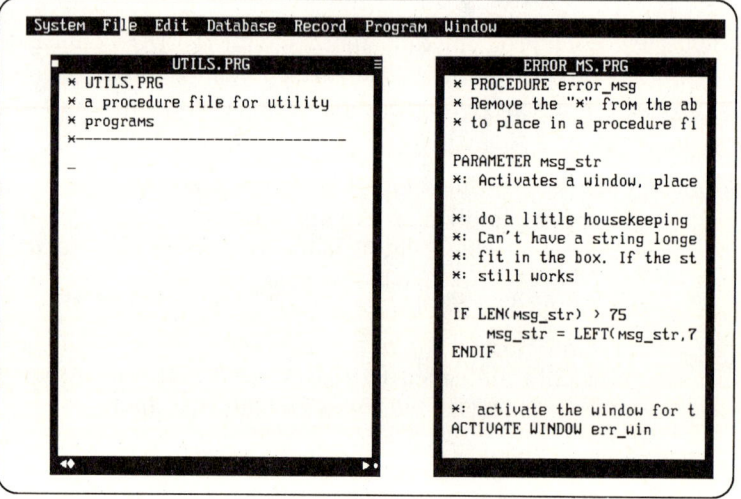

Move to the ERROR_MS.PRG window and delete the * that marks the first line as a comment. Then highlight all the lines in the program and choose Copy from the Edit menu. Now make the UTILS.PRG window active, make sure that the cursor is where you want to insert the program, and choose Paste. The ERROR_MS.PRG program is inserted into the procedure file. You can continue this process until all the program files you want in the procedure file are included.

Using Basic Utility Programs

Learning a new programming language, particularly if it's your first, can be a terribly frustrating experience. To ease this pain, here are some fairly simple, but quite useful, FoxPro programs that you can peruse and use. Although I don't claim to be the world's greatest FoxPro programmer, these programs do work and may form the basis for your own exploits in FoxPro programming.

Reading To Get a Valid Character

Often, you will want to get a character from the screen that must meet some criterion. You may, for example, ask the user whether he wants to file, edit, save, or quit from a data-entry screen, and want your program to accept a letter from the user which must be either F for file, E for edit, S for save, or Q for quit; any other letter must cause a message to appear explaining the situation. Here is a procedure that will receive a message string and a string against which to check the input. The procedure will return the valid character.

In pseudo-English, the procedure can be written as follows:

```
GET message, CHECK_STRING from calling program
open the window
DO WHILE the input character is not in the CHECK_STRING
   write the message on-screen
   GET the entered character
   if the entered character is not in the CHECK_STRING
      write an error message
   ENDIF
ENDDO
close the window
```

And the program itself is shown in figure 11.6.

Before this program can be called, you must issue a DEFINE WINDOW command. The DEFINE WINDOW commands tells FoxPro to set up in its memory a window, with a name, which can then be put on-screen with the ACTIVATE WINDOW command and taken off the screen with the DEACTIVATE WINDOW command. The format of the DEFINE WINDOW command for this routine is

DEFINE WINDOW MSG_WIN1 FROM 21,0 TO 24,79

Fig. 11.6.

The GET_CHAR procedure.

```
PROCEDURE get_char
PARAMETER msg_str, chk_str, ret_char
*: Activates a window, places the msg_str in it and waits for a
*: character input. Tests the character entered against the
*: chk_str and will not return until a valid character has been
*: entered.

*: do a little housekeeping
*: Can't have a string longer than 75 characters, because it
*: won't fit in the box. If the string is longer, truncate it so
*: the routine still works

IF LEN(msg_str) > 75
    msg_str = LEFT(msg_str,75)
ENDIF

*: set up the error message to be used if the user enters an
*: invalid character

err_msg = "You must enter one of these characters: " + chk_str

*: activate the window for the message
ACTIVATE WINDOW msg_win1

valid_char = .F.
DO WHILE .NOT. valid_char        && loop until users enters a
                                 && character that's in the chk_str

    *: Center the string on the first line of the box
    @ 0, (80 - (LEN(msg_str)+ 3))/2 SAY msg_str GET ret_char PICTURE '!
    READ

    IF UPPER(ret_char) $ UPPER(chk_str)
    *: user entered a valid character, exit the do while...enddo loop
        valid_char = .T.
        ELSE
            *: center the error message on the next line
            @ 1, (80-LEN(err_msg))/2 SAY err_msg
        ENDIF
ENDDO

DEACTIVATE WINDOW msg_win1

RETURN
```

This creates a window from row 21, column 0 to row 24, column 79 (across the bottom of the screen). A great advantage of using a window is that, should you decide to put the GET_CHAR input somewhere else on-screen, you only must change the row and column parameters in the DEFINE WINDOW command. The line,

    IF UPPER(RET_CHAR) $ UPPER(CHK_STR)

tells FoxPro to change the character entered (RET_CHAR) to uppercase, change all the characters in the check string to uppercase, and see whether the uppercase RET_CHAR exists in the uppercase CHK_STR. In this way, you can ensure that the user doesn't have to worry about whether he is entering an upper- or lowercase character; either will work. The $ symbol is FoxPro's shorthand for "is in"; you could read this command as if the uppercase RET_CHAR is in the uppercase CHK_STR.

The expression,

    ("80 − LEN(MSG_STR))/2 SAY"

centers the MSG_STR on a line. The program adds two to the length of the MSG_STR,

$$(``(80 - (LEN(MSG\_STR) + 2) /2 SAY"$$

to account for the space after the message and the space in which the GET will take place. By doing this, the entire line, message, and GET field will be centered on the line.

Using Memory Variables for Database Input

Most APPEND operations add a record as soon as the user moves out of the last field of the data-entry screen. Often, though, you will want to give the user the opportunity to edit the entered data before adding it to the database. This gives the user a chance to make sure that the data is correct, and gives you some assurance that data going into the database is right. It is always easier to correct data before it is added to a database file than afterward.

The program shown in figure 11.7 is a routine that uses memory variables and two DO WHILE..ENDDO loops to give the user the opportunity to change the entered data before it enters the database file.

Chapter Summary

In this chapter, you have learned quite a bit about FoxPro programming. You learned about the different programming constructs of DO WHILE..ENDDO, FOR..ENDFOR, DO CASE..ENDCASE, and SCAN..END-SCAN, and how these constructs tell FoxPro to react differently to different conditions. You learned the basics of FoxPro screen input and output with SAY and GET statements. And you have seen several sample programs that illustrate basic FoxPro programming.

Programming is not a mystic art. FoxPro programming is quite simple and, like all else about FoxPro, amazingly powerful. Experiment with it and have fun.

Fig. 11.7.
The
ADD_EDIT.PRG
program.

```
*: add_edit.prg
*: an append routine that enables the user to edit the record
*: on-screen until it is acceptable. At the end of entering data,
*: the user is asked if he wants to file, edit or quit without
*: filing. This routine enables you to take data from the screen
*: but not enter it into the database until it's correct.

SET TALK OFF
esc_pressed = 12   && READKEY() returns a 12 if escape key is pressed

SELECT 1
USE customer INDEX cust_num

*: loop while the user wants to enter records
entering = .T.
DO WHILE entering
    mCustName  = SPACE(25)
    mAddr1     = SPACE(25)
    mAddr2     = SPACE(25)
    mCity      = SPACE(25)
    mState     = SPACE(2)
    mZip       = SPACE(9)

    @ 0, 0 CLEAR
    @ 4, 10 SAY "Customer Name : "
    @ 5, 10 SAY "        Address : "
    @ 6, 10 SAY "                : "
    @ 7, 10 SAY "          City : "
    @ 8, 10 SAY "         State : "
    @ 9, 10 SAY "           Zip : "

    *: loop through the read/validate routine until user says it's ok
    *: to save in the database
    editing = .T.
    DO WHILE editing
        @ 4, 27 GET mCustName
        @ 5, 27 GET mAddr1
        @ 6, 27 GET mAddr2
        @ 7, 27 GET mCity
        @ 8, 27 GET mState FUNCTION "@!"
        @ 9, 27 GET mZip PICTURE "@R 99999-9999"

        READ

        IF READKEY() = esc_pressed
            editing = .F.
            entering = .F.
        ELSE
            choice = "F"
            DO get_char WITH "Do you want to Edit, File or Quit? (E/F/Q)
            DO CASE
                CASE choice = "E" && user wants to edit the data
                    editing = .T.
                    entering = .T.
                CASE choice = "F" && user wants to file the data
                    APPEND BLANK
                    REPLACE cust_name WITH mCustName
                    REPLACE addr_1    WITH mAddr1
                    REPLACE addr_2    WITH mAddr2
                    REPLACE city      WITH mCity
                    REPLACE state     WITH mState
                    REPLACE zip       WITH mZip
                    editing = .F.
                    entering = .T.
                CASE choice = "Q"  && user wants to quit without filing
                    editing = .F.
                    entering = .F.
            ENDCASE
        ENDIF
    ENDDO  && while editing
ENDDO  & while entering

USE
RETURN
```

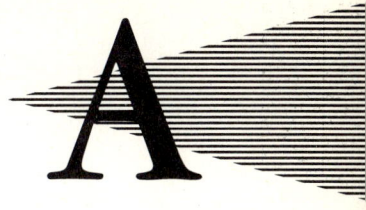

Installing FoxPro

The installation procedures for FoxPro could hardly be easier than they are. You enter a command, give the installation routine your version's serial number and activation key, and then swap disks as you're asked. Once the base system is installed, you can add nonessential parts of the system as you want.

This appendix leads you through the installation procedure. When you're finished, you will have FoxPro and the necessary optional systems installed properly.

System Requirements

FoxPro is one of a growing number of PC programs that almost require a hard disk drive. You could run FoxPro on a system with two high-capacity floppy disk drives (at least 1.2 megabytes per drive) but it would be very cumbersome and slow.

FoxPro did not follow the trend toward memory-hungry systems, though. Although more and more PC-based systems require the full 640K of system memory (some barely work with that), FoxPro continues to run "lean and mean." FoxPro will work well with 512K computer. This doesn't mean that FoxPro will not benefit from more memory, however. With 640K, you can add some memory-resident programs, and if your computer does have extended memory or expanded memory, FoxPro can use it well when accompanied by the appropriate memory drivers.

Using expanded and extended memory is a complicated topic. If you know how to set up your computer to do this, I refer you to the FoxPro manual for specific instructions. If "expanded memory," "extended memory," and "software drivers" are foreign terms to you, I suggest you enlist the aid of an expert.

Installing FoxPro

FoxPro's installation procedure is two part: in the first part, you install the base system, which is FoxPro itself, FoxView (the screen developer), Fox-Code (for advanced users), and FoxDoc (a program documentor). Once you have done that, you're given the chance to install additional programs you may want.

To install the base system, follow these procedures:

1. Copy the five original FoxPro disks to blank disks. If you have a one-drive PC, do this with the following command:

   DISKCOPY A: A:

   If you have a two-drive system, use this command:

   DISKCOPY A: B:

   In the first case, place the original disk in drive A: and enter the command. DOS will read the disk (the "source disk") and prompt you to enter the disk onto which you want to copy (the "destination disk"). In the second case, place the original disk in drive A: and the new disk in drive B: and issue the command.

Do this with each of the disks, then put the originals away. I know many readers will totally ignore this step, thinking that because they're putting FoxPro on the hard drive and never using the original disks, there's no need to copy the originals. I have never had an original disk go bad, so I understand that sentiment; but I have lost original disks and then had my hard drives crash. This is cheap insurance.

In your FoxPro package is a form showing the serial number and two activation keys. One activation key, called the Demonstration Activation Key, unlocks FoxPro so that you can test it, but severely limits the number of records FoxPro will allow. The second activation key, which you can read only by opening the sealed envelope, unlocks the full FoxPro system.

2. Next, write down your serial number and the regular activation key. I suggest you write both down on the original disks, the copy disks, in at least one of the manuals, in your address book, the family Bible, and three or four other safe places. I suggest that because it is easy to lose that sheet of paper with the serial number and activation keys, and when you accidentally erase your hard drive (yes, I have done that), you will need the serial number and activation key to reinstall FoxPro.

Now, finally, you're ready to install FoxPro. To install the FoxPro system, you need about 1 megabyte of space on your hard disk. The base system provides all FoxPro functions, but doesn't include FoxView, the tool used to develop sophisticated data-entry screens. Adding FoxView and the necessary programs will add 500K to your disk requirements. If you want to install everything included on the distribution disks (which includes demonstration and tutorial files along with several FoxPro programming tools), you will need 2.5 megabytes of space.

3. Create a FoxPro directory. If you are installing on a hard drive designated as the C: drive, type the following command at the C: prompt:

    MKDIR C:\FOXPRO CD C:\FOXPRO

    If you want to install FoxPro on a drive other than C:, replace the C: in this command with the appropriate drive letter designation.

4. Now, place Disk 1 in drive A: and type

    INSTALL C:

    If you're installing FoxPro on a drive other than C:, replace the C: with the correct drive letter. FoxPro displays the screen containing installation information. Press any key to continue.

5. Enter your serial number exactly as it appears on the envelope; uppercase and lowercase characters must be entered exactly as shown. When you're finished, you will see the screen shown in figure A.1, which asks for the activation key.

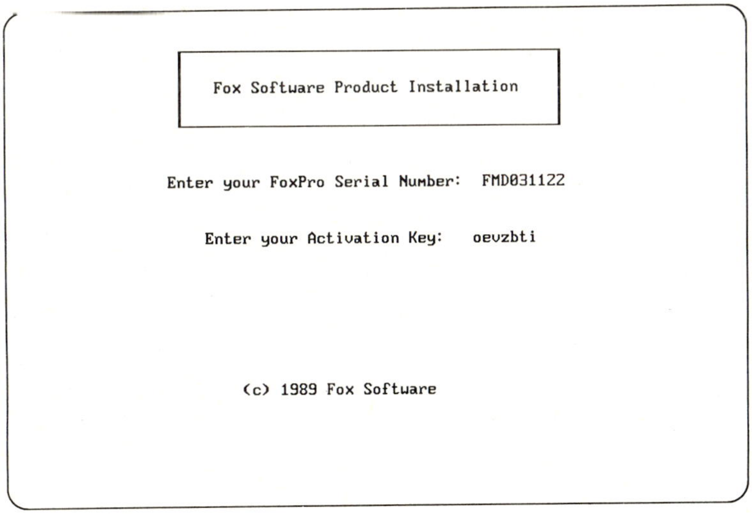

```
        ┌──────────────────────────────────────┐
        │   Fox Software Product Installation   │
        └──────────────────────────────────────┘


        Enter your FoxPro Serial Number:   FMD031122

          Enter your Activation Key:    oevzbti




             (c) 1989 Fox Software
```

Fig. A.1.
Entering the
Activation key.

6. Enter the activation key exactly as it appears on the envelope. You must enter upper- and lowercase letters exactly as they appear on the envelope. If you want to "test drive" FoxPro, enter the Demonstration Activation Key, otherwise enter the live key.

FoxPro will now lead you through the installation procedure, asking you to insert disks as necessary. When the base system is in place, you will see the screen shown in figure A.2.

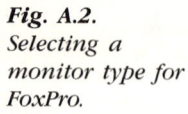

Fig. A.2.
Selecting a
monitor type for
FoxPro.

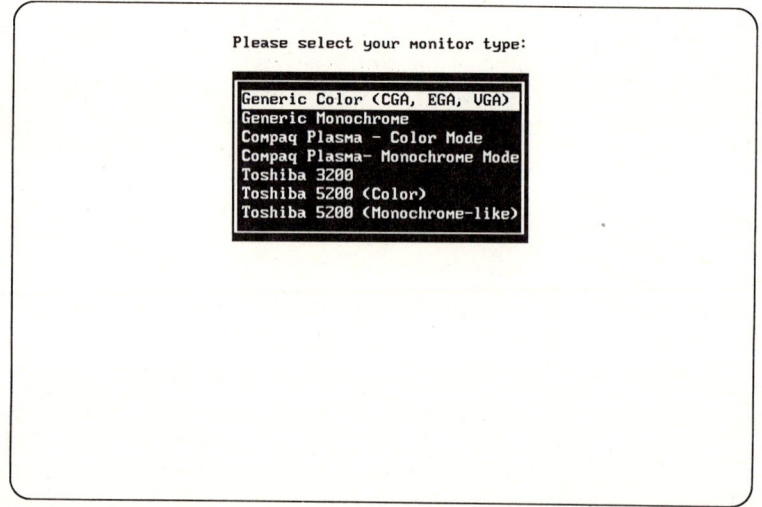

```
            Please select your monitor type:


         Generic Color (CGA, EGA, UGA)
         Generic Monochrome
         Compaq Plasma - Color Mode
         Compaq Plasma- Monochrome Mode
         Toshiba 3200
         Toshiba 5200 (Color)
         Toshiba 5200 (Monochrome-like)
```

You now have the opportunity to install FoxPro optional products. Some of these optional products are sample files and tutorial programs; others are near-essentials, such as FoxView (see fig. A.3).

7. In the window labeled CONTENTS, move the highlight up and down using the up- and down-arrow keys, and select what you want to install by pressing the space bar. When you have selected the programs you want to install, press Enter. Following is a summary of what is included in the Optional Products menu:

❏ Help File. This file is useful while you're learning FoxPro.

❏ Small Help File. This is a Help file with abbreviated command explanations. If you install the full-sized Help file, there's no need to install this one too. As you become more expert with FoxPro, you may want to replace the full Help file with this one to conserve disk space.

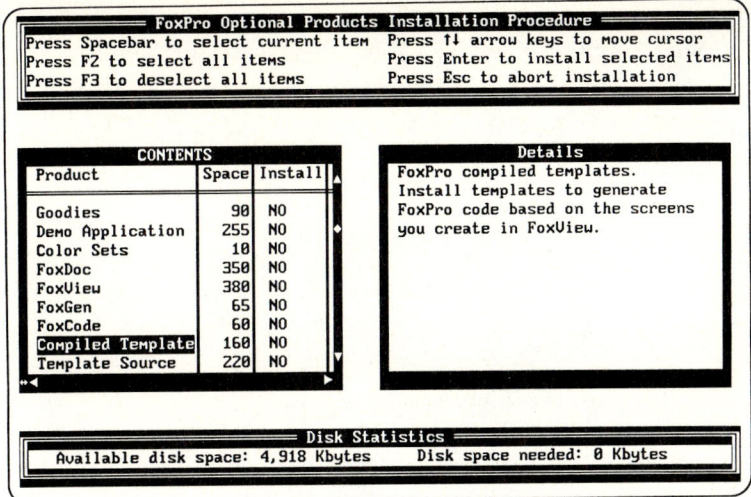

Fig. A.3.
The FoxPro
Optional
Products
installation
screen.

❏ Tutorial Files. A series of program and database files that form the FoxPro tutorial. If you're new to FoxPro, this is an excellent introduction.

❏ Goodies. Optional programs that you may use when you become quite familiar with FoxPro. You don't need these to start.

❏ Demo Application. A full application showing off FoxPro. It's interesting to play around with, but you will find yourself erasing it after several sessions.

❏ Color Sets. These are color sets for monitor types other than the one you already specified. No need to install these now. (If, however, you find your screen difficult to read, experiment with other color sets through the Window Color menu option. Choosing another color set may improve your screen readability.)

❏ FoxDoc. FoxDoc is a program that documents FoxPro application programs. If you're an experienced FoxBase+ or dBASE IV programmer and expect to be writing FoxPro code right away, install this. Otherwise, leave it off until you're ready to do some FoxPro programming.

❏ FoxView. FoxView is the FoxPro screen editing program. With it you create screens for FoxPro to use. This option is a necessity; install it.

❏ FoxGen. FoxView uses FoxGen to transform your screen designs to FoxPro code, so you should install this option.

❏ FoxCode. FoxCode goes with FoxGen.

❏ Compiled Templates. These are used by FoxGen to translate screen design to files that FoxPro can use. You should install these templates if you go beyond the bare-bones use of FoxPro.

❏ Template Source. These programs are what created the Compiled Templates. In Using FoxPro, you will make some changes to these source files, so install them also.

8. Once you have specified what optional products you want installed, press Enter and follow FoxPro's instructions for disk changes. When FoxPro is done, you are returned to the C: prompt, now in the directory you defined for FoxPro.

FoxPro has created the necessary directories for you. The directory structure is shown in figure A.4.

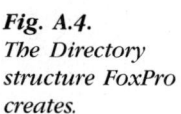

Fig. A.4.
The Directory structure FoxPro creates.

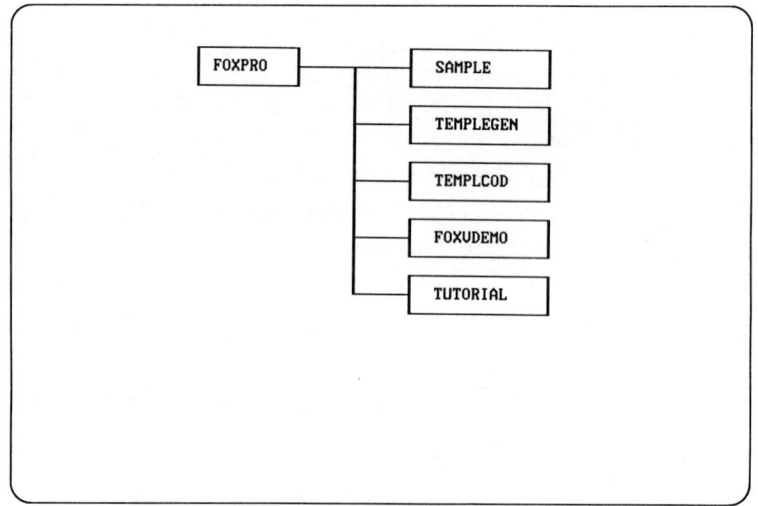

FoxPro is now ready to run. I suggest you create another directory for your FoxPro database files and other files you will create during the process of learning and using FoxPro. To create another file, enter the command

MKDIR C:\FOXPRO*dir_name*

where *dir_name* is the name of the directory you want to create. Then, move to this directory by typing

CD \FOXPRO*dir_name*

again where *dir_name* is the directory you just created.

Next, set a path so that DOS knows where to find FoxPro by typing

PATH = C:\FOXPRO

and enter the command

FOXPRO

You should see the FoxPro opening screen (see fig. A.5). Now turn to Quick Start 1 and have fun!

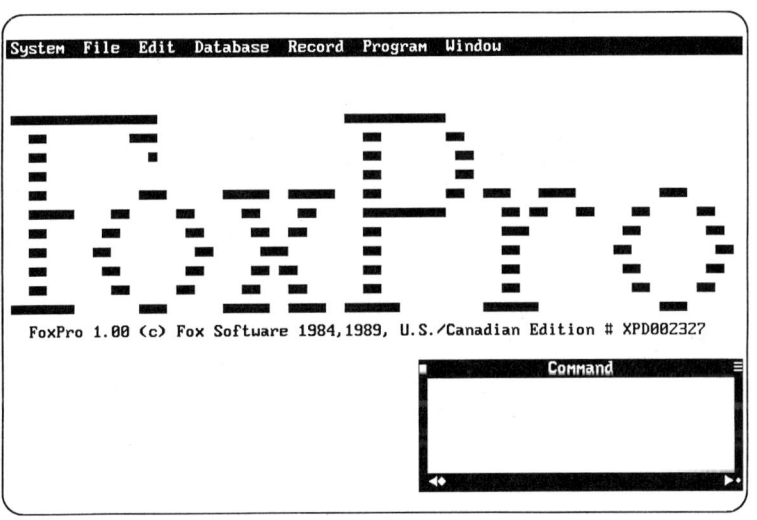

Fig. A.5.
The FoxPro opening screen.

Index

Free Catalog!

Mail us this registration form today, and we'll send you a free catalog featuring Que's complete line of best-selling books.

Name of Book _____

Name _____

Title _____

Phone ( ) _____

Company _____

Address _____

City _____

State _____ ZIP _____

Please check the appropriate answers:

1. Where did you buy your Que book?
   - ☐ Bookstore (name: _____)
   - ☐ Computer store (name: _____)
   - ☐ Catalog (name: _____)
   - ☐ Direct from Que
   - ☐ Other: _____

2. How many computer books do you buy a year?
   - ☐ 1 or less
   - ☐ 2-5
   - ☐ 6-10
   - ☐ More than 10

3. How many Que books do you own?
   - ☐ 1
   - ☐ 2-5
   - ☐ 6-10
   - ☐ More than 10

4. How long have you been using this software?
   - ☐ Less than 6 months
   - ☐ 6 months to 1 year
   - ☐ 1-3 years
   - ☐ More than 3 years

5. What influenced your purchase of this Que book?
   - ☐ Personal recommendation
   - ☐ Advertisement
   - ☐ In-store display
   - ☐ Price
   - ☐ Que catalog
   - ☐ Que mailing
   - ☐ Que's reputation
   - ☐ Other: _____

6. How would you rate the overall content of the book?
   - ☐ Very good
   - ☐ Good
   - ☐ Satisfactory
   - ☐ Poor

7. What do you like *best* about this Que book?
   _____
   _____

8. What do you like *least* about this Que book?
   _____
   _____

9. Did you buy this book with your personal funds?
   - ☐ Yes   ☐ No

10. Please feel free to list any other comments you may have about this Que book.
    _____
    _____
    _____

— QUE —

Order Your Que Books Today!

Name _____

Title _____

Company _____

City _____

State _____ ZIP _____

Phone No. ( ) _____

Method of Payment:

Check ☐ (Please enclose in envelope.)

Charge My: VISA ☐   MasterCard ☐

American Express ☐

Charge # _____

Expiration Date _____

Order No.	Title	Qty.	Price	Total

You can **FAX** your order to **1-317-573-2583**. Or call **1-800-428-5331, ext. ORDR** to order direct.
Please add $2.50 per title for shipping and handling.

Subtotal _____

Shipping & Handling _____

Total _____

— QUE —

BUSINESS REPLY MAIL

First Class Permit No. 9918   Indianapolis, IN

Postage will be paid by addressee

11711 N. College
Carmel, IN 46032

BUSINESS REPLY MAIL

First Class Permit No. 9918   Indianapolis, IN

Postage will be paid by addressee

11711 N. College
Carmel, IN 46032